Fodor's 07

CHICAGO

**Where to Stay and Eat
for All Budgets**

**Must-See Sights
and Local Secrets**

Ratings You Can Trust

Fodor's Travel Publications   New York, Toronto, London, Sydney, Auckland
www.fodors.com

FODOR'S CHICAGO 2007

Editors: Sarah Sper, Heidi Leigh Johansen

Editorial Production: Bethany Cassin Beckerlegge
Editorial Contributors: Kelly Aiglon, Thomas Connors, Elaine Glusac, Roberta Sotonoff, Judy Sutton Taylor, Jennifer Vanasco, Jessica Volpe
Maps & Illustrations: David Lindroth, *cartographer;* William Wu; Adam Cohen, *Earth Data Solutions;* Bob Blake and Rebecca Baer, *map editors.* Additional cartography provided by Henry Colomb, Mark Stroud, and Ali Baird, Moon Street Cartography
Design: Fabrizio La Rocca, *creative director;* Guido Caroti, *art director;* Moon Sun Kim, *cover designer;* Melanie Marin, *senior picture editor*
Production/Manufacturing: Colleen Ziemba
Cover Photo: (Millenium Park): Kim Karpeles

COPYRIGHT

ISBN-10:1–4000–1599–5

ISBN-13: 978–1–4000–1599–3

ISSN: 0743–9326

SPECIAL SALES

This book is available at special discounts for bulk purchases for sales promotions or premiums. Special editions, including personalized covers, excerpts of existing books, and corporate imprints, can be created in large quantities for special needs. For more information, write to Special Markets/Premium Sales, 1745 Broadway, MD 6-2, New York, New York 10019, or e-mail specialmarkets@randomhouse.com.

AN IMPORTANT TIP & AN INVITATION

Although all prices, opening times, and other details in this book are based on information supplied to us at press time, changes occur all the time in the travel world, and Fodor's cannot accept responsibility for facts that become outdated or for inadvertent errors or omissions. So **always confirm information when it matters,** especially if you're making a detour to visit a specific place. Your experiences—positive and negative—matter to us. If we have missed or misstated something, **please write to us.** We follow up on all suggestions. Contact the Chicago editor at editors@fodors.com or c/o Fodor's at 1745 Broadway, New York, NY 10019.

PRINTED IN THE UNITED STATES OF AMERICA

10 9 8 7 6 5 4 3 2 1

Be a Fodor's Correspondent

Your opinion matters. It matters to us. It matters to your fellow Fodor's travelers, too. And we'd like to hear it. In fact, we *need* to hear it.

When you share your experiences and opinions, you become an active member of the Fodor's community. That means we'll not only use your feedback to make our books better, but we'll publish your names and comments whenever possible. Throughout our guides, look for "Word of Mouth," excerpts of your unvarnished feedback.

Here's how you can help improve Fodor's for all of us.

Tell us when we're right. We rely on local writers to give you an insider's perspective. But our writers and staff editors—who are the best in the business—depend on you. Your positive feedback is a vote to renew our recommendations for the next edition.

Tell us when we're wrong. We're proud that we update most of our guides every year. But we're not perfect. Things change. Hotels cut services. Museums change hours. Charming cafés lose charm. If our writer didn't quite capture the essence of a place, tell us how you'd do it differently. If any of our descriptions are inaccurate or inadequate, we'll incorporate your changes in the next edition and will correct factual errors at fodors.com *immediately*.

Tell us what to include. You probably have had fantastic travel experiences that aren't yet in Fodor's. Why not share them with a community of like-minded travelers? Maybe you chanced upon a beach or bistro or B&B that you don't want to keep to yourself. Tell us why we should include it. And share your discoveries and experiences with everyone directly at fodors.com. Your input may lead us to add a new listing or highlight a place we cover with a "Highly Recommended" star or with our highest rating, "Fodor's Choice."

Give us your opinion instantly at our feedback center at www.fodors.com/feedback. You may also e-mail editors@fodors.com with the subject line "Chicago Editor." Or send your nominations, comments, and complaints by mail to Chicago Editor, Fodor's, 1745 Broadway, New York, NY 10019.

You and travelers like you are the heart of the Fodor's community. Make our community richer by sharing your experiences. Be a Fodor's correspondent.

Happy traveling!

Tim Jarrell, Publisher

CONTENTS

ABOUT THIS BOOK

Our Ratings

Sometimes you find terrific travel experiences and sometimes they just find you. But usually the burden is on you to select the right combination of experiences. That's where our ratings come in.

As travelers we've all discovered a place so wonderful that its worthiness is obvious. And sometimes that place is so unique that superlatives don't do it justice: you just have to be there to know. These sights, properties, and experiences get our highest rating, **Fodor's Choice** ★, indicated by orange stars throughout this book.

Black stars highlight sights and properties we deem **Highly Recommended** ★, places that our writers, editors, and readers praise again and again for consistency and excellence.

By default, there's another category: any place we include in this book is by definition worth your time, unless we say otherwise. And we will.

Disagree with any of our choices? Care to nominate a place or suggest that we rate one more highly? Visit our feedback center at www.fodors.com/feedback.

Budget Well

Hotel and restaurant price categories from ¢ to $$$$ are defined in the opening pages of each chapter. For attractions, we always give standard adult admission fees; reductions are usually available for children, students, and senior citizens. Want to pay with plastic? **AE, D, DC, MC, V** following restaurant and hotel listings indicate whether American Express, Discover, Diner's Club, MasterCard, and Visa are accepted.

Restaurants

Unless we state otherwise, restaurants are open for lunch and dinner daily. We mention dress only when there's a specific requirement and reservations only when they're essential or not accepted—it's always best to book ahead.

Hotels

Hotels have private bath, phone, TV, and air-conditioning and operate on the European Plan (aka EP, meaning without meals), unless we specify that they use the Continental Plan (CP, with a Continental breakfast), Breakfast Plan (BP, with a full breakfast), or Modified American Plan (MAP, with breakfast and dinner) or are all-inclusive (including all meals and

most activities). We always list facilities but not whether you'll be charged an extra fee to use them, so when pricing accommodations, find out what's included.

Many Listings
- ★ Fodor's Choice
- ★ Highly recommended
- ⊠ Physical address
- ✛ Directions
- ⌂ Mailing address
- ☎ Telephone
- 🖷 Fax
- ⊕ On the Web
- ✉ E-mail
- 🎫 Admission fee
- ☉ Open/closed times
- ▶ Start of walk/itinerary
- Ⓜ Metro stations
- ▭ Credit cards

Hotels & Restaurants
- 🏨 Hotel
- ⇱ Number of rooms
- ⟁ Facilities
- ⑂ Meal plans
- ✕ Restaurant
- ⟁ Reservations
- ⥑ Dress code
- ⤸ Smoking
- 🆎 BYOB
- ✕🏨 Hotel with restaurant that warrants a visit

Outdoors
- 🏌 Golf
- ⛺ Camping

Other
- ☺ Family-friendly
- 🔢 Contact information
- ⇨ See also
- ⊠ Branch address
- ☞ Take note

Experience Chicago

WORD OF MOUTH

"Take a boat ride on the lake and see the city skyline (preferably both day and night, but if you had to pick only one, night)—even if it's only the harbor taxi from the Museum Campus to Navy Pier or vice versa."

—exiledprincess

"Make sure you try some Chicago deep dish pizza. There are many options. Chicago is a great, clean city."

—closer52

CHICAGO PLANNER

The Second City?

New Yorkers will tell you theirs is the greatest city in the world. But Chicagoans beg to differ. Chicago's charm is indisputable—the impeccably clean streets; the Midwestern-friendly vibe; the alluring mixture of lush parks, Lake Michigan, and slick skyscrapers. It's what keeps the debate going (log onto the Fodors.com forum and check out one of the "favorite city" debates), and what keeps everyone coming back again and again.

Word of Mouth

"Chicago is fabulous! In every way! The architecture is positively amazing. The people are really, really friendly. We found the city very clean and very beautifully landscaped. Prices (hotel, restaurants, public transportation, visitor passes...) are more moderate than New York City. Though streets were busy and full of people, there weren't the mobs and mobs of New York."

–djkbooks

"While I love New York City, Chicago is amazing, especially around the holidays. Spend your time walking, taking the El train or the bus, and visiting the neighborhoods. If you want to include some great shopping, you must visit the Wicker Park neighborhood and Lincoln Park boutiques."

–allure

Getting Around

Chicago has an excellent network of buses and trains, called the El (for "elevated," which many of them are). The combination should bring you within a quarter-mile of anyplace you'd like to go. Those with city smarts will find it safe to take any train, any time. Others may want to avoid late weeknights after about 11 PM. Buses are almost always safe and there are several express buses running from downtown to destinations like the Museum of Science and Industry and the Museum Campus. Just sit up near the driver if you're uncomfortable.

As of this writing, the fare for any bus or train is $1.75 and a transfer is 25 cents, but the Chicago Transit Authority (CTA) is trying to raise the fee. Travelers may want to get a Visitor Pass at their hotel, the airport CTA stations, or any visitor center. These passes allow unlimited rides for a small fee and are worth it as long as you take three trips a day.

For directions to specific places via public transportation, for public transportation maps, and for locations to buy transit passes, see www.transitchicago.com.

A free trolley circulates around downtown attractions like the museums and Navy Pier every 20 minutes until 9 PM on weekdays and 11 PM on weekends. More information is at www.tylin.com.

Most neighborhoods are walkable, but to get between them, hail one of the many cabs on any main street. If you drive downtown, park in one of the giant city-owned parking lots underneath Millennium Park or by the Museum Campus, which charge a flat fee. Private lots usually cost double.

When to Go

June, September, and October are the golden months in Chicago—mild and sunny. November through March ranges from crisp to bitter, April and May are usually cold and soggy, and July and August can be either perfect or the deadly combo of high heat–high humidity. That said, the only thing certain about Chicago's weather, according to locals, is that it will change—sometimes there are 60-degree days in January, and sometimes August drops down to the 50s. If you head to Chicago in warmer months, you'll be able to catch some of the fantastic outdoor festivals; during the holiday season, the city's decked out in lights. To help you pick the best time to go, see Fabulous Festivals on page 25.

A Few of Our Favorite Things

What do Fodor's editors do when they head to Chicago? Here are a few of our personal picks. We love walking along the Chicago River and watching the boats ply the water, then strolling down State Street to the Carson Pirie Scott building to admire the gorgeous iron scrollwork. We gallery hop in River North, and duck in cute boutiques along Oak Street. We head to Hyde Park to gawk at the colorful, noisy monk parrots. We never leave without indulging in gooey deep-dish pizza (and, if we want to justify that indulgence, take a run along the lakefront first). We won't tell you which baseball team we cheer for, but we love going to the games. And at night? You can find us catching the blues at B.L.U.E.S., going to an outdoor concert (we've seen big ones in Soldier Field and small ones in Lincoln Park), howling at Second City improvers, or having drinks at the Signature Room at the John Hancock (hey, we're suckers for a great city view!).

Local Know-How

Most Chicago businesses are open 10–6. Some shops stay open as late as 9. Restaurants can be closed on Monday and usually stop serving around 10 PM on weeknights, 11 PM on weekends. There are a few 24-hour diners, but they're more rare than you might expect. Bars close at 2 AM or 4 AM.

You can avoid the long lines at Chicago museums by buying tickets at least a day in advance online. The most popular architecture tour, led by docents from the Chicago Architecture Foundation, always sells out—be sure to buy tickets when planning your trip. As in other cities, you'll need reservations for most three- and four-star restaurants for dinner and almost all theaters.

Visitor Centers

Chicago's two visitor centers provide maps, discounts to local attractions, and friendly information.

Chicago Cultural Center ✉ 77 E . Randolph St., at Michigan Ave. ☎ 312/744–2400 or 877/244–2246 ⊕ www.877chicago.com ⊙ Weekdays 10–6, Sat. 10–5, Sun. 11–5.

Chicago Water Works ✉ 163 E. Pearson St., at Michigan Ave. ☎ 877/244–2246or ⊕ www.877chicago.com ⊙ Daily 7:30–7:00.

TOP ATTRACTIONS

(A) Sears Tower Skydeck

Take the ear-popping ride to the 103rd-floor observatory, where, on a clear day, you can see to Michigan, Wisconsin, and Indiana. At the top, interactive exhibits tell about Chicago's dreamers, schemers, architects, musicians, writers, and sports stars. Kids love Knee-High Chicago, a 4-foot-high exhibit that has cutouts of Chicago sports, history, and cultural icons at a child's eye-level. Security is very tight, so figure in a little extra time for your visit to the Skydeck. ⇨ See Architecture

(B) John Hancock Center Observatory

The third-tallest building in Chicago has the most impressive panoramic views of the lake and surrounding skyline—it's high enough to see the tops of neighboring buildings in vivid 3-D, but not so remote that you feel like you're looking out from a plane. Our tip? Skip the observatory and head to the bar that adjoins the

Signature Room restaurant on the 95th floor—you'll spend your money on an exorbitantly priced cocktail instead of the entrance fee and enjoy the same view. Women, head to the 95th floor ladies' room for the best view in the whole building. ⇨ See Architecture

(C) Shopping on the Magnificent Mile

Exclusive shops, department stores, and boutiques line the northern half of swanky Michigan Avenue. Even better, the concentration of prestigious stores in vertical malls means you can get a lot of shopping done in winter without venturing into the bluster outside. ⇨ See Shopping

(D) The Blues Scene

Explore jumping North Side clubs, like Kingston Mines, or South Side venues, like the Checkerboard or Lee's Unleaded Blues (where greats like Muddy Waters and Buddy Guy first honed their talent), for the

sound Chicago gave birth to—the scintillating electric blues. If you're here in June, don't miss the Chicago Blues Festival, which packs fans in every summer. ⇨ See Entertainment

(E) Navy Pier

Yes, it's a little schlocky, but Navy Pier is fun, especially for families. Everyone can fan out to shop in the mall, play minigolf in the Crystal Ballroom in winter, see a movie at the IMAX Theater, or explore the Chicago Children's Museum. Plus, there's a stained-glass museum, a maze, and a 3-D ride that whizzes through scenes of Chicago. Meet up later at the Ferris wheel for a photo-op or just settle on the pier with a drink and enjoy the view.

(F) Art Institute of Chicago

This Chicago cultural gem has the country's best collection of impressionist and Post-impressionist art. It's also a great place to see all those paintings you've only seen on postcards, like *American Gothic* and *Nighthawks*. ⇨ See Museums

(G) Adler Planetarium & Astronomy Museum

How can you not enjoy the snazzy 3-D sky shows at the country's oldest planetarium? Older children and physics fanatics get geeked about the interactive science exhibits and the high-tech Sky Pavilion, while younger visitors get a kick out of the cultural exhibits. ⇨ See Museums

(H) Field Museum

Say hello to Sue, the Field's beloved gigantic T.rex, before immersing yourself in this extraordinary museum's collection of anthropological and paleontological artifacts and animal dioramas. The dinosaurs are the thing here, but surprising collections of items like Tibetan Buddhist alters and the re-creation of famous gems may entice you to linger for hours. ⇨ See Museums

(I) Museum of Science and Industry

Travel down an elevator to a "working" coal mine, walk down the cobblestone streets of old Chicago, explore the caves of a human heart, or watch quietly as a baby chick pecks its way out of its shell at this unusual museum. ⇨ See Museums

(J) Shedd Aquarium

We find the experience of watching entire universities—not just schools—of fantastically colored fish, as well as dolphins and whales, completely mesmerizing. Don't miss the Wild Reef exhibit, where stingrays slide quietly under the plexiglass at your feet. ⇨ See Museums

(K) Frank Lloyd Wright Architecture

Frank Lloyd Wright's Prairie School captured the flat, expansive Midwestern plains he saw around him. Oak Park, a Chicago suburb, has many fine examples, though one of the best is Robie House in Hyde Park, which is open for tours. ⇨ See Architecture

SOAKING IT ALL IN: RIVER & LAKE TOURS

Coursing through the heart of the Windy City is the majestic Chicago River, lined with some of the city's finest architecture and dotted with river walks and restaurants. Hop in a boat, kayak, canoe, or gondola and sail down for some of the prettiest views of the city. Some tours even head out to the Lake for a skyscraper-studded panorama.

Best Tour Companies

The **ArchiCenter of the Chicago Architecture Foundation** (✉ 224 S. Michigan Ave., Loop ☎ 312/922–3432 ⊕ www.architecture. org ☉ Tues.–Sun. 9:30–4) conducts excellent, docent-led boat tours of the Loop. Our favorites are the "Early Skyscrapers" tour and the "Modern and Beyond" tour. The ArchiCenter also has walking and bus tours and hosts exhibitions, lectures, and discussions.

TOUR ALTERNATIVES

■ Pinching pennies? Hop on a Shoreline water taxi and cruise down the river. You won't get the running narration that you'd get on one of the river tour boats, but it's less expensive (tickets are $6 one-way weekdays, $7 weekends) and less crowded.

■ For a more adventurous spin down the river, rent a canoe or a kayak and paddle yourself down the river. Just beware of large boats and crew shells, neither of which turn easily. **Chicago Canoe and Kayak** (✉ 3400 N. Rockwell St. ☎ 773/704–2663 ⊕ www.chicagoriverpaddle. com). **Chicagoland Canoe Base** (✉ 4019 N. Narragansett Ave. ☎ 773/777–1489 ⊕ www.chicagolandcanoebase. com).

Watch the panoply of Chicago's magnificent skyline slide by from the decks of *Chicago's First Lady* or *Chicago's Little Lady,* the fleet of the **Chicago Architecture Foundation River Cruise.** Make reservations in advance for the popular 90-minute tours. Ticketmaster (☎ 312/902–1500 ⊕ www. ticketmaster.com/illinois) sells tickets by phone, online, and at the Hot Tix booth in the Chicago Water Works Visitor Center. Ticketmaster fees apply at these outlets. You can also purchase tickets at the *Chicago's First Lady* ticket window or at the Chicago ArchiCenter (224 S. Michigan Ave.). ✉ *Southeast corner of Michigan Ave. Bridge* ☎ 847/358–1330 ⊕ *www. cruisechicago.com* ▣ *$23 Mon.–Thurs., $25 Fri.–Sun.* ☉ *May–Oct., daily; Nov., weekends.*

Other Recommended Companies

Shoreline Sightseeing. Shoreline's been plying these waters since 1939 and has tours of both the river and Lake Michigan. ✉ *West end of Navy Pier* ☎ 312/222–9328 ⊕ *www.shorelinesightseeing.com* ☉ *May–Oct., daily; Apr., Nov., weekends.*

Wendella Sightseeing. See the city just as the sun sets behind the glittering skyline on the Chicago at Sunset tour. There's also a river architecture tour and a combined river and lake tour. ✉ *400 N. Michigan Ave.* ☎ *312/337–1446* ⊕ *www.wendellaboats. com* ☉ *Apr.–Nov. daily.*

Mercury Cruises. Mercury does quirky tours, including Canine Cruises, where dogs are welcome, and Pirate Cruises for kids. ✉ *112 E. Wacker Dr.* ☎ *312/332–1353* ☉ *Schedule varies according to season.*

CITY ITINERARIES

Two Hours in Town

If you've only got a bit of time, do something classic and easy. If the weather's nice, stroll down State Street, the Magnificent Mile, or the lakefront outside the **Adler Planetarium** (it's one of the nicest skyline views in the city). If you're hungry, indulge in one of Chicago's three famous culinary treats—deep-dish pizza (head to **Pizzeria Due** to try to avoid the lines of **Giordano's**, **Gino's**, and **Pizzeria Uno**), garden-style hot dogs, or Italian beef sandwiches (See Chicago's Holy Trinity feature on page 199). If you don't mind whizzing through a museum, take a brisk walk around the **Art Institute** to see Grant Wood's *American Gothic,* Edward Hopper's *Nighthawks,* and any other impressionist paintings you see along the way. Or duck into the **Chicago Historical Society** for an entertaining look at the Great Chicago Fire and the World Fair of 1893. After dark? Hear some music at a local club. Catch blues at **Blue Chicago** to get a taste of authentic Chicago.

■ TIP→ Remember that museums are closed on Monday.

A Perfect Afternoon

Do the zoo. Spend some time at the free **Lincoln Park Zoo and Conservatory** (the tropical plants will warm you up in winter), take a ride on the exotic animal-themed carousel, and then spend a couple hours at the nearby **Chicago Historical Society** for a quirky look at the city's past. If you'd like to stay in the Lincoln Park neighborhood a bit longer, have dinner at one of many great local restaurants and then head to **The Second City,** the sketch comedy troupe that was the precursor to Saturday Night Live.

■ TIP→ The Second City offers free improvisation following the last performance every night but Friday.

Sightseeing in the Loop

State Street, that Great Street, is home to the old **Marshall Fields** building (now a Macy's), Louis Sullivan's ornate iron entrance to department store **Carson Pirie Scott,** and a nascent theater district, as well as great people-watching. Start at Harold Washington Library at Van Buren Street and State Street and walk north, venturing a block east to the beautiful **Chicago Cultural Center** when you hit Randolph Street. Grab lunch at the Museum of Contemporary Art's serene Wolfgang Puck café, **Puck's at the MCA,** and then spend a couple hours with in-your-face art. Go for steak at Morton's or The Palm before a night of Chicago theater. Broadway touring shows are on Randolph Street at the Oriental or the Ford, or head elsewhere downtown for excellent local theater—the Goodman, Steppenwolf, Lookingglass, and Chicago Shakespeare will each give you a night to remember.

Get Outdoors

Begin with a long walk (or run) along the lakefront, or rent a bike or inline skates and watch the waves on wheels. Then catch an El train north to **Wrigley Field** for Cubs baseball; grab a dog at the seventh-inning stretch and sing your heart out to "Take Me Out to the Ball Game." Afterward, soak up a little beer and atmosphere on the patio at one of the local sports bars. Finish up with an outdoor concert in **Grant or Millennium parks.**

Family Time

Start at **Navy Pier**—or heck, spend all day there. The **Chicago Children's Museum** is a main attraction, but there's also an IMAX Theater, a Ferris wheel, a swing ride, a fun house, a stained-glass museum, and in winter, Chicago-themed miniature golf in a sunny atrium. If the crowds at the Pier get to be too much, walk or take the free trolley to **Millennium Park,** where kids of all ages can ice-skate in winter and play in the fountain in summer, and where giant digital portraits of Chicagoans spit streams of water to help cool you off. Whatever the weather, make sure to get your picture taken in the mirrored center of the **Bean**—the sculpture that's formally known as Cloud Gate. At night in summertime, take a stroll by Buckingham Fountain, where the dancing sprays jump to music and are lit by computer-controlled color lights, or take a turn on the dance floor during Chicago's nightly Summerdance celebration.

■ TIP→ Fireworks explode near Navy Pier every Wednesday and Saturday night at 9 PM, Memorial Day through Labor Day.

City Scapes

Start at the top. Hit the heights of the **John Hancock Center** or the **Sears Tower Skydeck** for a grand view of the city and the lake. Then take a walking tour of downtown with a well-read docent from the **Chicago Architecture Foundation.** In the afternoon, wander north to the **Michigan Avenue Bridge,** where you can take an informative boat tour of the Chicago River. Enjoy the architecture as you float by, resting your weary feet.

Buy Chicago

Grab your bankroll and stroll the **Mag Mile** in search of great buys and souvenirs. Walking north from around the Michigan Avenue Bridge, window shop your way along the many upscale stores. Hang a left on **Oak Street** for the most elite boutiques. Dedicated shoppers will want to detour a little farther south to **State Street** in the Loop for a walk through the landmark Marshall Fields building, which has become a Macy's. For a culture buzz, check out the **Museum of Contemporary Art** (closed Monday). After making a tough restaurant choice (Prime rib at Smith & Wollensky's or Lawry's? Deep-dish pizza at Giordano's?), consider a nightcap at the **Signature Room** at the 95th bar on top of the John Hancock Center—the city will be spread beneath your feet.

GETTING OUTSIDE: PARKS & ZOOS

Chicago may not be the country's biggest city, but it's arguably the prettiest. Architect Daniel Burnham designed the city to have plenty of green space so city dwellers could relax and take in the bustle, and even the tiniest green outpost usually has some sort of public art. With winter never too far from thought, Chicagoans pour into the city's parks and zoos at the first hint of summer, or take to conservatories when the weather's less than ideal. The following are our favorite city parks and zoos.

Parks

Garfield Park Conservatory. One of the most exotic places to visit in winter has Victorian glass rooms of tropical palms, spiny cacti, turtle-filled ponds, and a children's garden with a slide that winds through trees. ⊠ *300 N. Central Park Ave., Garfield Park.*

★ **Fodor's Choice** **Grant Park & Buckingham Fountain.** Two of Chicago's greatest treasures reside in Grant Park—the Art Institute and Buckingham Fountain. Bordered by Lake Michigan to the east and a spectacular skyline to the west, the ever-popular Grant Park hosts many of the city's outdoor events, including the annual Taste of Chicago, a vast picnic featuring foods from more than 70 restaurants. The event precedes a fireworks show around July 4. The fountain is a wonderful place to people-watch.

The centerpiece of Grant Park is the gorgeous tiered **Buckingham Fountain** (⊠ Between Columbus and Lake Shore Drs. east of Congress Plaza), which has intricate designs of pink-marble seashells, water-spouting fish, and bronze sculptures of sea horses. It was patterned after a fountain at Versailles but is about twice as large

as its model. See it in all its glory between May 1 and October 1, when it's elaborately illuminated at night and sprays colorfully lighted waters. ⊠ *South Loop* ☎ *312/747–1534.*

Lincoln Park Conservatory. Green grows on green in the lush tropical main room of this refreshing city greenhouse. Stroll through permanent displays of orchids, palms, and ferns, or catch one of the special shows, like the fragrant Easter Lily show in March or April and the festive Chrysanthemum Show in November. The peacefulness and lush greenery inside the 1892 conservatory is a refreshing respite in the heart of this bustling neighborhood. ⊠ *2400 N. Stockton Dr., Lincoln Park* ☎ *312/742–7736* ⊠ *Free* ☉ *Daily 9–5.*

★ **Millennium Park.** The bean, the fountains, the Disney-esque music pavilion—all the pieces of this new park quickly stole the hearts of Chicagoans and visitors alike. This is one of our favorite places to while away a sunny day.

The showstopper here is Frank Gehry's stunning music pavilion, the **Jay Pritzker Pavilion.** Dramatic ribbons of stainless steel stretching 40 feet into the sky look like petals wrapping the stage. The sound system, suspended by a trellis that spans the great lawn, gives concert-hall sound outside. So what can you see on this beautiful stage? Take your pick. There's the Grant Park Music Festival—a free classical music series—as well as the city's popular free summer concerts, including the jam-packed Chicago Blues and Chicago Jazz Festivals.

Hot town? Summer in the city? Cool off by letting Chicagoans spit on you. Okay, they're just giant images rotating through on two huge (read: 50-foot-high) glass block tower-fountains. The genius behind the **Crown Fountain,** Spanish sculptor Jaume Plensa, made an opening where the mouths are on the photos, and water comes shooting out at random intervals. Kids love it, and we feel like kids watching it. It's at the southwest corner of the park.

You've seen the pictures. Now go, take your own. The **Cloud Gate,** otherwise known as "the Bean," awaits your delighted oohs and ahs as you stand beneath its gleaming seamless polished steel. It's between Washington and Madison streets. Go on, get camera happy.

If you're feeling artsy, you can find out if there's a show playing at the indoor, underground **Harris Theater for Music and Dance,** behind the Jay Pritzker Pavilion.

In summer, the carefully manicured plantings in the Lurie Garden bloom; in winter, the **McCormick Tribune Ice Rink** is open for public skates.

✉ *Bounded by Michigan Ave., Columbus Dr., Randolph Dr., and Monroe St., Loop* ⊕ *www. millenniumpark.org* ✉ *Free* ☉ *Daily 6 AM–11 PM.*

Zoos

★ **Brookfield Zoo.** Spend the day among nearly 3,000 animals at this gigantic zoo. The highlights? First, there's the popular **Tropic World,** a simulated tropical rain forest where monkeys, otters, birds, and other rain-forest fauna cavort in a carefully constructed setting of rocks, trees, shrubs, pools, and waterfalls. Next, test your "flying strength" in the **Be a Bird House** by

flapping your "wings" on a machine that decides what kind of bird you would be, based on how you flap. We also like the **Living Coast,** where you can venture through huge glassed-in passageways to see sharks, rays, jellyfish, and turtles swimming by. Daily dolphin shows are a favorite even for adults. Walruses, seals, and sea lions inhabit a rocky seascape exhibit. Don't worry if you don't want to trek around the grounds—you can hop aboard a "motorized safari" tram in warm weather ($2.50) or the heated *Snowball Express* tram in the cold (free).

GETTING THERE

The zoo is 3½ mi southwest of Oak Park (from Oak Park, take Harlem Avenue south 2 mi, turn west on Cermak Road 1 mi, then south on 1st Avenue to the zoo entrance). You can also take Metra's Burlington Northern Line from downtown's Union Station to the Zoo stop (Hollywood Station). It's a two-block walk from the train station to the zoo.

The two best educational exhibits are Habitat Africa and Swamp. In **Habitat Africa,** you can explore two very different environments. See such tiny animals as klipspringer antelope, which are only 22 inches tall, and rock hyraxes, which resemble prairie dogs, in the savannah exhibit, which also has a water hole, rock formations characteristic of the African savannah, and termite mounds. If you look closely in the dense forest exhibit, you might be able to find animals like the okapi. The **Swamp** is about as realistic as you would want an exhibit on swamps to be, with a springy

floor, push-button alligator bellows, and open habitats with low-flying birds vividly demonstrating the complex ecosystems of both southern and Illinois wetlands.

For hands-on family activities, check out the **Hamill Family Play Zoo** (✉ $3, children $2), where kids can learn to care for nature by playing zookeeper, gardener, or veterinarian. The **Children's Zoo** (✉ $1, children 50¢) includes a petting farm, excellent animal shows, and the Big Barn with its daily milking demonstrations. ✉ *1st Ave. and 31st St.* ☎ *708/485–0263 or 800/201–0784* ⊕ *www.brookfieldzoo. org* ✉ *Zoo $8 ($4 children, free on Tues. and Thurs. Oct.–Mar.); dolphin show $2.50; parking $8* ☉ *Jan.–Mar., daily 10–5; Apr. and Sept., weekdays 10–5; weekends 10–6; May–Aug., daily 9:30–6; Oct.–Dec., daily 10–5.*

★ **Fodor's Choice** | **Lincoln Park Zoo.** Lions and gorillas and bears, oh my! At this urban zoo, you can face-off with lions (separated by a window, of course) outside the Lion House, watch 24 gorillas go ape in the Great Ape House, or watch some rare and endangered species of bears, such as the spectacle bear (named for the eyeglasslike markings around its eyes). Animals both slithery (pythons) and cuddly (koalas) reside in the glass-dome Regenstein Small Mammal and Reptile House; if you're looking for the big guys (elephants, giraffes, black rhinos), they're in the large-mammal house. For youngsters, there are the children's zoo, the Farm in the Zoo (farm animals and a learning center with films and demonstrations), and the Conservation Station, with hands-on activities.

■ **DID YOU KNOW?**→ Begun in 1868 with a pair of swans donated by New York's Central Park, this zoo grew through donations of animals from wealthy Chicago residents and the purchase of a collection from the Barnum and Bailey Circus.

✉ *2200 N. Cannon Dr., Lincoln Park* ☎ *312/742–2000* ⊕ *www.lpzoo.com* ✉ *Free* ☉ *Daily 9–5.*

AUTHENTIC CHICAGO

So you've done the Art Institute and the Sears Tower—now it's time to put away your tourist hat and make like a local. Luckily, it's not hard to figure out what Chicagoans like to do in their spare time. Here's how to follow in their footsteps.

Visit an Ethnic Neighborhood

Chicago is a city of neighborhoods, and in many of them you can see traces of each successive immigrant group. Each neighborhood in the city has its own flavor, reflected in its architecture, public art, restaurants, and businesses, and most have their own summer or holiday festivals. Here are a few stand-out 'hoods.

Little Italy. Though most Italians moved to the West Side a couple of generations ago, Little Italy's Italian restaurants and lemonade stands still draw them back.

Andersonville. The charming diversity of the Swedish/Middle Eastern/gay mecca of Andersonville means you can have lingonberry pancakes for breakfast, hummus for lunch, and go to a club after dinner.

Chinatown. The Chinese New Year dragon parade is just one reason to visit Chinatown, which has dozens of restaurants and shops and a quiet riverfront park.

Devon Avenue. Devon Avenue turns from Indian to Pakistani to Russian Orthodox Jewish within a few blocks. Buy a sari, buy a bagel, or just people-watch—it's an excellent way to spend the afternoon.

Pilsen/Little Village. The best Mexican restaurants are alongside Pilsen's famous murals. Be sure to stop into the Mexican Fine Arts Museum, which will give you an even deeper appreciation of the culture.

Bronzeville. Bronzeville's famous local historic figures include Ida B. Wells, the founder of the NAACP, the trumpeter Louis Armstrong, and Bessie Coleman, the first African-American woman pilot. The area has nine landmark buildings and is rapidly gentrifying.

Enjoy the Lake

San Diego and LA might have the ocean, and New York its Central Park, but Chicago has the peaceful waters of Lake Michigan at its doorstep. Bikers, dog walkers, boaters, and runners crowd the lakefront paths on warm days; in winter the lake is equally beautiful, with icy towers formed from frozen sheets of water.

BIKE ALONG THE LAKESHORE

★ To bike any part of the gentle dips and swells of the Chicago's 20 mi **lakefront bicycle path** is to see the city: the skyline, the people, the water. The breeze from the lake mixes with the sounds of the city at play as you zoom by, carefree, whiling away an afternoon.

The **Chicago Park District** (☎ 312/742–7529 ⊕ www.chicagoparkdistrict.com) is a good source for bike maps. For information on biking in the city, contact the **Chicagoland Bicycle Federation** (✉ 650 S. Clark St., No. 300, South Loop ☎ 312/427–3325 ⊕ www.chibikefed.org).

Bike Chicago (✉ 600 E. Grand Ave., Near North ☎ 312/595–9600 or 773/327–2706 ⊕ www.bikechicago.com/home.asp) can deliver a bike to your hotel and pick it up after your ride. Fees start at $8.75 per hour and $34 a day. It also runs a free three-hour, lakefront bike tour daily, weather permitting.

You can rent a bike for the day or by the hour from **On the Route** (✉ 3146 N. Lincoln Ave., Lake View ☎ 773/477–5066), which stocks a large inventory of bicycles, including children's bikes. They also supply helmets and other safety equipment.

BOATING

Nothing beats the view of the Chicago skyline from the water, especially when the sun sets behind the sparkling skyscrapers. Plenty of boats are available to rent or charter, though you might want to leave the skippering to others if you're not familiar with Great Lakes navigation.

Sailboat lessons and rentals are available from the **Chicago Sailing Club** (✉ Belmont Harbor, Lake View ☎ 773/871–7245 ⊕ www.chicagosailingclub.com). The Chicago Sailing Club focuses on sailing instruction for all levels and includes a program on keeping your boat in tip-top shape. **Sailboats Inc.** (✉ Monroe Harbor, Loop ☎ 312/ 861–1757 or 800/826–7010 ⊕ www. sailboats-inc.com), one of the oldest charter certification schools in the country, prepares its students to charter any type of boat.

For a more placid water outing, try the paddleboats at **Lincoln Park Lagoon** (✉ 2021 N. Stockton Dr., Lincoln Park ☎ 312/742– 2038), just north of the Farm in the Zoo.

BEACHES

One of the greatest surprises in the city is the miles of sandy beaches that Chicagoans flock to in summer. The water becomes warm enough to swim in toward the end of June, though the brave will take an icy dip through the end of October. Chicago has about 20 mi of lakefront, most of it sand or rock beach. Beaches are open to the public daily from 9 AM to 9:30 PM, Memorial Day–Labor Day, and many beaches have changing facilities. The **Chicago Park District** (☎ 312/742–7529 ⊕ www.chicagoparkdistrict.com) provides lifeguard protection during daylight hours throughout the swimming season.

All references to north and south in beach listings refer to how far north or south of the Loop each beach is. In other words, 1600–2400 north means the beach begins 16 blocks north of the Loop (at Madison

BEACHES	Block	Best For	Bathrooms	Changing Facilities	Showers	Lifeguard
Far North Side						
Foster Beach	5200 N	Families	yes	no	no	yes
Montrose Beach	4400 N	Learning to sail	yes	no	yes	yes
Osterman Beach	5800 N	Quiet conversations	yes	no	yes	yes
Hyde Park						
South Shore Country Club	7100 S	Quieter beach	yes	yes	yes	yes
Jackson Beach Central	5700–5900 S	Beach trip after the Museum of Science and Industry	yes	no	no	yes
Lincoln Park						'
North Avenue Beach	1600–2400 N	Margaritas at the upstairs concession	yes	yes	yes	yes
Near North						
Oak Street Beach	600–1600 N	Singles scene	yes	no	no	yes
South Loop						
12th Street Beach	1200 S at 900 E	Post museum-hopping break	yes	no	yes	yes

Beaches

Osterman Beach

Foster Beach

Montrose Beach

North Avenue Beach

Oak Street Beach

12th Street Beach

Jackson Beach Central

South Shore Country Club

Street, which is the 100 block) and extends for eight blocks.

⚠ Along the lakefront you'll see plenty of broken-rock breakwaters with signs that warn NO SWIMMING OR DIVING. Although Chicagoans frequently ignore these signs, you shouldn't. The boulders below the water are slippery with seaweed and may hide sharp, rusty scraps of metal, and the water beyond is very deep. It can be dangerous even if you know the territory.

Brave the Cold

The city's brutal windy winters are infamous, but that doesn't keep Chicagoans from making the best out of the long cold months. Throw on a few layers, lace up your ice skates, and show those city dwellers what you're made of.

★ The rink at **Millennium Park** (✉ 55 N. Michigan Ave., Loop ☎ 312/742–5222) has free skating seven days a week and a lustrous view of the Chicago skyline. Skate rentals are $3 a session.

On snowiest days, some hardy souls **cross-country ski** and snow shoe on the lakeshore—bring your own equipment.

Loosen up by playing outdoor paddle tennis at **Midtown Tennis Club** (✉ 2020 W. Fullerton Ave. ☎ 773/235–2300 ⊕ www. midtowntennisclub.com). If it's snowing, they turn on the heated floors.

Holiday walk Chicago's windows during the **Magnificent Mile Lights Festival,** a weekend-long family-friendly event at the end of November. The celebration includes music, ice-carving contests, and stage shows, and ends in a parade and the illumination of more than one million lights along Michigan Avenue. *See* The Magnificent Mile In Focus feature *in the Shop chapter for more information.*

FREE THINGS TO DO

It's easy to spend money in the big city: shopping, museum-entrance fees, restaurants, theater. But if you'd like to put your wallet away for a while, here are some of our favorite options.

Free Art
- Chicago has some of the most famous public art in the country, including the **Picasso** in Daley Plaza, **Alexander Calder's Flamingo** in Federal Plaza, and the new **Cloud Gate** sculpture in Millennium Park. For a fairly comprehensive list, see www.chipublib.org.
- The **City Gallery** (✉ 806 N. Michigan Ave., ☎ 312/742–0808) in the Historic Water Tower hosts rotating exhibits of Chicago-theme photography.
- Five different galleries showcase contemporary visual art by local artists at the **Chicago Cultural Center** (✉ 78 E. Washington St., ☎ 312/744–6630, ⊕ www.cityofchicago.org.)

Free Concerts
- **Grant Park** and **Millennium Park** host regular classical and pop concerts in summer. For a schedule, pick up the Chicago Reader or buy a copy of TimeOut Chicago.
- Chicago is a festival town, celebrating blues, jazz, country, gospel, Celtic, and World Music during the warm months. For a schedule, see www.cityofchicago.org.
- Free jazz and classical concerts are performed Monday through Wednesday and Friday at 12:15 in the **Chicago Cultural Center** (✉ 78 E. Washington St., ☎ 312/744–6630, ⊕ www.cityofchicago.org).

Free Movies
Every Tuesday night in summer, **Grant Park** shows classic films at sundown on a giant screen. The films tend to be popular, so go early, spread out a blanket, and have a picnic a couple hours beforehand. There's even a free bike valet. Local library branches and parks also have free movies—check the city's Web site for details.

Free Dance Lessons
Learn to swing, polka, step, waltz, and salsa to the beat of a live band in Grant Park during the summer-long Chicago SummerDance Festival. Chicagoans of all ages and abilities sashay around the dance floor during the lessons and the free dancing afterward. For more information, see www.chicagoparkdistrict.com.

Free Fireworks
Every Wednesday and Saturday night in summer, Navy Pier puts on a showy display of colorful explosives. Watch from the pier or along the waterfront opposite Buckingham Fountain.

Free Trolley Rides
A free trolley circles downtown attractions like the museums and Navy Pier every 20 minutes until 9 PM on weekdays and 11 PM on weekends. For more information, call ☎ 877/244–2444.

Free Improv
The world-famous Second City comedy troupe has a free improv set following the last performance every night but Friday. For more information, go to www.secondcity.com or call ☎ 312/337–3992.

Free Museum Days
ALWAYS FREE
Jane Addams Hull-House Museum
Mexican Fine Arts Center
Museum of Contemporary Photography
Oriental Institute
Peace Museum
Smart Museum

SUNDAY:
DuSable Museum of African American History

MONDAY:
Adler Planetarium (Jan. and Feb. and Sept. through Dec.)

TUESDAY:
Adler Planetarium (Jan. and Feb. and Sept. through Dec.)
Art Institute of Chicago
Museum of Contemporary Art (5–8 PM only)
Swedish American Museum (second Tues. each month)

THURSDAY:
Chicago Children's Museum (5–8 PM only)
Peggy Notebaert Nature Museum

FRIDAY:
Spertus Museum (1–3 PM only)

Sightseeing Walks

THAT GREAT STREET

The Loop—defined by the oval created by the El tracks—is the heart of downtown, and the heart of downtown is State Street. Begin at the south end of the Michigan Avenue Bridge, with your back to the Chicago Tribune's gothic tower (take a moment to look at all the stolen stones in the walls that reporters have taken from famous world monuments). Walk west along the river past Marina City's iconic "corn cob" towers, perhaps taking the stairs down to the Riverwalk for a drink at one of the cafés. Once you're back to street level, make a left on State Street, cruising by the famous Chicago Theatre sign that marks the beginning of the theater district. Window shop at local landmarks Carson Pirie Scott and the old Marshall Field's (now a Macy's). If you don't stop to shop, the walk should take about an hour.

■ **Movie trivia time:** The Riverwalk runs along the newly reconstructed tunnel that is lower Wacker Drive, home of the infamous *Blues Brothers* chase scene.

ZOOTOPIA

In two hours on a beautiful day you can breeze through the Lincoln Park Zoo, stroll beside the park's lagoons, and explore the quaint, upscale neighborhood of Old Town. Beginning on North Avenue and Lake Shore Drive, walk north through the park next to the lagoons. Watch the crew shells try to navigate past the fishing lines, or throw a line into the stocked lagoon yourself. Take your time through the zoo or the Lincoln Park Conservatory and then circle west to Wells Street, where the Second City improv troupe's theater and a host of tony shops and restaurants line bricked streets. If you like, venture into the residential areas east of Wells where you find elegant Gold Coast homes, including the Cardinal's residence (North State Parkway and Lake Shore Drive).

FOR THE FANATICS

Michael Jordan, Scottie Pippen, Walter Payton, the Refrigerator, Ernie Banks, Sammy Sosa, Shoeless Joe Jackson. You can't mention Chicago without talking about sports. Chicagoans are fiercely devoted to their teams, whether it's baseball, basketball, or football—and whether their team's winning or losing. Come opening day for baseball season, die-hard Cubs and Sox fans take the day off of work to cheer on their teams; during football season, tailgaters chow down in the parking lot before kickoff, even if it's snowy and in the single digits. One of the most fun ways to get into the Chicago spirit is to go to a game, so throw on your team's colors and join the screaming fans.

Chicago Bears

Chicago football is messy and dirty and sometimes even exciting. Don't expect to be wowed by star quarterbacks and amazing passing, but do get ready for the team's smash-mouth style that reflects the city's blue-collar persona. Legends like Walter Payton have come and gone, but after several mediocre seasons, things have started to look up: The Bears won the NFC North division in 2005.

• **Where they Play:** Soldier Field, 425 E. McFetridge Dr., South Loop

• **Season:** August—December

• **How to Buy Tickets:** From the ticket office, 847/295–6000 or *www.chicagobears.com*

• **Most Notable Players:** Walter Payton, William "the Refrigerator" Perry, Jim McMahon

• **Past Highlights:** Superbowl XX championons, 1985; played in NFL Championship 10 times; NFC North Champions, 2005

Chicago Bulls

It's been years since Michael Jordan and Phil Jackson's "dynasty" teams played in the United Center, but the Bulls' six championships are still revered here. After Jordan's departure in 1998, the franchise became a shadow of its former self—but a new squad of fresh faces is starting to turn things around. Coach Scott Skiles and the "Baby Bulls" are back in the playoffs (2005 and 2006), and the United Center is starting to rock again.

• **Where they Play:** United Center, 1901 W. Madison St., near West Side

• **Season:** November—April

• **How to Buy Tickets:** From the ticket office, 312/455–4000 or *www.bulls.com*

• **Most Notable Players:** Michael Jordan, Dennis Rodman, Scottie Pippen, Toni Kukoc

• **Past Highlights:** Won six NBA Championship Trophies: 1991, 1992, 1993, 1996, 1997, 1998

• **Note:** Avoid leaving the game early or wandering around this neighborhood at night

Chicago Baseball

Take Me Out to the Ballgame   **See Page 19**

TAKE ME OUT TO THE BALLGAME

In a city where you can get a debate going about all sorts of things—best deep-dish pizza, best blues bar, best big city (Chicago or New York?)—nothing can inspire a passionate discussion quite like Chicago baseball, an argument that's been going strong since 1901.

Your favorite team says more about you than just whether you prefer the National or American League. The rivalry plays out along geographical and class lines. South Siders, who include everyone living south of the Loop, are die-hard Sox fans. North Siders sell out afternoon Cubbies games even when the team is losing—as they do most years.

And Sox fans and Cubs fans hate each other. When the Sox won the World Series in 2005 for the first time in 88 years, most Cubs fans didn't even watch the games. The traitors who did were called "BiSoxual." When the Cubs made the playoffs in 2003, Sox fans actively rooted for the other team (as the song "Ballad of the South Side Irish" goes, "When it comes to baseball there are two teams that I love, it's the go-go White Sox and whoever plays the Cubs.") One reason that the division has lasted so long is class tension. South Siders, besides the intellectual Hyde Park pocket, tend to be blue collar. North Siders tend to be professionals.

The teams have only played against each other once post-season: the 1906 World Series. The Cubs were favored, but the White Sox won. Fans on both the North and South sides agree on one thing: it would be "an El of a series" if the teams ever faced each other postseason again. As Cubs fans say, "You Gotta Believe."

NATIONAL LE... 1907

SCHULTE ZIMMERMAN REULBACH LUNDGREN PFEISTER HOWARD
KLING SHECKARD McCORMICK CHANCE mgr. STEINFELDT
...KER BROWN SLAGLE

CHICAGO CUBS

Just the Facts

Nickname: Lovable Losers

Mascot: None

Founded: 1870

Last World Series appearance: 1945

World Series wins: 1907 and 1908

Most famous players: Sammy Sosa, Ron Santo, Ryne Sandberg, Ernie Banks, Billy Williams

Original name: White Stockings

Did you know?

Most hated fan: Steve Bartman, who, in the eighth inning of Game 6 in the 2003 playoffs, reached for—and caught—a foul ball at the same time as left fielder Moises Alou. Before Bartman, the Cubs were five outs away from advancing to the World Series. After Bartman's catch, the Cubs fell apart, giving up eight runs.

Lifelong Chicagoans: The Cubs are the only team to play continually in the same city since the founding of the National League in 1876.

Curse: William Sianis, the old owner of the Billy Goat Tavern, bought two tickets for one of the 1945 Cubs–Tigers World Series games: one for himself, and one for his goat. The goat was turned away, and Sianis vowed that the Cubs would never again win a World Series.

HARRY CARAY: "HOLY COW!"

Beloved for his hoarse, off-key rendition of "Take Me Out to the Ballgame," the way he mashed up players names, and his infamous "Holy Cow!", the Cubs' exuberant play-by-play broadcaster, Harry Caray (1914–1998), was as much a fixture of Wrigley Field as the bleacher bums.

Caray broadcast 8,300 games in his 53-year career. (Don't tell Cubs fans—before he came to Wrigley field, he was the voice of the St. Louis Cardinals for 25 years, the White Sox for 10.) After his death in 1998, every single player wore a caricature of Caray—with his infectious smile and goggle glasses—on their sleeves.

The curse persists, it seems, even though the current Billy Goat owner, son Sam Sianis, occasionally drags a goat back onto the field.

Best seat in the house: The bleachers. Tradition has it that the most serious fans (known as bleacher bums) sit here, on either side of the ivy covered, hand-operated scoreboard. When rival teams hit a ball into the bleachers, the fans throw it back. As of this writing, Cubs fans are nervous; the Cubs' owners, The Chicago Tribune Company, are expanding the bleachers for the first time since 1938.

CHICAGO WHITE SOX

Just the Facts

Mascot: Southpaw, a fuzzy, green character of indeterminate origin. He appeared in 2004.

Founded: 1893 in Sioux City, Iowa. Moved to Chicago in 1900.

Last World Series appearance: 2005

World Series wins: 1906, 1917, 2005

Notable players: "Shoeless" Joe Jackson, Roberto Hernandez, Roberto Alomar, Johnny Mostil

Original name: White Stockings, which was also the first name of the Chicago Cubs. Charles Comiskey hoped to buy some goodwill for the new team by taking on the Cubs' former name.

Did you know?

Theme song: "Na Na Hey Hey (Kiss Him Goodbye)," is played every home game by organist Nancy Faust.

From White Sox to Black: Eight players—outfielder "Shoeless Joe" Jackson, outfielder Oscar "Happy" Felsch, pitchers Eddie Cicotte and Claude "Lefty" Williams, third baseman Buck Weaver, shortstop "Swede" Risberg, and infielders Fred McMullen and Arnold "Chick" Gandi—were accused of throwing the 1919 World Series on behalf of a group of gamblers. They were never convicted, though they were banned from baseball for life. That season's team has been known as the Black Sox ever since.

Most Famous Quote: As Shoeless Joe Jackson was leaving a Black Sox scandal hearing, a newsboy supposedly shouted out, "Say it ain't so, Joe!" This inspired headline writers after the 2005 World Series win to write: "Say it IS so!"

Strangest promotional event: Disco Demolition Night, July 12, 1979, at the old Comiskey Park. Fans were asked to bring unwanted disco records to the park for a Sox–Tigers double header; in return, the admission was lowered to a mere 98 cents. After the first game, chaos erupted—fans threw their records like Frisbees and ran onto the field where they started bonfires and mini-riots.

Fireworks: After every home run and every win, the Sox shoot fireworks into the sky from U.S. Cellular Field. They can be heard across the South Side.

WRIGLEY FIELD

Getting There

Address: 1060 West Addison St., at the corner of Addison St. and Clark St.

Phone: 773/404–CUBS

Public transportation: The Red Line's Addison stop is right outside the park. The #22 Clark bus stops at the entrance.

Driving directions: Try not to drive, but if you do, take Lake Shore Drive north to Belmont Avenue. Travel west on Belmont to North Clark Street, and north on Clark to Wrigley Field.

Parking: Parking is difficult to find around Wrigley, though business owners tend to open up their lots for exorbitant prices, as do lucky home owners with garages.

The Park: The Friendly Confines, as it's known, was built in 1914, which makes it the second-oldest ballpark in the country.

Tours: The Cubs offer 90-minute tours that provide an insider's look at 90 years of Wrigley history. Tickets are $20 per person and you must buy tickets in advance.

Renovations: As of this writing, Wrigley Field and its surroundings are being renovated. Ticket window hours and prices, and concession/ATM locations are currently unavailable.

What to bring: Don't forget your sunscreen and umbrella/rain gear if you're in the bleachers. Bring water—the container must be one liter or less. Don't bring hard-sided coolers, large bags, thermoses, bottles, cans, or alcoholic beverages.

PLAY BALL

Tickets: Prices can range between $14 to $55. Don't expect to score tickets on short notice—games sell out early in the season.

Wrigley Field Alternatives:
- Join the crowd at Harry Caray's Restaurant in River North (⇨ see Where to Eat chapter, pg. 222).
- Check out the ticketless fans in their lawnchairs on Sheffield Avenue.
- Opt for a White Sox game (tickets are easier to come by).

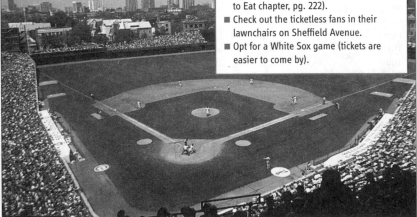

THE CELL

Getting There

Address: 333 W. 35th St.

Phone: 312/674–1000

Public transportation: Take the CTA Red Line to the 35th Street/Sox Park station of the CTA Red Line.

Driving directions: I-94 West to 35th Street; follow signs to "Sox Parking".

Parking: Parking is $17 in the lots surrounding the park. The lots open two hours prior to game time and close one hour after the game. There is no street parking.

About the name: Now it's "The Cell." But until 2003, when the White Sox made a deal to call it U.S. Cellular Field, it was Comiskey Park, named for former White Sox owner Charles A. Comiskey.

What to bring: Sunscreen and hats on hot days; jackets and small umbrellas if it looks like rain. Food in small, clear, see-through plastic bags and one sealed plastic bottle of water per person is OK—all other beverages, coolers, and large bags are not. Leave beach balls and large radios at home. The area around The Cell is sketchy—don't leave valuables in your car.

Tickets: Prices for tickets can range between $14 for a nosebleed seat to $55 for a box seat. Kids who are shorter than the turnstiles—about 36"—get in free but must sit in someone's lap. Monday home games are half price; get a second ticket free when you redeem an empty Pepsi product at ticket windows on the day of the game.

Box Office Hours:
Non-game days: Mon.–Fri., 10–6, Sat. and Sun., 10–4.
Game days: Mon.–Fri. 9–6 (day games); 9–9 (night games)

Sat. 9–6 (day games); 9–8 (night games) Sun. 9–4 (day games); 9–9 (night games).

Kids: Pontiac FUNdamentals, huge play area for kids, includes baseball and softball clinics, batting cages, and places to practice base running and pitching. It's above the left field concourse, opens 90 minutes before the game, and stays open throughout the game.

Speed pitch machine: Test your pitching speed and accuracy near section 164.

Fan Deck: Get a panoramic view of the field from a two-tiered deck. It's atop the center field concession stands. Free for all fans holding a main level ticket.

Baggage Check: Outside Gate 5 between parking lots A and B. $2 fee per bag.

ATMs: Sections 139, 531, centerfield, outside the Bullpen Sports Bar, and outside Gate 4.

Concessions: Burgers and veggie burgers, hot dogs and veggie hotdogs, and ice cream are available throughout the park. The Bullpen Sports Bar, offering more substantial food, is near ramp 2. For a small charge, you can sit in the two-tiered, open-air section. Ages 21 and over only.

FIRST GAME CERTIFICATE
The White Sox offer a certificate for guests to commemorate their first time at U.S. Cellular Field. Visit any Guest Relations Booth behind home plate to pick one up.

CHICAGO WITH KIDS

Chicago sometimes seems to have been designed with kids in mind. There are many places to play and things to do, from building sand castles at one of the lakefront's many beaches to playing indoor minigolf at the Navy Pier in winter. Here are some suggestions for ways to show kids the sights.

Museums

Several area museums are specifically designed for kids. At the **Chicago Children's Museum** (700 E. Grand Ave., Navy Pier), three floors of exhibits cast off with a play structure in the shape of a schooner, where kids can walk the gangplank and slide down to the lower level. Also at **Navy Pier** you'll find a Ferris wheel and Viennese swings (the kind that go around in a circle like a merry-go-round). In winter a Chicago-theme minigolf course is set up in the Crystal Ballroom, an atriumlike space with fountains that spring from one potted plant to another in synchronized motion.

Many other Chicago museums are also kid-friendly, especially the butterfly haven at the **Peggy Notebaert Nature Museum,** the replica coal mine at the **Museum of Science and Industry,** the dinosaur exhibits at the **Field Museum,** and the sharks at the **John G. Shedd Aquarium.** Less well known are the cool music and video booths where kids and adults can create their own compositions and harmonies using digital tools at **Echo,** the Eloise M. Martin Center of the Chicago Symphony Orchestra (67 E. Adams St. ☎ 312/294–3030).

Parks, Zoos & Outside Activities

Chicago's neighborhoods are dotted with area play lots that have playground equipment as well as several ice-skating rinks for winter months. On scorching days, visit the **63rd Street Beach House,** at 63rd Street and Lake Shore Drive in Woodlawn. The interactive spiral fountain in the courtyard jumps and splashes, leaving kids giggling and jumping. **Millennium Park** (55 N. Michigan Ave.) has a 16,000-square-foot ice-skating rink. Skaters have an unparalleled view of downtown as they whiz around the ice.

For more structured fun, there are two zoos: the free **Lincoln Park Zoo** (2200 N. Cannon Dr. at Lake Shore Dr. and Fullerton Pkwy.) and the large, suburban **Brookfield Zoo** (1st Ave. and 31st St., Brookfield), which has such surprising exhibits as a wall of pulsing jellyfish. The **Buccaneer Pirate Adventure Cruise** (Wagner Charter Cruise Co. Dock, Lower Wacker Dr. between Wells St. and Franklin/Orleans St. bridges) sets sail with wannabe pirates, teaching them about the river's locks and entertaining kids with magic tricks.

FABULOUS FESTIVALS

Chicago festivals range from local neighborhood get-togethers to citywide extravaganzas. People fly in for the Chicago Blues Festival, but try to catch a neighborhood street fair for some great people-watching and fried dough if you're in town between June and September. On some weekends, there are several festivals at once. For details, see ⊕ www.chicagoreader.com.

The **St. Patrick's Day parade** (☎ 312/942–9188) turns the city on its head: the Chicago River is dyed green, shamrocks decorate the street, and the center stripe of Dearborn Street is painted the color of the Irish from Wacker Drive to Van Buren Street. This is your chance to get your fill of bagpipes and green knee socks. You probably won't see the whole thing—the parade can clock in at over four hours.

The **Chicago Blues Festival** (☎ 312/744–3315), in Grant Park, is a popular four-day, three-stage event in June starring blues greats from Chicago and around the country. If you see only one festival in Chicago, this is the one. *See* Entertainment chapter for more information.

The medium-size **Chicago Gospel Fest** (☎ 312/744–3315) brings its joyful sounds to Grant Park in early June.

Taste of Chicago (✉ Grant Park, Columbus Dr. between Jackson and Randolph Sts. ☎ 312/744–3315) dishes out pizza, cheesecake, and other Chicago specialties to 3.5 million people over a 10-day period before the July Fourth holiday that includes top pop acts as well as novelties—like high divers who torpedo into small swimming pools.

The **Chicago Jazz Festival** (☎ 312/744–3315) holds sway for four days during Labor Day weekend in Grant Park.

At the **Celtic Fest,** Celtic food, art, storytelling, dance, and a bagpiper's circle celebrate everything Irish. It's held in Grant Park during the month of September.

At the weeklong **World Music Festival,** international artists play traditional and contemporary music at venues across the city in September.

Street Fairs are held every week in summer, but two stand out as the best. **Halsted Market Days,** in August, is the city's largest street festival. It's held in the heart of the gay community of Lakeview and has blocks and blocks of vendors as well as some wild entertainment such as zany drag queens and the radical cheerleaders. The **Taste of Randolph** is more sedate, featuring dishes from the fine restaurants lining the western end of Randolph Street in June.

GET OUT OF TOWN

You could spend a month or two just exploring the city of Chicago, but the surrounding towns are likewise rich in history, culture, and activity. The closest suburbs offer theaters and museums; the farther out you go, the more likely you are to find wooded parks and quiet places.

Brush up your Ernest Hemingway

Ernest Hemingway Birthplace. Part of the literary legacy of Oak Park, this three-story turreted Queen Anne Victorian, which stands in frilly contrast to the many streamlined Prairie-style homes elsewhere in the neighborhood, contains period-furnished rooms and many photos and artifacts pertaining to the writer's early life. Museum curators have redecorated rooms to faithfully depict the house as it looked at the turn of the 20th century; you can poke your head inside the room in which the author was born on July 21, 1899. ⊠ 339 N. Oak Park Ave. ☎ 708/848-2222 ⊕ www.hemingway.org ✉ Joint ticket with Hemingway Museum $7 ☉ Sun.–Fri. 1–5, Sat. 10–5.

Ernest Hemingway Museum. How did the author's first 20 years in Oak Park impact his later work? Check out the exhibits and videos here to find out. Don't miss his first "book," a set of drawings with captions written by his mother, Grace. Holdings include reproduced manuscripts and letters. ⊠ 200 N. Oak Park Ave. ☎ 708/848-2222 ⊕ www.hemingway.org ✉ Joint ticket with Hemingway Birthplace $7 ☉ Sun.–Fri. 1–5, Sat. 10–5.

For Frank Lloyd Wright's Oak Park **See Page 137**

Follow the Chicago Symphony Orchestra

If you enjoy music under the stars, the outdoor concerts at **Ravinia Park** are a stellar treat. The **Ravinia Festival** is the summer home of the Chicago Symphony Orchestra. Come for jazz, chamber music, pop, and dance performances. Pack a picnic and blanket and sit on the lawn for a little more than the cost of a movie ($15). Seats are also available in the pavilion for

---

ERNEST HEMINGWAY: OAK PARK PROTÉGÉ

It seems unlikely that the rough-and-tumble adventurer and writer was born in 1899 amid the manicured suburb of Oak Park, Illinois, a town he described as having "wide lawns and narrow minds." He excelled at writing for the high school paper—a skill that turned into his life's work. A volunteer stint as an ambulance driver introduced him to World War I and its visceral horrors—he used that experience and the lessons he learned as a reporter for the *Kansas City Star* to craft emotionally complex novels built from deceptively simple sentences, like his master work, *A Farewell to Arms.* Hemingway later lived in Toronto and Chicago. Though his return visits to Oak Park were infrequent, the residents celebrate him there to this day.

a significantly higher price ($20–$60). Restaurants and snack bars are on park grounds. Concerts start at 8 PM; be at the park at 6:30 to park and get settled. ✉ *Green Bay and Lake Cook Rds., in Highland Park, 26 mi north of downtown Chicago* ☎ *847/266–5100* 📠 *847/433–7983* ⊕ *www.ravinia.org.*

Unwind Outdoors

⭐ **Fodor's Choice** See the spectacular spring blooming season or the beautiful display of mid-June roses at the **Chicago Botanic Garden.** Among the 23 different gardens are a three-island Japanese garden, a waterfall garden, a sensory garden and a 4-acre fruit-and-vegetable garden. Three big greenhouses showcase a desert, a rain forest, and a formal garden with flowers that bloom all winter long. Standout special events are the Antiques and Garden Fair in April and the Railroad Garden in summer. ✉ *Lake Cook Rd. and U.S. 41* ☎ *847/835–5440* ⊕ *www.chicagobotanic.org* 🎫 *Free, parking $8.75, tram tour $4* 🕐 *Daily 8 AM–sunset; 45-min tours through Oct., daily 10–3, weather permitting.*

Take a quiet hike around the **Morton Arboretum,** full of woodlands, wetlands, and display gardens. Trees, shrubs, and vines flower year-round, but in spring the flowering trees are particularly spectacular. You can drive your car through some of the grounds, but we think it's much nicer to walk. There are lots of trails to take, and most take about 15–30 minutes. Don't miss the Daffodil Glade in early spring. Tours are scheduled most Sunday afternoons. ✉ *4100 Illinois Rte. 53, 25 mi southwest of downtown Chicago* ☎ *630/719–2400* ⊕ *www.mortonarb.org* 🎫 *$5, Wed. $3; tram tours $4* 🕐 *Daily 7–7 in* summer daylight savings time; until 5 in winter.

Samuel Insull, partner of Thomas Edison and founder of Commonwealth Edison, built the mansion at the **Cuneo Museum and Gardens** in 1916 as a country home. After Insull lost his fortune, John Cuneo Sr., the printing press magnate, bought the estate and fashioned it into something far more spectacular. The sky-lighted great hall in the main house resembles the open central courtyard of an Italian palazzo; the private family chapel has stained-glass windows; and a gilded grand piano graces the ballroom. The house is filled with antiques, porcelains, 17th-century Flemish tapestries, and Italian paintings. The gardens appeared in the film *My Best Friend's Wedding.*

To get to Cuneo by car (about a 45-minute drive from downtown Chicago), take I–94 West to IL Route 60 West. Turn right (north) onto IL Route 21 (Milwaukee Avenue). It's half a mile to the entrance. To get here by train, take Metra's Milwaukee District North Line from Union Station to Libertyville. Hail a cab to the mansion; it's about 5 mi from the station to Cuneo. ✉ *1350 N. Milwaukee Ave., 15 mi west of Lake Forest, 40 mi northwest of downtown Chicago.* ☎ *847/362–3042* ⊕ *www.cuneomuseum.org* 🎫 *$5 per car; $10 per person for mansion tours* 🕐 *Tues.–Sun. 10–5; guided mansion tours Feb.–Dec., Tues.–Sat. at 11, 1, and 3, self-guided on Sun.*

CHICAGO THEN & NOW

The Early Days

Before Chicago was officially "discovered" by the team of Father Jacques Marquette, a French missionary, and Louis Jolliet, a French–Canadian mapmaker and trader, in 1673, the area served as a center of trade and seasonal hunting grounds for several Native American tribes, including the Miamis, Illinois, and Potowatomis. Villages kept close trading ties with the French, though scuffles with the Fox tribe kept the French influence at bay until 1779. That year, black French trader Jean Baptiste Point du Sable built a five-room "mansion" by the mouth of the Chicago river on the shores of Lake Michigan.

The Great Fire

The city grew until 1871, when a fire in the barn of Catherine and Patrick O'Leary spread across the crowded wooden buildings of the city, destroying 18,000 structures within 36 hours. A year later, the city was on its way to recovery, and the fire led to an explosion of architectural innovation.

Gangsters to the Great Migration

World War I (aka the Great War) changed the face of Chicago. Postwar—and especially during Prohibition (1920–1933)—the Torrio–Capone organization expanded its gambling and liquor distribution operations, consolidating its power during the violent "beer wars" from 1924 to 1930. Hundreds of casualties include the seven victims of the infamous 1929 St. Valentine's Day massacre.

The Great War also led to the Great Migration, when African-Americans from the South moved to the northern cities between 1916 and 1970. WWI slowed immigration from Europe, but increased jobs in Chicago's manufacturing industry. More than 500,000 African-Americans came to the city to find work; the black population, which was 2% before the Great War, was 33% by 1970. By the mid-20th century, African-Americans were a strong force in Chicago's political, economic, and cultural life.

IMPORTANT DATES IN CHICAGO HISTORY

1673	Chicago discovered by Marquette and Jolliet
1779	Jean Baptiste Point du Sable, a "free Negro," and his wife Catherine, a Potowatami Indian, are the first Chicago settlers
1837	Chicago incorporated as a city
1860	First national political convention. Abraham Lincoln nominated as the Republican candidate for president
1871	Great Chicago Fire

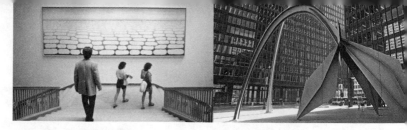

Mayor Daley and the Notorious 1968 Democratic Convention

The Daley dynasty began when Richard J. Daley became mayor in 1955. He was re-elected five times and his son, Richard M. Daley, currently runs the city.

The first Mayor Daley redrew Chicago's landscape, overseeing the construction of O'Hare International Airport, the expressway system, the University of Illinois at Chicago, and a towering skyline. He also helped John F. Kennedy get elected, thanks to his control of Chicago's Democratic party.

Despite these advances, Mayor Richard J. Daley is perhaps best known for his crackdown on student protesters during the 1968 Democratic National Convention. Americans watched on their televisions as the Chicago police beat the city's youth with sticks and blinded them with tear gas. That incident, plus his "shoot to kill" order during the riots that followed the assassination of Dr. Martin Luther King Jr., and his use of public funds to build giant, disastrous public housing projects like Cabrini–Green, eventually led to the temporary dissolution of the Democratic machine in Chicago after Daley's death and the win of Chicago's first black—and beloved—mayor, Harold Washington, in 1983.

Chicago Today

The thriving commercial and financial "City of Broad Shoulders" is spiked with gorgeous architecture and set with cultural and recreational gems, including the Art Institute, Millennium Park, 250 theater companies, and 31 mi of shoreline. Three million residents live within city limits. The current Mayor Daley gave downtown a makeover, adding wrought-iron street furniture, regular fireworks, and planters of flowers. Spectacular lights brighten buildings along Michigan Avenue after dark. There are always controversies, but most Chicagoans are proud to call the city home.

1885	First skyscraper in the country, Home Insurance Building (no longer standing), is built
1886	Haymarket Riot
1893	World's Columbian Exposition
1929	St. Valentine's Day Massacre
1968	Democratic National convention
1973	Sears Tower, tallest building in North America, completed
2005	Chicago White Sox win the World Series

BEHIND THE SCENES

For a look at what (or who) makes the city tick, check out the following activities.

Black & White & Read All Over
Chicago Tribune Freedom Center. Tour the Chicago Tribune's printing plant and the New York Times' Midwest distribution center. ✉ *777 W. Chicago Ave., West Loop* ☎ *312/222–2116* ✉ *Free, but call ahead.*

WORD OF MOUTH

I absolutely loved the tour. I remember him showing us how they could "stop the presses," dump the copy and destroy, then reprint totally different copy within a certain time frame. —JJ5

Movers & Shakers
Graceland Cemetery. A comprehensive guide available at the entrance walks you by the graves and tombs of the people who made Chicago great, including merchandiser

---

WORD OF MOUTH

We've heard about Graceland for years but had never visited. I'm so glad we finally got around to it. Very interesting. —CAPH52

Marshall Field and railroad car builder George Pullman. ✉ *4001 N. Clark St., Far North Side* ☎ *773/525–1105* ⊕ *www.gracelandcemetery.org* ✉ *Free.*

See Green
Federal Reserve Bank. Though they don't hand out money here, they sure do handle a lot of the green stuff. The facility processes currency and checks, scanning bills for counterfeit, destroying unfit currency, and repackaging fit currency. A visitor center in the lobby has permanent exhibits of old bills, counterfeit money, and a million dollars in $1 bills. One-hour tours explain how money travels and show a high-speed currency-processing machine. Call two months in advance for tour reservations, since it's often booked in spring and fall with school groups. ✉ *230 S. LaSalle St., Loop* ☎ *312/322–2400* ⊕ *www.chicagofed.org* ✉ *Free.*

Tour a Factory
Though Chicago isn't the industrial center it once was, you can still watch all sorts of things being made in the Chicago area, from cheesecakes to harps. Log on to ⊕ www.factorytoursusa.com for a complete list.

Neighborhoods

WORD OF MOUTH

"Lincoln Square is a charming old German community and Andersonville is the same for the Swedish. Also, explore Hyde Park—there's Jackson Park with the Japanese Gardens, a few small museums on the University of Chicago Campus, and the Robie House. The Mexican-American Museum in Pilsen is really cool, and there is of course some great Mexican food and shopping in the neighborhood."

—flamingomonkey

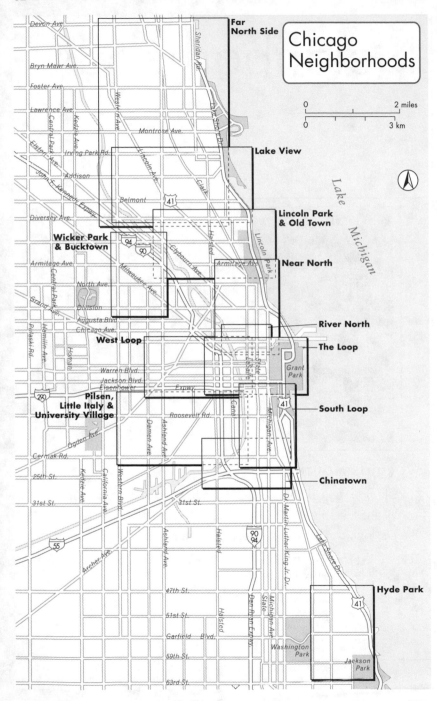

Far
North Side

Chicago
Neighborhoods

0   2 miles
0   3 km

Lake View

Lincoln Park
& Old Town

Wicker Park
& Bucktown

Near North

River North

The Loop

West Loop

South Loop

Pilsen,
Little Italy &
University Village

Chinatown

Hyde Park

LOOP

Sightseeing
★ ★ ★ ★
Dining
★ ★ ★
Lodging
★ ★ ★
Shopping
★ ★
Nightlife
★ ★ ★

The Loop is a living architectural museum, where shimmering modern towers stand side-by-side with 19th-century buildings. Striking sculptures by Picasso, Miró, and Chagall watch over plazas alive with music and farmers' markets in summer. There are noisy, mesmerizing trading centers, gigantic department stores, internationally known landmarks like the Sears Tower and the Art Institute, and the city's newest playground, Millennium Park. Rattling overhead, encircling it all, is the train system Chicagoans call the El.

Known as the Loop since the cable cars of the 1880s looped around the central business district, downtown Chicago comprises the area south of the Chicago River, west of Lake Michigan, and north of Congress Parkway/the Eisenhower Expressway. The western boundary used to be the Chicago River, but the frontier continues to push westward. Handsome skyscrapers now line every foot of South Wacker Drive east of the river, and investors have sent construction crews across the bridges in search of more land to fuel the expansion.

What's Here

Getting around the Loop is easy. It's laid out like a grid: State Street intersects north-south blocks, and Madison Street intersects east-west blocks. Where State and Madison converge is the zero point from where the rest of the city fans out. It's also where you find the department store **Carson Pirie Scott,** with its breathtaking decorative cast-iron façade—an outstanding example of Louis Sullivan's work. Farther north on State Street—the Loop's most famous thoroughfare—is a **Macy's** department store that until 2006 had been the flagship location for the much mourned Marshall Field's. Despite the name change, the landmark turn-of-the-20th-century building is still beguiling.

GETTING ORIENTED

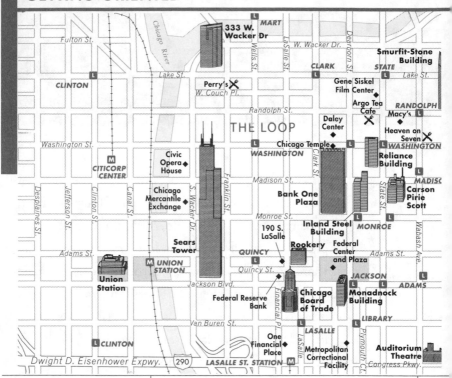

MAKING THE MOST OF YOUR TIME

If you have the time, give yourself a whole day to explore the Loop. You can easily spend half a day at the Art Institute. The rest of your day you can spend sunning yourself in Millennium Park, shopping up and down State Street, taking a trip to the top of the Sears Tower, or meandering among the architectural masterpieces and sculptures. And of course, you'll want to allow yourself time to stand in line for Garret Popcorn.

GETTING HERE

Take a bus to Michigan Avenue and Wacker Drive. From the north, you can take Bus 3, 145, 147, or 151. Coming from the south, you can take Bus 3, 6, 145, 146, 147, or 151. The Lake stop on the El's Red Line will put you at State and Lake Streets. The Brown, Green, and Purple lines stop at State, above ground, at Lake Street. If you arrive by car, you can park it in the subterranean Grant Park North Garage, with an entrance on Michigan Avenue. Most streets in the Loop prohibit parking weekdays from 6 AM to 6 PM.

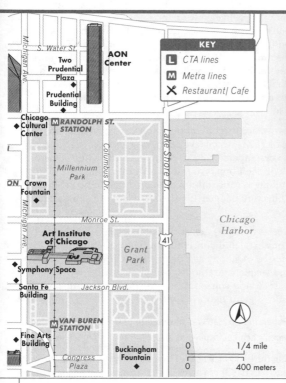

KEY

L *CTA lines*

M *Metra lines*

✗ *Restaurant/ Cafe*

S. Water St.

Michigan Ave.

Two Prudential Plaza

AON Center

Prudential Building

Chicago Cultural Center

M RANDOLPH ST. STATION

Columbus Dr.

Lake Shore Dr.

Millennium Park

Crown Fountain

Michigan Ave.

Monroe St.

Chicago Harbor

41

Art Institute of Chicago

Grant Park

Symphony Space

Santa Fe Building

Jackson Blvd.

M VAN BUREN STATION

Fine Arts Building

Congress Plaza

Buckingham Fountain

0   1/4 mile

0   400 meters

NEIGHBORHOOD TOP 5

1. Spend an afternoon with George Seurat and *A Sunday on La Grande Jatte* at the Art Institute.

2. Stand between the 50-foot faces screened onto the two towers of the Crown Fountain in Millennium Park and wait for them to spit.

3. Jump in a car and get lost in the underground world of Lower Wacker Drive.

4. Give a thumbs up—or a thumbs down—to a movie at the Gene Siskel Film Center.

5. Follow your nose and line up at one of the Loop locations of Garret Popcorn for a tub of the good stuff.

QUICK BITES

Heaven on Seven (✉ 111 N. Wabash Ave., 7th fl., Loop ☎ 312/263-6443) is a Loop legend, famous for casual Cajun breakfasts and lunches that have area office workers gladly lining up to chow down.

Sample one of dozens of exotic varieties of tea at **Argo Tea Cafe** (✉ 16 W. Randolph St., Loop ☎ 312/553-1551). Light lunch fare and sweet treats round out the menu.

Perry's (✉ 180 N. Franklin St., Loop ☎ 312/372-7557) is a hit as much for the trivia questions Perry announces over his deli's PA system as it is for the overstuffed sandwiches.

The lines form early and stay long throughout the day at **Garret Popcorn** (2 W. Jackson Blvd., Loop ☎ 312/360-1108).

Continuing on State, just north of Randolph Street, is the old theater district. First is the ornate 1921 Beaux Arts **Chicago Theatre,** a former movie palace that now hosts live performances. Across the street is the **Gene Siskel Film Center,** which screens art, industrial, foreign, and classic movies. West on Randolph Street is the **Ford Center for the Performing Arts–Oriental Theatre,** with its long, glitzy neon sign. On Dearborn is the **Goodman Theatre,** wrapped in the 1923 art deco facades of the landmark Harris & Selwyn Twin Theaters. One more block west is the **Cadillac Palace Theatre,** a renovated 1926 vaudeville house that still has its original marble lobby.

Much of the impressive architecture in the Loop can be credited to the Great Chicago Fire of 1871, which leveled the city and cleared the way for the building of skyscrapers using steel-frame construction. One of the best things to do in the Loop is to just stroll around and take in the different types of buildings. More information on the architecture in the Loop is in the Architecture chapter (page 115). Here are some neighborhood highlights.

On Washington Street is the **Daley Center,** an outdoor plaza that has holiday and farmer's markets, and concerts. Check out the unnamed Picasso sculpture, referred to simply as *The Picasso.* Opposite the Daley Center is the **Chicago Temple,** a Methodist church whose beautiful spire is so tall that it's best seen at some distance. Also on the south side of the street is Joan Miró's giant figure, *Chicago.*

DID YOU KNOW? Controversy swirled when the Picasso was unveiled in 1967—everyone wanted to know if it was a woman's head or inspired by one of the artist's Afghan hounds.

To the west, following the bend of Wacker Drive, is the art deco **Civic Opera House,** where Chicago's Lyric Opera gives its performances, and the pale-grape-color twin towers of the **Chicago Mercantile Exchange,** where action on the trading floors is frenetic. East on Monroe Street, the sunken, bi-level **Bank One Plaza** has room to rest in the shadow of the sweeping Bank One building that curves skyward in the shape of the letter "A." The Chagall mosaic, *The Four Seasons,* is at the northeast end of the plaza.

Back on Michigan Avenue, at the eastern end of the Loop, is **Millennium Park,** anchored by the immensely popular Bean structure. On the west side of the intersection of Randolph Street and Michigan Avenue is the **Chicago Cultural Center,** home to the **Chicago Office of Tourism Visitor Information Center.** At 200 East Randolph is the soaring **Aon Center,** the second-tallest building in Chicago. Directly west of the Aon Center is the **Prudential Building,** Chicago's tallest building until the late 1960s. Behind it rises the rocket ship–like **Two Prudential Plaza,** affectionately nicknamed Pru Two.

The southern part of the Loop balances the hub of the financial district with the fine arts. On one block is the **Art Institute of Chicago,** the grand-looking **Symphony Center** (home to the internationally acclaimed Chicago Symphony Orchestra), and the **Santa Fe Building** (where Daniel Burnham, the architect, had his offices). Farther south on Michigan Avenue is the **Fine Arts Building.**

On Dearborn Street is the **Federal Center and Plaza,** designed by Mies van der Rohe, and anchored by Alexander Calder's red mobile *Flamingo* sculpture. The beautiful **Rookery,** an imposing red-stone building that is one of the city's 19th-century showpieces, is on LaSalle Street; make sure to see the Frank Lloyd Wright lobby. Nearby is Phillip Johnson's **190 South LaSalle,** with striking gold-leaf ceilings. Across Quincy Street is the massive **Federal Reserve Bank.** Farther south at Jackson Boulevard the street seems to disappear in front of the commanding **Chicago Board of Trade,** which sits like a throne reigning over the financial district.

From Jackson Boulevard and LaSalle Street, look up to the west to see the hulking **Sears Tower,** the tallest building in North America.

At A Glance

SEE CORRESPONDING
CHAPTERS. SIGHTS ARE IN
THE EXPERIENCE CHAPTER.
SIGHTS
Sears Tower Skydeck
Millennium Park
ArchiCenter of the Chicago
  Architecture
  Foundation–River Tours
Chicago Architecture
  Foundation River
  Cruise
Sailboats Inc.–sailboat
  rentals
Federal Reserve Bank
ARCHITECTURE
2 Prudential Plaza
311 South Wacker Drive
333 West Wacker Drive
Aon Center
Auditorium Building
Carbide & Carbon Building
Carson Pirie Scott & Co
Chase Tower
Chicago Board of Trade
Chicago Cultural Center
Chicago Temple
Civic Opera House
Daley Center
Federal Center and Plaza
Fine Arts Building
Harold Washington Library
  Center
Hyatt Center
Inland Steel Building
James R. Thompson Center
Marquette Building
Monadnock Building

Reliance Building
Santa Fe Center
Sears Tower
Smurfit-Stone Building
Symphony Center
The Rookery
SHOPPING
DEPARTMENT STORES
Carson Pirie Scott
Filene's Basement
Macy's (formerly Marshall
  Field's)
BOOKS/PRINTED MATTER
Brent Books & Cards
Powell's Bookstore
Prairie Avenue Bookshop
Savvy Traveller
CAMERAS/FILM
Central Camera
CLOTHING & SHOES
Bates Design
Syd Jerome
Altman's Men's Shoes
  and Boots
JEWELRY, SOUVENIRS &
GIFTS
Chicago Watch Center
The Jeweler's Center at the
  Mallers Building
Museum Shop at the Art
  Institute of Chicago
Chicago Architecture
  Foundation ArchiCenter
  Shop & Tour Center
Gallery 37 Store
Garrett Popcorn
Illinois Artisans Shop

Harlan J. Berk
Iwan Ries and Co
MODERATE DINING
Atwood Café, *Contemp.*
Park Grill, *Contemp.*
The Berghoff, *German*
Petterino's, *Italian*
312 Chicago, *Italian*
Vivere, *Italian*
Nick & Tony's Italian
  Chophouse, *Italian*
The Grillroom, *Steak*
EXPENSIVE DINING
Rhapsody, *Contemp.*
Aria, *Eclectic*
Everest, *French*
Trattoria No. 10, *Italian*
Russian Tea Time, *Russian*
Nick's Fishmarket, *Seafood*
Catch 35, *Seafood*
The Palm, *Steak*
Morton's, The Steakhouse,
  Steak
ENTERTAINMENT
Encore, *Lounge*
Tasting Room, *Wine bar*
MODERATE HOTEL
Hyatt Regency Chicago
Hotel Monaco
Swissôtel
EXPENSIVE HOTEL
Palmer House Hilton
Fairmont
Hard Rock Hotel
Renaissance Chicago Hotel
W Chicago City Center
Hotel Burnham
Hotel Allegro Chicago

SOUTH LOOP INCLUDING PRINTER'S ROW, MUSEUM CAMPUS & BRONZEVILLE

Sightseeing
★ ★ ★ ★

Dining
★ ★ ★

Lodging
★ ★

Shopping
★

Nightlife
★ ★

The South Loop, bounded by Congress Parkway–Eisenhower Expressway on the north, Michigan Avenue on the east, Cermak Avenue on the south, and the Chicago River on the west, presents a striking contrast to the Loop, with its less trafficked streets and a more subdued—but also grittier—vibe. Though it was one of Chicago's first residential districts, the area eventually became a symbol of urban blight. A redevelopment boom is transforming it into a residential neighborhood again, this time attracting more and more residents who like its ethnic and racial mix and growing sense of community, as well as its proximity to the Loop, great museums, and hip restaurants.

Trips to the Museum Campus and Printer's Row district here are musts. Perched on the lakefront, Museum Campus is a glorious spot to take in the skyline and watch the boats go by. It's home to the **Field Museum,** the **John G. Shedd Aquarium,** and the **Adler Planetarium & Astronomy Museum,** all of which hold some of the most important and exciting exhibits and artifacts in the country. Printer's Row, a small enclave to the west, was once a thriving commercial area and the center of the printing trades in Chicago. Today it stands as a prime example of the South Loop renaissance with quaint coffeehouses, shops, and restaurants inhabiting the area's beautiful buildings. Farther afield, but worth a visit if there's time, is the Bronzeville area, a historic community originally settled by waves of African-Americans fleeing the South after World War I.

What's Here

The 57-acre Museum Campus is home to the Big Three—the **Field Museum**, the **John G. Shedd Aquarium**, and the **Adler Planetarium & Astronomy Museum**, all united in one pedestrian-friendly, parklike setting. Park your car in one of the lots just past the Field Museum on McFetridge Drive, or ride the free Museum Campus trolley (☎ 877/244–2246), which connects the three museums with other downtown tourist attractions and train stations. It operates daily from Memorial Day to Labor Day and on holidays, and runs only on weekends the rest of the year. On the west side of the campus is the Field Museum, which houses a staggering array of culture- and nature-focused exhibits that date from prehistoric times to the present. It's most famous is Sue, the largest and most complete T. rex skeleton in the world. No one's sure if Sue was actually a male or female. She's named for Sue Hendrickson, the fossil hunter who discovered her skeleton.

DID YOU KNOW? The large marble panel in the lobby of the Adler has bronze emblems representing each of the planets, but if you count them up, there are only eight. That's because the discovery of Pluto, the ninth planet, was announced after the panel had been installed in 1930.

The Shedd Aquarium, on the lakefront just past the Field Museum, has bizarre and fantastically beautiful fish, plus dolphins and beluga whales. On the east side of the campus, at the far end of a peninsula that juts out into Lake Michigan (and provides wonderful views and photo opportunities of Chicago's skyline), is the Adler Planetarium & Astronomy Museum—the first modern planetarium in the western hemisphere.

FRUGAL FUN If you're visiting all three museums, plus some of the city's other big attractions, buy a Chicago CityPass (adults $49, kids 3–11 $38). You'll avoid long lines and get access to the Field, the Shedd, and the Adler, plus the Art Institute of Chicago, the Hancock Observatory, and the Museum of Science and Industry.

Just south of Museum Campus is **Soldier Field,** the building with the massive columns reminiscent of ancient Greece and the home of the Chicago Bears. A modern glass addition, built in 2003, appears to grow out of the 1920s sports palace design.

The Printer's Row district is bounded by Congress Parkway on the north, Polk Street on the south, Plymouth Court to the east, and the Chicago River to the west. It fell into disrepair in the 1960s as the printing industry moved to other areas in the city because of changing needs for space. Sleazy bars, pawnbrokers, and pornography shops filled the area, but a neighborhood resurgence began in the late 1970s with renovations to some of the run-down loft and office buildings. You can still see examples here of buildings by the group that represented the First Chicago School of Architecture (including Louis Sullivan), as well as **Dearborn Station,** a Romanesque Revival-style structure that was once the city's main passenger train hub. These days this section of town is best

GETTING ORIENTED

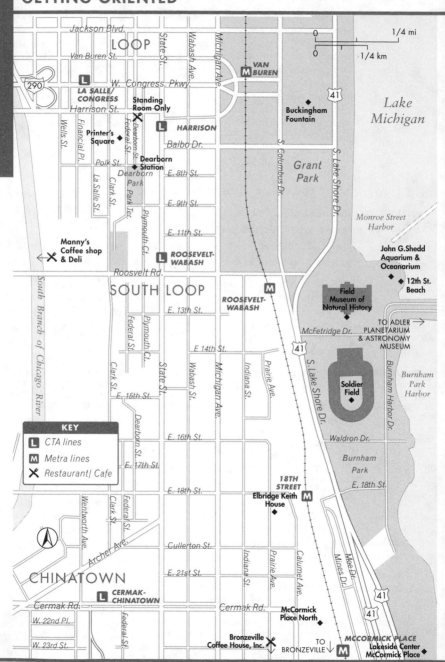

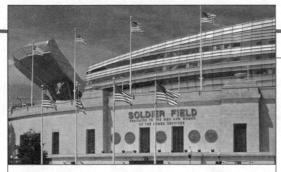

2

GETTING HERE

Buses 6, 12, and 146 take you to Museum Campus. If you drive, take Lake Shore Drive to the Museum campus exit. There's some coveted meter parking as well as pricier lots adjacent to the museums. For Printer's Row, take the El's Brown, Orange, or Purple line to the library stop, or the Red line to Harrison. Buses 6, 22, 36, and 145 will also get you there. Drivers can take Congress Parkway to Dearborn Street. Bronzeville can be easily accessed by buses 49 and 95. To get there by car, take Lake Shore Drive to 31st Street, then travel west to Martin Luther King Drive.

MAKING THE MOST OF YOUR TIME

Plan on at least a day for a visit to the three museums (you could spend a day at the mammoth Field Museum alone). Allow extra time to enjoy the spectacular skyline and lake views from Museum Campus and to stroll along the harbor. Note that traffic can get snarled and special parking rules go into effect around Museum Campus when the Chicago Bears are playing in neighboring Soldier Field. Prairie Avenue is a quick-hit, taking a couple of hours at most. A trip to Bronzeville can take from an hour or two to half-day, depending on whether you opt for one of the longer organized tours.

QUICK BITES

Have a corned beef sandwich all the other delis in town aim to beat at **Manny's Coffee Shop & Deli** (✉ 1141 S. Jefferson St., South Loop ☎ 312/939-2855).

"Da Mare" himself, Richard M. Daley, has stood up for the turkey burgers at the tiny **Standing Room Only (SRO Chicago)** (✉ 610 S. Dearborn St., South Loop ☎ 312/360-1776).

Bronzeville Coffee House, Inc. (✉ 538 E. 43rd St., South Loop ☎ 773/536-0494) is a comfy choice for coffee, smoothies, and baked goods.

SAFETY

The South Loop is a changing neighborhood. Some parts can still feel sketchy, so exercise caution, particularly at night, by sticking to populated and well-lit streets. Group tours of Bronzeville are recommended for those unfamiliar with the area.

TOURS

The **Chicago Office of Tourism** (312/742-1190) offers a half-day bus tour of Bronzeville. Other tours are offered by the **Black Metropolis Convention and Tourism Council** (773/548-2579), and **Tour Black Chicago** (773/684-9034). **Black CouTours** (773/233-8907) offers a 2½-hour excursion of black culture including Bronzeville and other highlights.

NEIGHBORHOOD TOP 5

1. Stand next to Sue the T. rex at the Field Museum and get an idea of how ants feel.

2. Catch some of the best live blues in the city at Buddy Guy's Legends—the man himself takes up residency on stage every January.

3. Tailgate in the parking lot before a Chicago Bears game at Solider Field.

4. Grab a corned beef sandwich and potato pancake with a cross-section of Chicago at Manny's Coffee Shop & Deli.

5. Take a step back in Chicago's rich African-American history with a guided tour of Bronzeville.

known for the annual **Printer's Row Book Fair,** a weekend-long literary celebration held each June.

That futuristic, cloudlike structure that seems to rise from the river west of Printer's Row on Polk Street is Marina City, a condominium complex and self-contained city within a city. It has its own private 1-acre park, market, clubhouse, dry cleaner, and boat slips.

The historic **Bronzeville** neighborhood, once known as Black Metropolis, roughly covers the area south of McCormick Place and north of Hyde Park between State Street and Cottage Grove Avenue. Following World War I, this neighborhood became a place where African-Americans who had migrated from the South could escape race restrictions prevalent in other parts of the city. Landmarks include the neighborhood's symbolic entrance, a tall statue at 26th Place and Martin Luther King Jr. Drive that depicts a new arrival from the South bearing a suitcase held together with string. The Victory monument at 35th Street and King Drive honors the all-black 8th Illinois Regiment in World War I. Walk along Martin Luther King Jr. Drive between 25th and 35th streets to follow a commemorative trail of more than 90 sidewalk plaques honoring the best and brightest of the community, including Pulitzer–prize winner Gwendolyn Brooks, whose first book of poetry was called *A Street in Bronzeville.*

At A Glance

SEE CORRESPONDING CHAPTERS. SIGHTS ARE IN THE EXPERIENCE CHAPTER.

SIGHTS
Grant Park & Buckingham Fountain
12th Street Beach
Soldier Field

MUSEUMS
Adler Planetarium & Astronomy Museum
Art Institute
Field Museum
John G. Shedd Aquarium
Museum of Contemporary Photography
National Vietnam Veterans Art Museum
Spertus Museum

ARCHITECTURE
Dearborn Station
Donohue Building
Franklin Building
Pontiac Building
River City
Illinois Institute of Technology (farther south)

SHOPPING

AUCTIONS
Susanin's Auctioneers and Appraisers

MODERATE DINING
Opera, *Chinese*

EXPENSIVE DINING
Chicago Firehouse Restaurant, *American–Casual*
Gioco, *Italian*

ENTERTAINMENT
Dance Center of Columbia College Chicago, *Theater*
Kitty O'Shea's, *Pub*
HotHouse, *Music club*
Cotton Club, *Jazz*
Velvet Lounge, *Jazz*

BUDGET HOTEL
Essex

MODERATE HOTEL
Holiday Inn & Suites Downtown Chicago
Hilton Chicago

2

WEST LOOP INCLUDING GREEKTOWN

Sightseeing
★

Dining
★ ★ ★ ★

Lodging
★

Shopping
★ ★

Nightlife
★ ★ ★ ★

Most of the West Loop languished for years as a waste-land peppered with warehouses and meatpacking plants. But now, many of the warehouses have been converted to urban lofts, and a thriving contemporary art scene has emerged around Fulton Market. Harpo Studios, the pro-duction house of Chicago's grande dame, Oprah Winfrey, is here, and there's also an ultrahip dining and nightclub scene. By day, it's a relatively quiet, concrete-laden area where plant workers, white-collar business types, and stroller-pushing power moms alike share the sidewalks. When night falls, the scenesters come out of the woodwork, and the too-cool-for-school vibe reigns.

Greektown, a five-block stretch of Halsted Street within the West Loop, is a world all its own. Here, tourists mingle with people from all over Chicago—they all come to the strip's restaurants, groceries, and shops for a taste of Greece that goes beyond plate breaking.

What's Here

The West Loop is bound by Ashland Avenue on the west, the Chicago River on the east, Grand Avenue on the north, and the Eisenhower Ex-pressway on the south.

Randolph Street is the neighborhood's restaurant row and home to some of the city's most notable dining spots, including French-inspired **Marché**, which many credit with jumpstarting the neighborhood's turnaround in the early 1990s, and **Blackbird**, a nouveau American hot spot lauded by critics worldwide as one of the best restaurants anywhere.

GETTING ORIENTED

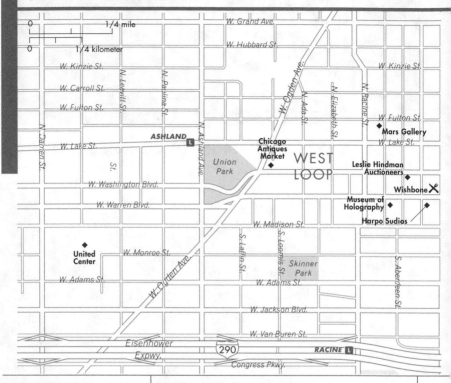

GETTING HERE	MAKING THE MOST OF YOUR TIME
By car, take the Kennedy Expressway to the Randolph Street exit. You can also get here by taking the 8 Halsted and 20 Madison buses, or the El's Green Line to Clinton. For Greektown, take the Blue Line to UIC–Halsted. The 8 Halsted and 20 Madison buses get you here, too. If you're driving to Greektown, exit the Kennedy Expressway at Randolph or Madison Street.	Start a visit to the West Loop in the late afternoon or early evening, so you have a few hours to browse the galleries before heading to one of the trendy neighborhood restaurants for dinner (plan to eat early if you don't have reservations), and a late-night club to cap off the evening.

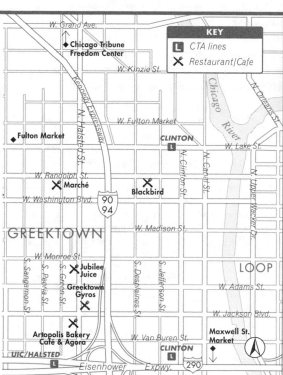

Map labels: W. Grand Ave. · ◆Chicago Tribune Freedom Center · W. Kinzie St. · KEY · **L** CTA lines · ✕ Restaurant/Cafe · Chicago River · N. Orleans St. · Kennedy Expressway · N. Halsted St. · W. Fulton Market · CLINTON **L** · W. Lake St. · ◆Fulton Market · N. Clinton St. · N. Canal St. · N. Upper Wacker Dr. · W. Randolph St. · ✕Marché · ✕Blackbird · W. Washington Blvd. · 90 94 · GREEKTOWN · W. Madison St. · W. Monroe St. · S. Sangamon St. · S. Peoria St. · S. Green St. · ✕Jubilee Juice · Greektown Gyros ✕ · S. Desplaines St. · S. Jefferson St. · LOOP · W. Adams St. · W. Jackson Blvd. · ✕ · Artopolis Bakery Café & Agora · W. Van Buren St. · Maxwell St. Market · CLINTON **L** · UIC/HALSTED **L** · Eisenhower Expwy. 290

NEIGHBORHOOD TOP 3

1. Take a picture outside of Harpo Studios, where Oprah films her talk show.

2. Check out the funky contemporary art along Fulton Market.

3. Order the *saganaki* (flaming cheese) and shout *Opaaa!* along with waiters who set it ablaze for you tableside in Greektown.

SAFETY

As you reach the western part of the neighborhood around Ashland Avenue, just a stone's throw from the United Center, the gentrification comes to a halt, and the streets around the Fulton Market area are deserted during off times. Exercise caution in both areas.

QUICK BITES

They come from all over town for the cheese grits, blue claw crab cakes, and other examples of "Southern Reconstructionist" cooking at **Wishbone** (✉ 1001 W. Washington Blvd., West Loop ☎ 312/850-2663). At breakfast and lunch, you can opt for a cafeteria line.

Smoothies and salads will fuel you up without weighing you down at the tiny **Jubilee Juice** (✉ 140 N. Halsted St., West Loop ☎ 312/491-8500).

For a quick and authentic taste of Greektown, or just a plain old burger and fries anytime day or night, stop in to **Greektown Gyros** (✉ 239 S. Halsted St., West Loop ☎ 312/236-9310), open 24 hours a day, seven days a week.

Artopolis Bakery, Café & Agora (✉ 306 S. Halsted St., West Loop ☎312/559-9000) has a light menu of salads, soups and sandwiches, and some of the best bread in the city.

▌DID YOU KNOW?

The corner of Randolph Street and Des Plaines Avenue is the site of the infamous Haymarket riot, when 11 people were killed in a melee sparked by protests for an eight-hour workday in Chicago. The event led to the creation of May Day, a worker's holiday still observed the first day in May throughout much of Europe. The neighborhood saw more strife in 1969 during the "Days of Rage" riots, which followed the famous trial of eight protestors charged with inciting riots at the Democratic National Convention here a year earlier.

On Carpenter Street between Randolph Street and Washington Boulevard is **Harpo Studios,** (✉ 1058 W. Washington Blvd., West Loop ☎ 312/591–9222 ⊕ www.oprah.com) the taping site for Oprah Winfrey's talk show. The studio isn't open to tours and tickets to the show can be near-impossible to score, so a stop here isn't much more than a fun photo-op. However, if you're a die-hard Oprah fan and want to attempt to get tickets, here's what you need to know. The show books audiences only for the current and following month. When you call—and if you're lucky enough to get through—a staffer will give you the taping schedule and a list of available dates. You can reserve up to four seats for any one taping (all attendees must be at least 18). If you can't get tickets in advance, check the Web site for occasional last-minute tickets via e-mail.

▌IN THE KNOW

If you keep your eyes peeled you might spot one of Winfrey's celebrity guests grabbing a bite in the neighborhood after a taping or an assistant walking one of her beloved cocker spaniels nearby.

Just to the west of Harpo on Washington is the **Museum of Holography,** where 10,000 square feet of exhibit space is dedicated to the advancement of—you guessed it—holography as an art form. East along Fulton Market, a number of art galleries continue to pop up among meatpacking warehouses. The art scene here includes all kinds of work—printmaking, sculpture, photography, paintings, and glass and metalwork. One of the pioneering forces in the art community, **Mars Gallery,** has showcased contemporary pop and outsider art since 1988.

The **Chicago Antique Market,** a seasonal indoor–outdoor flea market held May through September on the last Sunday of the month, has already established itself as this city's answer to London's famed Portobello Road market. Centered around Randolph Street and Ogden Avenue, you can find everything from mid-century furniture to vintage handbags.

Antiques hunters with fat wallets may want to also check the schedule at **Leslie Hindman Auctioneers,** (✉ 122 N. Aberdeen St., West Loop ☎ 312/280–1212) a fine art auctioneer on Aberdeen Street that's the fifth-largest auction house in the country.

Back on Halsted Street between Madison and Van Buren streets is **Greektown,** a small strip of the West Loop that may as well be half a world away. Greek restaurants are the main draw here.

At A Glance

2

NEAR NORTH INCLUDING THE GOLD COAST, MAGNIFICENT MILE & STREETERVILLE

Sightseeing
★ ★ ★ ★

Dining
★ ★ ★ ★

Lodging
★ ★ ★ ★

Shopping
★ ★ ★ ★

Nightlife
★ ★ ★ ★

The city's greatest tourist magnet reads like a to-do check-list: Navy Pier, the John Hancock Building, art museums and galleries, lakefront activities, and countless shops where you could spend a few dollars or thousands. The Magnificent Mile, a stretch of Michigan Avenue between the Chicago River and Oak Street, owes its name to the swanky shops that line both sides of the street. Shoppers cram the sidewalks in summer and keep the street bustling even in winter, when the trees are twined with thousands of white fairy lights and the buildings are lighted with colored flood lights.

East of the Magnificent Mile is upscale Streeterville, which began as a disreputable landfill that the notorious George Wellington "Cap" Streeter and his wife, Maria, claimed as their own. Along the Lake Michigan shoreline, from North Avenue on the north, Oak Street on the south, and LaSalle Street on the west, is the posh Gold Coast area. Made fashionable after the Great Chicago Fire of 1871 by the social-climbing industrialists of the day, today's Gold Coast neighborhood is still a ritzy place to live, work, shop, and mingle. Architectural styles along East Lake Shore Drive Historic District include Baroque, Renaissance, Georgian, and Beaux Arts—though varied, they blend together beautifully.

What's Here

The **Michigan Avenue Bridge** spans the Chicago River as a gateway to North Michigan Avenue from the south. On the east side of the river is the headquarters of the *Chicago Tribune,* in the crenellated **Tribune Tower,** and behind it the **NBC Tower.**

The base of Tribune Tower is studded with pieces from more than 120 famous sites and structures around the world, including the Parthenon, the Taj Mahal, and Bunker Hill.

2

Across the water and due for completion in 2007 is the much-hyped Trump International Hotel & Tower, a 90-story mixed-use behemoth on the site of the old *Chicago Sun-Times* headquarters. The construction project has been managed by the Donald's first *Apprentice,* hometown son Bill Rancic. North of the bridge on the west side of Michigan Avenue is the **Wrigley Building,** with its striking wedding-cake embellishments and clock tower. They mark the beginning of the **Magnificent Mile,** the famous stretch of shops. The tapering **John Hancock Center,** the third-tallest building in Chicago, and the elegant Fourth Presbyterian Church, with its peaceful courtyard, are near the north end of the Mile.

This stretch of Michigan Avenue was originally called the Magnificent Mile because of the architecture. Most of those elegant, small buildings are long gone, however, and the moniker now refers to the excellent shopping.

West of the Mag Mile, at Pearson and Rush streets, is Water Tower Park, a Chicago icon. The Water Tower and the matching Water Works Pumping Station across the street are among the few buildings to survive the Great Chicago Fire of 1871. One block east is the imposing **Museum of Contemporary Art,** which concentrates on 20th-century art, principally works created after 1945.

East of the Mag Mile, on Illinois Street and Lake Michigan, is **Navy Pier,** a wonderful place to enjoy lake breezes, hop on an afternoon or evening boat cruise, catch a concert or play, or ride on the giant Ferris wheel. The **Chicago Children's Museum** is part of the Navy Pier complex. North of Navy Pier, hugging Lake Shore Drive, is the Gold Coast neighborhood. Astor Street is the grande dame of Gold Coast promenades. On the northwest corner of Astor and Burton streets, you'll find the Georgian Patterson-McCormick Mansion (20 E. Burton Pl.), commissioned in 1891 by *Chicago Tribune* chief Joseph Medill. Where Astor Street jogs to meet Schiller Street stands the 1892 **Charnley–Persky House,** designed in part by Frank Lloyd Wright. On Goethe Street is the Ambassador East Hotel, home of the famous Pump Room restaurant. In its glory days, celebrities like Frank Sinatra, Humphrey Bogart, and Lauren Bacall held court in the famed Booth One. Where Dearborn Street meets Oak Street is the Gold Coast's famous shopping district. Past the former Playboy Mansion (1340 N. State St.), all the way to North Avenue, is a beautiful view of Lincoln Park.

If you're ever pressed for conversation in Chicago, just solicit opinions on how Goethe Street should be pronounced. Then sit back and enjoy the fireworks.

GETTING ORIENTED

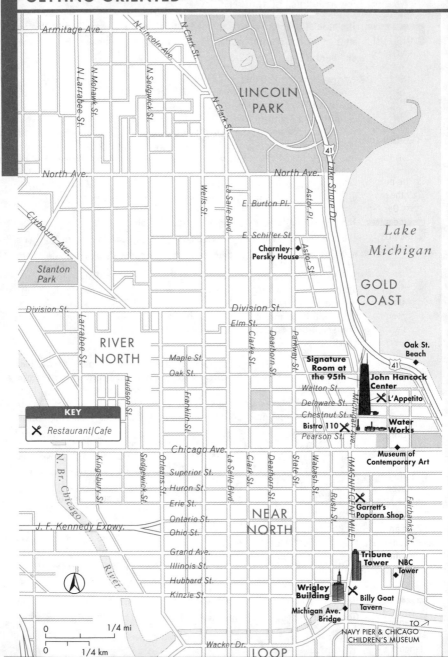

A GOOD WALK

At the north end of the Magnificent Mile on Walton Place, past the grand Drake Hotel, is one of Chicago's nicest walks: cross Oak Street in front of the Drake and take the underground passage that leads to Oak Street Beach and the lakefront promenade (watch out for speeding bicyclists, skateboarders, and in-line skaters).

GETTING HERE

If you're arriving from the north by car, take Lake Shore Drive south to the Michigan Avenue exit. From the south, you can start your exploring by exiting at Grand Avenue, the exit for Navy Pier. Numerous buses run along Michigan Avenue, including the 3, 4, 144, 145, 146, 167, and 151. Buses 29, 65, and 66 all service Navy Pier. If you're using the El, take the Red Line to Chicago Avenue to get closest to the action.

MAKING THE MOST OF YOUR TIME

You can spend a day at a number of the attractions (or just shopping), depending on your interests. Navy Pier takes a couple of hours (especially if you have children); you could spend a few hours in the Chicago Children's Museum alone. Art lovers will want to set aside at least one or two hours for the Museum of Contemporary Art. A stroll through the Gold Coast can be done in an hour, but what's the hurry? Make an afternoon of it. Our favorite times are weekend afternoons in spring or fall or just before dusk any day in summer, when the neighborhood's leafy tranquillity and big-city energy converge.

QUICK BITES

For an inexpensive, hearty lunch, try **L'Appetito** (✉ 875 N. Michigan Ave. ☎ 312/337–0691), a deli and grocery off the Hancock Center's lower-level plaza that has some of the best Italian sandwiches in Chicago.

Garrett's Popcorn Shop (✉ 670 N. Michigan Ave. ☎ 312/944–4730) is a Chicago institution that has been selling popcorn on the Mag Mile for more than 50 years. Tourists and locals alike line up outside—even in the frigid months—to buy tasty warm popcorn mixed with things like macadamia nuts and caramel. (Warning: The cheese and caramel combo is a well-known diet killer.)

Behind and one-level down from the Wrigley Building is the (in)famous **Billy Goat Tavern** (✉ 430 N. Michigan Ave. ☎ 312/222–1525), the inspiration for *Saturday Night Live*'s classic "cheezborger, cheezborger" skit and a longtime haunt of local journalists, most notably the late columnist Mike Royko. Grab a greasy burger (and chips, of course) at this no-frills grill, or just have a beer and absorb the comic undertones.

Make a meal out of appetizers at **Bistro 110** (✉ 110 E. Pearson St. ☎ 312/266–3110). The artichoke hearts are heavenly, and the gooey French onion soup is not to be missed. There are ample choices of wine by the glass. The front bar-café area is perfect for casual dining.

NEIGHBORHOOD TOP 3

1. Have a drink or a meal at the Signature Room at the 95th.

2. Sunbathe with the beautiful people at Oak Street Beach.

3. Take one of the Chicago Architecture Foundation's amazing boat tours along the river.

At A Glance

SEE CORRESPONDING CHAPTERS. SIGHTS ARE IN THE EXPERIENCE CHAPTER.

SIGHTS
John Hancock Center Observatory
Magnificent Mile
Navy Pier
Shoreline Sightseeing-River Tours
Wendella Sightseeing-River Tours
Oak Street Beach

MUSEUMS
Chicago Children's Museum of Contemporary Art

ARCHITECTURE
John Hancock Center
Michigan Avenue Bridge
Park Tower
Tribune Tower
Water Tower
Water Works Pumping Station
Wrigley Building
Fourth Presbyterian Church
Charnely-Persky House

SHOPPING
Fabulous shopping!
⇨ See Mag Mile p. 157
BOOKS/PRINTED MATTER
Europa Books
CRAFTS & TOYS
Tender Buttons
American Girl Place
Children in Paradise
CLOTHING & SHOES
adidas
Bis Designs
Madison and Friends
Jake
Ikram
Londo Mondo
GIFTS & HOME
Bloomingdale's Home & Furniture Store
City of Chicago Store
Quatrine
Room & Board

Museum of Contemporary Art Store and Bookstore
MUSIC
Jazz Record Mart

BUDGET DINING
Billy Goat Tavern, *American-Casual*
Fox & Obel, *Café*
Flat Top Grill, *Contemp.*

MODERATE DINING
RL, *American*
Joe's Be-Bop Cafe and Jazz Emporium, *Barbecue*
Pierrot Gourmet, *Café*
Heaven on Seven on Rush, *Cajun*
Caliterra, *Contemp.*
Bistro 110, *French*
Bistrot Margot, *French*
Roy's, *Hawaiian*
Kamehachi, *Japanese*
Salpicon, *Mexican*
Adobo Grill, *Mexican*
McCormick and Schmick's, *Seafood*
Gibsons Steakhouse, *Steak*
Mike Ditka's Restaurant, *Steak*
Big Bowl, *Thai*

EXPENSIVE DINING
Shanghai Terrace, *Chinese*
Avenues, *Contemp.*
NoMI, *Contemp.*
Seasons Restaurant, *Contemp.*
TRU, *Contemp.*
Pump Room, *Contemp.*
Signature Room at the 95th, *Contemp.*
The Dining Room, *French*
Les Nomades, *French*
Spiaggia, *Italian*
Heat, *Japanese*
Riva, *Seafood*
The Capital Grille, *Steak*
Morton's, The Steakhouse, *Steak*

ENTERTAINMENT
Chicago Shakespeare Theater, *Theater*
Butch McGuire's, *Bar*

Lodge, *Singles bar*
Original Mother's, *Bar*
Cru Café and Wine Bar, *Café*
Signature Room at the 95th, *Lounge*
Third Coast Café, *Café*
Second City, *Comedy club*
Zanies, *Comedy club*
Crobar, *Dance club*
Le Passage, *Dance club*
Coq d'Or, *Piano bar*
Howl at the Moon, *Piano bar*
Pump Room, *Piano bar*
Zebra Lounge, *Piano bar*
Signature Lounge, *Pub*
Whiskey Sky, *Pub*
Original Mother's, *Pub*

BUDGET HOTEL
Homewood Suites
Gold Coast Guest House
Red Roof Inn
Cass Hotel

MODERATE HOTEL
Embassy Suites Lakefront
Fitzpatrick Chicago Hotel
Holiday Inn Chicago City Centre
Hotel Indigo
Millennium Knickerbocker
Omni Chicago Hotel
Tremont

EXPENSIVE HOTEL
Drake Hotel
Peninsula Chicago
Ritz-Carlton
Sutton Place Hotel
Conrad Chicago
Four Seasons
Park Hyatt
Sofitel Chicago Water Tower
Talbott
Whitehall Hotel
Allerton Crowne Plaza
Doubletree Guest Suites
W Chicago Lakeshore
Hotel Inter-Continental Chicago
Omni Ambassador East
Westin Michigan Avenue

2

RIVER NORTH

Sightseeing
★ ★

Dining
★ ★ ★ ★

Lodging
★ ★ ★ ★

Shopping
★ ★ ★ ★

Nightlife
★ ★ ★ ★

Technically a part of Near North, River North is a neighborhood that commands a strong presence all its own. Bounded on the south and west by branches of the Chicago River, River North has eastern and northern boundaries that can be hard to define. As in many other Chicago neighborhoods, the limits have expanded as the area has grown more attractive; today they extend roughly to Oak Street on the north and Rush Street on the east. Richly served by waterways and railroad tracks that ran along its western edge, the neighborhood was settled by Irish immigrants in the mid-19th century. As the 20th century approached, the area developed into a busy commercial, industrial, and warehouse district.

But as economic conditions changed and factories moved away, the neighborhood deteriorated, and River North became just another down-on-its-luck urban area. In the 1970s, artists attracted by low rents and spacious abandoned storage areas and shop floors, began to move into the neighborhood, and it eventually became the go-to spot for art lovers to gallery hop. Then developers caught the scent and began buying up properties with an eye to renovation. Today, struggling artists might find it hard to afford a cup of coffee in this high-rent district dotted with tourist-pleasing restaurants and upscale retail shops.

What's Here

The huge **Merchandise Mart**, on the river between Orleans and Wells streets, is so commanding that it has its own stop on the El's Brown and Pur-

GETTING ORIENTED

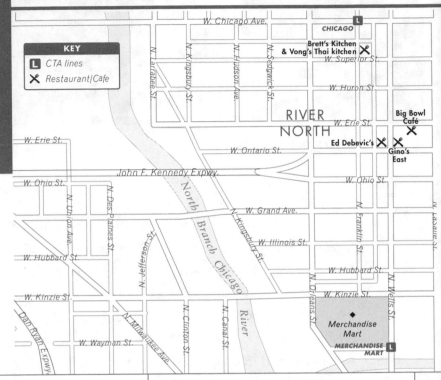

GETTING HERE

The Mart has its own stop on the El's Brown and Purple lines. By car, take Wells Street to Chicago Avenue to put you at the northern tip of the neighborhood. You can also walk west from the Mag Mile a few blocks to get to the area.

MAKING THE MOST OF YOUR TIME

You can see all there is to see in about two hours, but add another hour or more if you want to wander leisurely in and out of the shops at Tree Studios or the galleries on Superior Street and the surrounding area. A meal at one of the touristy restaurants can entail a wait on weekends and nice days. If you plan to hit the Museum of Broadcast Communications, add another hour. Most galleries are closed Sunday and Monday.

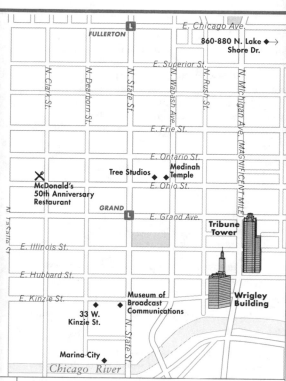

NEIGHBORHOOD TOP 5

1. Treat yourself to music at lunch at the infamous Andy's Jazz Club's Jazz at Noon series.

2. While away an afternoon browsing the art galleries.

3. Get a taste of history by tuning into some of the 85,000 hours of radio and television programs archived at the Museum of Broadcast Communications.

4. Pick up some ideas for your next home improvement project at LuxeHome in the Merchandise Mart.

5. Cheer on the Chicago Cubs from the comfort of a cozy bar stool at Harry Caray's Restaurant.

QUICK BITES

Nestled under the El tracks at Superior and Franklin streets is **Brett's Kitchen** (⊠ 233 W. Superior St., River North ☎ 312/664-6354), an excellent spot for a sandwich or an omelet Monday through Saturday.

The great John-Georges Vongerichten gets casual at **Vong's Thai Kitchen** (⊠ 233 W. Superior St., River North ☎ 312/664-6354), where sharing satays, noodle dishes, and curries is encouraged.

Want some fries to go with that shake, honey? The purposefully snarky waitstaff at **Ed Debevic's** (640 N. Wells St.), a '50s-style diner, keeps the crowds entertained.

For quality over kitsch, try the **Big Bowl Café** (159 W. Erie St.), or fill up on both while chowing down on yummy Chicago deep-dish pizza at the graffiti-covered, tourist-happy **Gino's East** (633 N. Wells St.).

ple lines. Miles of corridors on its top floors are lined with trade-only furniture and home-design showrooms. LuxeHome, a collection of 30 or so upscale stores with an emphasis on home design and renovation, take up the bottom two floors.

At Dearborn and Kinzie streets is the splendid ornamental brickwork of **33 West Kinzie Street**, the home of Harry Caray's restaurant. (The loud—and delicious—restaurant, filled with flags and giant drawings of the late Cubs broadcaster and his big glasses, is on "Harry Caray Drive," an honorary designation.) One block east, at the corner of State Street, is the new **Museum of Broadcast Communications**, one of only three broadcast museums in the United States. South of here, just shy of the bridge that crosses the Chicago River, you can see the distinctive twin corncobs of **Marina City**, a residential complex that also includes the House of Blues hotel and nightclub and a bowling alley. Fans of the old *Bob Newhart Show* may recognize Marina City from the backdrop in the show's opening credits.

A few blocks north, at the intersection of State and Ohio streets, is the **Tree Studios** shops and galleries, and the adjacent Medinah Temple, on Wabash Avenue, which houses a **Bloomingdale's Home & Furniture Store.**

DID YOU KNOW? The original Tree Studios were intended as living spaces for artists who were in town for the World's Columbian Exposition at the turn of the 20th century. They were used as live-work spaces by generations of creative types and were considered an artistic oasis until 2001, when a development group bought the studio buildings and the Medinah temple.

Head west on either Ohio or Ontario streets, and as you approach LaSalle, then Wells streets, see the neighborhood transform into something of a dining Disneyland, with enormous outposts of national chains like Rainforest Café, Hooters, and the Hard Rock Cafe. Tourists clog the streets, eager to mob them all.

Things get a little more civilized again north on Wells Street to Superior Street, where you run into the area known as the **River North Gallery District.** Dozens of art galleries show every kind of work imaginable in the area bounded by Wells, Orleans, Chicago, and Erie streets—in fact, virtually every building on Superior Street between Wells and Orleans streets houses at least one gallery. Galleries welcome visitors, so feel free to stop into any that catch your eye. On periodic Fridays throughout the year, the galleries coordinate their exhibitions and open their doors to the public for a special night to showcase new works. Art lovers take note: though River North is still a good bet for great art, a growing number of artists have ditched the high-rent district for the cheaper, more industrial West Loop neighborhood (*See* West Loop neighborhood section) a short hop to the south. If you can, try and browse both areas.

At A Glance

SEE CORRESPONDING
CHAPTERS.

MUSEUMS
Museum of Broadcast
Communications
ARCHITECTURE
860–880 N. Lake Shore
Drive
Marina City
SHOPPING

ACCESSORIES
Linda Campisano

ANTIQUES
Antiquarians Building
Christa's, Ltd
Fly-by-Nite Gallery
Jay Robert's Antique
Warehouse, Inc
Michael FitzSimmons
Decorative Arts
P.O.S.H
Rita Bucheit, Ltd

ART GALLERIES
Alan Koppel Gallery
Ann Nathan Gallery
Byron Roche
Carl Hammer Gallery
Catherine Edelman Gallery
Habatat
Primitive Art Works
Stephen Daiter Gallery

*BOOKS, PRINTED MATTER
& CRAFTS*
Pearl Art & Craft Supply
Abraham Lincoln Book
Shop
Paper Source

CHOCOLATE
Blommer Chocolate Outlet
Store

CLOTHING
Clever Alice

GIFTS & HOME
Cambium
The Chopping Block
Golden Triangle
Lightology
Luminaire
Manifesto
Modernica
Sawbridge Studios
Svenska Mobler

BUDGET DINING
Ed Debevic's, *American–
Casual*
Mr. Beef, *American–Casual*
Cafe Iberico, *Spanish*

MODERATE DINING
Ben Pao, *Chinese*
Allen's, *Contemp.*
Wildfire, *Contemp.*
Bin 36, *Contemp.*
Brasserie Jo, *French*
Kiki's Bistro, *French*
Cyrano's Bistrot Wine Bar
& Cabaret, *French*
Vermilion, *Indian*
Coco Pazzo, *Italian*
Harry Caray's, *Italian*
Maggiano's Little Italy,
Italian
Pizzeria Due, *Italian*
Pizzeria Uno, *Italian*
Scoozi!, *Italian*
Nacional 27, *Latin*
Frontera Grill, *Mexican*
Vong's Thai Kitchen, *Thai*

EXPENSIVE DINING
Fogo de Chao, *Brazilian*
Kevin, *Contemp.*
MK, *Contemp.*

Naha, *Contemp.*
Crofton on Wells,
Contemp.
SushiSamba Rio, *Contemp.*
Zealous, *Contemp.*
Le Lan, *Fusion*
Osteria via Stato, *Italian*
Japonais, *Japanese*
Topolobampo, *Mexican*
Blue Water Grill, *Seafood*
Joe's Seafood, Prime
Steaks & Stone Crab,
Seafood
Shaw's Crab House and
Blue Crab Lounge,
Seafood
Smith and Wollensky,
Steak
Gene and Georgetti, *Steak*
Keefer's, *Steak*
Ruth's Chris Steak House,
Steak

ENTERTAINMENT
Fado, *Pub*
Rockit's, *Lounge*
Excalibur, *Dance clubs*
Spy Bar, *Dance club*
Sound-Bar, *Dance club*
Gentry, *Gay/Lesbian*
Baton, *Music club*
House of Blues, *Music club*
Andy's, *Jazz*
Jazz Showcase, *Jazz*
Motel, *Pub*
Castaways, *Pub*

EXPENSIVE HOTEL
House of Blues Hotel
Embassy Suites
Westin Chicago River North

2

LINCOLN PARK & OLD TOWN

Sightseeing
★ ★ ★ ★

Dining
★ ★ ★ ★

Lodging
★ ★

Shopping
★ ★

Nightlife
★ ★ ★ ★

What began in the 1850s as a modest neighborhood of working-class German families, Old Town now accommodates a diverse population and has some of the oldest—and most expensive—real estate in Chicago. It's bordered by Division Street to the south, Armitage Avenue to the north, Clark Street on the east, and Larrabee Street on the west, but its heart lies at the intersection of North Avenue and Wells Street. Besides its notable architecture, Old Town is home to the famous comedy clubs Zanies and The Second City.

When you get to Lincoln Park, just north of Old Town, don't be confused: the neighborhood near the southern part of the city's oldest and most popular lakefront park also bears its name. Lincoln Park—the *park*—today extends from North Avenue to Hollywood Avenue. It became the city's first public playground in 1864, named after the then recently assassinated president. The neighborhood adjacent to the original park, bordered by Armitage Avenue on the south, Diversey Parkway on the north, the lake on the east, and the Chicago River on the west, also became known as Lincoln Park. It was a sparsely settled community of truck farms and orchards that grew produce for the city of Chicago, 3 mi to the south.

In some ways, Lincoln Park today epitomizes all the things that people love to hate about yuppified urban areas: stratospheric housing prices, teeny boutiques with big-attitude salespeople, and plenty of fancy-schmancy coffee shops, wine bars, and cafés. That said, it's also got some of the prettiest residential streets in the city, that gorgeous park, a great nature museum, and a thriving arts scene. So grab a nonfat half-caf easy foam extra shot grande latte and go with the flow—you'll be happy you did.

What's Here

There's a lot going on in Old Town and Lincoln Park. The yuck-it-up comedy clubs on Wells Street and raucous nightlife along North Lincoln Avenue and Halsted Street are a sharp contrast to the tranquillity at the lagoon in Lincoln Park at Fullerton Parkway, where sometimes, all the noise you hear is the flapping wings of the resident waterfowl. Between the two are plenty of historic landmarks as well as some cultural gems.

You can hear the laughs emanating from Wells Street in Old Town most any night of the week. **Zanies** has been hosting stand-up shows by some of the country's most famous comics, from Jay Leno to Dave Chappelle, for 30 years. Just up the street is **The Second City,** the legendary improv company that's served as a training ground for generations of would-be superstars.

FRUGAL FUN

Whether or not you go to a show, visit the lobby at The Second City to check out the who's who collection of photographs and caricatures of past troupe members: Alan Alda, John Belushi, Bonny Hunt, Mike Meyers, Steve Carell, and Amy Sedaris represent just a few of the famous funny alums.

The **Chicago Historical Society,** (✉ 160 N. Clark St., Old Town ☎ 312/642–4600) at North Avenue and Clark Street, is housed in a Georgian structure built in 1932. The beautiful people strut their stuff just to the east along the lake at **North Avenue Beach,** while the beasts roar nearby on Stockton Drive at **Lincoln Park Zoo,** which is free to the public. A few blocks ahead, there's a rather inconspicuous patch of grass where a garage once stood bearing the address **2122 N. Clark St.** There's no marker, but it's the site of the infamous St. Valentine's Day massacre, when seven men were killed on the orders of Al Capone on February 14, 1929.

DID YOU KNOW?

Another infamous Lincoln Park locale is the **Biograph Theater,** (✉ 2433 N. Lincoln Ave., Lincoln Park ☎ 312/348–4123) where notorious bank robber John Dillinger was shot and killed by the FBI in 1934.

One of the largest Catholic universities in the country, **DePaul University** has a 28-acre campus in Lincoln Park, bounded roughly by Webster Avenue on the south, Fullerton Avenue on the north, Halsted Street on the east, and Racine Avenue on the west. It serves more than 17,000 students, and has four other campuses in the Loop and suburbs. You might have a celebrity sighting or two on Halsted Street if you time a visit right to **Steppenwolf Theatre Company,** where ensemble members including Joan Allen, John Mahoney, Gary Sinese, and John Malkovich often perform or direct. The **Notebaert Nature Museum,** back in the park at Fullerton Parkway, is geared to kids, but outdoorsy type adults will dig it, too.

OUR TIP

All ages get especially wide-eyed in the Notebaert's Judy Istock Butterfly Haven, where you get to comingle with 75 different species of free-flying, brightly colored beauties—roughly 1,000 at any time.

GETTING ORIENTED

Altgeld St. · Cafe Luigi ✗ · Orchard Ave. · Burling St.
Ashland Ave. · Greenview Ave. · Southport Ave. · Fullerton Ave. · Clifton Ave. · Kenmore Ave. · Biograph Theater ◆ · Lincoln Ave. · Larrabee St.
◆ Facets Cinematheque · DePaul University ◆
Belden Ave.
North Clybourn Ave. · Wayne Ave. · Lakewood Ave. · Magnolia Ave. · Racine Ave. · Webster Ave. · Sheffield Ave. · Bissell St. · Fremont St. · Dayton St. · Halsted St. · Oz Park · Mohawk St.
Seminary Ave. · ✗ Nookies Too
Dickens Ave.
ARMITAGE
Elston Ave. · Cortland Ave. · **CLYBOURN** · Armitage Ave. **L**
90 · 94 · N Br. Chicago River · Maud · North Clybourn Ave. · Poe · Wisconsin St. · Burling St. · Orchard St. · Howe St. · Larrabee St.
Kingsbury · Willow St. · Vine St.
Sheffield Ave. · Steppenwolf Theatre Company ◆
NORTH/ CLYBOURN
L

KEY
L CTA lines
M Metra lines
✗ Restaurant/Cafe

GETTING HERE

Take the Howard (Red Line) train or the Ravenswood (Brown Line) train to either Armitage or Fullerton avenues. Sheffield Avenue will be the nearest north–south street in both cases. Buses 11, 22, 36, and 151 take you through the area, too. If you're driving, take Lake Shore Drive to Fullerton Avenue and drive west on Fullerton Avenue to Sheffield Avenue. Parking is scarce, especially evenings and weekends, so public transit or a cab is recommended.

MAKING THE MOST OF YOUR TIME

You could spend an hour or a whole day in Lincoln Park, depending on how you prefer to spend your time. Set aside at least a couple of hours if you plan on a leisurely shopping experience along Armitage, Halsted, and Webster avenues. Tack on a couple more for the Notebaert Nature Museum, especially with kids. And if it's a beautiful summer day, ditch whatever else you had planned and surrender yourself to hours of frolicking in the park and on the beach.

2

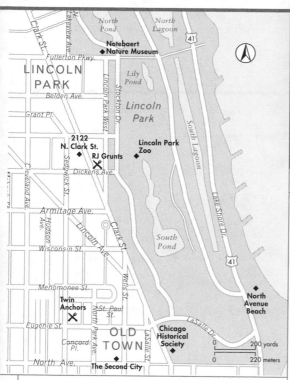

NEIGHBORHOOD TOP 5

1. Take a walk—or a run, or a bike ride—along the lakefront path heading south from North Avenue beach, and take in the breathtaking views of the city along Lake Michigan.

2. Catch the free improv after the show every night except Friday at The Second City.

3. See some of Hollywood's greats come home to their roots to perform in a play at the Steppenwolf Theatre Company.

4. Satisfy your late-night cravings after a stint at the bars with a stop at the Weiner Circle, where the surly service is part of the fun.

5. For a very different dining experience, splurge on a degustation at the Charlie Trotter's.

QUICK BITES

Nookies, too (⊠ 2114 N. Halsted St., Lincoln Park ☏ 773/327-1400), is open 24 hours on Friday and Saturday and serves heaping breakfasts anytime, making it a favorite of the neighborhood's late-night partying crowd. Cash only.

Twin Anchors (⊠ 1655 N. Sedgwick St., Lincoln Park ☏ 312/266-1616 ☉ No lunch weekdays), a popular Old Town restaurant and tavern for more than 60 years, is famous for its barbecued ribs.

Cafe Luigi (⊠ 2548 N. Clark St., Lincoln Park ☏ 773/404-0200) is a blink-and-you'll-miss-it storefront that sells New York–style pizza slices, calzones, and sausage rolls to grateful East Coast ex-pats.

Just outside the park, **R. J. Grunt's** (⊠ 2056 N. Lincoln Park W, Lincoln Park ☏ 773/929-5363) has been serving killer milkshakes and burgers and stocking a salad bar for healthy types since 1971.

Film buffs shouldn't leave Lincoln Park without a visit to **Facets Cinematheque,** which presents an eclectic selection of artistically significant films from around the world on its two screens. It also has a well-stocked video store (Facets Videotheque) that's got more than 60,000 foreign, classic, and cult films.

At A Glance

SEE CORRESPONDING
CHAPTERS. SIGHTS ARE IN
THE EXPERIENCE CHAPTER.

SIGHTS
Lincoln Park Conservatory
Lincoln Park Zoo
North Avenue Beach

MUSEUMS
Chicago Historical Society
Peggy Notebaert Nature
  Museum

ARCHITECTURE
Louis Sullivan row houses

SHOPPING

ACCESSORIES, PERFUME &
  COSMETICS
Isabella Fine Lingerie
The Left Bank
Mint
1154 Lill Studio
Aroma Workshop
Endo-Exo Apothecary

BOOKS & PRINTED
  MATTER
Gramaphone Records
Transitions Bookplace

CLOTHING & SHOES
Lori's Designer Shoes
O & I
Davis for Men
Guise
Active Endeavors
Barneys New York CO-OP

Out of the West
Uncle Dan's
Betsey Johnson
Cynthia Rowley
Fox's
Jane Hamill
Palazzo
Shopgirl
Studio 910
Swell

GIFTS
Barker & Meowsky
Paul Frank Store
Vosges Haut-Chocolat

HOME & FURNITURE
Ancient Echoes
Bedside Manor
CB2
Crate&Barrel
Crate&Barrel Outlet
Jayson Home & Garden
A New Leaf
Rachel Ashwell's Shabby
  Chic
Tabula Tua
For Kids
Bellini
Land of Nod
Little Strummer Music
  Store
LMNOP
Piggy Toes
Spoiled . . . but Not
  Rotten

MODERATE DINING
Geja's, *French*
Mon Ami Gabi, *French*
Café Ba-Ba-Reeba!,
  Spanish

EXPENSIVE DINING
Alinea, *Contemp.*
Charlie Trotter's,
  Contemp.
North Pond, *Contemp.*
Boka, *Contemp.*
Ambria, *Italian*

ENTERTAINMENT
Victory Gardens Theater,
  Theater
John Barleycorn, *Pub*
Red Lion, *Pub*
Webster's Wine Bar, *Wine*
  bar
Clybar, *Lounge*
Elbo Room, *Music club*
Gamekeepers, *Sports bar*
North Beach Chicago,
  Sports bar
Jet Vodka Lounge, *Pub*
Old Town School of Folk
  Music, *Folk*

BUDGET HOTEL
Belden-Stratford
Days Inn Lincoln Park
  North

2

WICKER PARK & BUCKTOWN

Sightseeing
★ ★

Dining
★ ★ ★ ★

Lodging
★

Shopping
★ ★ ★ ★

Nightlife
★ ★ ★ ★

Creative types still cluster in Bucktown and Wicker Park, a hip, somewhat grungy enclave of side-by-side neighborhoods centered on Milwaukee, Damen, and North avenues. But they no longer lay exclusive claim to this funky part of town. These days, you'll find young families, twentysomething working types, and university students thrown into the mix along with the immigrant communities that have lived here for generations. Within this Petri dish of gentrification, there are also cutting-edge galleries, coffeehouses, nightclubs, and a bizarre bazaar of shops. A sign of the changing times: chains like American Apparel and Urban Outfitters have opened outposts in this neighborhood, once considered a haven from corporate retail. Still, this definitely ain't where you'll find anything akin to your momma's suburban strip malls.

Bucktown—which is said to have taken its name from the goats kept by the area's original Polish and German immigrants—encompasses the neighborhood surrounding Milwaukee Avenue north of North Avenue. The area south of North Avenue to Division Street is Wicker Park. Farther south still is Ukrainian Village, where the artsy types are now encroaching, but which still has a number of sights that are a testimony to the ethnic roots that remain strong in this neighborhood. If you're ambitious, in one afternoon's walk you can visit Bucktown and Wicker Park and even make a detour into Ukrainian Village.

GETTING ORIENTED

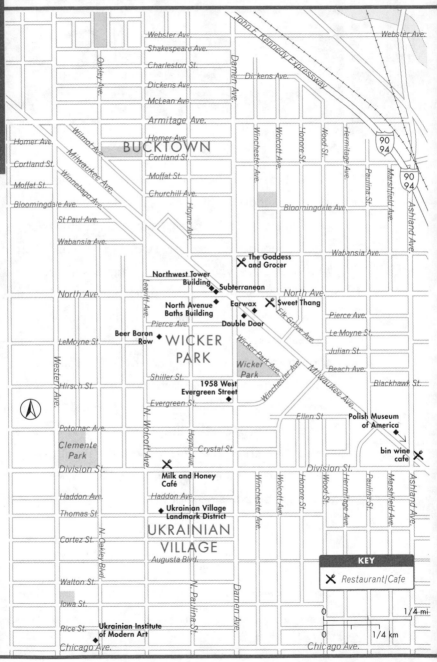

Webster Ave.

Shakespeare Ave.

Charleston St.

Dickens Ave.

Dickens Ave.

McLean Ave.

Armitage Ave.

Webster Ave.

Oakley Ave.

Damen Ave.

John F. Kennedy Expressway

90 94

90 94

Ashland Ave.

BUCKTOWN

Homer Ave.

Homer Ave.

Cortland St.

Cortland St.

Moffat St.

Moffat St.

Bloomingdale Ave.

St Paul Ave.

Wabansia Ave.

Churchill Ave.

Milwaukee Ave.

Wilmot Ave.

Winnebago Ave.

Hoyne Ave.

Bloomingdale Ave.

Wabansia Ave.

Winchester Ave.

Wolcott Ave.

Honore St.

Wood St.

Hermitage Ave.

Paulina St.

Marshfield Ave.

The Goddess and Grocer

Northwest Tower Building

Subterranean

North Ave.

North Avenue Baths Building

Earwax

Sweet Thang

North Ave.

Pierce Ave.

Le Moyne St.

Pierce Ave.

Double Door

Beer Baron Row

LeMoyne St.

WICKER PARK

Julian St.

Beach Ave.

Blackhawk St.

Western Ave.

Leavitt Ave.

N. Wolcott Ave.

Wicker Park Ave.

Wicker Park

Milwaukee Ave.

Winchester Ave.

Elk Grove Ave.

Shiller St.

Hirsch St.

1958 West Evergreen Street

Evergreen St.

Ellen St.

Polish Museum of America

Potomac Ave.

Clemente Park

Hoyne Ave.

Crystal St.

bin wine cafe

Division St.

Division St.

Winchester Ave.

Wolcott Ave.

Honore St.

Wood St.

Hermitage Ave.

Paulina St.

Marshfield Ave.

Ashland Ave.

Milk and Honey Café

Haddon Ave.

Haddon Ave.

Thomas St.

Ukrainian Village Landmark District

N. Oakley Blvd.

Cortez St.

UKRAINIAN VILLAGE

Augusta Blvd.

Hoyne Ave.

N. Paulina St.

Damen Ave.

Walton St.

Iowa St.

Rice St.

Ukrainian Institute of Modern Art

Chicago Ave.

Chicago Ave.

KEY
✗ Restaurant/Cafe

0   1/4 mi

0   1/4 km

GETTING HERE

If you're driving, take the Kennedy to North Avenue, then go west on North Avenue until you reach the triangular intersection where North meets Milwaukee and Damen avenues. Metered street parking is available. By El train, take the Blue Line to the Damen–North Avenue stop.

QUICK BITES

Fuel up with fluffy French croissants, palmiers, and cappuccinos at **Sweet Thang** (⊠ 1921 W. North Ave., Bucktown ☎ 773/772–4166), a cute little bistro with a rich red sofa in the window and red-leather chairs with heart-shape backs. If you want to practice your French, place your order for a slice of quiche or a croque monsieur in *la belle langue*. Then settle back and imagine you're in gay Paris.

bin wine cafe (⊠ 1559 N. Milwaukee Ave., Wicker Park ☎ 773/486–2233) is a cozy little storefront where you can pair top-notch wines by the glass with global menu options.

A sunny spot with a fireplace for cold winter days, **Milk and Honey Café** (⊠ 1920 W. Division St., Wicker Park ☎ 773/395–9434) packs in neighborhood types who crave the French toast at breakfast and inventive lunchtime sandwiches served with house-made potato chips.

To us, former caterer to the stars Debby Sharpe is both **The Goddess and Grocer** (⊠ 1646 N. Damen Ave., Bucktown ☎ 773/342–3200), serving up to-die-for sandwiches and salads that please vegans and carnivores alike at her gourmet takeout shop. You can eat at the small dining room next door.

NEIGHBORHOOD TOP 3

1. Order a cup of coffee or a glass of wine and perch yourself at the windowseat in a café–or at an outdoor table in warm weather–and get ready for some of the best people-watching in the city.

2. Catch some cutting-edge music at the Double Door.

3. Shop for funky finds at the shops along Division Street, Milwaukee Avenue, and Damen Avenue.

MAKING THE MOST OF YOUR TIME

The best times for people-watching are in the evenings when the clubs and bars draw a crowd, or during Sunday brunch when the restaurants do steady business. May through October you can take your place at an outdoor patio to savor the view of hipsters and young families strolling by, soaking up the sun. The most lively times to visit are late August, when Bucktown hosts its annual Arts Fest, and early September, during the Around the Coyote Arts Festival.

What's Here

The anchor of the North-Milwaukee-Damen intersection is the striking triangular Northwest Tower Building, used as a reference point from miles around. The beautiful facade of the **North Avenue Baths Building,** (✉ 2039 W. North Ave., Bucktown) near the intersection of Milwaukee and Damen avenues, is a clue to its past life when it was a storied meeting spot for politicians who cut deals in the hot steam rooms, where it was difficult to plant wire taps. Across the street is **Subterranean,** (✉ 2011 W. North Ave., Bucktown ☎ 773/278–6600) a bar and dance club resting atop tunnels once used to flee authorities in the Prohibition era. Also near this intersection is the **Double Door,** a late-night music venue where homegrown acts like Veruca Salt and Liz Phair and legends like the Rolling Stones have played, and the colorful **Earwax Cafe,** a vegan and vegetarian friendly hangout with a video rentals department.

FRUGAL FUN

Art spills onto the streets of Bucktown and Wicker Park every September, when the weekend-long Around the Coyote Fall Arts Festival attracts thousands of collectors, dealers, and browsers who scour every nook and cranny of the neighborhood.

For a reality television fix, check out the building at the corner of Winchester and North avenues, a former *Real World* house. Back on Damen, head north for some shopping—window or otherwise—at a collection of shops selling wares you won't likely find elsewhere. Hip fashionistas from around the city head to **p. 45** to check out the latest finds from up-and-coming designers, while homebodies oooh and ahhh over the luxurious tabletop finds at **Stitch.** The neighborhood's well known to antique hunters, too, who hunt for treasures at shops like **Bleeker Street** and **Pagoda Red.**

DID YOU KNOW?

As you're walking the neighborhood, note the Anglophile street names (Webster, Shakespeare, Dickens, Churchill). These were changed around the time of World War I, to distance the neighborhood from its Russian, German, and Polish roots.

Along Hoyne and Pierce streets you'll find some of the biggest and best examples of Chicago's Victorian-era architecture. So many brewery owners built homes in this area that it was once dubbed **"Beer Baron Row."**

DID YOU KNOW?

Novelist Nelson Algren, whose book *Chicago: City on the Make* still wins praise for capturing the essence of the city, lived in the three-story home at **1958 West Evergreen Street.**

For a glimpse of how the working class lived at the turn of the 20th century, head a little farther south to the **Ukrainian Village Landmark District** (on Haddon Avenue and Thomas and Cortez streets between Damen and Leavitt avenues), a well-preserved group of worker cottages and flats. Another place to glimpse the old immigrant populations' squat leaded-glass brick homes is on Homer Street between Leavitt and Oakley streets. Nearby on Chicago Avenue is the **Ukrainian Institute of Modern**

Art (✉ 2320 W. Chicago Ave. ☎ 773/227–5522), which has three galleries that focus on sculpture, mixed media, and paintings.

At A Glance

2

SEE CORRESPONDING
CHAPTERS.

MUSEUMS
Polish Museum of America
Ukrainian Institute of
    Modern Art

SHOPPING

ACCESSORIES
Paper Doll
Ruby Room
Tatine

ANTIQUES
Bleeker Street
Modern Times
Pagoda Red
Pavilion

MUSIC
Beat Parlor
Myopic Books
Reckless Records

CLOTHING & SHOES
Psycho Baby
The Red Balloon Company
Apartment Number 9
Bynum & Bang
Eurotrash
John Fluevog
Hejfina
Noir
Public I
Softcore
The T-Shirt Deli

Belly Dance Maternity
G Boutique
Helen Yi
Jade
Pump
p. 45
Robin Richman
Saffron
Tangerine
Una Mae's Freak Boutique
Vive La Femme

GIFTS & HOME
Casa Loca
Dubby's Buy the Ounce
Embelezar
For Dog's Sake
Jean Alan Upholstered
    Furniture and
    Furnishings
Kachi Bachi
Lille
Orange Skin
Stitch

SPORTING GOODS
Shred Shop

BUDGET DINING
Milk & Honey Café, *Café*
Piece, *Pizza*

MODERATE DINING
Smoke Daddy, *Barbecue*
Hot Chocolate, *Café*
Café Absinthe,
    Contemp.

Spring, *Contemp.*
Feast, *Contemp.*
Le Bouchon, *French*
Mirai Sushi, *Japanese*
Mas, *Latin*
Adobo Grill, *Mexican*

EXPENSIVE DINING
Meritage Café and Wine
    bar, *Contemp.*

ENTERTAINMENT
Map Room, *Café*
Silver Cloud Bar & Grill,
    Bar
Caffe de Luca,
    Cafés–Nightlife
The Hideout, *Club, Country
    music*
California Clipper, *Club, DJs*
Northside Bar & Grill, *Bar*
Sonotheque, *Lounge*
Vintage Wine Bar, *Wine
    bar*
Earwax, *Café*
Café Ballou's, *Café*
Funky Buddha Lounge,
    Dance club
Double Door, *Rock club*
Empty Bottle, *Rock club*
Davenport's, *Piano bar*
Matchbox, *Pub*
Rainbo Club, *Pub*

LAKE VIEW INCLUDING WRIGLEYVILLE

Sightseeing
★ ★

Dining
★ ★ ★ ★

Lodging
★

Shopping
★ ★ ★ ★

Nightlife
★ ★ ★ ★

Lake View is a massive North Side neighborhood made up of smaller enclaves that each have their own distinct personalities. There's the beer-swilling, Cubby-blue-'til-we-die sports bar fanaticism of Wrigleyville, home of the esteemed Wrigley Field; the out-and-proud colors of the gay bars, shops, and clubs along Halsted Street in Boys Town; and an air of urban chicness along Southport Avenue (a street that's really a bit too far west to enjoy any lake views, but part of the neighborhood still the same), where young families stroll amid the trendy boutiques and ice-cream shops. It's a mix that means that a few blocks' walk in one direction or another will surely lead to some interesting finds.

Lake View's first white settler was Conrad Sulzer, a grim-looking Swiss native and the son of a Protestant minister. Sulzer arrived in 1837, but the community was really established in the 1850s by James E. Rees and E. E. Hundley. Rees and Hundley built the Hotel Lake View—from which the neighborhood got its name—and then its first main road, which is now Broadway. By 1889 Chicago took the town for its own. Lake View had, and continues to have, a large Irish population, with pubs dotting many of its streets. It's also an area that's densely populated with young urban professionals and one of the main centers of Chicago's gay and lesbian community.

What's Here

The venerable **Wrigley Field,** the ivy-covered home of the Chicago Cubs and the nation's second-oldest major league ballpark, is on the corner of Addison and Clark streets. Check out the **Harry Caray statue** commemorating the late Cubs announcer and sing "Take Me Out to the Ballgame" in his honor. Diagonally across the street is the **Cubby Bear Lounge** (1059 W. Addison St. ☎773/327–1662), a Chicago institution since 1953.

FRUGAL FUN

If you look up along Sheffield Avenue on the eastern side of the ballpark, you can see the rooftop patios where baseball fans pay high prices to root for the home team. Ticketless fans sit in lawn chairs on Sheffield during the games, waiting for foul balls to fly their way.

A long fly ball north of Wrigley is **Metro** (3730 N. Clark St.), a former theater that's been converted to one of the city's best live-music venues. The Smashing Pumpkins got their start here. East on Grace Street is the 3800 north block of **Alta Vista Terrace**, a lovely residential street where 40 town houses completed as part of a single development in 1904 mirror one another diagonally across the block for a striking, harmonious effect. North again on Clark Street is **Graceland Cemetery**, which has crypts that are almost as strikingly designed as the city skyline.

DID YOU KNOW?

The names on the gravesites at Graceland read like a who's who from a Chicago history book: Marshall Field, George Pullman, Louis Sullivan, and Daniel Burnham are a few of the notables buried here. You can buy a walking-tour map at the entrance Monday through Saturday to explore on your own.

Right on Halsted Street is "Boys Town," as locals often call it. Distinctive rainbow pylons line the street between Belmont and Addison avenues, marking the gay district. In June, Halsted is a sea of people when Chicago's gay pride parade floats merrily down the block.

Belmont Avenue is a strip with a different character entirely. There are tattoo parlors and vintage clothing stores, and just past the El tracks at Sheffield is the **Vic Theatre**, originally a luxurious vaudeville theater. Today it's a live music venue that's most popular for Brew & View nights, when second- or third-run movies are screened, three bars are open, and the mood is festive.

LOCAL LIFE

Where Belmont meets up with Clark Street is a place the locals like to call "Punkin' Donuts." It's just a plain old Dunkin' Donuts, really, on a strip where lots of heavily pierced, spiky-haired types hang out.

A few blocks farther west you hit Southport Avenue, where the shopping seems to get more interesting all the time. There's not a Gap or Pottery Barn in sight—rather, the streets that travel north to Irving Park Road are lined with independent shops, many of which cater to well-dressed young women with money to burn. **Red Head Boutique** and neighboring **Krista K** are big favorites. Hipsters of both sexes, meanwhile, drool over the goods at **Jake.** Southport's main claim to fame, though, is the **Music Box Theatre,** a 1929 movie house where you can still see twinkling stars and clouds on the ceiling and hear live organic music before the independent and classic films are shown on its two screens.

GETTING ORIENTED

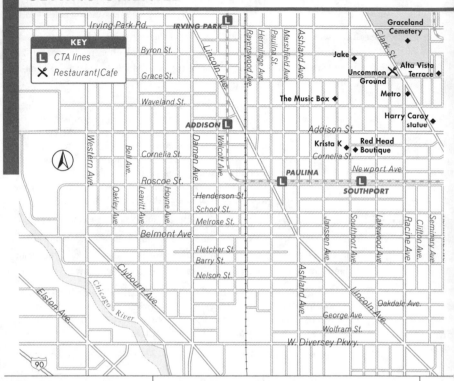

KEY

L CTA lines
✗ Restaurant/Cafe

GETTING HERE

If you're driving, take Lake Shore Drive north from the Loop to Belmont, but keep in mind that parking can be scarce. Buses 22 and 26 will bring you here from points downtown, as will the Red Line and Brown lines to Belmont or the Red to Addison.

MAKING THE MOST OF YOUR TIME

A quick walk through Wrigleyville and Lake View will take about an hour and a half. Add another half-hour if you're wading through the post-Cubs-game crowds. If you want to get a feel for the rest of the neighborhood, head to Graceland Cemetery—allot about an hour to two hours for a visit— or go shopping along Southport Avenue. A few hours more are necessary for an afternoon game at Wrigley Field, one of the best ways to experience the real Chicago.

NEIGHBORHOOD TOP 5

1. If you can score a ticket, sit in the bleachers with the locals at Wrigley Field—and be ready to throw the ball back onto the field if the opposing team nearly hits a homer into the stands.

2. If you can't score a ticket, hang out with the fans on Sheffield Avenue, who wait there to catch one of the long fly balls out of the park.

3. Catch a vintage flick at the vintage Music Box Theatre.

4. Indulge in a scoop of Daley's (as in Mayor Richard J. Daley's) Fudge Addiction at the homegrown Bobtail Soda Fountain.

5. Thumb through the extensive selection of vintage vinyl and new tracks at Reckless Records.

QUICK BITES

The original Swedish **Ann Sather** (✉ 929 W. Belmont Ave., Lakeview ☎ 773/348-2378) has legendary breakfasts: lingonberry pancakes or giant cinnamon buns.

The **Chicago Diner** (✉ 3411 N. Halsted St., Lakeview ☎ 773/935-6696) is known for its yummy vegetarian food.

Bobtail Soda Fountain (✉ 2951 N. Broadway, Lakeview ☎ 773/880-7372) serves ice cream based on an old family recipe, with specialty flavors like Lakeview Bourbon Barhopper and Daley Fudge Addiction.

Goose Island Wrigleyville (✉ 3535 N. Clark St., Wrigleyville ☎ 773/832-9040) has a variety of their own beers and root beers on tap, plus good burgers.

Uncommon Ground (✉ 3800 N. Clark St., Wrigleyville ☎ 773/929-3680) might look like a typical neighborhood coffeehouse, until you check out the menu: Jamaican jerk pork chops and baked Guinness French onion soup.

At A Glance

FAR NORTH SIDE

Sightseeing
★ ★

Dining
★ ★ ★ ★

Lodging
★

Shopping
★ ★ ★ ★

Nightlife
★ ★ ★

The north side of Chicago is home to several of the city's most colorful, eclectic neighborhoods. History-rich Uptown was a once-thriving entertainment district, and you can take in the beautiful architecture and striking old marquees. Though it's been a bit gritty for decades, new condo developments and chains like Borders and Starbucks are revitalizing the area. The neighborhood is predominantly African-American, though there is a large Asian contingent, especially along Argyle Street, which is known as Little Saigon.

Andersonville was named for the Swedish community that settled near Foster Avenue and Clark Street in the 1960s, and the area still has one of the largest concentrations of Swedes in the United States. A water tower above Clark Street is painted with the colors of the Swedish flag and a bunch of businesses sell goodies like strudels and lingonberry pancakes.

Devon Avenue is a spicy mix of immigrant communities. In places its double street signs attest to its diversity: for a while it's Gandhi Marg, then Golda Meir Avenue. By any name, it's a sensory safari best undertaken on foot.

One of the best ways to explore the ethnic diversity of these areas is by sampling the offerings at restaurants and food stores, so set out hungry. Uptown is just north of Lake View, and Andersonville is north and west of Uptown. Devon Avenue is the farthest north and west of the three.

GETTING ORIENTED

Three Sisters Delicatessen
Udupi Palace
Tiffin
Rosemblum's Wold of Judaica
Rosemont Ave.

Granville Ave.

Glenlake Ave.

Peterson St.

Thorndale Ave.

Ardmore Ave.

Hollywood Ave.

Bryn Mawr St.

Catalpa Ave.

Balmoral Ave.

ROSEHILL

Berwyn Ave.

Foster Ave.

Carmen Ave

Winnemac Park

Winnemac Ave.

Ainslie St.

Gunnison Ave.

Lawrence Ave.

RAVENSWOOD

Leland Ave.

Wilson Ave.

Sunnyside Ave.

Welles Park

MONTROSE L

Montrose Ave.

Cullom Ave.

Berteau Ave.

Belle Plaine Ave.

Irving Park Rd.

IRVING PARK L

Byron St.

Grace St.

Waveland Ave.

ADDISON L

Cornelia St.

Roscoe St.

School St.

Belmont St.

Barry Ave.

California Ave.

Western Ave.

Damen Ave.

Lincoln Ave.

Ashland Ave.

Rosehill Cemetery

41

Devon Ave.

Ridge Ave.

14

EDGEWATER

Lake Michigan

Bryn Mawr St.

BRYN MAWR L

Catalpa Ave.

ANDERSONVILLE

BERWYN L

Balmoral Ave.

Women & Children First
Swedish Bakery
Reza's
Swedish American Museum Center
Ann Sather

ARGYLE L
Green Mill Lounge

Argyle Strip

St Boniface Cemetery
UPTOWN

Lawrence Ave.
Aragon Ballroom

Riviera Theater
LAWRENCE L

WILSON L

Graceland Cemetery

Montrose Ave.
Montrose Beach

41

Irving Park Rd.

SHERIDAN L

WRIGLEYVILLE

Wrigley Field
ADDISON L

Clark St.

Racine Ave.

Southport

SOUTHPORT

PAULINA L

LAKE VIEW

BELMONT L

WELLINGTON L

Ashland Ave.

Lincoln Ave.

Halsted St.

Clark St.

Ridge Ave.

Ravenswood Ave.

Clark St.

Glenwood Ave.

Broadway

Sheridan Rd.

Sheridan Rd.

Broadway

Lincoln Park

KEY

L   CTA lines

M   Metra lines

✕   Restaurant/Cafe

0   1/2 mile

0   1/2 kilometer

GETTING HERE

Take the El's Red Line north from the Loop (toward Howard) and get off at the Lawrence stop for Uptown. In a car, take Lake Shore Drive north to Lawrence Avenue for Uptown or Foster Avenue for Andersonville. Drivers should take Foster Avenue west to Western Avenue. Devon Avenue is reachable via the El's Red Line (exit at the Morse Avenue station), then the 155 (Devon Avenue) bus. By car, head north up Western Avenue.

MAKING THE MOST OF YOUR TIME

If you're planning on hitting all three neighborhoods, allow most of a day. Uptown will take about an hour; allow a couple of hours for Andersonville if you pop into the shops, and another hour to see the Swedish Museum. Devon Avenue takes about two hours—the street is crowded, especially on evenings and weekends, so walking is slow going there.

LOCAL LIFE

Andersonville is one of the best places in Chicago to stock up on Swedish and other European foods and treats. If you have a sweet tooth, try the **Swedish Bakery** (✉ 5348 N. Clark St., Far North Side ☎ 773/561-8919). Among its delicious baked goods are Swedish limpa and Jutland bread, *pepparkakor* (gingerbread) cookies, and flaky strudels and turnovers.

SAFETY

Be cautious in all of Uptown, especially at night. The neighborhood is slowly undergoing a resurgence, but there's still quite a bit of gang activity. Nevertheless, daytime walking, especially in pairs or groups, is just fine if you stick to the main drags of Broadway and Argyle.

QUICK BITES

Ann Sather (✉ 5207 N. Clark St., Far North Side ☎ 773/271-6677) carries what may be the world's most tender, delicious cinnamon rolls (you can buy some to carry out) and light lingonberry pancakes.

At **Reza's** (✉ 5255 N. Clark St., Far North Side ☎ 773/561-1898), you can dine on such outstanding Persian cuisine as kebabs, *dolmeh* (stuffed grape leaves), pomegranate juice, and charbroiled ground beef with Persian rice.

The decor is reminiscent of a hotel lobby, and the music sounds like Indian Muzak, but the South Indian vegetarian cuisine is scrumptious at **Udupi Palace** (✉ 2543 W. Devon, Far North Side ☎ 773/338-2152).

Another consistent favorite down the street is **Tiffin** (✉ 2536 W. Devon, Far North Side ☎ 773/338-2143), where the consistent crowds are a good testament to the quality of the curry.

NEIGHBORHOOD TOP 3

1. Gorge yourself on cinnamon buns at Ann Sather.

2. Haggle over the prices of electronics, fabric, and jewelry on Devon Avenue.

3. Catch a Sunday night poetry slam at the Green Mill, where it all began.

What's Here

Uptown is filled with an interesting mix of entertainment venues that attract, well, a pretty interesting mix of people to the area on any given night. Just outside the Lawrence train station is the **Aragon Ballroom,** (⊠ 1106 W. Lawrence Ave., Far North Side ☎ 773/561–9500), its large sign heralding upcoming bands—who play everything from metal to mariachi—in its dreamy, piazzalike setting. South is the marquee of the **Riviera Theatre,** (⊠ 4746 N. Racine Ave., Far North Side ☎ 773/275–6800) which draws a mosh-pit-diving crowd to see grungy bands.

The Green Mill, a cramped jazz club that has drawn top names for over a century, also sparked the national Poetry Slam movement.

Nearby, Little Saigon is a part of the **Argyle Strip,** which is anchored by the El's Argyle Street stop with its red pagoda. The Strip is teeming with storefront noodle shops and groceries. Roasted ducks hang in shop windows and fish peer out from large tanks.

Andersonville, just north of Uptown, still shows many signs of the Swedish settlers who founded the neighborhood. The **Swedish-American Museum Center** has an interesting mix of exhibits, a separate museum complete with a Viking ship for kids, and a gift shop packed with Scandinavian items. The section of Clark Street north and just to the south of Foster Avenue is a lively mix of restaurants, bakeries, delicatessens, and boutiques. Victorian-looking street lamps and bricked crosswalks complement the well-kept storefronts. An anchor of the area is the **Women & Children First** bookstore, which stocks an extensive selection of feminist and children's books.

Farther north, **Devon Avenue** is where Chicagoans go when they crave Indian food, or, as the avenue moves west, a good Jewish challah. The Indian restaurants and shops start popping up just east of Western Avenue. Besides authentic, inexpensive Indian and Pakistani food, you find the latest Bollywood flicks, electronics, jewelry, and beautifully embellished saris and fabrics. Restaurants and stores change over rapidly, however, so if the place you're looking for has closed, simply step into the next alluring spot you find. At Talman Avenue, the multicultural wares transform to Jewish specialties. There are butchers and bakers and windows decorated with Russian newspapers and handmade *matrioshkas* (nesting dolls), evidence of this section's concentration of Russian Jews. At **Interbook** (⊠ 2754 W. Devon Ave. ☎ 773/973–5536) you can listen to rowdy rebel Russian rock or read recent romances. At **Three Sisters Delicatessen** (⊠ 2854 W. Devon Ave. ☎ 773/973–1919), you can pick up an imported teapot or a doll with your Russian rye. Pick up menorahs, mezuzahs, and even stuffed matzo ball dog toys at **Rosenblum's World of Judaica** (⊠ 2906 W. Devon Ave. ☎ 773/262–1700).

At A Glance

SEE CORRESPONDING CHAPTERS. SIGHTS ARE IN THE EXPERIENCE CHAPTER.

SIGHTS
Montrose Beach
Graceland Cemetery

MUSEUMS
Swedish-American Museum Center

ARCHITECTURE
Baha'i House of Worship (north of the city)

BUDGET DINING
Ann Sather, *Scandinavian*
Svea, *Swedish*

MODERATE DINING
Square Kitchen, *American-Casual*
Café Selmarie, *Café*
Tomboy, *Contemp.*
La Tache, *French*
Chicago Brauhaus, *German*
La Donna, *Italian*

ENTERTAINMENT
Holiday Club, *Bar*
Hopleaf, *Bar*
Kopi, a Traveler's Cafe, *Café*
Big Chicks, *Gay/Lesbian*
Carol's Pub, *Country club*
Green Mill, *Jazz club*
The Abbey, *Rock club*
Martyrs', *Rock club*
Lakeview Lounge, *Pub*
Green Mill, *Pub*

PILSEN, LITTLE ITALY & UNIVERSITY VILLAGE

Sightseeing
★ ★

Dining
★ ★ ★ ★

Lodging
★

Shopping
★ ★

Nightlife
★

Stretching from the South Branch of the Chicago River to the Eisenhower Expressway (I-290) this area West of the Loop on the south side of the city is a jumble of ethnic neighborhoods that has been home to immigrants of all cultures over the 20th century, most notably the Mexican community of Pilsen and the enclaves of Italian-Americans living in the shadow of the University of Illinois's Medical District and its Circle Campus.

Formerly a neighborhood of immigrants from Bohemia, Czechoslovakia, the enclave of Pilsen is now home to the largest Mexican community in the Midwest—making up roughly 85% of the neighborhood's population. Pilsen is known for its dramatic, colorful murals that show scenes from Mexican history, culture, and religion. It's also home to a thriving arts community—if you're a gallery-hopping art collector, you must visit this neighborhood. Pilsen is bordered by Halsted Street on the east and Western Avenue on the west and extends from 16th Street to the south branch of the Chicago River.

Chicago's Little Italy is to the north of Pilsen. This traditional ethnic neighborhood has been encroached upon by the expansion of the nearby university in recent years, but there are still plenty of yummy Italian restaurants, bakeries, groceries, and sandwich shops to explore. Stretching to Ashland Avenue on the west and Roosevelt on the south, Little Italy blends into University Village in its northeast corner.

The University of Illinois at Chicago anchors University Village. This booming residential area lies west of Roosevelt Road, primarily made up of a massive new mixed-use development that centers around Halsted Street and spans south to 14th Street.

What's Here

The **Mexican Fine Arts Center Museum,** the nation's largest Latino museum, has traditional and contemporary creations by international and local artists. Its annual Day of the Dead celebration around Halloween is the largest in the city.

The murals of Pilsen are one of the things that give this neighborhood its distinctive flair. You'll run into their bright colors and bold images at many turns during a walk through the neighborhood. At Ashland Avenue and 19th Street are two large murals ruminating on Latino family life and Latinos at work. More murals created by community youth groups and local artists brighten up the blocks along 18th to the east, and Aztec sun god inserts are on the sidewalk stones.

Pilsen's main commercial strip, 18th Street, is loaded with tempting restaurants, bakeries, and Mexican grocery stores. East on 18th past the BIENVENIDOS A PILSEN sign is **Nuevo Leon,** a brightly painted family restaurant that has been an anchor in the neighborhood since the Guiterrez family set up shop in 1962. Inhale deeply if the doors to the tortilla factory next door are open.

NEED A BREAK? If you have a sweet tooth or have kids in tow keep an eye out for **Bomboncito Candy & Party Store** (⊠ 1653 W. 18th St. ☎ 312/733–3201), which stocks a mind-boggling array of treats with a Latino verve to them.

Halsted near 18th Street is home to an ever-growing cluster of art galleries that have put Pilsen on the map with the West Loop and River North as a go-to gallery destination. But while the other neighborhoods have defined themselves as homes to contemporary and fine art, respectively, the Pilsen community doesn't represent a definitive style.

In Little Italy, the main thoroughfare is **Taylor Street,** which is best known for its Italian restaurants, though Thai food, tacos, and other ethnic food options are starting to fill in the street as well. The **National Italian American Sports Hall of Fame** (⊠ 1431 W. Taylor St., Little Italy ☎ 312/226–5566) pays tribute to athletes like Rocky Marciano, Yogi Berra, and Phil Rizzuto.

NEED A BREAK? If you visit Taylor Street from May to early September, be sure to stop at **Mario's Italian Lemonade** (1068 W. Taylor St., no phone) where everyone from politicians like Jesse Jackson to neighborhood families lines up for old-fashioned slush-like Italian ices.

On Polk Street is **St. Basil Greek Orthodox Church,** (⊠ 733 S. Ashland Ave., Little Italy ☎ 312/243–3738) a gorgeous Greek-revival building originally used as a Jewish synagogue. The bronze statue of Italian explorer Christopher Columbus that anchors **Arrigo Park** on Loomis Street was cast in Rome and brought to Chicago for the 1893 World's Columbian Exposition.

In University Village, new luxury town homes and loft conversions intermix with row houses and two-flats on a stretch of the city that not

GETTING ORIENTED

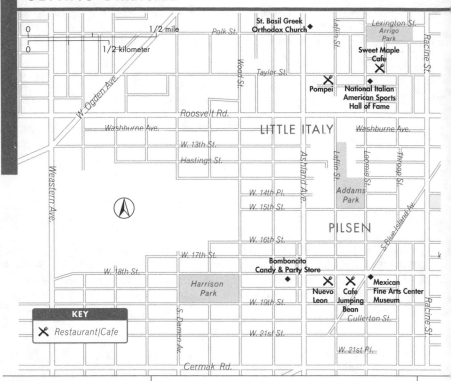

MAKING THE MOST OF YOUR TIME

Pilsen is busiest on weekends and on the first weekend of August during the Fiesta del Sol festival. Little Italy is busier at night when the restaurants and bars draw crowds. A visit to the University Village area is most rewarding on weekdays when there's plenty of student activity on campus, or on Sunday when you can check out the nearby Maxwell Street Market.

GETTING HERE

Take I-290 west to the Damen Street exit. Go south on Damen to 19th Street. There's parking at the Mexican Fine Arts Center Museum. You can also take the El's Blue Line from downtown to 18th Street station. It's covered with colorful murals and when you reach street level, take a look at the mosaic mural depicting Mexican women from pre-Columbian time to now.

To get to University Village, take the Blue line to UIC/Halsted. The 9 Ashland bus will take you to UIC and Little Italy. If you're driving to Little Italy and University Village, take the Kennedy Expressway from either direction to the Taylor Street exit, then head west.

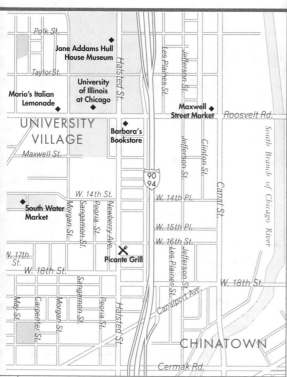

2

NEIGHBORHOOD TOP 4

1. Try the Italian lemonade—really a slushy Italian ice that comes in a rainbow of flavors—at Mario's Lemonade Stand on Taylor Street.

2. Gallery hop on Second Fridays in Pilsen, the monthly event when the art galleries stay open late.

3. Haggle over everything from TVs to tube socks at the legendary Maxwell Street Market on Sunday.

4. Three words—tres leches cake. At Bomboncito in Pilsen. Yum.

QUICK BITES

Cafe Jumping Bean (✉ 1439 W. 18th St., Pilsen ☎ 312/451-0019), a cozy neighborhood coffee shop, displays original art by local artists on its walls. This eclectic gathering place has hot chocolate with Mexican spices, panini pizzas, and fresh sandwiches.

Pompei (✉ 1531 W. Taylor St., Little Italy ☎ 312/421-5179) started as a bakery selling thick, bready squares of pizza back in 1909. Today it's a part of a growing local empire of restaurants that serve salads, housemade pasta, and that same delicious pizza.

Sweet Maple Cafe (✉ 1339 W. Taylor St., Little Italy ☎ 312/243-8908) has a loyal following for Southern-inspired breakfast. If you can stand the crowds on the weekends, it's worth the wait for grits, salmon cakes, and sweet-milk biscuits.

Picante Grill (✉ 1626 S. Halsted St., Pilsen ☎ 312/455-8500) is an upscale taqueria.

SAFETY

The area between Pilsen and Little Italy is railway tracks and vacant lots, and it isn't safe to walk between the two neighborhoods. If at all possible, try to drive to this area, park your car as you explore each individual neighborhood, and drive between the two. Cabs aren't too common in this area.

long ago was considered a wasteland. Retailers, including **Barbara's Bookstore,** (✉ 1218 S. Halsted St., University Village ☎ 312/413–2665) a small local chain, have been lured to the area along with the new residents. The Jane Addams Hull-House Museum on the UIC campus (✉ 800 S. Halsted St., University Village ☎ 312/413–5353) is a city landmark as well as a memorial to Jane Addams, who launched innovative settlement house programs. Nearby, you find the new home of the legendary **Maxwell Street Market,** which was not-so-gently nudged to the east at Canal Street and Roosevelt Road to make way for the new development. The year-round Sunday flea market is where odds and ends are sold at hundreds of stalls operated mostly by Latino immigrants. There's also live blues and food.

DID YOU KNOW?

The **Jane Addams Hull-House Museum** is filled with exhibits about the first Hull House settlement, an innovative model for urban reform at the turn of the 20th century.

At A Glance

SEE CORRESPONDING CHAPTERS.	BUDGET DINING	Tuscany, *Italian*
	Nuevo Leon, *Mexican*	Francesca's on Taylor,
MUSEUMS	Pompeii, *Italian*	*Italian*
Jane Addams Hull-House Museum	**MODERATE DINING**	
Mexican Fine Arts Center Museum	Chez Joel, *French*	
	New Rosebud Cafe, *Italian*	

2

PRAIRIE AVENUE & CHINATOWN

Sightseeing
★ ★ ★

Dining
★ ★ ★ ★

Lodging
★

Shopping
★ ★

Nightlife
★

Geography is the main thing linking the Prairie Avenue Historic District and Chinatown. Prairie Avenue (two blocks east of Michigan Avenue, between 18th and 22nd streets) was Chicago's first Gold Coast. Many prominent merchants and manufacturers, including George Pullman and Marshall Field, built their homes here in the 1870s through the 1890s. Today only a handful of buildings recall this vanished era, and this stretch of Prairie Avenue is a neighborhood in flux. New condominium construction has helped give this neighborhood more of its old vim, but it's nothing compared to the compact commotion to the west in Chinatown, a neighborhood packed-in with restaurants and shops. Tour the historic commercial district along Wentworth and Archer avenues and you might just forget you're in a Midwestern city.

What's Here

The **National Vietnam Veterans Art Museum,** on the corner of 18th Street and Indiana Avenue, shows art inspired by combat and created by veterans, providing a unique view of war. Explore a different period in history at the **Clarke House,** half a block south on Indiana Avenue. Built in 1836, it holds the distinction of being the oldest still-standing building in Chicago. Today it functions as a museum, revealing what life was like for a middle-class family in the early part of the 19th century.

GETTING ORIENTED

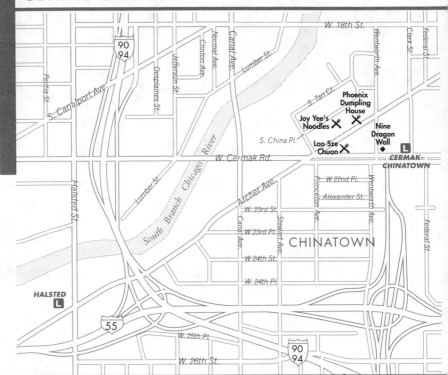

GETTING HERE

To get to Chinatown by car, drive south on Michigan Avenue and take a left at 18th Street, and travel four blocks to Cermak Road/E. 22nd Street. For the Prairie Avenue Historic District, take Michigan Avenue to E. 21st Street, then travel west to Prairie Avenue. Buses 1, 3, and 4 cover both of these areas, or you can take the El's Red Line to the Cermak–Chinatown stop.

MAKING THE MOST OF YOUR TIME

You can easily spend a few hours browsing the shops and sampling the goodies along Wentworth Avenue or at Chinatown Square. Add an hour or two more if you're going to tour one or more of the Prairie Avenue homes. Chinatown is particularly busy on weekends throughout the year but the big draws are Chinese New Year in January or February and the summer fair in July.

SAFETY

Both of these areas are a little removed from the heart of the city and bordered by slowly gentrifying neighborhoods, so be wary of walking around here at off hours.

2

NEIGHBORHOOD TOP 3

1. Forgo traditional weekend brunch for dim sum with the locals.

2. Check out the digs where Chicago greats like Marshall Field and George Pullman lived in the Prairie Avenue Historic District.

3. Shop for tea and learn about ancient traditions at Chinatown shops like Ten Ren Tea & Ginseng Co.

TOURS

Package guided tours of both the Clarke House and the Glessner House Museum are available Wednesday through Sunday, and are free on Wednesday (312/326–1480). The Chinatown Chamber of Commerce (312/326–5320) conducts one-hour walking tours in English and can even help you arrange lunch at a neighborhood restaurant.

QUICK BITES

Phoenix Dumpling House (⊠ 2131 S. Archer Ave., Chinatown ☎ 312/328–1205) is the plainer ground-floor offshoot of the widely popular Phoenix upstairs, and a perfect choice for soul-satisfying soup dumplings and pot stickers. The food's all about comfort, but we'll warn you that the service isn't.

Lao Sze Chuan (⊠ 2172 S. Archer Ave., Chinatown ☎ 312/326–5040) is the go-to spot for the best Szechuan in town. Try the twice-cooked pork and dry chili string beans. They're served super-fast.

Joy Yee's Noodles (⊠ 2159 S. China Pl., in Chinatown Square Mall, Chinatown ☎ 312/328–0001) has a mile-long menu of Pan-Asian dishes that arrive in a flash and claims to have introduced bubble teas to Chicagoland. Who are we to argue while we sip away?

Clarke House has been moved three times from its original location on Michigan Avenue between 16th and 17th streets. The last time, in 1977, it had to be hoisted above the nearby elevated train tracks.

Just around the corner to the east on Prairie Avenue is the main entrance to the **Glessner House Museum.** Designed by Henry Hobson Richardson, who also designed Trinity Church in Boston, it evokes the revolutionary Richardson Romanesque style (stone construction and short towers).

At the intersection of Calumet and Cullerton avenues is the **Wheeler Mansion,** another of the area's great mansions that was nearly replaced by a parking lot before it was saved and painstakingly restored in the late 1990s. Today it's a contemporary boutique hotel, and a fun alternative to more traditional chain lodging options nearby. ⊠ *2020 S. Calumet Ave., Prairie Avenue* ☎ *312/945–2020.*

Three blocks farther west, on Michigan Avenue, is the handsome Gothic Revival **Second Presbyterian Church.** (⊠ 1936 S. Michigan Ave., Prairie Avenue ☎ 312/225–4951). Be sure to go inside this national historic landmark and take a look at the Tiffany stained-glass windows—one of the largest collections anywhere. If your spirits still need lifting after the church visit, walk south another block on Michigan Avenue for a tour of the **Willie Dixon's Blues Heaven Foundation,** housed in the former Chess Records office and studios (⊠ 2120 S. Michigan Ave.), where a cadre of music legends, from Etta James and Bo Diddley to Aretha Franklin and John Lee Hooker, have recorded.

The Rolling Stones immortalized this address in a blues track they recorded here in 1964 entitled—you guessed it—"2120 S. Michigan Avenue."

South of the Prairie Avenue district, where Wentworth Avenue and Cermak Road/22nd Street meet, is the entrance to Chinatown. Our favorite part about Chinatown is the plethora of gift shops spilling over with eye candy in **Chinatown Square** on bustling Archer Avenue and the mouth-watering smells from the area's many restaurants and bakeries. The 11-block neighborhood is anchored by the Chinatown Gate and the enormous green-and-red pagoda towers of the Pui Tak Center, a church-based community center, in the former On Leong Tong Building. Be sure to see the **Nine Dragon Wall,** one of only four replicas worldwide of the Beijing original, and **Ping Tom Memorial Park** (⊠ 300 W. 19th St., Chinatown) a multi-acre site dedicated to a neighborhood civic leader that has views of the Chicago River and incorporates Chinese landscaping elements.

At A Glance

2

HYDE PARK

Sightseeing
★ ★ ★ ★
Dining
★ ★
Lodging
★
Shopping
★
Nightlife
★ ★

Hyde Park is something of a haul from downtown and the usual tourist haunts in Chicago, but it's worth the extra effort. Best known as the home of the University of Chicago, the neighborhood only began to see significant growth in the late 19th century, when the university opened in 1892 and the Columbian World's Exposition attracted an international influx a year later. The exposition spawned the Midway Plaisance and numerous Classical Revival buildings, including the behemoth Museum of Science and Industry. The Midway Plaisance, which surrounded the heart of the fair, still runs along the southern edge of the University of Chicago's original campus. Sprawling homes were soon erected for school faculty in neighboring Kenwood, and the area began to attract well-to-do types who commissioned famous architects to build them spectacular homes.

Today the neighborhood is considered a vibrant, eclectic part of the city. A number of architecturally riveting buildings are here, including two by Frank Lloyd Wright, the **Robie House** and **Heller House.** There's also a thriving theater scene and several art and history museums. Most impressive, though, is the diverse population with a strong sense of community pride and fondness for the neighborhood's pretty tree-lined streets, proximity to the lake, and slightly-off-the-beaten path vibe.

What's Here

To get a good overview of the neighborhood, stop by the **Hyde Park Historical Society** (⊠ 5529 S. Lake Park Ave., Hyde Park ☎ 773/493–1893 ⊘ Weekends 2–4), which sponsors lectures and tours.

DID YOU KNOW?

The tall bronze sculpture, Nuclear Energy (on the east side of Ellis Avenue between 56th and 57th streets), marks the site where Enrico Fermi and other physicists set off the first controlled nuclear chain reaction on December 2, 1942. It occurred under the bleachers of what was then Stagg Field. The sculpture is said to represent both a human skull and an atomic mushroom cloud.

One of Hyde Park's gems is **Jackson Park** (⊠ Bounded by E. 56th and 67th Sts., S. Stony Island Ave., and the lakefront), which was designed by Frank Law Olmsted (who also designed Central Park in New York City) for the World's Columbian Exposition of 1893. It has lagoons, a Japanese garden with authentic Japanese statuary, and the Wooded Island, a nature retreat with wildlife and 300 species of birds.

DID YOU KNOW?

Jackson Park has a notable parrot population. It all started back during the World's Columbian Exposition of 1893, when parrots were imported for an exhibit. The Exposition left, but the parrots settled right down and seem to brave the cold winters just fine.

The **University of Chicago** (⊠ S. Ellis Ave. ☎ 773/702–1234) dominates the physical and cultural landscape of Hyde Park and South Kenwood, and it's visually arresting. Much of the original campus was designed by Henry Ives Cobb. Especially of note is the International House and the Rockefeller Memorial Chapel, which has a carillon with 72 bells; a university carillonneur gives regular performances. The university's stately Gothic-style quadrangles look like something straight out of Cambridge and Oxford.

DID YOU KNOW?

"The toasters" are two apartment buildings that sit on an island in the middle of the street, so named because, fittingly enough, the buildings look like two pieces of toast. They were designed by I. M. Pei, architect for the Louvre's controversial glass pyramids.

Frank Lloyd Wright's **Robie House** is a Prairie-style masterpiece and one of the most remarkable designs in modern American architecture. **Heller House,** nearby on Harper Avenue between 52nd and 53rd streets, was designed by Wright in 1897, 12 years prior to Robie House. Though not open to the public, the exterior is a good indication of his progression toward the Prairie Style he achieved with Robie. The area is loaded with other architecturally significant buildings, including the **Windermere House and Promontory Apartments.**

DID YOU KNOW?

Robie House literally sits on a pedestal. Wright abhorred basements, which he considered unhealthy.

Hyde Park has a bunch of smaller museums that stand in the shadow of the **Museum of Science and Industry. The DuSable Museum of African Amer-**

GETTING ORIENTED

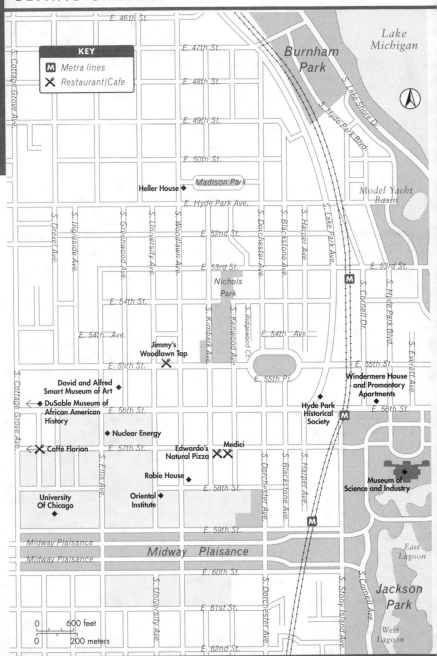

KEY

Ⓜ *Metra lines*
✕ *Restaurant/Cafe*

E. 46th St.

E. 47th St.

E. 48th St.

E. 49th St.

E. 50th St.

Madison Park

Heller House ◆

E. Hyde Park Ave.

E. 52nd St.

E. 53rd St.

Nichols Park

E. 54th St.

E. 54th Ave.

E. 54th Ave.

Jimmy's Woodlawn Tap ✕

E. 55th St.

E. 55th Pl.

David and Alfred Smart Museum of Art ◆

←◆ DuSable Museum of African American History

E. 56th St.

◆ Nuclear Energy

✕ Caffè Florian

E. 57th St.

Edwardo's Natural Pizza ✕

Medici ✕

Robie House ◆

E. 58th St.

University Of Chicago ◆

Oriental Institute ◆

E. 59th St.

Midway Plaisance

Midway Plaisance

Midway Plaisance

E. 60th St.

E. 61st St.

E. 62nd St.

Windermere House and Promontory Apartments ◆

E. 56th St.

Hyde Park Historical Society ◆

Ⓜ

Museum of Science and Industry ◆

Lake Michigan

Burnham Park

S. Lake Shore Dr.

S. Hyde Park Blvd.

Model Yacht Basin

E. 53rd St.

Ⓜ

East Lagoon

Jackson Park

West Lagoon

S. Cottage Grove Ave.

S. Drexel Ave.

S. Ingleside Ave.

S. Greenwood Ave.

S. University Ave.

S. Woodlawn Ave.

S. Kimbark Ave.

S. Kenwood Ave.

S. Ridgewood Ct.

S. Dorchester Ave.

S. Blackstone Ave.

S. Harper Ave.

S. Lake Park Ave.

S. Cornell Dr.

S. Hyde Park Blvd.

S. Everett Ave.

S. Ellis Ave.

S. Cottage Grove Ave.

S. University Ave.

S. Dorchester Ave.

S. Blackstone Ave.

S. Harper Ave.

S. Stony Island Ave.

S. Cornell Ave.

0　　600 feet

0　　200 meters

GETTING HERE

If you're arriving by car, take Lake Shore Drive south to the 57th Street exit and turn left into the parking lot of the Museum of Science and Industry. You can also take the Metra Railroad train from Randolph Street and Michigan Avenue; get off at the 55th Street stop and walk east through the underpass two blocks, then south two blocks. Or, for a longer trip that snakes through more of the city, take the El's Red Line to the State Street and Lake Street stop, then pick up either the No. 6 or No. 10 bus heading southward.

MAKING THE MOST OF YOUR TIME

If you're visiting the Museum of Science and Industry, you'll probably be spending a good chunk of your day there, especially if you have kids. Try to go during the week to avoid crowds. You could wind down the day meandering through Jackson Park or walking around the University of Chicago (it's most fun to visit during the week, when it bustles with students). If you're not interested in the museum, you could spend the morning checking out the Frank Lloyd Wright buildings.

QUICK BITES

You'll find several spots on 57th Street where you can get a quick bite and relax. **Medici** (✉ 1327 E. 57th St., Hyde Park ☎ 773/667–7394) has served up its specialty pizzas, burgers, and sandwiches to generations of University of Chicago students who've carved their names into the tables.

The deep-dish pies at **Edwardo's Natural Pizza** (✉ 1321 E. 57th St., Hyde Park ☎ 773/241–7960) are considered by some to be the best in the city.

Caffé Florian (✉ 1450 E. 57th St., Hyde Park ☎ 773/752–4100) serves pizza and Italian entrées as well as hearty sandwiches, homemade soups and salads, decadent desserts, and lots of java.

Jimmy's Woodlawn Tap (✉ 1172 E. 55th St., Hyde Park ☎ 773/643–5516 ☉ Daily 11 AM–2 AM) is a favored spot where locals and university students gather for a spoken-word reading or jazz concert along with pub grub.

SAFETY

Hyde Park is bordered to the west, south, and north by some less prosperous, and at times dangerous, areas. Use caution, especially in the evening, if you're uncertain about where you're heading.

TOURS

Tours of Frank Lloyd Wright's Robie House are conducted daily. (☎ 773/834–1847). A self-guided tour of University of Chicago architecture, *A Walking Guide to the Campus*, is available for purchase in the University of Chicago Bookstore. ✉ *Visitor Center: Reynolds Club 5706 S. University* ☎ *773/702–9739* ⊕ *www.uchicago.edu* ☉ *Weekdays 9–5.*

NEIGHBORHOOD TOP 4

1. Get lost in the massive wonder of the Museum of Science and Industry.

2. Do some exotic-bird watching in Jackson Park, where a tropical parrot population roosts.

3. Tour Frank Lloyd Wright's fantastic Robie House.

4. Pack a picnic and enjoy the views from the beautiful Promontory Point.

At A Glance

SEE CORRESPONDING CHAPTERS. SIGHTS ARE IN THE EXPERIENCE CHAPTER.	DuSable Museum of African American History Museum of Science and Industry	ENTERTAINMENT Checkboard Lounge, *Blues* Lee's Unleaded Blues, *Blues*
SIGHTS South Shore Country Club Beach Jackson Beach Central	Oriental Institute ARCHITECTURE Robie House	
MUSEUMS David and Alfred Smart Museum of Art	Isidore Heller House MODERATE DINING La Petite Folie, *French*	

ican History has a notable permanent exhibit on slavery, and offers a cinema series and jazz and blues concerts, as well as children's programs. The **David and Alfred Smart Museum of Art** houses the fine art collection of the University of Chicago. **The Oriental Institute,** also a part of the university, is filled with art and artifacts from the ancient Near East, many that are more than 3,000 years old.

DID YOU KNOW?

Hyde Park was one of the first communities in the country to go through the urban-renewal process. Developers razed entire blocks and built town houses designed by I. M. Pei and Harry Weese in their place.

Museums

WORD OF MOUTH

"Shedd Aquarium has a great exhibit of beluga whales—so fun to watch them swimming and playing. We're big fans of the Adler Planetarium, in addition to the Museum of Science and Industry."

—SusanEva

"Art Institute is great, all the major museums are great, and Shedd Aquarium is fun."

—fishee

MUSEUM PLANNER

Free Days

Always free:
Jane Addams Hull-House
  Museum
Mexican Fine Arts Center
Museum of Contemporary
  Photography
Oriental Institute
Peace Museum
Smart Museum

Sunday:
DuSable Museum of African
  American History

Monday:
Adler Planetarium (selected
  months only)
Field Museum (selected months
  only)

Tuesday:
Adler Planetarium (selected
  months only)
Art Institute of Chicago
Field Museum (selected months
  only)
Museum of Contemporary Art
  (5–8 PM only)
Swedish American Museum
  (second Tues. each month)

Thursday:
Chicago Children's Museum
  (5–8 PM only)
Peggy Notebaert Nature
  Museum

Friday:
Spertus Museum (1–3 PM only)

Save Money

All the major museums are expensive; consider purchasing a Chicago CityPass instead of buying a single ticket. For about the price of admission to two museums, the pass lets you bypass the long lines and visit all of the big five—the Art Institute, Field Museum, Museum of Science and Industry, Adler Planetarium, and the Shedd Aquarium—plus the Hancock Observatory, anytime within nine days. For more information, see citypass.com.

Late Hours

Adler Planetarium, First Friday of the month to 10 PM
Art Institute, Thursday to 8 PM
Chicago Children's Museum, Thursday and
  Saturday to 8 PM
Museum of Contemporary Art, Tuesday to 8 PM
Museum of Contemporary Photography, Thursday to 8 PM
Oriental Institute, Wednesday to 8:30 PM
Smart Museum, Thursday to 8 PM

Special Events

Sonic Vision at the Adler Planetarium is a roller-coaster ride of alternative music and 3-D imagery, which was developed with Moby and MTV2. The play list is available on Adler's Web site (⊕ www.adlerplanetarium.org). Fri. and Sat. at 7, 8, 9, and 10. $10. Shows are often sold out; purchase tickets in advance.

Tuesdays on the Terrace is a weekly summer event for mingling and live local jazz at the Museum of Contemporary Art. Cash bar. June–Sept., Tues. 5:30–8.

DJs and local bands get things going at the Museum of Contemporary Art's First Fridays, a monthly preview of new work by Chicago artists. First Friday of every month, 6–10. $14.

Feel like dinner, drinks, live jazz, and a view of the lake and the skyline? Get thee to Shedd Aquarium's Jazzin at the Shedd on the museum's terrace. June–Sept., Thurs. 5–10. $10.

How Much Time?

Less than an hour:
Balzekas Museum of Lithuanian Culture
Museum of Contemporary Photography
Museum of Holography
National Vietnam Veterans Art Museum
Peace Museum
Polish Museum of America
Smart Museum of Art

1–2 hours:
DuSable Museum of African American History
Jane Addams Hull-House Museum
Museum of Broadcast Communications
Oriental Institute

2–3 hours:
Adler Planetarium
Chicago Children's Museum
Chicago Historical Society
Mexican Fine Arts Center Museum
Peggy Notebaert Nature Museum

Half-Day:
Museum of Contemporary Art
Shedd Aquarium

Full Day:
Art Institute of Chicago
Field Museum
Museum of Science and Industry

Best Gift Shops

Art Institute of Chicago. Find silk scarves, fine jewelry, glass paperweights, and other items that are reproduced from art works in the museum.

Field Museum. Everything dinosaur is sold in Field gift shops, but our guilty pleasure is the Mold-A-Rama vending machines on the lower level. These 1960s relics take heated colorful plastic and inject it into dinosaur molds.

Museum of Science and Industry. The Big Idea gift shop, on the entrance level, is packed with objects to tickle your mind, including chemistry sets, radio-controlled blimps, robot kits, and a kinetic solar system model.

Museum of Contemporary Art. Pick up a Calder mobile or soap designed to look like a person—you know, the stuff you never knew you always wanted.

Best Quirky Exhibits

Judy Istock Butterfly Haven, Peggy Notebaert Nature Museum. More than 20 local and international species of butterfly flutter through the small butterfly room. Hundreds of butterflies land gently on brightly colored clothes, on hair, and sometimes, if you're lucky, on hands. Even more interesting are the cocoons in various stages of development. You might even catch a butterfly struggling out of its chrysalis.

Colleen Moore's Fairy Castle, Museum of Science and Industry. The MSI is full of quirky exhibits that kinda make us wonder if we're still in a technology museum—there are live baby chicks and a moving exhibit of circus wagon miniatures—but one of the most beloved is the Fairy Castle. Built between 1928 and 1935, the final cost for this 8-foot-high palace with its 2,000 miniatures was $500,000.

Mesopotamian gallery, Oriental Institute. The OI's largest gallery covers the entire sweep of Mesopotamian history, and includes a caveman's axe with the first trace of human blood and tablets that trace the history and development of writing.

Thorne Miniature Rooms, Art Institute. The 68 dollhouselike rooms were designed by a Chicago socialite to display the miniatures she collected through her travels in Europe and America. They have working artifacts and showcase the architecture and interior design from the 16th century to the 1930s.

By Jennifer Vanasco

Chicago's museums are the cultural heart of the city—so vital that a few years ago the mayor rerouted Lake Shore Drive to create a verdant Museum Campus for the Adler Planetarium, Shedd Aquarium, and Field Museum. Treasures in Chicago's museums include Grant Wood's iconic painting *American Gothic*, at the Art Institute; "Sue," the largest T. rex ever discovered, at the Field Museum; and the only German U-boat captured during World War II, at the Museum of Science and Industry.

Just the Highlights, Please . . .

Head to the Art Institute for a quick art-fix. For a tour of superlatives, see *Sky Above Clouds IV*, Georgia O'Keefe's largest painting; the largest holding of Monet's *Grainstacks* anywhere; and *A Sunday on La Grande Jatte—1884*, Georges Seurat's greatest piece.

Culture Vulture . . .

Tour the world without leaving the city. First stop? Europe. Hit the **The Balzekas Museum of Lithuanian Culture,** the **Swedish-American Museum,** the **Polish Museum,** and the **Ukranian Museum of Modern Art.** Swing by the **Oriental Institute** for all things Asian, or brush up on Latino history at the **Mexican Fine Arts Center.**

If You Have Kids . . .

Besides the Chicago Children's Museum, these are our favorite kids' exhibits, sure to capture the imagination of your young ones. Don't miss the **Fairy Castle** at the Museum of Science and Industry; **"Sue,"** the T. rex, at the Field Museum; the **dolphin show** at the Shedd Aquariums' Oceanarium; and the **Television Center,** where you can pretend to be a news anchor, at the Museum of Broadcast Communications. If the weather's nice, **chase butterflies** at the Peggy Notebaert Nature Museum.

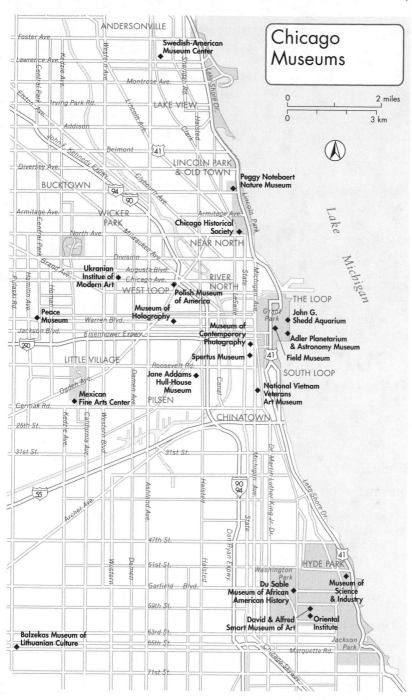

Chicago Museums

0   2 miles

0   3 km

ANDERSONVILLE

Foster Ave.

Lawrence Ave.

Swedish-American
Museum Center

Montrose Ave.

Irving Park Rd.

LAKE VIEW

Addison

Belmont

41

Diversey Ave.

LINCOLN PARK
& OLD TOWN

BUCKTOWN

94

Peggy Notebaert
Nature Museum

90

Armitage Ave.

WICKER
PARK

Armitage Ave.

North Ave.

Chicago Historical
Society

Division

NEAR NORTH

Augusta Blvd.

Ukranian
Institue of
Modern Art

Chicago Ave.

RIVER
NORTH

WEST LOOP

Polish Museum
of America

Museum of
Holography

THE LOOP

Peace
Museum

Warren Blvd.

John G.
Shedd Aquarium

Jackson Blvd.

Eisenhower Expwy.

Museum of
Contemporary
Photography

Adler Planetarium
& Astronomy Museum

290

LITTLE VILLAGE

Roosevelt Rd.

Spertus Museum

41

Field Museum

Jane Addams
Hull-House
Museum

SOUTH LOOP

Mexican
Fine Arts Center

PILSEN

National Vietnam
Veterans
Art Museum

Cermak Rd.

25th St.

CHINATOWN

31st St.

31st St.

55

90
94

Archer Ave.

47th St.

51st St.

HYDE PARK

Garfield Blvd.

41

Washington
Park

Museum of
Science
& Industry

Du Sable
Museum of African
American History

59th St.

David & Alfred
Smart Museum of Art

Oriental
Institute

Balzekas Museum of
Lithuanian Culture

63rd St.

65th St.

Jackson
Park

Marquette Rd.

71st St.

Lake
Michigan

A GUIDE TO THE ART INSTITUTE

The Art Institute of Chicago, nestled between the contemporary public art showplace of Millennium Park and the Paris-inspired walkways of Grant Park, is both intimate and grand, a place where the rooms are human-scale and the art is transcendent.

Come for the sterling collection of Impressionists and Old Masters (an entire room is dedicated to Monet), linger over the extraordinary and comprehensive photography collection, take in a number of fine American works, and discover paintings, drawings, sculpture, design, and photography spanning the ancient to the contemporary world.

The Institute is more than just a museum; in fact, it was originally founded by a small group of artists in 1866 as a school with an adjoining exhibition space. Famous alumni include political cartoonist Herblock and artists Grant Wood and Ed Paschke. Walt Disney and Georgia O'Keeffe both took classes, but didn't graduate. The School of the Art Institute of Chicago, one of the finest art schools in the country, is across the street from the museum; occasionally there are lectures and discussions that are open to the public.

ORIENTATION TO THE MUSEUM

✉ 111 S. Michigan Ave., South Loop

☎ 312/443-3600

🌐 www.artic.edu/aic/

💳 Suggested $12, Students and Seniors $7, Free Tuesdays

🕐 Mon.-Wed. and Fri. 10:30-4:30, Thu. 10:30-8, Sat.-Sun. 10-5

Take in the museum's grandeur.

Photo op: Pose with one of the two bronze lions.

The Art Institute is a complicated jumble of three difficult-to-navigate buildings—you can only change buildings on the first level of the museum, and the map the museum gives out isn't very helpful. Here are some tips to help you find your way around:

- On the lower level are textiles, decorative arts, the Thorne Miniature Room, and the Kraft Education Center. The first level includes the non-European galleries, contemporary art, and American art to 1890. The second level holds American art from 1900 to 1950, European art from all periods, and Impressionism.

- Pinpoint the five or six works you'd really like to see or pick two or three galleries and wander around after getting yourself there.

- Guards expect visitors to ask for directions, so don't be shy.

- Buy the audio tour ($6) by the coatroom as you enter—it provides descriptions for every gallery and work in the museum. All you do is key in the gallery number and the voices of curators will guide you around the room.

- Note that a massive construction project, due to be completed in 2009, may cause the temporary closure of some exhibits (including the celebrated Chagall stained glass windows) or the relocation of some galleries.

FOR THE KIDS

Kids love the Kraft Education Center, which has rotating exhibits of child-friendly art (like paintings from picture books) and a permanent, interactive exhibit called *Faces, Places & Inner Spaces* that helps teach children how to look at different kinds of art. There's also a small stage with Kabuki costumes, actual paintings hung at kid-friendly levels, and computer-enhanced games. Nearby is the Touch Gallery, which was originally designed for the blind. You can run your fingers over several bronze works. For more suggestions, check out *Behind the Lions: A Family Guide to the Art Institute of Chicago*, available at the museum bookstore.

BEST PAINTINGS

AMERICAN GOTHIC (1930). GALLERY 263
Grant Wood won $300 for his iconic painting of a
solemn farmer and his wife (really his sister and his
dentist). Wood saw the work as a celebration of solid,
work-based Midwestern values, a statement that rural
America would survive the Depression and the massive migration to cities.

American Gothic (1930).

NIGHTHAWKS (1942). GALLERY 262
Edward Hopper's painting of four figures in a diner
on the corner of a deserted New York street is a noir
portrait of isolated lives and is one of the most recognized images of 20th-century art. The red-haired
woman is the artist's wife, Jo.

THE CHILD'S BATH (1893). GALLERY 273
Mary Cassatt was the only American to become an
established Impressionist and her work focused on the
daily lives of women and children. In this, her most
famous work, a woman gently bathes a child who is
tucked up on her lap. The Bath was unconventional
when it was painted because the bold patterns and
cropped forms it used were more often seen in Japanese prints at the time.

Nighthawks (1942).

SKY ABOVE CLOUDS IV (1965). GALLERY 249
(not pictured) Georgia O'Keeffe's massive painting,
the largest canvas of her career, is of clouds seen from
an airplane. The rows of white rectangles stretching
toward the horizon look both solid and ethereal, as
if they are stepping stones for angels.

THE OLD GUITARIST (1903/04). GALLERY 263
(not pictured) One of the most important works of
Pablo Picasso's Blue Period, this monochromatic
painting is a study of the crooked figure of a blind and
destitute street guitarist, singing sorrowfully. When he
painted it, Picasso was feeling particularly empathetic
toward the downtrodden—perhaps because of a
friend's suicide—and the image of the guitarist is one
of dignity amid poverty.

The Child's Bath (1893).

GRAINSTACK (1890/91). GALLERY 206
The Art Institute has the largest collection of Monet's
Grainstacks in the world. The stacks rose 15 to 20 feet
tall outside Monet's farmhouse in Giverny and were
a symbol to the artist of sustenance and survival.

Grainstack (1890/91)

3

A SUNDAY ON LA GRANDE JATTE 1884 (1884-86). GALLERY 205

Georges Seurat's greatest work has inspired generations of painters and even spawned a musical—Stephen Sondheim's *Sunday in the Park with George*. A precise pattern of tiny dots creates a scene of mixed-class serenity in Paris, with rounded figures of soldiers, genteel women, children, and a monkey.

SELF-PORTRAIT (1887). GALLERY 205

Twenty-four self portraits were painted by Vincent Van Gogh, and this early example is an expressive picture made up of colorful dots and dashes. The artist's intense eyes gaze directly into yours, inviting you into his soul.

A Sunday on La Grande Jatte 1884 (1884–86).

Self-Portrait (1887).

OTHER DON'T-MISS EXHIBITS

PAPERWEIGHT COLLECTION. GALLERY 69

In the mid-nineteenth century, a newly dependable mail service made writing implements and desk accessories chic—including glass paperweights. The Art Institute's famous Arthur Rubloff Collection houses over 1,400 of these surprisingly intricate paperweights, with examples from all periods, techniques, designs, and manufacturers.

STOCK EXCHANGE TRADING ROOM.

Architects Louis Sullivan and Dankmar Adler used art glass and stenciled decorations to build a glorious trading room for the Chicago Stock Exchange. Though the Exchange was demolished in 1972, it's recreated here with pieces from the original.

TADAO ANDO. GALLERY 109

Many visitors miss this serene room of pottery and painted screens, half hidden behind a closed glass door in the Asian galleries on the first floor. The room, designed by Japanese architect and artist Tadao Ando, is notable for its rows of large wooden columns; Ando said he wanted viewers to "feel as if the wind is passing through."

THORNE MINIATURE ROOMS. GALLERY 11

68 tiny rooms showcase interior design and decorative arts from the 13th century to 1940. Master craftsmen built them (1932–1940) for Mrs. James Ward Thorne to a scale of one inch to one foot. The rooms look like tiny, perfect dollhouses.

Paperweight collection.

Thorne Miniature Rooms.

ADLER PLANETARIUM & ASTRONOMY MUSEUM

✉ 1300 S. Lake Shore Dr., South Loop

☎ 312/922-7827

🌐 www.adlerplanetarium. org

💲 $13 museum admission and 1 show, $18 museum admission and 2 shows. Free Mon. and Tues. Jan., Feb., and mid-Sept.-3rd wk Dec.

🕐 Weekdays 9:30 AM-4:30 PM (except 1st Fri. of month when open until 10 PM), weekends 9 AM-4:30 PM.

Navigate your way through the solar system with interactive and state-of-the-art exhibits that appeal to planetarium traditionalists as well as technology-savvy kids and adults. The museum uses computer games, videos, short films, and hands-on devices to teach physics and astronomy basics like the Doppler effect. Two different planetariums unlock the mysteries of the stars.

TIPS

■ Additional charges apply for the Sky Theater planetarium shows and the StarRider interactive shows (see admission prices above), but don't skip them—they're the reason to go.

■ Take a quick (free) ride in the Atwood Sphere, a large metal globe with punched-out stars. It provided the nation's very first planetarium experience.

■ On weekend nights, you can experience SonicVision, where trippy electronic music is accompanied by beautiful computer-generated 3-D patterns in the StarRider Theater.

■ No need to purchase the museum's audio tour. The signs in the museum are comprehensive and the narrative doesn't add much to the experience.

HIGHLIGHTS

The Adler's traditional in-the-round Zeiss planetarium (called the Sky Theater) shows constellations and planets in the night sky. It's been around since the Adler opened in 1930 as the first public planetarium in the western hemisphere.

In the cultural astronomy section, kids can dress up like ancient astronomers, navigate a simulated skiff using slowly wheeling stars, figure out when to plant crops, or predict the future of a kingly reign based on eclipses and the positions of planets.

Take a digital journey into space on the interactive StarRider Theater, inside the high-tech Sky Pavilion. For some shows, you use control buttons on your armrest to vote for what you see on screen. (Part of the technology is based on aircraft flight simulators.) Other shows wrap you in a 3-D universe of stars. Also in the Sky Pavilion are a telescope terrace and interactive exhibition galleries that include computer animations of the Milky Way and of the birth of the solar system.

CHICAGO CHILDREN'S MUSEUM

✉ Navy Pier, 700 E. Grand
  Ave., Near North
☎ 312/527-1000
🌐 www.chichildrens
  museum.org
🎫 $7, free Thurs. 5–8
🕐 Sun.-Wed. and Fri. 10–5,
  Thurs. and Sat. 10–8.

TIPS

■ The museum issues read-mission bracelets that let you leave the museum and come back on the same day—great idea for weary families that want to take a break to get a bite to eat, or simply explore other parts of Navy Pier before coming back to the museum.

■ Grab a bite at the nearby space-themed McDonald's (312/832-1640), or bring a picnic and grab a sunny seat outside (in warm weather) or gather in the Crystal Ballroom (amid tropical plants and fountains).

■ Most families spend an average of three hours visiting the museum.

■ Hour-long Artabounds workshops are free.

■ The museum is designed for children 2 to 12 years.

■ Try each of the artist-created benches to figure out which one makes music when you sit on it.

"Hands-on" is the operative concept for this brightly colored Navy Pier anchor. Kids play educational video games, climb through multilevel tunnels, run their own TV stations, and, if their parents allow it, get soaking wet.

HIGHLIGHTS

Kids can don raincoats before they start splashing around in the WaterWays exhibit, which has oversize water tubs with waterwheels, pumps, brightly colored pipes, and splashing fountains. If everyone pumps hard enough, water squirts 50 feet into the air.

In the Big Backyard exhibit, children "shrink" to the size of bugs amid giant giggling flowers. Butterflies seem to flutter around their bodies and water appears to splash down on their heads, all through the magic of a tall video screen.

Parents, get ready for a workout. You and your children can scurry up a three-story-high rigging complete with crow's nest and gangplank on the Kovler Family Climbing Schooner. It's reminiscent of the boats that once sailed Lake Michigan. If you make it to the rope tunnels at the top, you can take in bird's-eye views of the museum, then slide back down to the lower level, where there are tanks of fish.

Crouch beside your child to search for fossils in the Dinosaur Expedition. Brush away dirt to discover the bones of a Suchomimus, a kind of fish-eating dinosaur that's on display nearby. The exhibit re-creates a trip to the Sahara led by University of Chicago paleontologist Paul Sereno.

Collaboration is the watchword at Kraft Artabounds studio, where kids participate in rotating group art projects that include activities like creating a castle out of clay.

FIELD MUSEUM

✉ 1400 S. Lake Shore Dr., South Loop

☎ 312/922-9410

🌐 www.fieldmuseum.org

🎟 $10, free Mon. and Tues. Jan., Feb., and Sept.-3rd wk of Dec.

🕐 Daily 9-5.

TIPS

■ It's impossible to see the entire Field in one visit. Try to get tickets to the special exhibit of the season (go to the Web site if you'd like to order in advance) and then choose a couple subjects you'd like to explore, like North American birds or Chinese jade.

■ The DinoStore sells a mind-boggling assortment of dinosaur-related merchandise.

■ Bring young ones to 20-minute story times, when staff and volunteers read a dinosaur-themed book and direct an art project (weekends year-round and daily July and August).

■ As of this writing, the museum's showpiece exhibit on evolution was to reopen in March 2006.

■ The lobby of the museum includes the Corner Bakery. The dining room tucked in the back has sparkling views of the lake and the Museum Campus.

■ Check the Web site for up-to-date details on special performances and lectures.

★ More than 6 *acres* of exhibits fill this gigantic world-class museum, which explores cultures and environments from around the globe. Interactive exhibits examine such topics as the secrets of Egyptian mummies, the people of Africa and the Pacific Northwest, and the living creatures in the soil. Originally funded by Chicago retailer Marshall Field, the museum was founded in 1893 to hold material gathered for the World's Columbian Exposition; its current classical-style home opened in 1921.

HIGHLIGHTS

Shrink to the size of a bug to burrow beneath the surface of the soil in the Underground Adventure exhibit ($7 extra). You'll come face-to-face with a giant, animatronic wolf spider twice your size, listen to the sounds of gnawing insects, and have other encounters with the life that teems under our feet.

Spend a couple hours taking in contemporary and ancient Africa. Dioramas let you feel like you're stepping inside the homes and lives of Africans from Senegal, Cameroon, and the Sahara, while the remarkable Inside Ancient Egypt complex includes a working canal, a living marsh where papyrus is grown, a shrine to the cat goddess Bastet, burial-ceremony artifacts, and 23 mummies.

The Field's dinosaur collection is one of the world's best. You can't miss 65-million-year-old "Sue," the largest and most complete Tyrannosaurus rex fossil ever found—it's on permanent exhibit in the lobby.

Figure out which exhibit is your favorite. Some of the most popular are the Pawnee Earth Lodge, a reconstruction of a Great Plains Native American dwelling; the man-eating Lions of Tsavo; and McDonald's Fossil Preparation Laboratory, where you can watch paleontologists clean up bones.

MUSEUM OF CONTEMPORARY ART

✉ 220 E. Chicago Ave., Near North

☎ 312/280-2660

⊕ www.mcachicago.org

🎟 $10, free Tues. evenings 5–8

🕐 Tues. 10–8, Wed.–Sun. 10–5.

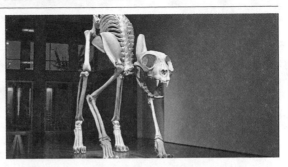

3

TIPS

■ The back of the MCA is one of the best spots to have lunch or Sunday brunch in the city. Run by Wolfgang Puck and called Puck's Café at the MCA, it not only has a tasty menu, but overlooks gardens, a park, and street life.

■ Try to catch one of the cutting-edge music and theater performances; one year, for example, the entire front of the museum was turned into a puppet theater. Performances happen quite frequently; check the Web site for information on what will be happening when you're in town.

■ In summer come for Tuesdays on the Terrace and be serenaded by local jazz bands. There's a cash bar from 5:30 to 8 PM and a full menu at the café.

■ On the first Friday of every month the museum hosts a party ($14) with live music and hors d'oeuvres from 6 PM to 10 PM.

★ A group of art patrons who felt the great Art Institute was unresponsive to modern work founded the MCA in 1967, and it's remained a renegade art museum ever since. It doesn't have any permanent exhibits; even the works from its collection are constantly rotating. This gives it a feeling of freshness, but it also makes it impossible to predict what will be on display at any time. Special exhibits are devoted mostly to original shows you can't see anywhere else—past exhibits have included solo shows by light artist Dan Flavin and photographer Catherine Opie, and group shows with new work from China and Brazil. See the MCA Web site for details.

HIGHLIGHTS

The MCA's dramatic quarters were designed by Berlin architect Josef Paul Kleihues. Even from the outside, the building looks like a home for modern art—it's made of square metal plates, with round bolts in each corner.

The MCA's growing 7,000-piece collection, which includes work by René Magritte, Alexander Calder, Bruce Nauman, Sol LeWitt, Franz Kline, and June Leaf, makes up about half the museum. The other half is dedicated to temporary exhibitions.

The museum showcases work in all media, including paintings, sculpture, works on paper, photography, video, film, and installations.

The MCA Store is the place to go for well-designed jewelry and items for the home, from a cake server that looks like a high heel to a clock with a face that's a psychedelic swirl of color.

MUSEUM OF SCIENCE AND INDUSTRY

✉ 5700 S. Lake Shore Dr.,
Hyde Park

☎ 773/684-1414

🌐 www.msichicago.org

🎟 $9, museum and
Omnimax admission $15;
parking $12

🕐 Memorial Day–Labor
Day, Mon.–Sat. 9–5:30,
Sun. 11–5:30; Labor
Day–Memorial Day,
Mon.–Sat. 9:30–4,
Sun. 11–4.

TIPS

■ Use the museum map to
plan out your visit. Your best
bet is to hit a couple of highlights (the U-boat tour alone
will take at least an hour)
and then see a couple of
quirky exhibits.

■ If the kids get grouchy,
bring them to the Idea
Factory, a giant playroom
where they can play with
water cannons, blocks, and
cranks. Limited to ages 10
and younger.

■ Relax with some ice
cream in the old-fashioned
ice-cream parlor, tucked
away in a genteel re-creation
of an Illinois main street.

■ On nice days, hordes of
sunbathers and kite-flyers
camp out on the giant lawn
out front—it's almost as entertaining as the museum itself. Lake Michigan is across
the street.

■ The museum has free-ad-
mission days, but the schedule changes often. Check the
Web site for details.

★ **Fodor's Choice** The beloved MSI is one of the most visited sites in Chicago, and for good reason. The sprawling open space has 2,000 exhibits on three floors, with new exhibits added constantly. The museum's high-tech interior is hidden by the classical revival exterior; it was designed in 1892 by D. H. Burnham & Company as a temporary structure to house the Palace of Fine Arts for the World's Columbian Exposition. It's the fair's only surviving building. On a nice day, take a walk behind the museum to the beautifully landscaped Jackson Lagoons and the hidden Japanese Tea Garden.

HIGHLIGHTS

Descend into the depths of a simulated coal mine on a "miner"-led tour that explores the technology behind digging energy out of the ground.

Get a close-up view of a plane's flaps and wheels as a cantilevered Boeing 727 "takes off" above visitors every hour. Former United pilots explain what's going on to those sitting inside the jet as the airplane flaps raise and lower and the wheels retract.

The opulent and detailed-as-a-film-set Fairy Castle (really a giant dollhouse) has tiny chandeliers that flash with real diamonds and floors that are laid with intricate stone patterns. It's enough to make us daydream about the world fairy-tale characters might have lived in.

Tour the cramped quarters of the only U-505 German submarine captured during World War II (there's an additional fee). Don't feel like waiting in line? Explore just the free interactive exhibits surrounding the sub, which give stunning insight into the strategy behind the war at sea.

Learn how scientists can make frogs' eyes glow or watch baby chicks tap themselves out of their shells at the "Genetics–Decoding Life" exhibit.

The Omnimax Theater shows science- and space-related films on a giant screen.

JOHN G. SHEDD AQUARIUM

✉ 1200 S. Lake Shore Dr., South Loop

☎ 312/939-2438

🌐 www.sheddaquarium. org

🎟 $21 all-access pass; $13 Mon. and Tues.

🕑 Memorial Day-Labor Day, daily 9-6, Thurs. until 10; Labor Day-Memorial Day, weekdays 9-5, weekends 9-6.

TIPS

■ Catch live jazz on the Shedd's north terrace on Thursday evenings from 5 to 10 PM June through September. A gorgeous view of the lake and skyline can make for a magical night. Food and a bar are available.

■ Lines for the Shedd often extend all the way down the neoclassical steps. Buy a ticket in advance to avoid the interminable wait, or spring for a CityPass.

■ Soundings restaurant is an elegant stop for lunch. The menu is pricey, but the quiet tables look over Lake Michigan—and there are very few Chicago eateries that can say that.

★ **Fodor's Choice** | Take a plunge into an underwater world at the world's largest indoor aquarium. Built in 1930, the Shedd is one of the most popular aquariums in the country, housing more than 8,000 aquatic animals in realistic waterscapes.

HIGHLIGHTS

"Amazon Rising" gives you an up-close look at the animals of the Amazon River, including piranhas, snakes, and stingrays.

Sharks swim by in their 400,000 gallon tank as part of the new permanent exhibit "Wild Reef," which explores the marine biodiversity and coral reefs in the Indo-Pacific. Wild Reef also has colorful corals, stingrays that slide by under your feet, and other surprising creatures, all from the waters around the Philippines.

Stare down one of the knobby-headed beluga whales (they love to people-watch), observe Pacific white-sided dolphins at play, and explore the simulated Pacific Northwest nature trail in the spectacular Oceanarium, which has pools that seem to blend into Lake Michigan. We like the daily educational dolphin presentation, during which the playful animals show off their natural behaviors, including vocalizing, breaching, and tail-walking, for delighted audiences. Be sure to get an underwater glimpse of the dolphins and whales through the viewing windows on the lower level, where you can also find a bunch of information-packed, hands-on activities.

In the 90,000-gallon Caribbean Reef exhibit in the main building, divers feed sharks, stingrays, a sea turtle, and other denizens of the deep.

NICHE MUSEUMS

Sometimes the best museums are ones that you can see in an hour or less. We like Chicago's smaller museums for the unexpected, interesting, and simply fun things you can find. Some of them highlight the diverse origins that built the city; others dedicate their space to history, archaeology, or specific types of art.

FOR HIDDEN GEMS **Balzekas Museum of Lithuanian Culture.** Though many of the people who come here do so for research (the museum is a large repository for genealogical information), the Balzekas has a stunning collection of Lithuanian amber. Other exhibits—armor, rare maps, stamps, and coins—chronicle Lithuanian history. ⌂ *6500 S. Pulaski Rd., Englewood* ☎ *773/582–6500* ✉ *$5, free Mon.* ☉ *Daily 10–4.*

CHECK OUT OLD LADY LEARY ★ **Chicago Historical Society.** The Historical Society is one of the coolest smaller museums in the city. The permanent exhibits include the much-loved Diorama Room, which portrays scenes from Chicago's history (where else could you see the apocryphal Mrs. O'Leary's cow knocking over the lamp that started the Chicago Fire?). Fun exhibits on the Chicago World's Fair, a great Civil War collection that includes Lincoln's deathbed, and Chicago's first locomotive—which is open for boarding—make for an intriguing afternoon. As of this writing, the Chicago Historical Society was closed for extensive renovations and set to reopen sometime in 2007. Call ahead to see if it's open. ⌂ *1601 N. Clark St., Lincoln Park* ☎ *312/642–4600* ⊕ *www.chicagohistory.org.*

David and Alfred Smart Museum of Art. If you want to see some art masterpieces but don't want to spend a long day wandering one of the major art museums, the Smart may be just your speed. The diverse, 8,000-piece permanent collection includes works by old masters; photographs by Walker Evans; furniture by Frank Lloyd Wright; sculptures by Degas, Matisse, Rodin, and Henry Moore; ancient Chinese bronzes; and modern Japanese ceramics. Temporary exhibits are a great way to see startlingly good art in a smaller, intimate space. ⌂ *5550 S. Greenwood Ave., Hyde Park* ☎ *773/702–0200* ⊕ *www.smartmuseum.uchicago.edu* ✉ *Free* ☉ *Tues., Wed., and Fri. 10–4, Thurs. 10–8, weekends 11–5.*

DuSable Museum of African American History. The DuSable is a colorful—and haunting—exploration of the African-American experience, set alongside the lagoons of Washington Park. There are handwritten lyric sheets from MoTown greats, letters and memorabilia of scholar W. E. B. Du Bois and poet Langston Hughes, and a significant African-American art collection. The most moving exhibit is one on slavery; the poignant, disturbing artifacts include rusted shackles used on slave ships. ⌂ *740 E. 56th Pl., Hyde Park* ☎ *773/947–0600* ⊕ *www.dusablemuseum.org* ✉ *$3, free Sun.* ☉ *Mon.–Sat. 10–5, Sun. noon–5.*

Jane Addams Hull-House Museum. The redbrick Victorian Hull House was the birthplace of social work, which makes it an American landmark. Social welfare pioneers and peace advocates Jane Addams and Ellen Gates Starr started the American settlement house movement in this house in 1889 and wrought near miracles in their surrounding community, which

QUIET SPACES

North Terrace, Shedd Aquarium. The entire aquarium is mesmerizing; you might find yourself staring at placidly swimming fish for hours without getting bored. But for a truly peaceful experience during mild weather, push through the doors of the North Terrace and sit at a table overlooking Lake Michigan and the city skyline. The terrace is usually deserted even on the busiest summer days.

Mammal dioramas, Field Museum. Few visitors linger amid the long, darkened hallways of the North American mammal dioramas. Take a seat on a curved wooden bench and you won't be disturbed—unless the sight of stuffed and mounted bears and buffalo makes you queasy.

Main Street theater and the Jackson Park Lagoons, Museum of Science and Industry. Olde Chicago is re-created in a corner of the MSI, complete with cobblestones and iron lamps. At the end of the street is a small theater showing silent shorts of Buster Keaton. If you'd rather be in the sunshine, take a walk around the lagoons and bridges behind the museum, one of the most peaceful—and overlooked—spots in all of Chicago.

was then a slum for new immigrants. Pictures and letters add context to the two museum buildings, which re-create the homey setting the residents experienced. ⊠ *800 S. Halsted St., University Village* ☎ *312/413–5353* ⊕ *www.uic.edu/jaddams/hull* 🎫 *Free* ☉ *Tues.–Fri. 10–4, Sun. noon–5.*

IF YOU ONLY HAVE TIME FOR ONE ★ **Mexican Fine Arts Center Museum.** This sparkling site, the largest Latino museum in the country, is half art museum, half cultural exploration. After the big downtown museums, this is the one you shouldn't miss. Galleries house impressive collections of contemporary, traditional, and meso-American art from both sides of the border, as well as vivid exhibits that trace immigration woes and political fights. Every fall, the giant Day of the Dead exhibit stuns Chicagoans with its altars from artists across the country. ⊠ *1852 W. 19th St., Pilsen* ☎ *312/738–1503* ⊕ *www.mfacmchicago.org* 🎫 *Free* ☉ *Tues.–Sun. 10–5.*

Museum of Broadcast Communications. How could a museum dedicated to TV and radio *not* be fun? Check out the Television Center, where you can don anchor jackets, read from teleprompters, and anchor your own newscast—with a professional-quality videotape to prove it. You can see broadcasting memorabilia like microphones and toys or watch commercial clips from around the world. If you'd like to while away the afternoon, check out the extensive public archives collection of more than 75,000 hours of television and radio programs and commercials. The museum, one of only three broadcast museums in America, closed its Loop location doors in 2003 to move to a new space on Kinzie Street. At this writing, it was scheduled to reopen in 2006; call for details. ⊠ *9 W. Kinzie St., River North* ☎ *312/245–8200* ⊕ *www.museum.tv.*

Museum of Contemporary Photography. "Contemporary" is defined here as anything after 1959—the date of Robert Frank's seminal work *The Americans,* which anchors the museum. Over 4,000 works from American-born and American-resident photographers make this an impressive collection. Don't-miss works include exhibits by Dorothea Lange, Ansel Adams, and Nicholas Nixon. Curators constantly seek out new talent and under-appreciated established photographers, which means that there are artists here you probably won't see elsewhere. Rotating exhibits have included photojournalism and scientific photography; the permanent collection contains works from Dorothea Lange, Ansel Adams, and Nicholas Nixon. ⊠ *600 S. Michigan Ave., South Loop* ☎ *312/663–5554* ⊕ *www.mocp.org* ⊠ *Free* ☉ *Mon.–Wed. and Fri. 10–5, Thurs. 10–8, Sat. noon–5.*

Museum of Holography. Holography seems almost quaint in our age of 3-D digital renderings. Still, it's fun to spend an hour walking from side to side in front of these glowing, three-dimensional, laser-etched portraits and pictures. ⊠ *1134 W. Washington Blvd., West Loop* ☎ *312/226–1007* ⊕ *www.holographiccenter.com* ⊠ *$4* ☉ *Wed.–Sun. 12:30–4:30.*

National Vietnam Veterans Art Museum. The chimelike sounds of more than 58,000 imprinted dog tags hanging from the ceiling entranceway are a melancholy memorial to the soldiers who lost their lives in the unpopular war. Take in the visual journal of the experiences of more than 122 artists who served in Vietnam through the 1,000-plus pieces of art on display here. ⊠ *1801 S. Indiana Ave., South Loop* ☎ *312/326–0270* ⊕ *www.nvvam.org* ⊠ *$10, free to service members* ☉ *Tues.–Fri. 11–6, Sat. 10–5, Sun. noon–5.*

MAKE LIKE
INDIANA JONES
Oriental Institute. This gem began with artifacts collected by University of Chicago archaeologists in the 1930s (one is rumored to have been the model for Indiana Jones) and has expanded into an interesting, informative museum with a jaw-dropping collection from the ancient Near East, including the largest U.S. collection of Iraqi antiquities. There are amulets, mummies, limestone reliefs, gold jewelry, ivories, pottery, and bronzes from the 4th millennium BC through the 13th century AD. You won't be able to miss the 40-ton sculpture of a winged bull from an Assyrian palace—it looks like it's about to take off through the ceiling. ⊠ *1155 E. 58th St., Hyde Park* ☎ *773/702–9520* ⊕ *www.oi. uchicago.edu* ⊠ *$5* ☉ *Tues. and Thurs.–Sat. 10–6, Wed. 10–8:30, Sun. noon–6.*

Peace Museum. An exhibit at the Peace Museum in the 1980s inspired U2 to write two songs: "The Unforgettable Fire" and "Pride (In the Name of Love)." You might get inspired, too, as you take in the artifacts on display here—the most interesting include a John Lennon guitar and manuscripts by Bono of U2 and Joan Baez; there are also posters, banners, and buttons in this museum dedicated to promoting peace through the arts. Exhibits focus on peacemakers, the horrors of war, domestic violence, and other issues. The museum is in the gorgeous Gold Dome building in Garfield Park, near the Garfield Park Conservatory. Please note:

CLOSE UP

The Local Art Scene

YOU DON'T NEED TO BE AN ART EXPERT to explore the city's growing web of local neighborhood galleries. Just do like a local and ready yourself with a free copy of *The Chicago Reader,* which has gallery and exhibition listings (available in many street dispensers, coffee shops, and record stores), or grab the *Chicago Gallery News* (or check it out on the Web at ⊕ www.chicagogallerynews. com)—it's the best source for maps, gallery information, and exhibition listings. Most galleries provide complimentary copies.

Here's the skinny: Chicago is divided into gallery "districts," or communities. They each have their own feel and flavor. Stop by anytime during gallery hours—no need to make an appointment—even if you're just browsing. Gallery directors and staff are always available to answer questions or provide further information on their artists.

RIVER NORTH DISTRICT
The city's first organized art neighborhood remains a vibrant community and the hub of the gallery scene.

Zolla/Lieberman (✉ contemporary multimedia, 325 W. Huron St. ☎ 312/944-1990).

Roy Boyd (✉ contemporary painting and sculpture, 739 N. Wells St. ☎ 312/642-1606).

Carl Hammer (✉ American folk and outsider, 740 N. Wells St. ☎ 312/266-8512).

Ann Nathan Gallery (✉ contemporary painting and sculpture, 212 W. Superior St. ☎ 312/664-6622).

Stephen Daiter Galery (✉ vintage black-and-white photography, 311 W. Superior St. ☎ 312/787-3350).

WEST LOOP DISTRICT
Lots of galleries have opened in multilevel warehouses on Randolph Street and throughout the rest of the neighborhood.

3

Aron Packer (✉ contemporary painting, 118 N. Peoria St. ☎ 312/226-8984).

Rhona Hoffman (✉ established and emerging contemporary artists, 118 N. Peoria St. ☎ 312/455-1990).

Donald Young Gallery (✉ local and international contemporary art, 933 W. Washington Blvd. ☎ 312/455-0100).

EAST PILSEN DISTRICT
Most artists live in their galleries in this district south and west of the Loop, and the line between reality and fantasy is often outrageously blurred.

Unit B (✉ contemporary, artist-run, 1733 S. Des Plaines ☎ 312/491-9384) and **Dubhe Carreño Gallery** (✉ contemporary ceramic art, 1841 S. Halsted St. ☎ 312/666-3150).

WICKER PARK/BUCKTOWN
The area is home to a respectable chunk of the city's artists, but most show their work privately or in independent group shows. You can still see artists' studios if you wander around the **Flat Iron Building** (✉ 1714 N. Damen Ave.). Check out **Pagoda Red** (✉ Chinese and Tibetan art objects, 1714 N. Damen Ave. ☎ 773/235-1188).

the park is not safe at night. ⊠ *100 N. Central Park Ave., Garfield Park* ☎ *773/638–6450* ⊕ *www.peacemuseum.org* ⊠ *Free* ⊙ *Wed.–Fri. 10–4, Sun. 11–3.*

★ **Peggy Notebaert Nature Museum.** Walk among hundreds of Midwest species of butterflies and learn about the impact of rivers and lakes on daily life at this modern museum washed in natural light. Like Chicago's other science museums, it's geared to kids, with educational computer games to play and water tubes to get wet in. But even jaded adults will be excited when bright yellow butterflies land on their shoulders. The idea is to study nature inside without forgetting graceful Lincoln Park outside. ⊠ *2430 N. Cannon Dr., Lincoln Park* ☎ *773/755–5100* ⊕ *www.chias.org* ⊠ *$7, free Thurs.* ⊙ *Weekdays 9 AM–4:30 PM, weekends 10–5.*

POLISH YOUR **Polish Museum of America.** Chicago has the largest Polish population of
POLISH any city outside Warsaw, and this museum in Ukranian Village, just south of Wicker Park, celebrates that fact. Take a trip to the old country by strolling through exhibits of folk costumes, memorabilia from Pope John Paul II, Hussar armor, American Revolutionary War heros Tadeusz Kosciuszko and Casimir Pulaski, pianist and composer Ignacy Paderewski, and an 8-foot-long sleigh in the shape of a dolphin that's carved from a single log. It's also a good place to catch up on your reading; the library has 60,000 volumes. ⊠ *984 N. Milwaukee Ave., Wicker Park* ☎ *773/384–3352* ⊕ *pma.prcua.org* ⊠ *$5* ⊙ *Fri.–Wed. 11–4.*

Spertus Museum. This museum addresses an intellectual puzzle: what does it mean to be Jewish in the modern world? Contemporary and traditional art and ritual objects illustrate daily life; a sobering Holocaust memorial with many photos and a tattered concentration camp uniform remind us to remember. A hands-on children's museum called the **Rosenbaum ARTiFACT Center** has a simulated archaeological dig, in which junior archaeologists can search for pottery underneath the sand. ⊠ *618 S. Michigan Ave., South Loop* ☎ *312/322–1747* ⊕ *www.spertus.edu* ⊠ *$5, free Fri.* ⊙ *Sun.–Wed. 10–5, Thurs. 10–7, Fri. 10–3; ARTiFACT Center: Sun.–Thurs. 1–4:30, Fri. 1–3.*

★ **Swedish-American Museum Center.** Though this tiny and welcoming museum does have changing exhibits that focus on the art and culture of Sweden, you don't have to be Swedish to find it interesting—much of the museum focuses on the immigrant experience. On permanent display, for example, are trunks immigrants brought with them to Chicago, and a map showing where in the city different immigrant groups settled. On the third floor, in the only children's museum in the country dedicated to immigration, kids can climb aboard a colorful Viking ship or "milk" a wooden cow, pulling rubber udders to collect streams of water in a bucket. ⊠ *5211 N. Clark St., Far North Side* ☎ *773/728–8111* ⊕ *www.samac.org* ⊠ *$4, free 2nd Tues. of month* ⊙ *Tues.–Fri. 10–4, weekends 11–4.*

Ukrainian Institute of Modern Art. Modern and contemporary art fans head out to this small museum at the far western edge of the Ukrainian Village, near Wicker Park. Three permanent galleries feature mixed media, sculpture, painting, and even some digital art. Some of the most interesting works are abstract or playful versions of Old World themes, like Evan Prokopov's 1998 abstract bronze of a mother cradling her child. ⊠ *2320 W. Chicago Ave., Wicker Park* ☎ *773/227–5522* ⊕ *www. uima-art.org* ⊠ *Free* ☼ *Wed., Thurs., and weekends noon–4.*

3

Architecture

WORD OF MOUTH

"I love walking on Michigan Avenue and the lakefront early in the morning. Hardly anyone is out except photographers. You can slow down and really appreciate some of the details of the buildings."
—buttercup

"Chicago is such a wonderful city and has so much to offer. One thing you and your kids would enjoy is going to the top of the John Hancock building, which has an incredible view of the city and the lake from its observation deck."
—lisa

ARCHITECTURE PLANNER

In a Chicago Mood

Chicago has long been known as America's Second City, but, as a visit here makes clear, this is no burg. A metropolis if there ever was one, Chicago hums with activity while its lakeside location lends a relaxed, breezy ambience. A great way to take advantage of this intermingling is to sit a spell in Millennium Park or Grant Park and enjoy the march of buildings up Michigan Avenue. Known as the "Michigan Avenue Cliff," this stretch just west of the parks comprises a slew of noteworthy structures, including the Auditorium Building, the Santa Fe Center, and the Chicago Cultural Center.

Good Reads

Architecture geeks won't need much introduction to the city's architectural history, but if you don't count yourself among that special breed, you might pick up *Chicago Architecture and Design*, a beautifully illustrated book with a good perspective by George A. Larson and Jay Pridmore. For a more in-depth yet highly readable study of some of the big names who worked here, check out Peter Blake's *The Master Builders*. And if you don't mind a bit of murder with your history lesson, there's Erik Larson's magnificent *The Devil in the White City*.

Walking Tours

The Chicago Architecture Foundation has a gigantic selection of expertly guided tours. Chicago Greeter and InstaGreeter are two free services that match savvy Chicagoans with visitors for neighborhood tours. Friends of the Chicago River leads Saturday-morning tours during the warmer months. **Chicago Architecture Foundation** ⊠ Santa Fe Bldg., 224 S. Michigan Ave. ☎312/922–3432 ⊕www.architecture.org. **Chicago Greeter/InstaGreeter** ⊠ Visitor Information Center at Chicago Cultural Center, 77 E. Randolph St. ☎ 312/744–8000 ⊕ www.chicagogreeter.com. **Friends of the Chicago River** ⊠407 S. Dearborn St., Suite 1580 ☎ 312/939–0490 ⊕ www.chicagoriver.org.

Bus & Trolley Tours

A narrated bus or trolley tour is a fun way to enjoy Chicago's architecture. Tours cost roughly $20 and last about two hours. **American Sightseeing** ☎ 312/251-3100 ⊕ www.americansightseeing.org/chicago.htm. **Chicago Architecture Foundation** (*See* Walking Tours.) **Chicago Trolley and Double Decker Co.** ☎ 773/648-5000 ⊕ www.chicagotrolley.com.

Boat Tours

The Chicago Architecture Foundation river tour on *Chicago's First Lady* is the most authoritative. You can purchase tickets at the Chicago ArchiCenter, 224 S. Michigan Avenue or through Ticketmaster at 312/902–1500 or www.ticketmaster.com. The boat-tour season usually runs from the end of April to mid-November—always call ahead. Other options include:

Mercury Chicago Skyline Cruiseline ☎ 312/332-1353 ⊕www.mercuryskylinecruiseline.com. **MetroDucks** ☎800/298-1506 ⊕ www.metroducks.com. **Shoreline Marine** ☎ 312/222-9328 ⊕ www.shorelinesightseeing.com. **Wendella Sightseeing Boats** ⊠ 400 N. Michigan Ave. ☎ 312/337-1446 ⊕ www.wendellaboats.com. **Windy of Chicago Ltd** ☎ 312/595-5555 ⊕ www.tallshipwindy.com.

4

By Thomas
Connors

Every great city has great buildings, but Chicago *is* its great buildings. Art, culture, food, and diversion are all part of the picture here, but everything Chicagoans do is framed by some of the most remarkable architecture to be found anywhere. From the sky-scraping of its tall towers to the horizontal sweep of the Prairie School, Chicago's built environment is second to none.

Decisions, Decisions, Decisions . . .

Even if you're pressed for time, you can't leave town without seeing a few of the city's important buildings. The lovely **Reliance Building** on State Street (home to trendy Hotel Burnham) is steps away from **Carson Pirie Scott** and just blocks from the Art Institute and Millennium Park. Mies van der Rohe's **860–880 North Lake Shore Drive** buildings are right on the lake and not too far from high-end shopping on the Magnificent Mile.

With so many significant skyscrapers packed into the Loop, it's tough to elevate any one above the rest. When it comes to early buildings, the **Rookery** is hard to beat. Looking like an impenetrable terra-cotta mass from the street, its heart is a graceful, covered court done up by Frank Lloyd Wright. And no matter how much you may dislike modern architecture, the **Inland Steel Building** is a beauty. Also worth a visit is the dizzying atrium of the squat **James R. Thompson Center,** a bold interpretation of a public building. Finally, for a swanky art deco number, stop by the **Carbide & Carbon Building,** home to the Hard Rock Hotel.

A Tall Order . . .

If you came looking for tall buildings, Chicago certainly won't let you down. Among the tallest are the famous **Sears Tower,** with its 103rd-floor observatory (on clear days you can see four states); the instantly recognizable **John Hancock Center,** with its crisscross braces and two huge antennae (not to mention cocktail hour on the 95th floor); and the formidable **Aon Center,** which towers over Millennium Park. And no building proclaims its skyscraping ambition quite like **311 South Wacker Drive,** whose Gothic crown is ablaze with light at night.

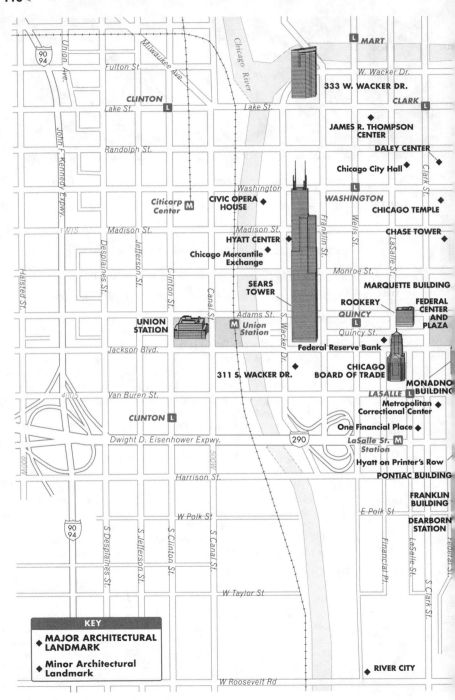

90 94
Union Ave.
Milwaukee Ave.
Fulton St.
Chicago River
MART
W. Wacker Dr.
333 W. WACKER DR.
CLINTON
Lake St.
Lake St.
CLARK
JAMES R. THOMPSON
CENTER
DALEY CENTER
John F. Kennedy Expwy.
Randolph St.
Chicago City Hall
Clark St.
Washington
Citicorp
Center
CIVIC OPERA
HOUSE
WASHINGTON
CHICAGO TEMPLE
90 WIS
Madison St.
Madison St.
CHASE TOWER
Franklin St.
Wells St.
LaSalle St.
HYATT CENTER
Desplaines St.
Jefferson St.
Clinton St.
Chicago Mercantile
Exchange
Monroe St.
MARQUETTE BUILDING
SEARS
TOWER
ROOKERY
FEDERAL
CENTER
AND
PLAZA
Halsted St.
Canal St.
QUINCY
Adams St.
UNION
STATION
Union
Station
S. Wacker Dr.
Quincy St.
Federal Reserve Bank
Jackson Blvd.
311 S. WACKER DR.
CHICAGO
BOARD OF TRADE
MONADNO
BUILDING
400S
Van Buren St.
LASALLE
Metropolitan
Correctional Center
CLINTON
One Financial Place
Dwight D. Eisenhower Expwy.
290
LaSalle St.
Station
500W
Hyatt on Printer's Row
Harrison St.
PONTIAC BUILDING
300W
FRANKLIN
BUILDING
90 94
W Polk St
E Polk St
DEARBORN
STATION
S Desplaines St.
S Jefferson St.
S Clinton St.
S Canal St.
Financial Pl.
LaSalle St.
Federal St.
S Clark St.
W Taylor St
KEY
MAJOR ARCHITECTURAL
LANDMARK
Minor Architectural
Landmark
RIVER CITY
W Roosevelt Rd

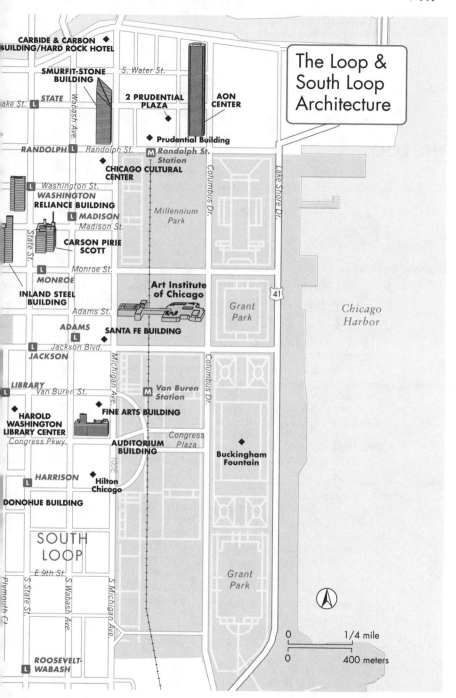

CARBIDE & CARBON ◆
BUILDING/HARD ROCK HOTEL

SMURFIT-STONE
BUILDING

S. Water St.

2 PRUDENTIAL
PLAZA

AON
CENTER

STATE Ⓛ

Wabash Ave.

ake St.

◆ Prudential Building

RANDOLPH Ⓛ   Randolph St.   Ⓜ Randolph St.
Station

The Loop &
South Loop
Architecture

◆
CHICAGO CULTURAL
CENTER

Ⓛ Washington St.
WASHINGTON
RELIANCE BUILDING

Ⓛ MADISON
Madison St.

CARSON PIRIE
SCOTT

State St.

Ⓛ
MONROE   Monroe St.

INLAND STEEL
BUILDING

Millennium
Park

Columbus Dr.

Lake Shore Dr.

Chicago
Harbor

Art Institute
of Chicago

Adams St.

ADAMS
Ⓛ

SANTA FE BUILDING

41

Grant
Park

Ⓛ Jackson Blvd.
JACKSON

LIBRARY
Ⓛ   Van Buren St.

Michigan Ave.

Ⓜ Van Buren
Station

Columbus Dr.

◆
HAROLD
WASHINGTON
LIBRARY CENTER
Congress Pkwy.

FINE ARTS BUILDING

Congress
Plaza

AUDITORIUM
BUILDING

◆
Buckingham
Fountain

100 E

HARRISON   ◆ Hilton
Ⓛ   Chicago

DONOHUE BUILDING

SOUTH
LOOP

E 9th St.

Plymouth Ct.

S State St.

S Wabash Ave.

S Michigan Ave.

Grant
Park

ROOSEVELT-
WABASH
Ⓛ

0   1/4 mile

0   400 meters

It's Worth the Trip . . .

Nearby **Oak Park** is Frank Lloyd Wright's old stomping ground. The leafy community is chock-full of his work, from early examples of Prairie Style to a fascinating church.

A visit to **Glessner House**—H. H. Richardson's masterpiece in the Prairie Avenue Historic District—offers the voyeuristic appeal of poking through a great home. It's enough to motivate even those who don't know an I beam from a flying buttress.

THE LOOP

Defined by the El (the elevated train that makes a circuit around the area), the Loop is Chicago at its big-city best. A hub of retail, cultural, financial, and governmental activity, it's also home to the city's most notable skyscrapers. Ambitious walkers can cover a good part of the Loop and the surrounding areas in a day, but even a relatively short stroll will reveal some top sites.

Historic Buildings

★ **Auditorium Building.** Hunkered down across from Grant Park, this 110,000-ton granite-and-limestone behemoth was an instant star when it debuted in 1889, boasting a 400-room hotel, offices, and a 4,300-seat theater. It didn't hurt the careers of its designers, Dankmar Adler and Louis H. Sullivan, either. The state-of-the art theater included electric lighting and an air-conditioning system that used 15 tons of ice per day. Adler managed the engineering—the theater's acoustics are renowned—while Sullivan ornamented the space using mosaics, cast iron, art glass, wood, and plaster. During World War II, the building was conscripted for use as a Servicemen's Center. Then Roosevelt University moved in. Thanks to Herculean restoration efforts, the Auditorium Theatre is once again one of the city's premiere performance venues. If you can't book a performance, call for tour details. ⊠ *50 E. Congress Pkwy., Loop* ☎ *312/431–2389* ⊕ *www.auditoriumtheatre.org* ⊠ *Tour $6.*

Fodor'sChoice
★ **Carson Pirie Scott & Co.** Old-fashioned department stores may be dying, but one of the most famous, built in 1899, remains open for business on State Street. The work of one of Chicago's most renowned architects, the flagship of Carson Pirie Scott & Co. combines Louis H. Sullivan's visionary expression of modern design with intricate cast-iron ornamentation. The eye-catching rotunda and the 11 stories above it are actually an addition Sullivan made to his original building. In later years, D. H. Burnham & Co. and Holabird & Root extended Sul-

---

FOR SULLIVAN FANS

Bear north to Lincoln Park to see the **Louis Sullivan row houses.** The love of geometric ornamentation that Sullivan eventually brought to such projects as the Carson Pirie Scott building is already visible in these row houses built in 1885. The terra-cotta cornices and decorative window tops are especially noteworthy. E 1826–1834 N. Lincoln Park W, Lincoln Park.

livan's smooth, horizontal scheme farther down State Street. Sullivan could be achingly poetic when discussing architecture, so it's not surprising that he gave new meaning to the expression "window shopping" by surrounding the street-level windows with cast-iron frames, turning the parade of product displays into a true gallery of goods. ⊠ *1 S. State St., Loop* ☏ *312/641–7000.*

★ **Chicago Cultural Center.** Built in 1897 as the city's original public library,
WORLD'S LARGEST this huge building houses the **Chicago Office of Tourism Visitor Infor-**
TIFFANY DOME **mation Center,** as well as a café, galleries, and a concert hall. Designed by the Boston firm Shepley, Rutan & Coolidge—the team behind the Art Institute of Chicago—it's a palatial affair of Carrara marble, mosaics, gold leaf, and the world's largest Tiffany glass dome. Building tours are offered Wednesday, Friday, and Saturday at 1:15 PM. There's live music every weekday at 1:00 PM in the café. ⊠ *78 E. Washington St., Loop* ☏ *312/346–3278 or 312/744–6630* ⊕ *www.ci.chi.il.us/Tourism/Cultural Center/* ⊙ *Mon.–Thurs. 10–7, Fri. 10–6, Sat. 10–5, Sun. 11–5.*

Fine Arts Building. This creaky building was constructed in 1895 to house the showrooms of the Studebaker Company, then makers of carriages. Publishers and artists have used its spaces; today the principal tenants are professional musicians. Take a look at the handsome exterior then step inside the marble-and-woodwork lobby. The motto engraved as you enter says, ALL PASSES—ART ALONE ENDURES. The building has an interior courtyard, across which strains of piano music and soprano voices compete with tenors as they run through exercises. There's also a gallery on the fourth floor (open Wed.–Sun. noon to 6). ⊠ *410 S. Michigan Ave., Loop* ☏ *312/913–0537.*

CHECK OUT THE **Marquette Building.** Like a slipcover over a sofa, the clean, geometric fa-
CHICAGO cade of the Marquette Building expresses what lies beneath: in this
WINDOWS case, a structural steel frame. Sure, the base is marked with roughly cut stone and a fancy cornice crowns the top, but the bulk of the building mirrors the cage around which it is built. Inside is another story. The intimate lobby of this 1895 Holabird & Roche building is a jewel box of a space, where a single Doric column stands surrounded by a Tiffany glass mosaic depicting the exploits of Jesuit missionary Jacques Marquette, an early explorer of Illinois. The building is a clear example of Chicago architecture, from the steel skeleton to the Chicago Windows to the terra-cotta ornamentation. ⊠ *140 S. Dearborn St., Loop.*

Monadnock Building. Built in two segments a few years apart, the Monadnock captures the turning point in high-rise construction. Its northern half, designed in 1891 by Burnham & Root, was erected with traditional load-bearing masonry walls (6 feet deep at the base). In 1893, Holabird & Roche designed its southern half, which rose around the soon-to-be-common steel skeleton. The building's stone and brick exterior, shockingly unornamented for its time, led one critic to liken it to a chimney. The lobby is equally Spartan: lined on either side with windowed shops, it's essentially a corridor, but one well worth traveling. Walk it from end to end and you'll feel like you're stepping back in time. ⊠ *53 W. Jackson Blvd. at S. Dearborn St., Loop.*

Fodor'sChoice **Reliance Building.** The clearly expressed, gleaming verticality that char-
★ acterizes the modern skyscraper was first and most eloquently articu-
A CHICAGO lated in this steel-frame tower in the heart of the Loop. Completed in
LANDMARK 1895 and now home to the stylish **Hotel Burnham,** the building was a
crumbling eyesore until the late 1990s, when the city initiated a major
restoration. Don't be misled when you go looking for this masterpiece—
a block away, at State and Randolph streets, a dormitory for the School
of the Art Institute of Chicago shamelessly mimics this trailblazing original by Burnham, Root, and Charles Atwood. Once you've found the
real thing, don't miss the mosaic floor and ironwork in the reconstructed elevator lobby. The building boasts early examples of the
Chicago Window, which define the entire building's facade by adding
a shimmer and glimmer to the surrounding white terra-cotta. ⊠ 1 W.
Washington St., Loop ☎ 312/782–1111 ⊕ www.burnhamhotel.com.

Fodor'sChoice **The Rookery.** This 11-story structure, with its eclectically ornamented fa-
★ cade, got its name from the pigeons and politicians who roosted at the
city hall that once stood on this site. Designed in 1885 by Burnham &
Root, who used both masonry and the more modern steel-frame construction, the Rookery was one of the first buildings in the country to
feature a central court that brought sunlight into interior office spaces.
Frank Lloyd Wright, who kept an office here for a short time, renovated
the two-story lobby and light court, eliminating some of the ironwork
and terra-cotta and adding marble scored with geometric patterns detailed in gold leaf. The interior endured some less tasteful alterations
after that, but it has since been restored to the way it looked when Wright
completed his work in 1907. ⊠ 209 S. LaSalle St., Loop.

Santa Fe Building. Also known as the Railway Exchange Building, this
structure was designed in 1904 by Daniel Burnham, who later moved
his office here. The SANTA FE sign on its roof was put up early in the 20th
century by the Santa Fe Railroad, one of several railroads that had offices here when Chicago was the rail center of the country. The fantastic **ArchiCenter of the Chicago Architecture Foundation** (☎ 312/922–
3432 ⊕ www.architecture.org ☉ Tues.–Sun. 9:30–4) occupies this historic space. ⊠ 224 S. Michigan Ave., Loop.

WHAT ARE YOU LOOKIN' AT?

Terra-cotta, a baked clay that can be produced as tiles or shaped orna-
mentally, was commonly used by Chicago architects after the Great Fire
of 1871.

Heat resistant and malleable, the material proved an effective and attractive fireproofing agent for the metal-frame buildings that otherwise would melt and collapse. The fa-
cade of the Marquette Building at 140 S. Dearborn Street is a particularly fine example.

WORLD'S COLUMBIAN EXPOSITION OF 1893

In 1893 the city of Chicago hosted the **World's Columbian Exposition.** The fair's mix of green spaces and Beaux Arts buildings offered the vision of a more pleasantly habitable metropolis than the crammed industrial center that rose from the ashes of the Great Fire. However, a ruffled Louis Sullivan prophesied that "the damage wrought to this country by the Chicago World's Fair will last half a century." He wasn't entirely wrong

in his prediction—the classicist style vied sharply over the next decades with the native creations of the Chicago and Prairie schools, all the while incorporating their technical advances. One of Hyde Park's most popular destinations—the Museum of Science and Industry—was erected as the fair's Palace of Fine Arts. It's the exposition's only building that is still standing.

4

Symphony Center. Orchestra Hall, home to the acclaimed Chicago Symphony Orchestra (CSO), lies at the heart of this music center. The hall was built in 1904 under the supervision of Daniel Burnham. The Georgian building has a symmetrical facade of pink brick with limestone quoins, lintels, and other decorative elements. Backstage tours are available by appointment for groups of 10 or more. ⊠ *220 S. Michigan Ave., Loop* ☎ *312/294–3000.*

Finding the Art Deco

★ **Carbide & Carbon Building.** Designed in 1929 by Daniel and Hubert Burnham, sons of the renowned architect Daniel Burnham, this is arguably the jazziest skyscraper in town. A deep-green terra-cotta tower rising from a black granite base, its upper reaches are embellished with gold leaf. The original public spaces are a luxurious composition in marble and bronze. The story goes that the brothers Burnham got their design inspiration from a gold-foiled bottle of champagne. So perhaps it's fitting that the building now houses a **Hard Rock Hotel,** party central for those who wouldn't be caught dead at the Four Seasons. ⊠ *230 N. Michigan Ave., Loop.*

FROM BUBBLY
INSPIRATION

★ **Chicago Board of Trade.** Rising dramatically at the end of LaSalle Street—heart of the city's financial district—Holabird & Root's building is a streamlined giant from the days when art deco was all the rage. The artfully lit marble lobby soars three stories; atop the roof stands Ceres, the Roman goddess of agriculture. Erected in 1930, this 45-story structure reigned as the city's tallest skyscraper until 1955, when the Prudential Center grabbed that title. ⊠ *141 W. Jackson Blvd., Loop* ☎ *312/435–3590.*

Civic Opera House. The handsome home of the Lyric Opera is grand indeed, with pink-and-gray Tennessee marble floors, pillars with carved capitals, crystal chandeliers, and a sweeping staircase to the second floor. Designed by Graham, Anderson, Probst & White, it combines lavish art deco details with classical touches. And the show goes on, with

Continued on page 128

THE SKY'S THE LIMIT

Talk about baptism by fire. Although Chicago was incorporated in 1837, it wasn't until after the Great Fire of 1871 that the city really started to take shape. With four square miles gone up in flames, the town was a clean slate. The opportunity to make a mark on this metropolis drew a slew of architects, from Adler & Sullivan to H. H. Richardson and Daniel H. Burnham—names renowned in the annals of American architecture. A Windy City tradition was born: the city's continuously morphing skyline is graced with tall wonders designed by architecture's heavy hitters, including Mies van der Rohe; Skidmore, Owings & Merrill; and, if he has his way, Santiago Calatrava. In the next four pages, you'll find an eye-popping sampling of Chicago's great buildings and how they've pushed—and continue to push—the definition of even such a lofty term as "skyscraper."

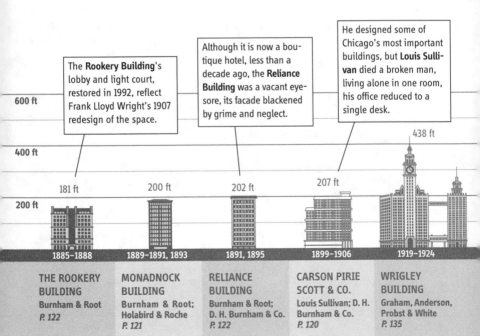

The **Rookery Building**'s lobby and light court, restored in 1992, reflect Frank Lloyd Wright's 1907 redesign of the space.

Although it is now a boutique hotel, less than a decade ago, the **Reliance Building** was a vacant eyesore, its facade blackened by grime and neglect.

He designed some of Chicago's most important buildings, but **Louis Sullivan** died a broken man, living alone in one room, his office reduced to a single desk.

600 ft

438 ft

400 ft

181 ft | 200 ft | 202 ft | 207 ft

200 ft

1885–1888 | 1889–1891, 1893 | 1891, 1895 | 1899–1906 | 1919–1924

THE ROOKERY BUILDING
Burnham & Root
P. 122

MONADNOCK BUILDING
Burnham & Root; Holabird & Roche
P. 121

RELIANCE BUILDING
Burnham & Root; D. H. Burnham & Co.
P. 122

CARSON PIRIE SCOTT & CO.
Louis Sullivan; D. H. Burnham & Co.
P. 120

WRIGLEY BUILDING
Graham, Anderson, Probst & White
P. 135

THE BIRTH OF THE SKYSCRAPER

Houses, churches, and commercial buildings of all sorts rose from the ashes after the blaze of 1871, but what truly put Chicago on the architectural map was the tall building. The earliest of these barely scrape the sky—especially when compared to what towers over us today—but in the late 19th century, structures such as William Le Baron Jenney's ten-story Home Insurance Building (1884) represented a bold push upward. Until then, the sheer weight of stone and cast-iron construction had limited how high a building could soar. But by using a lighter yet stronger steel frame and simply sheathing his building in a thin skin of masonry, Jenney blazed the

way for ever taller buildings. And with only so much land available in the central business district, up was the way to go.

Although the Home Insurance Building was razed in 1931, Chicago's Loop remains a rich trove of early skyscraper design. Some of these survivors stand severe and solid as fortresses, while others manifest an almost ethereal quality. They—and their descendants along Wacker Drive, North Michigan Avenue, and Lake Shore Drive—reflect the technological, economic, and aesthetic forces that have made this city on the prairie one of the most dramatically vertical communities in the country.

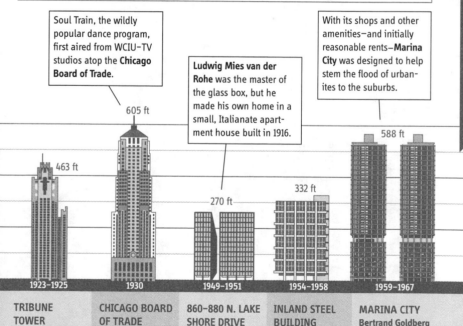

Soul Train, the wildly popular dance program, first aired from WCIU–TV studios atop the **Chicago Board of Trade.**

Ludwig Mies van der Rohe was the master of the glass box, but he made his own home in a small, Italianate apartment house built in 1916.

With its shops and other amenities—and initially reasonable rents—**Marina City** was designed to help stem the flood of urbanites to the suburbs.

605 ft

463 ft

270 ft

332 ft

588 ft

1923–1925	1930	1949–1951	1954–1958	1959–1967
TRIBUNE TOWER	CHICAGO BOARD OF TRADE	860–880 N. LAKE SHORE DRIVE	INLAND STEEL BUILDING	MARINA CITY
Howells & Hood	Holabird & Root	Ludwig Mies van der Rohe	Skidmore, Owings & Merrill	Bertrand Goldberg Associates
P. 134	P. 123	P. 143	P. 129	P. 143

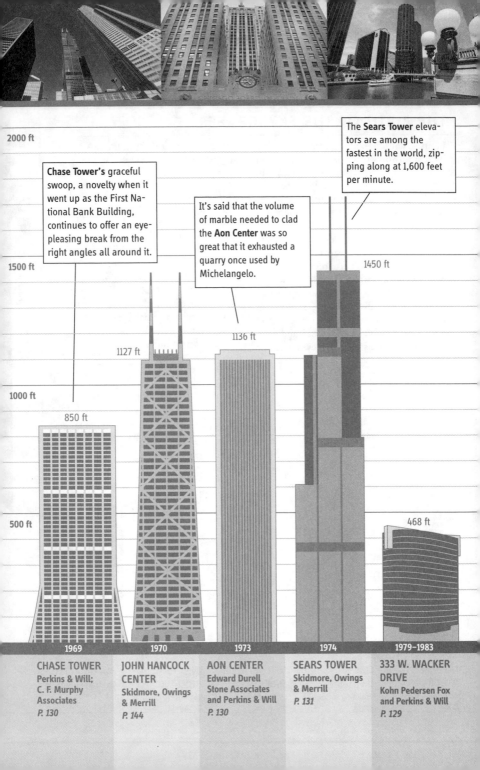

The **Sears Tower** elevators are among the fastest in the world, zipping along at 1,600 feet per minute.

Chase Tower's graceful swoop, a novelty when it went up as the First National Bank Building, continues to offer an eye-pleasing break from the right angles all around it.

It's said that the volume of marble needed to clad the **Aon Center** was so great that it exhausted a quarry once used by Michelangelo.

2000 ft

1500 ft

1450 ft

1136 ft

1127 ft

1000 ft

850 ft

500 ft

468 ft

1969	1970	1973	1974	1979–1983
CHASE TOWER Perkins & Will; C. F. Murphy Associates *P. 130*	**JOHN HANCOCK CENTER** Skidmore, Owings & Merrill *P. 144*	**AON CENTER** Edward Durell Stone Associates and Perkins & Will *P. 130*	**SEARS TOWER** Skidmore, Owings & Merrill *P. 131*	**333 W. WACKER DRIVE** Kohn Pedersen Fox and Perkins & Will *P. 129*

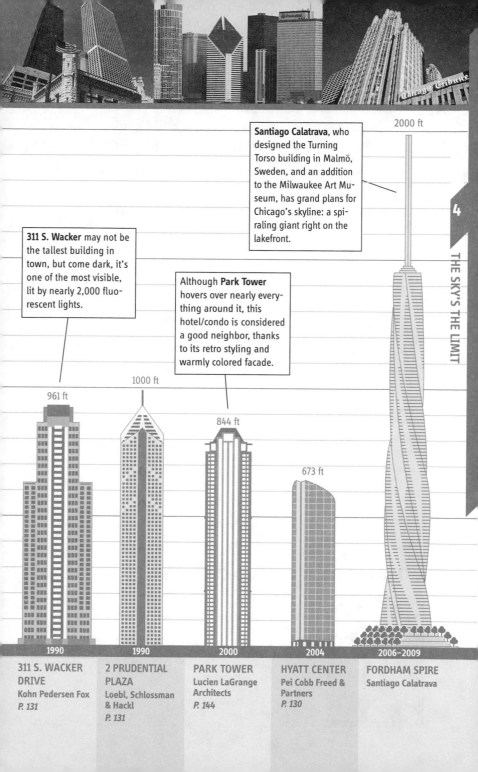

2000 ft

4

THE SKY'S THE LIMIT

Santiago Calatrava, who designed the Turning Torso building in Malmö, Sweden, and an addition to the Milwaukee Art Museum, has grand plans for Chicago's skyline: a spiraling giant right on the lakefront.

311 S. Wacker may not be the tallest building in town, but come dark, it's one of the most visible, lit by nearly 2,000 fluorescent lights.

Although **Park Tower** hovers over nearly everything around it, this hotel/condo is considered a good neighbor, thanks to its retro styling and warmly colored facade.

1000 ft

961 ft

844 ft

673 ft

1990	1990	2000	2004	2006–2009
311 S. WACKER DRIVE	**2 PRUDENTIAL PLAZA**	**PARK TOWER**	**HYATT CENTER**	**FORDHAM SPIRE**
Kohn Pedersen Fox	Loebl, Schlossman & Hackl	Lucien LaGrange Architects	Pei Cobb Freed & Partners	Santiago Calatrava
P. 131	P. 131	P. 144	P. 130	

the Lyric Opera performing regularly on the great stage within. ✉ *20 N. Wacker Dr., Loop* ☎ *312/419–0033 Civic Opera House, 312/332–2244 Lyric Opera* ⊕ *www.civicoperahouse.com.*

1950s & Beyond: Meet Modernism

Daley Center. Named for the late mayor Richard J. Daley, this boldly plain high-rise is the headquarters of the Cook County court system, but it's best known as the site of a sculpture by Picasso. Known simply as *The Picasso,* this monumental piece provoked an outcry when it was installed in 1967; baffled Chicagoans tried to determine whether it represented a woman or an Afghan hound. In the end, they gave up guessing and simply embraced it as a unique symbol of the city. The building was constructed in 1965 of Cor-Ten steel, which weathers naturally to an attractive bronze. In summer the building's plaza is the site of concerts, political rallies, and a weekly farmers' market (Thursday); during the holidays, the city's official Christmas tree is erected here. ✉ *Bounded by Washington Blvd., Randolph, Dearborn, and Clark Sts., Loop.*

> **GREAT CORNERS TO LOOK UP!**
>
> • North Michigan Avenue and East Wacker Drive
> • West Adams and South LaSalle Streets
> • North Michigan Avenue and East Chestnut Street

★ **Federal Center and Plaza.** Designed
MIES MEETS CALDER in 1959, but not completed until 1974, this severe constellation of buildings around a sweeping plaza was Mies van der Rohe's first mixed-use urban project. Fans of the International Style will groove on this pocket of pure modernism, while others can take comfort in the presence of the Marquette Building, which marks the north side of the site. In contrast to this dark ensemble are the great red arches of Alexander Calder's *Flamingo.* The piece was dedicated on the same day in 1974 that the artist's *The Universe* was unveiled at Sears Tower. Calder went from one event to the other, riding through the streets in a brightly colored circus wagon accompanied by calliopes. The area is bound by Dearborn, Clark, and Adams streets and Jackson Boulevard. ✉ *Dirksen: 219 S. Dearborn St., Loop* ✉ *Kluczynski: 230 S. Dearborn St., Loop.*

WHAT ARE YOU LOOKIN' AT?

The Chicago Window, a popular window design used in buildings all over America (until air-conditioning made it obsolete) consists of a large fixed central pane with smaller movable windows on each side. The picture window offered light, while the double-hung windows let in the Lake Michigan breeze. Developed in Chicago by engineer and architect William Le Baron Jenney, who pioneered the use of metal frame construction in the 1880s, the Chicago Window helps to define buildings across the city.

★ **Inland Steel Building.** A runt compared to today's tall buildings, this crisp, sparkling structure from Skidmore, Owings & Merrill was a trailblazer back in the late 1950s. It was the first skyscraper built with external supports (allowing for wide-open, unobstructed floors within); the first to employ steel pilings (driven 85 feet down to bedrock); the city's first fully air-conditioned building; and the first to feature underground parking. As for looks, well, you might say it combines the friendly scale of the Reliance Building with the cool rigor of a high-rise by Mies. ⊠ *30 W. Monroe St., Loop.*

Late Modernism Gives Way to Post-Modernism

★ **James R. Thompson Center.** People either hate or love the center: former

ENJOY THE governor James Thompson, who selected the Helmut Jahn design for
17-STORY ATRIUM this state government building, hailed it in his dedication speech in 1985 as "the first building of the 21st century." For others, it's a case of postmodernism run amok. A bowl-like form topped by a truncated cylinder, the building's sky-blue and salmon color scheme scream 1980s. But the 17-story atrium, where exposed elevators zip up and down and sunlight casts dizzying patterns through the metal-and-glass skin, is one of the most animated interiors to be found anywhere in the city. The sculpture in the plaza is Jean Dubuffet's *Monument with Standing Beast*. It's nearly as controversial as the building itself. The curved shapes, in white with black traceries, have been compared to a pile of melting Chicago snow. The **Illinois Artisans Shop** (☎ 312/814–5321), on the second level of the Center, sells crafts and folk art by Illinois artists. ⊠ *100 W. Randolph St., Loop.*

Smurfit-Stone Building. Some wags have said this building, with its diamond-shape top, looks like a giant pencil sharpener. The slanted top carves through 10 floors of this 1984 building. The painted, folded aluminum sculpture in the plaza is Yaacov Agam's *Communication X9.* You'll see different patterns in the sculpture depending on your vantage point. ⊠ *150 N. Michigan Ave., Loop.*

333 West Wacker Drive. This green-glazed beauty doesn't follow the rules. Its riverside facade echoes the curve of the Chicago River just in front of it, while the other side of the building is all business, conforming neatly to the straight lines of the street grid. This 1983 Kohn Pedersen Fox design is roughly contemporary to the James R. Thompson Center—but it has enjoyed a much more positive public reception. ⊠ *333 W. Wacker Dr., between W. Lake Street and N. Orleans St., Loop.*

★ ☺ **Harold Washington Library Center.** Gargantuan and almost goofy (the

CHECK OUT THE huge sculptures atop the building look like something out of Harry Pot-
ROOF OWLS ter), this granite-and-brick edifice is a uniquely postmodern homage to Chicago's great architectural past. The heavy, rusticated ground level recalls the Rookery; the stepped-back, arched windows are a reference to the great arches in the Auditorium Theatre; the swirling terra-cotta design is pinched from the Marquette Building; and the glass curtain wall on the west side is a nod to 1950s modernism. The library was named for the first African-American mayor of Chicago, and the primary architect was Thomas Beeby, of the Chicago firm Hammond, Beeby & Babka.

The excellent **Children's Library** on the second floor, an 18,000-square-foot haven, has vibrant wall-mounted figures by Chicago imagist Karl Wirsum. Works by noted Chicago artists are displayed along a second-floor walkway above the main lobby. There's also an impressive Winter Garden with skylights on the ninth floor. Free programs and performances are offered regularly at the center. ⌗ *400 S. State St., Loop* ☏ *312/747–4300* ⊕ *www.chipublib.org* ⊙ *Mon.–Thurs. 9–7, Fri. and Sat. 9–5, Sun. 1–5.*

Sky-High Sanctuary

Chicago Temple. The Gothic-inspired headquarters of the First United Methodist Church of Chicago were built in 1923 by Holabird & Roche, complete with a first-floor sanctuary, 21 floors of office space, a sky-high chapel, and an eight-story spire (best viewed from the bridge across the Chicago River at Dearborn Street). Outside, along the building's east wall at ground level, stained-glass windows relate the history of the church in Chicago. Joan Miró's sculpture *Chicago* (1981) is in the small plaza just east of the church. ⌗ *77 W. Washington St., Loop.*

Up, Up, Up: The Skyscrapers

Aon Center. With the open space of Millennium Park at its doorstep, the Aon Center really stands out—even if its appearance isn't much to write home about. Originally built as the Standard Oil Building, the structure has changed names and appearances twice. Not long after it went up, its marble cladding came crashing down and the whole building was resheathed in granite. The massive building sits on a handsome (if rather sterile) plaza, where Harry Bertoia's wind-chime sculpture in the reflecting pool makes interesting sounds when a breeze blows. ⌗ *200 E. Randolph Dr., Loop.*

PLAZA BLISS: VISIT THE MARC CHAGALL MOSAIC **Chase Tower.** This building's graceful swoop—a novelty when it went up—continues to offer an eye-pleasing respite from all the right angles surrounding it. And its spacious plaza, with a mosaic by Marc Chagall called **The Four Seasons,** is one of the most enjoyable public spaces in the neighborhood. Designed by Perkins & Will and C. F. Murphy Associates in 1969, the building has been home to a succession of financial institutions (its most recent name was Bank One Plaza); names aside, it remains one of the more distinctive buildings around, not to mention one of the highest buildings in the Loop's true heart. ⌗ *Bounded by Dearborn, Madison, Clark, and Monroe Sts., Loop.*

Hyatt Center. At 48 stories, the headquarters of this hospitality group is no giant, but it more than makes its mark on South Wacker Drive with a bold elliptical shape, a glass-faced street-level lobby rising 36 feet, and a pedestrian-friendly plaza. One of the city's newer towers, it displays a noticeable tweaking of the unrelieved curtain wall that makes many city streets forbidding canyons. Designed by Pei Cobb Freed & Partners, the building was completed in 2004. ⌗ *71 S. Wacker Dr., Loop.*

Sears Tower. In Chicago, size matters. This soaring 110-story skyscraper,
Fodor's Choice   designed by Skidmore, Owings & Merrill in 1974, was the world's tallest
★   building until 1996 when the Petronas Towers in Kuala Lumpur,
OBSERVE THE   Malaysia, claimed the title. However, the folks at the Sears Tower are
CITY FROM THE   quick to point out that Petronas counts its spire as part of the building.
103rd FLOOR   If you were to measure the 1,450-foot-high Sears Tower in terms of highest occupied floor, highest roof, or highest antenna, the Sears Tower would
win hands down.

Those bragging rights aside, the **Skydeck** is really something to boast
about. Enter on Jackson Boulevard to take the ear-popping ride to the
103rd-floor observatory. Video monitors turn the 70-second elevator
ride into a fun-filled, thrilling trip. On a clear day a whopping four states
are visible: Illinois, Michigan, Wisconsin, and Indiana. (Check the visibility ratings at the security desk before you decide to ride up and take
in the view.) At the top, interactive exhibits tell about Chicago's dreamers, schemers, architects, musicians, and sports stars. Computer kiosks
in six languages help international travelers key into Chicago hot spots.
Knee-High Chicago, a 4-foot-high exhibit with cutouts of Chicago
sports and history at a child's eye-level, will entertain the kids. The Sears
Tower also has spruced up the lower level with a food court, new exhibits, and a short movie about the city. Security is very tight, so figure
in a little extra time for your visit to the Skydeck. Before you leave, don't
miss the spiraling Calder mobile sculpture *The Universe* in the ground-
floor lobby on the Wacker Drive side. ⊠ *233 S. Wacker Dr.; for the Skydeck, enter on Jackson Blvd. between Wacker Dr. and Franklin St., Loop*
☎ *312/875–9696* ⊕ *www.theskydeck.com* 🎫 *$11.95* ⊗ *May–Sept., daily
10–10; Oct.–Apr., daily 10–8.*

★   **311 South Wacker Drive.** The first of three towers intended for the site,
NIGHT LIGHTS   this pale pink building is the work of Kohn Pedersen Fox, who also de-
SUPREME   signed 333 West Wacker Drive, a few blocks away. The 1990 building's
most distinctive feature is its Gothic crown, blindingly lighted at night.
During migration season so many birds crashed into the illuminated tower
that the building management was forced to tone down the lighting. The
building has an inviting atrium, with palm trees and a splashy, romantic fountain. ⊠ *333 S. Wacker Dr. at W. Jackson Blvd., Loop*
⊕ *www.311southwacker.com.*

2 Prudential Plaza. Nicknamed "Two Pru," this glass-and-granite giant
is the older sibling of the 1955 tower at its feet (looking very 1950s indeed). Together with their neighbors they form a block-long business-
oriented minicity. Two Prudential is the tallest reinforced concrete
building in the city, and its blue detailing and beveled roof are instantly
recognizable from afar. ⊠ *180 N. Stetson Ave., Loop* ⊕ *www.
pruplazachicago.com.*

SOUTH LOOP

Heading south from the heart of the Loop, you'll find Printer's Row, where lofts that once clattered with linotype machines are now luxury real estate morsels, as well as Dearborn Park, a residential enclave reclaimed from old rail yards.

Historic Buildings

Dearborn Station. Chicago's oldest standing passenger train station, a South Loop landmark, now serves as a galleria. Designed in Romanesque Revival style in 1885 by the New York architect Cyrus L. W. Eidlitz, it has a wonderful clock tower and a redsandstone and redbrick facade ornamented with terra-cotta. Striking features inside are the marble floor, wraparound brass walkway, and arching wood-frame doorways. ⊠ *47 W. Polk St., South Loop* ☎ *312/554–8100* ⊙ *Daily 7–9.*

Donohue Building. The first major printing facility in Printers Row, this 1883 building's main entrance is flanked by marble columns topped by ornately carved capitals, with tile work over the entrance set into a splendid granite arch. Note the beautiful ironwork and woodwork ornamenting the first-floor retail establishments. ⊠ *711 S. Dearborn St., South Loop.*

> ### CURVES ON THE MARINA
>
> **River City.** These concrete curves may look familiar; the complex was built in 1986 by Bertrand Goldberg, who also built the "corncobs" of Marina City. This apartment complex features a 10-story atrium, commercial space, and 62-slip marina. It has great views of the water from the lobby. ⊠ *800 S. Wells St., South Loop.*

Franklin Building. Built in 1888 and initially the home of the Franklin Company, a printing concern, this building has intricate decoration. The tile work on the facade leads up to *The First Impression*—a medieval scene illustrating the first application of the printer's craft. Above the entryway is a motto: THE EXCELLENCE OF EVERY ART MUST CONSIST IN THE COMPLETE ACCOMPLISHMENT OF ITS PURPOSE. ⊠ *720 S. Dearborn St., South Loop.*

OLD-SCHOOL HOLABIRD & ROCHE **Pontiac Building.** An early Chicago School skyscraper—note its classic rectangular shape and flat roof—the simple, redbrick, 14-story Pontiac was designed by Holabird & Roche in 1891 and is their oldest existing building in Chicago. ⊠ *542 S. Dearborn St., South Loop.*

PRAIRIE AVENUE & BEYOND

Heading even farther south parallel to the lakeshore, you'll find the Prairie Avenue Historic District; this was the neighborhood of choice for the city's movers and shakers in the mid-19th century. If you're a die-hard Mies van der Rohe fan, continue your journey south to check out his buildings on the campus of the Illinois Institute of Technology.

MIES VAN DER ROHE, KOOLHAAS & JAHN

Illinois Institute of Technology. "Less is more" claimed Mies van der Rohe, but for fans of the master's work, more is more at IIT. The campus holds an array of the kind of glass-and-steel structures for which he is most famously known. Crown Hall is the jewel of the collection and has been designated a national historic landmark, but don't overlook the Robert F. Carr Memorial Chapel of St. Savior. Additions to the campus include the

McCormick Tribune Campus Center, designed by Dutch architect Rem Koolhaas and new student housing by Helmut Jahn. The campus is about 1 mi west of Lake Shore Drive on 31st Street. Or take the El train's Green or Red Line to the 35th Street stop, and walk east two blocks to campus. ⊠ *S. State St. between 31st and 35th Sts., Douglas, south of Chinatown* ☎ *312/567–3000* ⊕ *www.iit.edu.*

4

Historic Buildings

Clarke House. This Greek Revival dates from 1836, making it Chicago's oldest surviving building. It's a clapboard house in a masonry city, built for Henry and Caroline Palmer Clarke to remind them of the East Coast they left behind. The Doric columns and pilasters were an attempt to civilize Chicago's frontier image. The everyday objects and furnishings inside reveal a typical 1830s–60s middle-class home. ⊠ *1827 S. Indiana Ave., Prairie Avenue District* ☎ *312/745–0040* ⊠ *$10; see Glessner House listing for combo-ticket information* ☉ *Tours: Wed.–Sun. at noon, 1, and 2.*

Fodor'sChoice **Glessner House.** This fortresslike, Romanesque Revival 1886 residence
★ is the only surviving building in Chicago by architect H. H. Richardson, who also designed Boston's Trinity Church. It's also one of the few great mansions left on Prairie Avenue, once home to such heavy hitters as retailer Marshall Field and meat packing magnate Philip Armour. The area has lately seen the arrival of new, high-end construction, but nothing beats a tour of Glessner House, a remarkable relic of the days when merchant princes really lived like royalty. Enjoy the lavish interiors and the many artifacts, from silver pieces and art glass to antique ceramics and Isaac Scott carvings and furnishings. ⊠ *1800 S. Prairie Ave., Prairie Avenue* ☎ *312/326–1480* ⊕ *www.glessnerhouse.org* ⊠ *$10. Combined admission to Glessner and the nearby Clarke House $15. Free Wed.* ☉ *Tours Wed.–Sun. at 1, 2, and 3.*

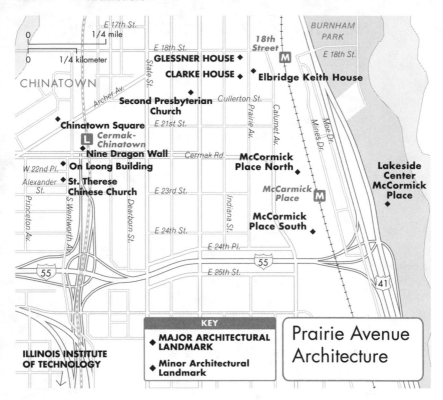

E 17th St.

0   1/4 mile

0   1/4 kilometer

CHINATOWN

E 18th St.

E 18th St.

18th Street

E 18th St.

BURNHAM PARK

GLESSNER HOUSE ◆

CLARKE HOUSE ◆

Elbridge Keith House

Second Presbyterian Church

Cullerton St.

Chinatown Square

E 21st St.

Cermak-Chinatown

Nine Dragon Wall

Cermak Rd.

On Leong Building

W 22nd Pl.

Alexander St.

St. Therese Chinese Church

E 23rd St.

McCormick Place North ◆

McCarmick Place

Lakeside Center McCormick Place ◆

McCormick Place South ◆

E 24th St.

E 24th Pl.

55

55

E 25th St.

41

ILLINOIS INSTITUTE OF TECHNOLOGY

KEY

◆ **MAJOR ARCHITECTURAL LANDMARK**

◆ **Minor Architectural Landmark**

Prairie Avenue Architecture

NEAR NORTH & RIVER NORTH

Just a hop, skip, and a jump from the Loop's northern reaches and across the Chicago River are the Near North and River North neighborhoods. The magnet for most folks is North Michigan Avenue—aka the Magnificent Mile—a glittering stretch studded with shops and hotels. Saunter up this thoroughfare from the Michigan Avenue Bridge (or head south from Oak Street) and you'll see such sights as the Wrigley Building, the Tribune Tower, the historic Water Tower, and the John Hancock Center.

Historic Buildings

Tribune Tower. In 1922 *Chicago Tribune* publisher Colonel Robert McCormick chose a Gothic design for the building that would house his paper, after rejecting a slew of functional modern designs by such notables as Walter Gropius, Eliel Saarinen, and Adolf Loos. Embedded in the exterior walls of the tower are chunks of material taken from famous sites around the world. Look for bits from the Parthenon, Westminster Abbey, the Alamo, St. Peter's Basilica, the Taj Mahal, and the Great Wall of China. On the ground floor are the studios of WGN radio, part of the *Chicago Tribune* empire, which also includes WGN-TV, cable-television stations, and the Chicago Cubs. (Modesty was not one of Colonel McCormick's prime traits: WGN stands for the *Tribune*'s self-bestowed nickname, World's Greatest Newspaper). ⊠ *435 N. Michigan Ave., Near North* ☎ *312/222-3232* ⊕ *www.chicagotribune.com.*

Water Tower. This famous Michigan Avenue structure, completed in 1867, was originally built to house a 137-foot standpipe that equalized the pressure of the water pumped by the similar pumping station across the street. Oscar Wilde uncharitably called it "a castellated monstrosity" studded with pepper shakers. Nonetheless, it remains a Chicago landmark and a symbol of the city's spirit of survival following the Great Chicago Fire of 1871. The small gallery inside has rotating art exhibitions of local interest. ⊠ *806 N. Michigan Ave. at Pearson St., Near North* 🔳 *Free* ⊙ *Daily 10–6:30.*

Water Works Pumping Station. Water is still pumped to some of the city residents at a rate of about 250 million gallons per day from this Gothic-style structure, which, along with the Water Tower across the street, survived the Great Chicago Fire of 1871. The acclaimed **Lookingglass Theatre** calls this place home. The station also houses a **Chicago Office of Tourism Visitor Information Center** (☎ 877/244–2246 ⊕ www.877chicago.com ⊙ Daily 7:30–7), which has a sandwich shop. ⊠ *163 E. Pearson St. at Michigan Ave., Near North.*

★ **Wrigley Building.** Two structures built several years apart and later con-
A NOD TO   nected, the gleaming white Wrigley Building sports a clock tower in-
SEVILLE   spired by the bell tower of the grand cathedral in Seville, Spain. The landmark headquarters of the chewing gum company—designed by Graham, Anderson, Probst & White—was instrumental in transforming Michigan Avenue from an area of warehouses to one of the most desirable spots in the city. Be sure to check it out at night, when lamps bounce light off the gleaming terra-cotta facade. ⊠ *400 and 410 N. Michigan Ave., Near North* ⊕ *www.wrigley.com/wrigley/about/about story_building.asp.*

A REVERED SCHOOL

The **Chicago School** had no classrooms, no curriculum. It didn't confer degrees. The Chicago School wasn't an institution at all, but a name given to the collection of architects whose work, beginning in the 1880s, helped free American architecture from the often rigid styles of the past. Nonetheless, a number of their buildings echoed a classical column, with the lower floors functioning as the base, the middle floors as the shaft, and the cornice on top being the equivalent of a capital. In pioneering the "tall building," these architects utilized steel-frame construction; they also reduced ornamentation. Alumni include Daniel Burnham, William Le Baron Jenney, Louis Sullivan, Dankmar Adler, John Root, William Holabird, and Martin Roche.

Continued on page 143

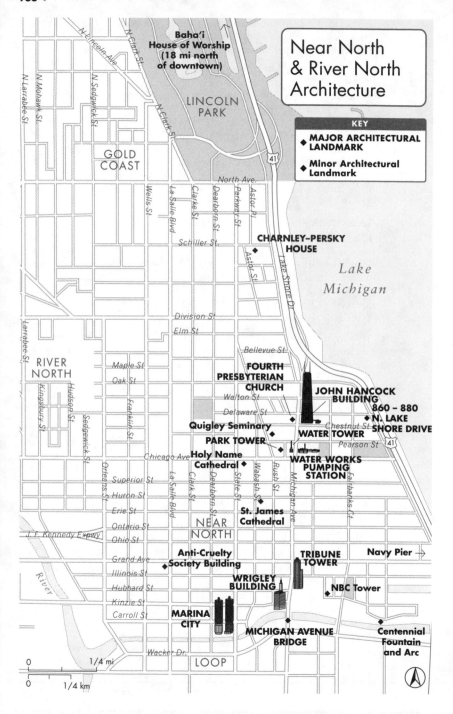

N. Lincoln Ave.

N. Clark St.

N. Sedgwick St.

N. Mohawk St.

N. Larrabee St.

Baha'i House of Worship (18 mi north of downtown)

LINCOLN PARK

N. Clark St.

41

Near North & River North Architecture

KEY

◆ MAJOR ARCHITECTURAL LANDMARK

◆ Minor Architectural Landmark

GOLD COAST

North Ave.

Wells St.

La Salle Blvd.

Clarke St.

Dearborn St.

Parkway St.

Astor Pl.

Schiller St.

Astor St.

Lake Shore Dr.

◆ **CHARNLEY–PERSKY HOUSE**

Lake Michigan

Larrabee St.

RIVER NORTH

Kingsbury St.

Hudson St.

Sedgwick St.

Orleans St.

Franklin St.

Maple St

Oak St

Division St

Elm St

Bellevue St.

Walton St.

Delaware St.

La Salle Blvd.

Clark St.

Dearborn St.

State St.

Wabash St.

Rush St.

Michigan Ave.

Chestnut St

Pearson St

Fairbanks Ct.

41

FOURTH PRESBYTERIAN CHURCH

■ **JOHN HANCOCK BUILDING**

◆ **860 – 880 N. LAKE SHORE DRIVE**

Quigley Seminary ◆

PARK TOWER ◆

◆ **WATER TOWER**

Holy Name Cathedral ◆

Chicago Ave

■ **WATER WORKS PUMPING STATION**

Superior St

Huron St

Erie St

Ontario St

Ohio St

J. F. Kennedy Expwy

NEAR NORTH

St. James Cathedral

Grand Ave

Illinois St

Hubbard St

Kinzie St

Carroll St

River

Anti-Cruelty Society Building ◆

■ **TRIBUNE TOWER**

Navy Pier →

WRIGLEY BUILDING

◆ **NBC Tower**

■ **MARINA CITY**

MICHIGAN AVENUE BRIDGE

◆ **Centennial Fountain and Arc**

Wacker Dr.

LOOP

0   1/4 mi

0   1/4 km

FRANK LLOYD WRIGHT

1867–1959

The most famous American architect of the 20th century led a life that was as zany and scandalous as his architectural legacy was great. Behind the photo-op appearance and lordly pronouncements was a rebel visionary who left an unforgettable imprint on the world's notion of architecture. Nowhere else in the country can you experience Frank Lloyd Wright's genius as you can in Chicago and its surroundings.

Born two years after the Civil War ended, Wright did not live to see the completion of his late masterpiece, the Guggenheim Museum. His father preached and played (the Gospel and music) and dragged the family from the Midwest to New England and back before he up and left for good. Wright's Welsh-born mother, Anna Lloyd Jones, grew up in Wisconsin, and her son's roots would run deep there, too. Although his career began in Chicago and his work took him as far away as Japan, the home Wright built in Spring Green, Wisconsin—Taliesin—was his true center.

Despite all his dramas and financial instability (Wright was notoriously bad with money), the architect certainly produced. He was always ready to try something new—as long as it fit his notion of architecture as an expression of the human spirit and of human relationship with nature. By the time he died in 1959, Wright had designed over 1,000 projects, more than half of which were constructed.

Robie House, Chicago

WELCOME TO OAK PARK!

Oak Park is a leafy, quiet community just 10 miles west of downtown Chicago. When you arrive, head to the **Oak Park Visitors Center** (⊠ 158 N. Forest Ave. ☎ 708/848–1500 ⊕ www.visitoakpark. com ☉ Daily 10–4, until 5 in summer) and get oriented with a free map.

Next wander to the **Frank Lloyd Wright Home and Studio** (⊠ 951 Chicago Ave. ☎ 708/848–1976 ᙙ 708/848–1248 ⊕ www.wrightplus.org ᙙ $12; walking tour $12; combined $20 ☉ Weekday tours at 11, 1, and 3; weekend tours 11–3:30, every 20 mins. Tickets can be purchased in advance via the Web site). From the outside, the shingle-clad structure may not appear all that innovative,

but it's here that Wright developed the architectural language that still has the world talking.

Financed with a $5,000 loan from his mentor, Louis Sullivan, Wright designed the home when he was only 22. The residence manifests some of the spatial and stylistic characteristics that became hallmarks of Wright's work: there's a central fireplace from which other spaces seem to radiate and an enticing flow to the rooms. In 1974, the local Frank Lloyd Wright Home and Studio Foundation, together with the National Trust for Historic Preservation, embarked on a 13-year restoration that returned the building to its 1909 appearance.

GETTING HERE

To get to the heart of Oak Park by car, take the Eisenhower Expressway (I-290) west to Harlem Avenue. Head north on Harlem and take a right on Lake Street to get to the Oak Park Visitors Center at Forest Avenue and Lake Street (158 N. Forest Avenue), where there's ample free parking. You can also take the Green Line of the El to the last stop, the Harlem Avenue exit, or Metra's Union Pacific West Line from the Ogilvie Transportation Center in Citicorp Center downtown (500 W. Madison) to the Oak Park stop at Marion Street.

WOMEN, FIRE, SCANDAL ... AND OVER 1,000 DESIGNS

The southeast entrance to the Frank Lloyd Wright Home & Studio in Oak Park.

1885   Wright briefly studies engineering at the University of Wisconsin.

1887   Wright strikes out for Chicago. He starts his career learning the basics with J. L. Silsbee, a residential architect. Later he joins the office of Adler & Sullivan as a drafter, just as the firm begins work on the massive Auditorium building.

1889   Wright marries Catherine Tobin; he builds her a home in suburban Oak Park, and they have six children together.

> "WHILE NEW YORK HAS REPRODUCED MUCH AND PRODUCED NOTHING, CHICAGO'S ACHIEVEMENTS IN ARCHITECTURE HAVE GAINED WORLD-WIDE RECOGNITION AS A DISTINCTIVELY AMERICAN ARCHITECTURE."

Strolling Oak Park

A leisurely stroll around the neighborhood will introduce you to plenty of **Frank Lloyd Wright houses.** All are privately owned, so you'll have to be content with what you can see from the outside. Check out 1019, 1027, and 1031 Chicago Avenue. These are typical Victorians that Wright designed on the sly while working for Sullivan.

For a look at the "real" Wright, don't miss the **Moore–Dugal Home** (1895) at 333 N. Forest Avenue, which reflects Wright's evolving architectural philosophy with its huge chimney and overhanging second story. Peek also at numbers 318, 313, 238, and 210, where you can follow his emerging modernism. Around the corner at 6 Elizabeth Court is the **Laura Gale House,** a 1909 project whose cantilevered profile foreshadows the thrusting planes Wright would create at Fallingwater decades later.

Between 1889 and 1913, Wright erected over two dozen buildings in Oak Park, so unless you're making an extended

A landmark profile: the eastern facade of the architect's home and studio, Oak Park.

visit, don't expect to see everything. But don't leave town without a visit to his 1908 **Unity Temple** (✉ 875 W. Lake St. ☎ 708/383–8873), a National Historic Landmark. Take a moment to appreciate Wright's fresh take on a place of worship; his bold strokes in creating a flowing interior; his unfailing attention to what was outside (note the skylights); and his dramatic use of concrete, which helps to protect the space from traffic noise.

Interior, Unity Temple, Oak Park

1893 Wright launches his own practice in downtown Chicago.

1898 As his practice grows, Wright adds a studio to his Oak Park residence.

1905 Wright begins designing the reinforced concrete Unity Temple.

1908 Construction begins on the Robie House in Chicago's Hyde Park neighborhood.

4

FRANK LLOYD WRIGHT

Guided Tours

A great way to get to know Oak Park is to take advantage of the guided tours. Well-informed local guides take small groups on tours throughout the day, discussing various architectural details, pointing out artifacts from the family's life, and often telling amusing stories of the rambunctious Wright clan. Reservations are required for groups of 10 or more for the home and studio tours. Note that you need to arrive as early as possible to be assured a spot. Tours begin at the **Ginkgo Tree Bookshop**, which is part of the home and studio. The shop carries architecture-related books and gifts. You can pick up a map ($3.95) to find other examples of Wright's work that are within easy walking or driving distance, or you can join a guided tour of the neighborhood led by volunteers.

The Hemingway Connection

Frank Lloyd Wright wasn't the only creative giant to call Oak Park home. Ten years after Wright arrived, Ernest Hemingway was born here in 1899 in a proper Queen Anne, complete with turret. Wright was gone by the time Hemingway began to sow his literary oats. Good thing, too. It's doubtful the quiet village could have handled two such egos. *See* Get Out of Town: Brushing up your Ernest Hemingway pg. 26.

Frank Lloyd Wright's distinctive take on a modern dining room.

TIPS

Tickets go on sale every March 1 for the eagerly awaited annual **Wright Plus Benefit Housewalk**, your chance to see the interiors of some of Oak Park's most architecturally notable homes. Check out ⊕ www.wrightplus.org for more details.

Note that you can save time (or rest your feet) on the free **Oak Park Shuttle** (☎ 708/615-1830). Operated by PACE and the Village of Oak Park, the shuttle bus runs every 30 minutes and makes 20 stops at Oak Park sights. Regular hours are 10-5:30 daily. You can catch the shuttle outside the Frank Lloyd Wright Home and Studio.

Interior, Rookery Building, Chicago

1909	Wright leaves for Europe with Mamah Cheney, the wife of a former client; this puts an abrupt end to his family life, but Mrs. Wright does not consent to a divorce.
1911	Wright and Cheney settle at Taliesin, in Spring Green, Wisconsin.
1914	Mrs. Cheney, her two children, and several other people are killed by a deranged employee, who also sets fire to Taliesin. Wright rebuilds, as he does when the house burns again in 1922.
1915	With new mistress Miriam Noel in tow, the architect heads for Japan to oversee the building of the Imperial Hotel.

PRAIRIE STYLE PRIMER

Primarily a residential mode, Wright's Prairie style is characterized by ground-hugging masses; low-pitched roofs with deep eaves; and ribbon windows. Generally, Prairie houses are two-story affairs, with single story wings and terraces that project into the landscape. Brick and stone, earth tones, and unpainted wood underscore the perception of a house as an extension of the natural world. Wright designed free-flowing living spaces defined by alternating ceiling heights, natural light, and architectural screens. Although a number of other Chicago architects pursued this emerging aesthetic, Wright became its

> "ALL FINE ARCHITECTURAL VALUES ARE HUMAN VALUES, ELSE NOT VALUABLE."

acknowledged master. Though Wright designed dozens of Prairie style homes, the most well-known is Robie House, in Chicago's Hyde Park neighborhood. A dynamic composition of overlapping planes, it seems both beautifully anchored to the ground and ready to sail off with the arrival of a sharp breeze.

4

FRANK LLOYD WRIGHT

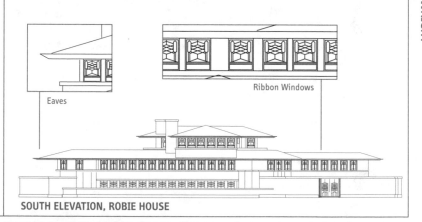

Eaves

Ribbon Windows

SOUTH ELEVATION, ROBIE HOUSE

The architect discusses a project with his assistants in Oak Park, 1958.

1922 Wright and his wife Catherine divorce.

1924 Wright marries Miriam Noel, but Noel is emotionally unsteady and the marriage implodes three years later.

1928 Wright marries Olga (Olgivanna) Lazovich Milanoff, who remains a compelling helpmate for the remainder of his life. They have one daughter together.

1930 The Taliesin Fellowship is launched; eager apprentices arrive at Spring Green to learn from the master.

WRIGHT BACK IN THE CITY

If you can't make it to Oak Park, there are a handful of notable—and memorable—Frank Lloyd Wright experiences to be had in the city.

★ **Fodor's Choice** Long and low, **Robie House** (1908–1910) grabs the ground and sends the eye zipping westward. Massive overhangs shoot out from the low-pitched roof and windows run along the facade in a glittering stretch. Inside, Wright's "open plan" echoes the great outdoors, as one space flows into another, while sunlight streaming through decorative leaded windows bathes the rooms in patterns. Robie House is midway through a 10-year renovation but remains open to visitors. ⊠ 5757 S. Woodlawn Ave., Hyde Park ☎ 773/834–1847 ☜ $12 ☉ Tour weekdays at 11, 1, and 3; weekends every ½ hr 11–3:30.

When he designed the **Isidore Heller House** in 1897, Frank Lloyd Wright was still moving toward the mature Prairie style achieved in the Robie House. As was common with Wright—and very uncommon then and now—the entrance to the Heller House is on the side of the structure. The house is not open to the public. ⊠ 5132 S. Woodlawn Ave., Hyde Park.

Frank Lloyd Wright designed the **Charnley–Persky House** with his mentor Louis Sullivan. This almost-austere residence represents one of Wright's first significant forays into residential design. Historians still squabble about who designed what here, but it's easy to imagine that the young go-getter had a hand in the cleanly rendered interior. Note how the geometric exterior looks unmistakably modern next to its fussy neighbors. ⊠ 1365 N. Astor St., Near North ☎ 312/915–0105 ☜ Free Wed., $10 for Sat. tour that includes Madlener House ($5 for Charnley-Persky House only). ☉ Apr.–Nov., tours Wed. at noon, Sat. at 10 AM and 1 PM; Dec.–Mar., 10 AM only. For larger groups, make reservations well in advance.

Stand outside the **Rookery Building** with its dizzyingly detailed facade and you'll think you've taken a wrong turn in your search for Wright. This early high-rise was designed by Burnham & Root. In 1905, Wright was hired to spruce up the building's interior court, which he lightened up by replacing terra-cotta with gilded white marble; adding pendant light fixtures; and gracing the stairway with urns, one of his favorite motifs. ⊠ 209 S. LaSalle St., Loop.

A New York icon: Wright's Guggenheim Museum.

1935	Fallingwater, the country home of Pittsburgh retailer Edgar J. Kaufmann, is completed at Bear Run, Pennsylvania.
1937	Wright begins construction of his winter getaway, Taliesin West, in Scottsdale, Arizona.
1956	Wright designs the Guggenheim Museum in New York. It is completed in 1959.
1957	Wright joins preservationists in saving Robie House from demolition.
1959	Wright dies at the age of 91.

Two Interpretations of "Twins"

FodorsChoice ★ **860–880 N. Lake Shore Drive.** These twin apartment towers overlooking Lake Michigan were an early and eloquent realization of Mies van der Rohe's "less is more" credo, expressed in the high-rise. I beams running up the facade underscore the building's verticality while, inside, mechanical systems are housed in the center so as to leave the rest of each floor free and open to the spectacular views. Completed in 1951, the buildings were built in the famed International Style, which played a key role in transforming the look of American cities. ⊠ *860–880 N. Lake Shore Dr. at E. Chestnut St., River North.*

SOME CALL THEM CORNCOBS **Marina City.** Likened to everything from corncobs to the towers of Antonio Gaudi's Sagrada Familia in Barcelona, Goldberg's twin towers were a bold departure from the severity of the International Style, which began to dominate high-rise architecture beginning in the 1950s. Completed in 1967, the towers house condominium apartments (all pie-shape, with curving balconies). In addition to the apartments and marina, the complex now has four restaurants, the House of Blues nightclub and hotel, and a huge bowling alley. ⊠ *329 N. Dearborn St., River North* ☎ *312/923–2000.*

OFF THE BEATEN PATH: HARMONY UP NORTH

About 18 mi north of downtown Chicago (in Wilmette), rising near the lake, the ★ **Baha'i House of Worship** is an intriguing, nine-sided building that incorporates architectural styles and symbols from many of the world's religions. With its delicate lacelike details and massive dome, the Louis Bourgeois design emphasizes the 19th-century Persian origins of the Baha'i religion. As symmetrical and harmonious as the building are the formal gardens that surround it. The temple is the U.S. center of the Baha'i faith, which advocates spiritual unity, world peace, race unity, and equality of the sexes. The visitor center has exhibits explaining the Baha'i faith; here you can also ask for a guide to show you around. ⊠ *100 Linden Ave.* ☎ *847/853–2300* ⊕ *www.us.bahai.org* ✉ *Free* ☉ *Daily 10–5.*

4

WHAT ARE YOU LOOKIN' AT?

"Curtain Wall" is the term for the largely glass exterior surface of many modern buildings. Unlike masonry construction, in which stone or brick support the weight of the building, a curtain wall is not a load-bearing system; rather, it is hung on the steel or concrete frame that holds the building up. The Reliance Building (an early example), the Sears Tower, and 333 W. Wacker Drive are all curtain-wall buildings.

Bridge of Bridges

★ **Michigan Avenue Bridge.** Chicago is a city of bridges, and this is one of its most graceful. Completed in 1920, it features impressive sculptures on its four pylons representing major Chicago events: its exploration by Marquette and Joliet, its settlement by trader Jean Baptiste Point du Sable, the Fort Dearborn Massacre of 1812, and the rebuilding of the city after the Great Chicago Fire of 1871. The site of the fort, at the southeast end of the bridge, is marked by a commemorative plaque. As you stroll Michigan Avenue, be prepared for a possible delay; the bridge rises regularly to allow boat traffic to pass underneath. ⊠ *Michigan Ave. at Wacker Dr., Near North.*

> For more information about the city's architectural treasures, contact the Chicago Architecture Foundation at 312/922-8687 or 312/922-3432 (online at ⊕ www.architecture.org) or the Chicago Convention and Tourism Bureau at 312/567-8500 (online at ⊕ www.choosechicago.com/architecture.html).

Skyscrapers Deluxe

Fodor'sChoice

★

SKY-HIGH

"BIG JOHN"

John Hancock Center. Designed by the same team that designed the Sears Tower (Skidmore, Owings & Merrill), this multi-use skyscraper is distinguished by its tapering shape and the enormous X braces, which help stabilize its 100 stories. Soon after it went up in 1970, it earned the nickname "Big John." No wonder: at 1,127 feet (1,502 feet counting the antennae at the top), 2.8 million square feet, and 46,000 tons o' steel, there's nothing little about it. Packed with retail, parking, offices, a restaurant, and residences, it has been likened to a city within a city. Impressive from any angle, it offers mind-boggling views from a 94th floor observatory (as with the Sears Tower, you can see to four states on clear days). For anyone afflicted with vertigo, a sensible option is a seat in the bar of the 95th floor Signature Room. The tab will be steep, but you'll be steady on your feet—*maybe.* ⊠ *875 N. Michigan Ave., Near North* ☎ *312/751-3681* ⊕ *www.hancock-observatory.com and www.johnhancockcenterchicago.com* 🎫 *Observatory $9.95* ☉ *Daily 9–11; last ticket sold at 10:45 PM.*

Park Tower. A relative newcomer to the neighborhood (2000), this high-end hotel–condo combines retro touches (note the pitched roof) and quirky contemporary flourishes (check out the protruding bank of windows on the 7th floor). Designed by Lucien LaGrange Architects, the 67-story tower seems even taller than it really is (almost 900 feet), thanks to its unobstructed location across from the small park where the historic Water Tower stands. ⊠ *800 N. Michigan Ave. at Chicago Ave., Near North* ⊕ *www.parkhyatt.com.*

Chicago's Answer to a Gothic Revival Church

REST YOUR FEET

IN THE GRASSY

COURTYARD

Fourth Presbyterian Church. A welcome visual and physical oasis amid the high-rise hubbub of North Michigan Avenue, this Gothic Revival house of worship was designed by Ralph Adams Cram. Local architect

Charles van Doren Shaw devised the cloister and companion buildings. The first big building erected on the avenue after the Chicago Fire, it counted among its congregants the city's elite. Noontime concerts are given every Friday in the sanctuary. ✉ *126 E. Chestnut St., Near North* ☎ *312/787–4570* ⊕ *www.fourthchurch.org.*

4

Shopping

WORD OF MOUTH

"Check out the boutique shopping in neighborhoods like Lincoln Park, where you'll find smaller, non-chain, funkier stores. Not cheap, but much more affordable than Oak Street."

—jlm—mi

"Definitely have a drink at the top of the Hancock Building, then a little retail therapy along Michigan Avenue."

—parisandelle

SHOPPING PLANNER

Itineraries for the Obsessed

Short on time? Get focused! If art is your thing, then head to River North and the West Loop, which are quick cab rides from one another and loaded with fabulous galleries.

If you're looking to head home with funky fashions, spend your time in Bucktown and Wicker Park. Must-hits include **p. 45** (*1643 N. Damen Ave., 773/862-4523*) for the hippest women's styles; **G Boutique** for va-va-va-voom lingerie (*2131 N. Damen Ave., 773/235-1234*); and **Lille** (*1923 W. North Ave., 773/342-0563*) for pretty-but-practical accessories. Men shouldn't miss **Apartment Number 9** (*1804 N. Damen, 773/395-299*) and **Bynum & Bang** (*2143 W. Division St., 773/384-4546*).

Need to buy some things for the little ones in your life? Look no further than Lincoln Park, and the stores in and around the Clybourn Corridor area. Be sure to check out **Spoiled . . . but not Rotten** (*1207 W. Webster Ave., 773/935-1399*); **LMNOP** (*2570 N. Lincoln Ave., 773/975-4055*); and **Active Kids** (*838 W. Armitage Ave., 773/281-2002*). **The Little Strummer Music Store** (*909 W. Armitage Ave., 773/751-3410*) is the perfect place to pick up presents for budding musicians. For stuff for the home, best bets are **Bellini** (*2100 N. Southport Ave., 773/880-5840*) and **Land of Nod** (*900 W. North Ave., 312/475-9903*), for stylish bedding, bath items, books, and toys.

Cold Weather Considerations

Visiting during winter or one of Chicago's chilly days? Don't let a little chill keep you from scoring some serious stash. Take a cue from weather-savvy local shoppers, who hit indoor urban malls like Water Tower Place and 900 North Michigan on the Mag Mile when the winds whip up.

If you're willing to brave the elements, dress wisely. The weather can change on a dime here, so wear layers that are easy to peel off and carry—something that'll make dressing-room acrobatics go quicker, too. We're talking warm undershirt, long-sleeved shirt, sweater or warm jacket, and windbreaker—substitute heavy winter coat for that last one if you're visiting in the dead of winter, along with the necessary accoutrements (scarf, hat, gloves). Happily, you'll find plenty of places along the way to stop for a hot cocoa or tea if the cold is getting the best of you.

Getting Around

Second only in size to that of New York City, the public transportation system in Chicago serves roughly 1.5 million riders a day and can get you to the city's main shopping drags with relative ease. With so many riders, it can get pretty crowded during weekday rush hours, so plan accordingly.

■ Fares are $1.75 for both the bus and train (called the El, for the elevated tracks that run around the Loop); transfers are 25 cents.

■ If you plan on riding frequently, buy a transit card at any El station vending machine.

■ Some of the neighborhoods we mention here are easy to walk between, like the Mag Mile and River North, and parts of Lincoln Park and Lake View, but it's best to consult a map to determine whether the distances you're planning to travel warrant wheels.

Chicago Hours

Keep these timing tips in mind as you plan out your day:

■ Most stores keep traditional retail hours, opening around 10 AM and closing at 6 or 7 PM, though different neighborhood styles and street traffic can dictate otherwise. In Bucktown and Wicker Park, for example, many shops don't open until 11 AM or noon, and may stay open later in the evenings.

■ Count on mall stores to keep later hours, usually until 8 or 9 PM. Most are open (with shorter hours than other days) on Sunday.

■ If there's a particular boutique you want to visit, call ahead. Simply flip through this chapter and you'll find all the contact information you'll need.

Pamper Your Pet

Chicago is a pet-lover's city, and it's filled with fun places to shop for them. Check out **The Down Town Dog** (111 N. State St., 312/782–4575), a delightful boutique stocked with everything the urban pooch (and kitty) need to lead a fashionable life. In Bucktown, **For Dog's Sake** (2257 W. North Ave., 773/278–4355) sells only the most healthful food and treats, in addition to plush beds and accessories for pets (mood ring collars) and their humans (dog-adorned baseball hats and T-shirts). If your dog comes along for the trip, there are some retail stores that let well-behaved pups on leashes do a little browsing. Our favorite: **Neiman Marcus** (737 N. Michigan Ave., 312/642–5900), where pedigree types can peruse Burberry carriers and other fancy items.

Word of Mouth

"Even if you are coming to Chicago on a budget, you have to do a shopping day-even if you don't buy anything. I window-shop in Chicago all the time. If you are coming around Christmastime, you might want to check out all the ornaments and stores on State Street. Then head to North Michigan Avenue and hit Saks, and Disney Store and American Girl Place (if you're holiday shopping for little ones), Water Tower Place, and Bloomingdales. You'll have a great time! Walking down Michigan Avenue during the holidays is a great feeling."

—Vanessa

5

Updated by
Judy Sutton
Taylor

A potent concentration of famous retailers around Michigan Avenue and neighborhoods bursting with one-of-a-kind shops combine to make Chicago a shopper's city. Michigan Avenue's world-class Magnificent Mile lures thousands of avid shoppers every week. How often can you find Neiman Marcus, Macy's, Nordstrom, Saks Fifth Avenue, Lord & Taylor, and Barneys New York within walking distance of one another? Neighborhood shopping areas, like fun-but-sophisticated Lincoln Park or the hipster haven of Bucktown/Wicker Park, have singular stores for specialty interests, whether Prairie-style furniture, cowboy boots, or outsider art. Those averse to paying retail won't have to venture far to unearth bargains on everything from fine jewelry to business attire. When it comes to shopping, this is one city that has it all.

Be forewarned that a gulp-inducing 9% city sales tax is added to all purchases except groceries and prescription drugs. Neighborhood shops on the North Side, especially those in Bucktown and Wicker Park, tend to open late—around 11 or noon. Most stores, particularly those on North Michigan Avenue and the North Side, are open on Sunday, although this varies by type of business; where applicable, more information is provided at the beginning of each area or category.

The Loop & South Loop

This area—named for the elevated train track that encircles it—is the heart of Chicago's business and financial district. Two of the city's major department stores, Macy's (formerly Marshall Field's) and Carson Pirie Scott, anchor **State Street,** which has been striving to regain the stature it enjoyed when it was immortalized as "State Street, that great street." It's certainly more enticing for shoppers than it was in the 1980s and early 1990s, particularly for those interested in discount department stores, but State Street is still a far cry from the shopping mecca that is the Mag Mile. The blocks surrounding the intersection of Wabash Avenue and Madison Street are designated as Jewelers Row; five high-rises cater to the wholesale trade, but many showrooms sell to the public at prices 25%–50% below retail. Despite the preponderance of working moms who spend their weekday lunch hours shopping in the area, the Loop lacks a strong presence of retail for kids, with some of the discount chains even pulling their children's lines from Loop outposts. Not all Loop stores maintain street-level visibility: several gems are tucked away on upper floors of office buildings.

Department stores and major chains are generally open on Sunday. Smaller stores are likely to be closed on Sunday and keep limited Saturday hours. Loop workers tend to start their day early, so many stores keep pace by opening by 8:30 and closing at 5 or 6.

Department Stores

Carson Pirie Scott. Famed Chicago architect Louis Sullivan designed this longtime Chicago emporium; the building is worth visiting just to see the iron scrollwork on the northwest door, at the corner of State and Madison streets. The emphasis is on moderately priced goods, including clothing, housewares, accessories, and cosmetics. It's also a good place to pick up Chicago souvenirs. ⊠ *1 S. State St., Loop* ☎ *312/ 641–7000.*

Filene's Basement. Patience can pay off at Filene's, where shoppers flip through racks of discounted clothing for a great find or two. Women can do well at either the State Street or Michigan Avenue location, but men will find a superior selection of designer names at State Street. Watch newspaper ads midweek for special shipments and events such as the infamous annual "Running of the Brides" bridal gown sale held every summer, which attracts hordes of brides willing to do just about anything to snag their dream dress at a deep discount. ⊠ *1 N. State St., Loop* ☎ *312/553–1055* ⊠ *830 N. Michigan Ave., Magnificent Mile* ☎ *312/482–8918.*

★ **Macy's (formerly Marshall Field's).** In the fall of 2006 Chicago's most famous—and perpetually struggling—department store became a Macy's. The Loop location stands as a glorious reminder of how grand department stores used to be. Founder Marshall Field's motto was "Give the lady what she wants!" and for many years both ladies and gentlemen have been able to find everything from furs to personalized stationery on one of the store's nine levels. The ground floor and lower level were refashioned in the model of European department stores to include leased boutiques. These stores-within-the-store include national companies like Yahoo, selling Internet service and computer equipment, and an Yves St. Laurent accessories boutique, as well as local retailers like Merz Apothecary, a pharmacy that opened on the North Side of Chicago in 1875 and specializes in homeopathic remedies. The latest addition is a World of JLo boutique—the first of its kind in the United States, which will feature the pop star's array of retail goods, from body-hugging fashions to perfume. Even with all these changes, some things remain the same. You can still buy Field's famous Frango mints (though they're no longer made locally), and the Walnut Room restaurant on the seventh floor is still a magical place to dine at Christmas. And, the famous Tiffany Dome—designed in 1907 by Louis Comfort Tiffany—is visible from the fifth floor. ⊠ *111 N. State St., Loop* ☎ *312/781–1000* ⊠ *Water Tower Place, 835 N. Michigan Ave., Magnificent Mile* ☎ *312/335–7700.*

Specialty Stores

BOOKS, MUSIC & ART

Brent Books & Cards. Adam Brent learned from his father, legendary Chicago bookstore owner Stuart Brent, to care for local customers with services like free downtown delivery and reading groups. ⊠ *309 W. Washington St., Loop* ☎ *312/364–0126* ⊠ *316 N. Michigan Ave., Loop* ☎ *312/920–0940.*

Museum Shop at the Art Institute of Chicago. Museum reproductions in the form of jewelry, posters, striking tabletop accents, and decorative accessories, as well as books and toys, fill the Art Institute's gift shop. If you're keen on one of the museum's current big exhibits, chances are you'll find some nifty souvenirs to take away. ⊠ *111 S. Michigan Ave., Loop* ☎ *312/443–3583.*

Powell's Bookstore. Marxism, the occult, and philosophy all have their own sections at Powell's, which focuses on used books and remainders with an intellectual bent. ⊠ *828 S. Wabash Ave., South Loop* ☎ *312/ 341–0748* ⊠ *1501 E. 57th St., Hyde Park* ☎ *773/955–7780.*

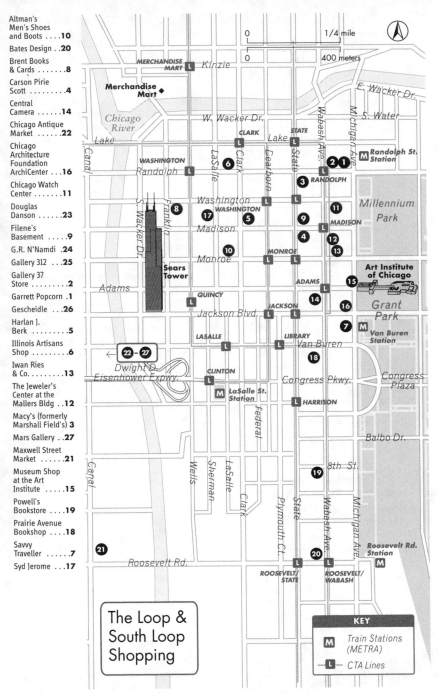

Prairie Avenue Bookshop. Massive tables amid architectural artifacts in the Prairie-style interior give browsers room to peruse nearly 20,000 new, rare, and out-of-print titles on architecture, interior design, and urban planning. ✉ *418 S. Wabash Ave., Loop* ☎ *312/922–8311.*

Savvy Traveller. You'll find an impressive selection of gadgets to improve the quality of life on the road, along with travel books, maps, luggage, and videos for everyone from on-the-go business executives to traveling toddlers. ✉ *310 S. Michigan Ave., Loop* ☎ *312/913–9800.*

Fodor'sChoice ★
FOR
SHUTTERBUGS

Central Camera. This century-old, third-generation-owned store is a Loop institution, stacked to the rafters with cameras and darkroom equipment at competitive prices. ✉ *230 S. Wabash Ave., Loop* ☎ *312/427–5580.*

CLOTHING &
SHOES

Altman's Men's Shoes and Boots. Altman's is usually packed with men trying on everything from Timberland and Tony Lama boots to Allen-Edmonds and Alden oxfords, all at a decent discount. Don't be deceived by the store's minuscule size—the stockrooms hold more than 50,000 pairs of men's shoes in sizes from 5 to 19 and in widths from AAAA to EEE. ✉ *120 W. Monroe St., Loop* ☎ *312/332–0667.*

Bates Design. Barbara Bates has been designing upscale fashions with a distinct urban edge since 1986 for a who's-who client list that includes Oprah Winfrey, Michael Jordan, Will Smith, and Mary J. Blige. But she's still invested in her community: her eponymous foundation donates custom prom dresses and tuxedos to disadvantaged inner-city teens set to graduate high school. This new studio showcases her couture and traditional labels. ✉ *1130 S. Wabash Ave., Suite 407, South Loop* ☎ *312/427–0284.*

Syd Jerome. Board of Trade types who like special attention and snazzy designers come to this legendary clothier for Giorgio Armani, Ermenegildo Zegna, and on-the-spot custom alterations. Home and office consultations are available. ✉ *2 N. LaSalle St., Loop* ☎ *312/346–0333.*

DISCOUNT
JEWELRY &
WATCHES

Chicago Watch Center. This large street-side booth in the Wabash Jewelers Mall has one of the city's most outstanding inventories of used luxury watches. ✉ *Wabash Jewelers Mall, 21 N. Wabash Ave., Loop* ☎ *312/609–0003.*

The Jeweler's Center at the Mallers Building. The largest concentration of wholesale and retail jewelers in the Midwest has been housed in this building since 1921 and is now open to the general public. Roughly 185 retailers span 13 floors, offering all kinds of jewelry, watches,

THREE SURE-SHOTS FOR ONE-OF-KIND SOUVENIRS

Chicago Architecture Foundation ArchiCenter Shop & Tour Center *(224 S. Michigan Ave., Loop, 312/922–3432)* is chock-full of treasures to remind you of the city's glorious architecture.

Garrett Popcorn *(26 E. Randolph St., Loop, 312/630–0127; see chapter listing for other locations)* lures people off the street with its mouth-watering aromas. We're partial to the cheese-and-caramel combo at this local chain.

City of Chicago Store *(163 E. Pearson St., Near North, 312/742–8811)* makes you forget the snow globes and lets you bring home something really authentic—like an old city parking meter.

and related repairs and services. ⊠ *5 S. Wabash Ave., Loop* ☎ *312/424–2664.*

Fodor'sChoice
★
SOUVENIRS OF
CHICAGO

Chicago Architecture Foundation ArchiCenter Shop & Tour Center. Daniel Burnham's 1904 Santa Fe Building is a fitting home for the Chicago Architecture Foundation. Chock-full of architecture-related books, home accessories, and everything and anything related to Frank Lloyd Wright, the store is also the place to sign up for one of the foundation's acclaimed walking tours conducted by foot, bus, bicycle, and river cruise. ⊠ *224 S. Michigan Ave., Loop* ☎ *312/922–3432.*

★ **Gallery 37 Store.** The works of student artists in the nonprofit Gallery 37 programs are for sale here, and proceeds are pumped back into the arts organization. Selection varies greatly but may include hand-painted birdbaths or small ceramics, all at affordable prices, especially considering you may be purchasing the early work of a soon-to-be superstar. ⊠ *66 E. Randolph St., Loop* ☎ *312/744–7274.*

★ **Garrett Popcorn.** Bring home a tub of Chicago's famous popcorn instead of a giant pencil or T-shirt, and you'll score major points. The lines can be long, but trust us—this stuff is worth the wait. ⊠ *26 E. Randolph St., Loop* ☎ *312/630–0127* ⊠ *4 E. Madison St., Loop* ☎ *312/263–8466* ⊠ *2 W. Jackson Blvd., Loop* ☎ *312/360–1108* ⊠ *670 N. Michigan Ave., Near North Mile* ☎ *312/944–2630.*

Illinois Artisans Shop. This store run by the Illinois State Museum culls the best jewelry, ceramics, glass, and dolls from craftspeople around the state and sells them at very reasonable prices. There are also exhibits on anything from quilting to Celtic design. ⊠ *James R. Thompson Center, 100 W. Randolph St., Suite 2–100, Loop* ☎ *312/814–5321* ⊙ *Closed weekends.*

SPECIAL STOPS **Harlan J. Berk.** Travel back to antiquity amid this wondrous trove of classical Greek, Roman, and Byzantine coinage and artifacts. Don't miss the gallery rooms in the back. ⊠ *31 N. Clark St., Loop* ☎ *312/609–0016.*

★ **Iwan Ries & Co.** Iwan Ries did not just jump on the cigar bandwagon; the family-owned store has been around since 1857. Cigar smokers are welcome to light up in the smoking area, which also displays antique pipes. ■ TIP→ **Almost 100 brands of cigars are available, as are 10,000 or so pipes, deluxe Elie Bleu humidors, and all manner of smoking accessories.** ⊠ *19 S. Wabash Ave., 2nd fl., Loop* ☎ *312/372–1306.*

West Loop

Art aficionados and gallery owners are taking some new direction in Chicago. After years of doing business in River North and along Michigan Avenue, their new credo is to go west—specifically, to the West Loop, an area just west of downtown marked by Halsted Street to the east, Fulton Market (still a busy meat-packing center) to the north, Ogden Avenue to the west, and Roosevelt Avenue to the south. Large former warehouses and loft spaces coupled with more reasonable rents have led many galleries from more established neighborhoods to join what was once a sparse number of experimental artists and dealers here. Most are clustered around the northern section of the neighborhood.

Art Galleries

Douglas Dawson. Douglas Dawson has added 8,000 square feet of space plus a sculpture garden in his new West Loop space to showcase ancient and historic art from Africa, Oceania, and the Americas. ⊠ *400 N. Morgan St., West Loop* ☎ *312/226–7975.*

G.R. N'Namdi. This gallery represents contemporary painters and sculptors, with an emphasis on African-American and Latin-American artists. ⊠ *110 N. Peoria St., West Loop* ☎ *312/563–9240.*

Gallery 312. This nonprofit, artist-run collective shows new art forms and work by young, emerging artists. ⊠ *845 W. Fulton Market, West Loop* ☎ *312/850–1234.*

Gescheidle. Susan Gescheidle recently moved her gallery from River North to the West Loop but has kept the focus on representational paintings and drawings. Veteran Chicago artist Michael Paxton is represented here. ⊠ *118 N. Peoria St., West Loop* ☎ *312/226–3500.*

Mars Gallery. A neighborhood pioneer that showcases contemporary pop and outsider artwork, Mars Gallery shows work by Peter Mars and other well-known locals like Kevin Luthardt. ⊠ *1139 W. Fulton Market, West Loop* ☎ *312/226–7808.*

Notable Markets

Fodor'sChoice
★
Chicago Antique Market. This indoor–outdoor flea market is a newer, urban version of the popular monthly sale in downstate Sandwich, Illinois, where city folks have been trekking for years. On the last Sunday of the month in season, more than 200 stalls line Randolph Street selling furniture, jewelry, books, and more. ■ TIP→ **The vibe is more funky fashions and vintage treasures than tube socks and refurbished vacuums.** In 2005 an Indie Designer Fashion Market was added, showcasing one-of-a kind wearables by up-and-coming local designers. Children under 12 get in free. ⊠ *Randolph St. between Ogden Ave. and Ada St., West Loop* 🖃 *$8* ☉ *May–Oct., last Sun. of month.*

Maxwell Street Market. A legendary outdoor bazaar that is part of the cultural landscape of the city, the Maxwell Street Market was closed by the city of Chicago amid much controversy in the 1990s. Soon after it reopened in its current location as the New Maxwell Street Market, where it remains a popular spot, particularly for Latino immigrants, to buy and sell wares. The finds aren't so fabulous, but the atmosphere sure is fun: live blues and stalls selling Mexican street food keep things lively. ⊠ *Intersection of Canal St. and Roosevelt Rd., West Loop* ☎ *312/922–3100* 🖃 *Free* ☉ *Sun. 7 AM–3 PM.*

Near North

The Near North section of Chicago encompasses the Gold Coast, which, yes, is as swanky as its name suggests. Filled with old, exclusive apartment buildings, luxury hotels, and top-notch restaurants, it also has some of the best shopping in the city. This is where you'll find the Magnificent Mile, Chicago's most famous shopping strip, as well as a bevy of significant shopping streets in the surrounding area. Check out the boutiques on booming Rush Street, which offers something for everyone—from young hipsters to ladies who lunch. Along the big avenues like Chicago and Ohio you'll find hyper-sized versions of familiar fare.

Specialty Stores

BOOKS, MUSIC & ART

Europa Books. Europa is the place for foreign-language books, newspapers, and magazines. This well-stocked bookstore carries French, Spanish, German, and Italian titles and is known for its selection of Latin-American literature. ⊠ *832 N. State St., Near North* ☎ *312/335–9677.*

Jazz Record Mart. Billing itself as the world's largest jazz record store, this "mart" sells tens of thousands of new and used titles on CD, vinyl, and cassette. You'll also find a broad selection of world music. Who are we to argue? A vast, in-depth selection of jazz and blues and knowledgeable sales staff make the store a must for music lovers. Sometimes you can catch a live performance here on a Saturday afternoon. ⊠ *25 E. Illinois St., Near North* ☎ *312/222–1467.*

Museum of Contemporary Art Store & Bookstore. This outstanding museum gift shop has out-of-the-ordinary decorative accessories, tableware, and jewelry, as well as a superb collection of books on modern and contemporary art. The shop has its own street-level entrance. ⊠ *220 E. Chicago Ave., Near North* ☎ *312/397–4000* ☯ *Closed Mon.*

BUTTONS

Tender Buttons. You can find lots and lots of anything-but-routine buttons here. These antique and vintage works of art will up the style quotient of any clothing they grace, and are priced accordingly. ⊠ *946 Rush St., Near North* ☎ *312/337–7033.*

FOR KIDS

American Girl Place. American Girl attracts little girls from just about everywhere with their signature dolls in tow. There's easily a day's worth of activities here—shop at the boutique, take in a live musical revue, and have lunch or afternoon tea at the café, where dolls can partake in the meal from their own "sassy seats." ⚠ **Brace yourself for long lines just to get into the store during high shopping seasons.** ⊠ *111 E. Chicago Ave., Near North* ☎ *877/247–5223.*

Children in Paradise. Young readers will think they are in paradise at this bookstore dedicated solely to children. There's also a good selection of kid-oriented DVDs and CDs. ⊠ *909 N. Rush St., Near North* ☎ *312/951–5437.*

Madison & Friends. Mini Mag Mile shoppers get their own high-end shopping experience at this boutique, which stocks labels like Hannah Banana and Les Tout Petits in newborn through junior sizes. They also carry top-of-the-line strollers and accessories. Adults can shop in the Denim Lounge downstairs, where the latest styles from Miss Sixty, True Religion, and other of-the-moment brands are available. ⊠ *940 N. Rush St., Near North* ☎ *312/642–6403.*

CLOTHING & SHOES

Adidas. Old school sneakers and fashions for a fresh generation of fans are the draw here. ⊠ *923 N. Rush St., Near North* ☎ *312/932–0651.*

Ikram. A household name in chichi Gold Coast high-rises, this 4,000-square-foot store named for owner Ikram Goldberg carries an assortment of new and old fashion icons, from Alexander McQueen and Jean Paul Gaultier to Narciso Rodriguez and Zac Posen. There's also a carefully edited selection of vintage designs. ⊠ *873 N. Rush St., Near North* ☎ *312/587–1000.*

Continued on page 163

THE MAGNIFICENT MILE: A SHOPPER'S SHANGRI-LA

One mile. More than 460 shops. Four vertical malls.
Art galleries, haute couture, bargains, and boutiques.
Does it get any better than this?

We've got news for shopaholics who consider the Midwest nothing but flyover country: If you haven't shopped Chicago's Magnificent Mile, dare we say, you simply haven't shopped.

With four lavish malls and more than 460 stores along the stretch of Michigan Avenue that runs from the Chicago River to Oak Street, the Mag Mile is one of the best shopping strips the world over. (Swanky Oak Street is also considered part of the Mag Mile, though neighboring streets technically are not. Shops on those streets are listed in this chapter under "Near North.")

Chanel, Hermès, Gucci, and Armani are just a few of the legendary fashion houses with fabulous boutiques here. Other no-

tables like Anne Fontaine, Kate Spade, and Prada also have Mag Mile outposts, recognizing the everybody-who's-anybody importance of the address.

Shoppers with down-to-earth budgets will find there's plenty on the Mag Mile, as well, with national chains making an extra effort at their multi-level megastores here. But the Mag Mile is much more than a paradise for clothes horses, with stores for techies, furniture fiends, sports fans, art collectors, and almost anyone else with money to spend.

Following is a selective guide to stores in the area. Hours generally run from 10 AM to 7 or 8 PM Monday through Saturday, with shorter hours on Sunday.

The Disney Store. This Mecca to the Mouse has everything little Disney disciples need for a fix: giant monitors playing Walt's classics, plus a plethora of plush toys, videos, games, and other goodies. ⊠ 717 N. Michigan Ave. ☎ 312/654-9208.

Lord & Taylor. Moderate to upscale clothing for men and women, plus shoes and accessories, form the inventory here, frequently at sale prices. ⊠ Water Tower Place, 835 N. Michigan Ave. ☎ 312/787-7400.

Neiman Marcus. Prices may be high, but they're matched by the level of taste. The selection of designer clothing and accessories is outstanding, and the gourmet top-floor food area tempts with hard-to-find delicacies and impeccable hostess gifts. ⊠ 737 N. Michigan Ave. ☎ 312/642-5900.

Nordstrom. This is a lovely department store with a killer shoe department. Note the Nordstrom Spa on the third floor. ⊠ Westfield North Bridge, 520 N. Michigan Ave. ☎ 312/464-1515.

Saks Fifth Avenue. The smaller, less-crowded cousin of the New York flagship doesn't scrimp on its selection of designer clothes. A men's specialty store is directly across the street. ⊠ Chicago Place, 700 N. Michigan Ave. ☎ 312/944-6500 ⊠ Men's Store, 717 N. Michigan Ave. ☎ 312/944-6500.

DEPARTMENT STORES

Barneys New York. A smaller version of the Manhattan store known for austere fashions, this one's heavy on private-label merchandise, though you'll find Donna Karan and several European designers. A Vera Wang salon caters to brides. The cosmetics and Chelsea Passage gift areas have plenty of plum choices. ⊠ 25 E. Oak St. ☎ 312/587-1700.

Bloomingdale's. Chicago's Bloomie's is built in an airy style that is part Prairie School, part postmodern

(quite unlike its New York City sibling), giving you plenty of elbow room to sift through its selection of designer labels. The new Space on 5 has trendier fashions. ⊠ 900 North Michigan Shops ☎ 312/440-4460.

CLOTHING FOR WOMEN

Anne Fontaine. The French designer's famous takes on the classic white shirt sport hefty price tags, thanks to her attention to detail. ✉ 909 N. Michigan Ave. ☎ 312/943–0401.

Chanel Boutique. Ensconced in the Drake Hotel, this shop carries the complete line of Chanel products, including ready-to-wear, fragrances, and cosmetics. ✉ 935 N. Michigan Ave. ☎ 312/787–5500.

Sugar Magnolia. Named for the Grateful Dead song, Sugar Magnolia has clothes and accessories that tap into trends with a romantic, Bohemian spin. Prices are high, but not over the top. ✉ 34 E. Oak St. ☎ 312/944–0885.

Ultimo. Check out the well-edited selection of designer goods from such names as John Galliano, Michael Kors, Chloe, and Manolo Blahnik. Oprah is a customer! ✉ 114 E. Oak St. ☎ 312/787–1171.

CLOTHING FOR MEN

Ermenegildo Zegna. The sportswear, softly tailored business attire, and dress clothes of this Italian great are gathered all under one roof. ✉ 645 N. Michigan Ave. ☎ 312/587–9660.

Hugo BOSS. Men will find modern, well-cut suits with attention to tailoring, as well as other signature Boss clothing and accessories here. ✉ Westfield North Bridge, 520 N. Michigan Ave. ☎ 312/660–0056.

Saks Fifth Avenue Men's Store. Spread over 30,000 square feet and three levels, Saks is the city's leading retailer for menswear. With a swanky look that emulates a 1930s luxury ocean liner and a huge selection, this is one place that has it all. ✉ 717 N. Michigan Ave. ☎ 312/944–6500 or 888/643–7257.

FOR YOUR HOME

Elements. A home-design leader in Chicago, this tempting store has decorative accessories, linens, and tableware from Europe and the United States. Check out the prime selection of European modernist and deco furnishings and the irresistible artisan jewelry. ✉ 102 E. Oak St. ☎ 312/642-6574.

CLOTHING FOR MEN & WOMEN

Brooks Brothers. The bastion of ready-to-wear conservative fashion still sells boatloads of their classic 1837 navy blazer. But this one-stop shop for oxfords and khakis also sneaks in the occasional bold color. ✉ 713 N. Michigan Ave. ☎ 312/915-0060.

Burberry. The label once favored by the conservatively well-dressed is now hot with young fashionistas, who can't get enough of the label's signature plaid on everything from bikinis to baby gear. ✉ 633 N. Michigan Ave. ☎ 312/787-2500.

Chasalla. Chasalla isn't for the timid—the bold, sexy clothes and accessories of European couture houses such as Dolce & Gabbana, Gianni Versace, and Hugo Boss are the norm here. ✉ 70 E. Oak St. ☎ 312/640-1940.

Giorgio Armani. An airy, two-floor space displays Armani's discreetly luxurious clothes and accessories, including the top-priced Black Label line. ✉ 800 N. Michigan Ave. ☎ 312/751-2244.

Gucci. Though the prices aren't for the faint of heart, there are plenty of pieces here that will last a lifetime. ✉ 900 North Michigan Shops ☎ 312/664-5504.

H&M. Bargain-savvy fashionistas around the world love the cheap-n-chic styles on offer; the constant crowds at the Mag Mile store prove Chicagoans are no different. ✉ 840 N. Michigan Ave. ☎ 312/640-0060.

Hermès of Paris. The well-heeled and very well-paid shop here for suits, signature scarves, and leather accessories. ✉ 110 E. Oak St. ☎ 312/787-8175.

Jil Sander. This line has captured the devotion of the fashion flock for its minimalist designs and impeccable tailoring. Prices are at the upper end of the designer range. ✉ 48 E. Oak St. ☎ 312/335-0006.

Mark Shale. Here you'll find two floors filled with stylish suits and separates from an international array of designers. ✉ 900 North Michigan Shops ☎ 312/440-0720.

Prada. The store has a spare, cool look that matches its modern inventory of clothing, shoes, and bags. In fact, unless you're a Miuccia devotee, the three-story shop can seem almost bare. ✉ 30 E. Oak St. ☎ 312/951-1113.

Polo/Ralph Lauren. Manor house meets mass marketing. The upper-crust chic covers men's, women's, and children's clothes and housewares. Fabrics are often enticing (suede, silk, cashmere), but expect to pay a pretty penny. ✉ 750 N. Michigan Ave. ☎ 312/280-1655.

TECH STUFF

Apple Store. It's a multilevel fantasyland for Mac users, complete with the full range of products—from computers to iPods to digital cameras. There's an Internet café where PC fans can get a glimpse of life on the other side. ✉ 679 N. Michigan Ave. ☎ 312/981-4104.

SHOES & ACCESSORIES

Avventura. Professional basketball players in need of European-style footwear stop here for sizes up to 16! ✉ Water Tower Place, 835 N. Michigan Ave. ☎ 312/337-3700.

Coach. Well-designed leather goods, in the form of purses, smart shoes, briefcases, and cell phone and PDA holders, are Coach's specialty. ✉ 625 N. Michigan Ave. ☎ 312/587-3167 ✉ 900 North Michigan Shops ☎ 312/440-1777.

Kate Spade. The goddess of handbags has filled her two-floor boutique in the middle of Oak Street with adorable shoes, pajamas, small leather goods, men's accessories from the Jack Spade line, and, of course, her to-die-for purses. ✉ 101 E. Oak St. ☎ 312/654-8853.

Louis Vuitton. Here you have it all under one roof—the coveted purses, leather goods, and luggage bearing the beloved logo, plus men's and women's shoes and jewelry. ✉ 919 N. Michigan Ave. ☎ 312/944-2010.

Salvatore Ferragamo. The shoes have been the classic choice of the well-heeled for generations, but it's the handbags, with a fresh, contemporary sensibility, that are generating excitement of late. ✉ 645 N. Michigan Ave. ☎ 312/397-0464.

Tod's. Choose from a wide selection of the signature handbags and driving moccasins that made Tod's famous, as well as newer additions to the line, including high heels. ✉ 121 E. Oak St. ☎ 312/943-0070 or 800/457-8637.

GET SPORTY

Niketown. This is one of Chicago's top tourist attractions. Many visitors—including professional athletes—stop here to take in the sports memorabilia, road test a pair of sneakers, or watch the inspirational videos. ✉ 669 N. Michigan Ave. ☎ 312/642-6363.

ART GALLERIES

Colletti Gallery. Fine antique posters, a serious collection of European ceramics and glass, and an eclectic selection of furniture transport you to the late 19th century. ✉ 67 E. Oak St. ☎ 312/664-6767.

Joel Oppenheimer, Inc. Established in 1969, this gallery in the Wrigley Building has an amazing collection of Audubon prints and specializes in antique natural-history pieces. ✉ 410 N. Michigan Ave. ☎ 312/642-5300.

R. H. Love Galleries. For three decades, this gallery has specialized in museum-quality American art from the colonial period to the early 20th century. ✉ 645 N. Michigan Ave., 2nd fl. entrance on Erie St. ☎ 312/640-1300.

R. S. Johnson Fine Art. More than 50 museums can be counted among the clients of R. S. Johnson, a Mag Mile resident for 50 years. The family-run gallery sells old masters along with art by modernists like Pablo Picasso,

Edgar Degas, and Goya. ✉ 645 N. Michigan Ave., 2nd fl. entrance on Erie St. ☎ 312/943-1661.

Richard Gray Gallery. This gallery lures serious collectors with pieces by modern masters such as David Hockney and Roy Lichtenstein. ✉ John Hancock Center, 875 N. Michigan Ave., Suite 2503 ☎ 312/642-8877.

NOT LIKE THE ONE BACK HOME

On the Mag Mile, everything seems bigger and better—even chain stores, which make an extra effort in this larger-than-life atmosphere. Here are our favorites:

Banana Republic
✉ 744 N. Michigan Ave. ☎ 312/642-0020.

Crate&Barrel
✉ 646 N. Michigan Ave. ☎ 312/787-5900.

The Gap
✉ 555 N. Michigan Ave. ☎ 312/494-8580.

Pottery Barn
✉ 734 N. Michigan Ave. ☎ 312/587-9602.

Victoria's Secret
✉ 830 N. Michigan Ave. ☎ 312/951-8324.

Williams-Sonoma
✉ 900 North Michigan Shops ☎ 312/587-8080.

MIGHTY VERTICAL MALLS

Forget all your preconceived notions about malls being suburban wastelands. Four decidedly upscale urban malls dot the Mag Mile.

The toniest of the four is 900 North Michigan, with a dazzling list of tenants, plus live weekend piano serenades. A more casual but no less entertaining shopping mecca is just blocks away at Water Tower Place. Fuel up there with a snack from **Wow Bao**, which sells steamed meat and vegetable buns that are *delish.*

Check out the beautiful views from Chicago Place's airy top-floor food court. The newest kid on the block is Westfield North Bridge, which opened in 2000.

Chicago Place. Saks Fifth Avenue is the big tenant here, and there's also a multilevel Ann Taylor. Several boutiques carry distinctive art for the home, including Chiaroscuro, Design Toscano, and Kashmir Handicrafts. ✉ 700 N. Michigan Ave. ☎ 312/642–4811.

900 North Michigan Shops. There's a ritzy feel to the mall that houses the Chicago branch of Bloomingdale's along with dozens of boutiques and specialty stores, such as Gucci, Coach, Lalique, and Fogal. ✉ 900 N. Michigan Ave. ☎ 312/915–3916.

Water Tower Place. The Ritz-Carlton Hotel sits atop this mall, which contains branches of Macy's and Lord & Taylor, as well as seven floors of shops. The more unusual spots here include Teavana (a modern tea shop) and Jacadi (children's wear). **Foodlife,** a step above usual mall food-court fare, is a fantastic spot for a quick bite. ✉835 N. Michigan Ave. ☎ 312/440–3165.

Westfield North Bridge. The big draw here is Nordstrom. Chains like Sephora and Ann Taylor Loft share space with specialty stores like Vosges Haut-Chocolat, a local chocolatier with an international following. The third floor is for tots, with a LEGO Store, a play area, and Oilily Kids. ✉ 520 N. Michigan Ave. ☎ 312/327–2300.

THE ANNUAL LIGHTS FESTIVAL

Chicago's holiday season officially kicks off every year at the end of November with the **Magnificent Mile Lights Festival,** a weekend-long event consisting of family-friendly activities that packs the shopping strip to the gills. Music, ice-carving contests, and stage shows kick off the celebration, which culminates in a parade and the illumination of more than one million lights along Michigan Avenue. Neighborhood stores keep late hours to accommodate the crowds. For more information, check out ⊕ www.themagnificentmile.com.

CLOTHING FOR
MEN & WOMEN
★
Jake. The motto here is "fashion without victims," an[ ] have taken heed to stock clothes for both sexes by up-a[ ] signers you don't see elsewhere. This shop is the newer [ ] wildly popular Southport Avenue store in Lakeview. ⊠ [ ] *St., Near North* ☎ *312/664–5533.*

Londo Mondo. Check out the great selection of swimwear for buff beach-ready bodies. You can also find workout gear and men's and women's in-line skates. ⊠ *1100 N. Dearborn St., Near North* ☎ *312/751–2794* ⊠ *2148 N. Halsted St., Lincoln Park* ☎ *773/327–2218.*

FOR THE HOME
Quatrine. The washable upholstered and slipcovered furniture for dining rooms, living rooms, and bedrooms here looks decidedly chic and not at all what you'd consider child- or pet-friendly. ⊠ *944 N. Rush St., Near North* ☎ *312/649–1700.*

Room & Board. Straightforward yet stylish pieces with a modern sensibility blend quality craftsmanship and materials with affordable pricing. ⊠ *55 E. Ohio St., Near North* ☎ *312/222–0970.*

Fodor'sChoice
★
SOUVENIRS OF
CHICAGO
City of Chicago Store. Nab unusual souvenirs of the city here—anything from a street sign to a real parking meter. It's also a good source for guidebooks, posters, and T-shirts. ⊠ *Chicago Waterworks Visitor Information Center, Michigan Ave. at E. Pearson St., Near North* ☎ *312/ 742–8811.*

Spotlight: Navy Pier

Extending more than ½ mi onto Lake Michigan from 600 East Grand Avenue, Navy Pier treats you to spectacular views of the skyline, especially from a jumbo Ferris wheel set in slow motion. Stores and carts gear their wares to families and tourists and most don't merit a special trip. But if you're out there, check out **Oh Yes Chicago!** for souvenirs and the **Chicago Children's Museum Store** for educational kids' toys. Many stores are open late into the evening, especially in summer.

River North

Contained by the Chicago River on the south and west, Clark Street on the east, and Oak Street on the north, River North is home to art galleries, high-end antiques shops, home furnishings stores, and a few clothing boutiques. The biggest news in this neighborhood is the resurrection of Tree Studios, part of a controversial restoration project to a building originally designed as an artist's colony. On the verge of demolition a few years ago, the building is again housing retail and tenants involved in the arts, though they are no longer permitted to live here. Most of the businesses in River North have a distinctive style that fits in with this art-minded area. Strangely, it's also a wildly popular entertainment district; touristy theme restaurants such as Ed Debevic's and Rainforest Café peddle logo merchandise as aggressively as burgers.

Merchandise Mart

This massive marketplace between Wells and North Orleans streets just north of the Chicago River is more notable for its art deco design than its shopping. Much of the building is reserved for the design trade, meaning that only interior design professionals have access to its wares.

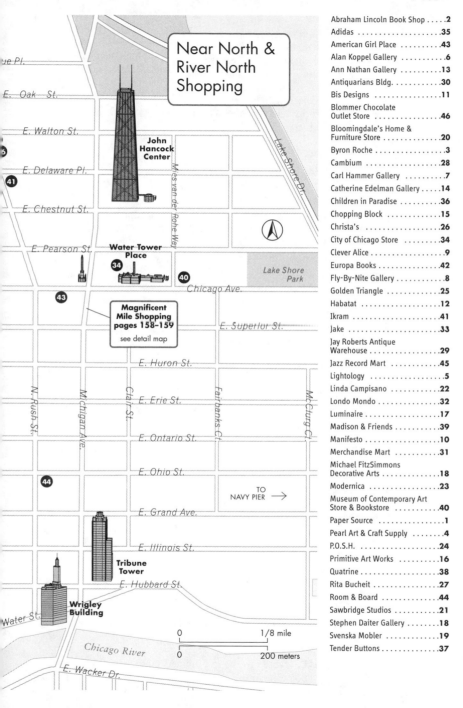

Near North &
River North
Shopping

John
Hancock
Center

E. Oak St.

E. Walton St.

E. Delaware Pl.

E. Chestnut St.

E. Pearson St.

Water Tower
Place

Lake Shore
Park

Chicago Ave.

Magnificent
Mile Shopping
pages 158–159
see detail map

E. Superior St.

E. Huron St.

E. Erie St.

E. Ontario St.

E. Ohio St.

TO
NAVY PIER →

E. Grand Ave.

E. Illinois St.

Tribune
Tower

E. Hubbard St.

Wrigley
Building

Water St.

Chicago River

E. Wacker Dr.

0   1/8 mile
0   200 meters

However, the first two floors have been turned into retail with the unveiling of LuxeHome, a group of 24 high-end kitchen, bath, and building showrooms that are open to the public as well as the design trade. Tenants include de Giulio kitchen design, Waterworks, and Christopher Peacock Cabinetry. In the fall of 2005, The Chopping Block, a local culinary school with a loyal fan base, moved from its cramped Lincoln Park headquarters to more spacious digs here. The Mart is usually closed on Sunday, and stores keep relatively short Saturday hours.

> **WORD OF MOUTH**
>
> "Check out The Chopping Block. Merchandise Mart's location is great. The cooking classes are awesome. Can be a bit pricey, but worth it!"
>
> —ethiokoko

Specialty Stores

ACCESSORIES **Linda Campisano.** Exceptionally detailed bridal headpieces, as well as custom hats for men, women, and children, are stocked at the designer's new space in Tree Studios. ⊠ *Tree Studios, 4 E. Ohio St., River North* ☎ *312/896–3395.*

ANTIQUES & **Antiquarians Building.** Five floors of dealers in Asian and European antiques display their wares; some examples of modernism and art deco are thrown in for good measure. ⊠ *159 W. Kinzie St., River North* ☎ *312/527–0533.*

Christa's, Ltd. Chests, cabinets, tables, and bureaus are stacked three and four high, creating narrow aisles that are precarious to negotiate but make for adventurous exploring. Look in, over, and under each and every piece to assess the gems stashed in every possible crevice. ⊠ *217 W. Illinois St., River North* ☎ *312/222–2520.*

Fly-by-Nite Gallery. Exceptional decorative and functional art objects (circa 1890–1930) are chosen with a curatorial eye. Fly-by-Nite is especially known for European art glass and pottery and antique jewelry. ⊠ *714 N. Wells St., River North* ☎ *312/664–8136.*

Jay Roberts Antique Warehouse, Inc. Jay Roberts has enough antique merchandise to fill a 50,000-square-foot showroom on his own. He specializes in 19th-century European pieces, and has many large-scale armoires, dining sets, sideboards, fireplace mantels, and clocks. ⊠ *149 W. Kinzie St., River North* ☎ *312/222–0167.*

Michael FitzSimmons Decorative Arts. Works by Frank Lloyd Wright, Louis Sullivan, and Gustav Stickley, along with some quality reproductions, are displayed in a homelike environment. FitzSimmons' collection of furniture and artifacts from the British and American Arts and Crafts movements is renowned. ⊠ *311 W. Superior St., River North* ☎ *312/787–0496.*

P.O.S.H. A move to Tree Studios from Southport Avenue has not made it easier to resist the charming displays of piled-up, never-been-used, vintage hotel and restaurant china here. There's also an impressive selection of silver gravy boats, creamers, and flatware that bear the marks of ocean liners and private clubs. ⊠ *Tree Studios, 613 N. State St., River North* ☎ *312/280–1602.*

Rita Bucheit, Ltd. Devoted to the streamlined Biedermeier aesthetic, this shop carries choice furniture and accessories from the period along with art deco and modern pieces that are perfect complements to the style. ✉ *449 N. Wells St., River North* ☎ *312/527–4080.*

ART GALLERIES The contemporary art scene continues to thrive in River North, despite losing some of its residents to a slightly lower rent warehouse district in the nearby West Loop. The neighborhood is chock-full of galleries, most open Tuesday through Saturday. ■ TIP→ Every Saturday morning at 10:45, the Chicago Art Dealers Association offers complimentary gallery tours. Groups meet at the Starbucks at 750 N. Franklin Street and are guided each week by a different gallery owner or director from the area. For more information and to check holiday weekend schedules, call 312/649–0065.

Alan Koppel Gallery. An eclectic mix of works by modern masters and contemporary artists is balanced by a selection of French and Italian Modernist furniture from the 1920s to 1960s. ✉ *210 W. Chicago Ave., River North* ☎ *312/640–0730.*

5

Ann Nathan Gallery. The specialty here is contemporary paintings, but the gallery also showcases sculpture and singular artist-made furniture. ✉ *212 W. Superior St., River North* ☎ *312/664–6622.*

Byron Roche. Contemporary paintings and drawings, many by Chicago artists, are exhibited. ✉ *750 N. Franklin St., River North* ☎ *312/654–0144.*

Carl Hammer Gallery. Lee Godie, Henry Darger, and Jordan Mozer are among the outsider and self-taught artists whose work is shown at this gallery. ✉ *740 N. Wells St., River North* ☎ *312/266–8512.*

Catherine Edelman Gallery. This gallery of contemporary photography explores the work of emerging, mixed-media, photo-based artists such as Maria Martinez-Canes and Jack Spencer. ✉ *300 W. Superior St., River North* ☎ *312/266–2350.*

Habatat. Collectors of fine studio art glass are drawn here by luminaries such as Dale Chihuly. ✉ *222 W. Superior St., River North* ☎ *312/440–0288.*

★ **Primitive Art Works.** A longtime neighborhood favorite, this gallery showcases ethnic and tribal art, including textiles, furniture, and jewelry. ✉ *706 N. Wells St., River North* ☎ *312/943–3770.*

Stephen Daiter Gallery. This space showcases stunning 20th-century European and American photography, particularly avant-garde photojournalism. ✉ *311 W. Superior St., River North* ☎ *312/787–3350.*

ART SUPPLIES & **Abraham Lincoln Book Shop.** In business since 1938, the shopowner here
BOOKS buys, sells, and appraises books, paintings, documents, and other paraphernalia associated with American military and political history. ✉ *357 W. Chicago Ave., River North* ☎ *312/944–3085.*

Pearl Art & Craft Supply. Pearl is the name synonymous with the best selection of art supplies at the best prices. Paints and palettes, crafts, portfolios, tools, easels—it's all here, and it's all discounted. ✉ *225 W. Chicago Ave., River North* ☎ *312/915–0200.*

CHEAP **Blommer Chocolate Outlet Store.** "Why does River North smell like freshly
CHOCOLATE baked brownies?" is a question you hear fairly often. The oh-so-sweet reason: it's close to the Blommer Chocolate Factory, which has been making wholesale chocolates here since 1939. More important, it's close to

the retail outlet store, where you can get Blommer chocolates and candies at a discount—a handy tip to know when those smells give you a case of the munchies. ⊠ *600 W. Kinzie St., River North* ☎ *312/226–7700.*

Bis Designs. This private-label line of classy, high-quality (but slightly subdued) reinterpretations of the day's latest trends has a good price-to-quality ratio. ⊠ *732 N. Wells St., River North* ☎ *312/988–9560.*
Clever Alice. This women's boutique recently moved from Lincoln Park to this new location, but it still carries the same well-chosen inventory of fashion, from designers like Alice in Oz, James Jeans, and Rebecca Beeson. ⊠ *750 N. Franklin St., River North* ☎ *312/587–8693.*

Bloomingdale's Home & Furniture Store. The Medinah Temple once occupied this space, and Bloomie's kept the historically significant exterior intact but gutted the inside to create its first stand-alone furnishings store in Chicago. Naturally, it's stocked to the rafters with everything you need to eat, sleep, and relax in your home in high style. ⊠ *600 N. Wabash Ave., Near North* ☎ *312/324–7500.*
Cambium. A particularly expansive line of kitchen fittings and accoutrements is one of many temptations at this home furnishings store. ⊠ *113–119 W. Hubbard St., River North* ☎ *312/832–9920.*
★ **The Chopping Block.** New and seasoned chefs appreciate an expertly edited selection of pots and pans, bakeware, gadgets, and ingredients here. The intimate cooking classes are hugely popular and taught by a fun, knowledgeable staff. The Lincoln Square location has a wine shop. ⊠ *Merchandise Mart Plaza, Suite 107, River North Park* ☎ *312/644–6360* ⊠ *4747 N. Lincoln Ave., Lincoln Square* ☎ *773/472–6700.*
Golden Triangle. At the outskirts of River North, this is a must for anyone enamored with the East-meets-West aesthetic. There are 11,000 square feet of choice pieces, including antique Chinese and British colonial Raj furniture from Burma, Asian accessories, and idiosyncratic pieces from Thailand. ⊠ *72 W. Hubbard St., River North* ☎ *312/755–1266.*
Lightology. This 20,000-square-foot showroom of modern light designs is an essential stop for designers and architects, not to mention passersby drawn to the striking designs visible from the windows. It's the brainchild of Greg Kay, who started out as a roller disco lighting designer in the 1970s and made a name for himself in Chicago with Tech Lighting, a contemporary design gallery. ⊠ *215 W. Chicago Ave., River North* ☎ *312/944–1000.*
Luminaire. The city's largest showroom of international contemporary furniture includes pieces by Philippe Starck, Antonio Citterio, Alberta Meda, and Shiro Kuromata. Sleek kitchen designs are from Italian manufacturer Bofi, and a large home accessories section has equally edgy offerings from Alessi, Zani & Zani, Rosenthal, and Mono. ⊠ *301 W. Superior St., River North* ☎ *312/664–9582.*
Manifesto. In an expansive, street-level space, one of the largest design ateliers in the city showcases work by furniture designer (and owner) Richard Gorman, plus contemporary furniture from Italy, Austria, Spain, and Mexico and streamlined Finnish accessories. ⊠ *755 N. Wells St., River North* ☎ *312/664–0733.*

Modernica. Price tags aren't stratospheric for the Modernist mid-century American furnishings shown here. ⊠ *555 N. Franklin St., River North* ☎ *312/222–1808.*

★ **Sawbridge Studios.** Sawbridge Studios displays custom handcrafted furniture by about 40 American artisans. The specialties include Frank Lloyd Wright reproductions, newly designed pieces with an Arts and Crafts or Shaker aesthetic, and contemporary pottery. ⊠ *153 W. Ohio St., River North* ☎ *312/828–0055.*

Svenska Mobler. This store carries a hand-picked selection of Swedish antique furniture, lighting, and art, all accompanied by high price tags. ⊠ *516 N. Wells St., River North* ☎ *312/595–9320.*

★ **Paper Source.** Reams and reams of different types of paper are sold here; PAPER much of the paper is eclectic and expensive. There are a custom invitation department and a good selection of rubber stamps and bookbinding supplies. Ask about the classes offered. ⊠ *232 W. Chicago Ave., River North* ☎ *312/337–0798* ⊠ *919 W. Armitage Ave., Lincoln Park* ☎ *773/ 525–7300.*

Wicker Park & Bucktown

Artists and musicians were the first to claim this once run-down area near the intersection of North, Damen, and Milwaukee avenues; trendy coffeehouses, nightclubs, and restaurants followed. Young, hip families were next, and shopping has since snowballed. Now scads of edgy clothing boutiques, art galleries, home design ateliers, alternative music stores, and antiques shops dot the area. Hipsters are squawking about gentrification with the opening of an Urban Outfitters on Milwaukee Avenue, but this is still a one-of-a kind shopping destination that deserves a solid chunk of time. The stretch of Division Street between Ashland and Western avenues is the newest hot spot, with eclectic stores selling all kinds of creative wares from custom rugs to motor scooters.

Many stores don't open until at least 11 AM, some shops are closed on Monday and Tuesday, and hours can be erratic. Spend a late afternoon shopping before settling in for dinner at one of the neighborhood's popular restaurants. To get here from downtown on the El, take the Blue Line toward O'Hare and exit at Damen Avenue.

Specialty Stores

ACCESSORIES & **Paper Doll.** Doll up your gift with an unusual card and handmade wrapGOODIES ping paper from this Wicker Park shop, where colorful paintings of canines line the walls and Maude, the owners' pug, holds court on the floor. Finger puppets, candles, and other gift items are also stocked. ⊠ *1747 W. Division St., Wicker Park* ☎ *773/ 227–6950.*

Ruby Room. This Wicker Park spa–boutique sells an eclectic mix of bath and body products from brands like Sage Spirit, Phytologie, and Surly Girl Studios. Check out the spa ser-

> **WORD OF MOUTH**
>
> "Definitely hit Bucktown & Wicker Park (my neighborhood) for some unique, funky boutiques and designers that aren't as well known."
> —Vittrad

vices, too—anything from intuitive astrology and pet healing to brow waxing and facials. ⊠ *1743–45 W. Division St., 2nd fl., Wicker Park* ☎ *773/635–5000.*

Tatine. It's hard to decide which luscious-smelling candle to choose with eclectic scents like sake, rose tabac, and ginger lily among the offerings. Margo Breznik makes all the candles in this pretty shop herself using soy wax, which is said to burn cleaner than traditional paraffin wax. ⊠ *1742 W. Division St., Wicker Park* ☎ *773/342–1890.*

ANTIQUES &
COLLECTIBLES

Bleeker Street. Rich in British, Irish, and French provincial home and garden wares, Bleeker Street's strong suits are home accessories that were proper in their day but look fanciful now, such as painted Victorian mirrors and sets of cigarette cards. In summer, garden items are displayed in an inviting backyard. ⊠ *1946 N. Leavitt St., Bucktown* ☎ *773/862–3185.*

Modern Times. This 2,500-square-foot showroom has been on the must-hit list since 1991 for designers and collectors of home furnishings from the 1900s, particularly the '40s, '50s, and '60s. They also stock a good selection of vintage jewelry. ⊠ *1538 N. Milwaukee Ave., Wicker Park* ☎ *773/772–8871.*

Pagoda Red. Prime, exceptionally well-priced Asian furnishings pack this open loft space, including Chinese deco chairs, Nepalese rugs, antique lanterns, and a rare collection of 20th-century Chinese advertising posters. ⊠ *1714 N. Damen Ave., Bucktown* ☎ *773/235–1188.*

Pavilion. The specialty here is French, Italian, and Scandinavian antiques, but you'll be lured in by the altogether uncommon mix of industrial and decorative furnishings, accessories, and fixtures. The eclectic selection reflects the collecting acumen of its two idiosyncratic owners, who scour Europe and the Midwest for items in the perfect state of intriguing decay. ⊠ *2055 N. Damen Ave., Bucktown* ☎ *773/645–0924.*

BOOKS & MUSIC

Beat Parlor. If dance music is the soundtrack to your life, you've found a home at Beat Parlor. DJs and groovin' hipsters head to this spot for its impressive collection of rare dance and hip-hop scores. There are turntables for testing out old, poorly labeled LPs, and a great selection of Japanese cartoons and Hong Kong martial arts flicks, too. ⊠ *1653 N. Damen Ave., Bucktown* ☎ *773/395–2887.*

★ **Myopic Books.** One of Chicago's largest used-book dealers stocks more than 80,000 titles and buys books from the public on Friday evenings and all day Saturday. ■ TIP➔ A community mainstay, Myopic also hosts regular music and poetry events and is the meeting spot for the Wicker Park Chess Club. ⊠ *1564 N. Milwaukee Ave., Wicker Park* ☎ *773/862–4882.*

Reckless Records. Look for a varied selection of music at this sister store to the Lake View flagship, including lots of rare stuff and rock paraphernalia. ⊠ *1532 N. Milwaukee Ave., Bucktown* ☎ *773/235–3727.*

FOR KIDS

Psycho Baby. The best-dressed urban tykes send their parents to this shop to spend a pretty penny on funky duds by designers like Imps & Elves, Rabbi's Daughters, and Paper Denim & Cloth. There's a great selection of shoes, plus toys and books, and a story hour every Monday and Wednesday for parents brave enough to tote their tykes along. ⊠ *1630 N. Damen Ave., Bucktown* ☎ *773/772–2815.*

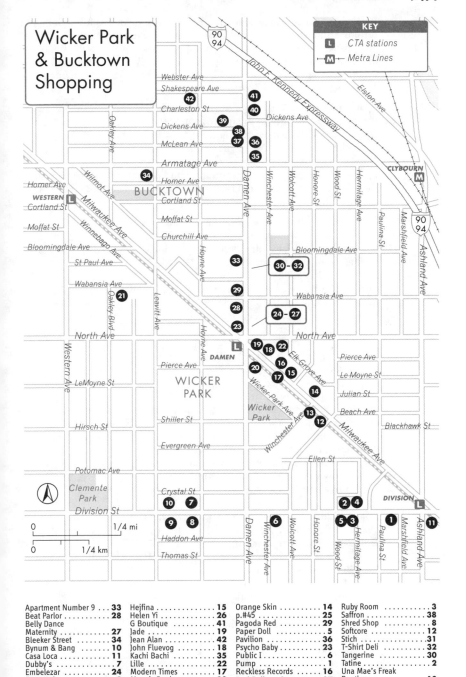

Wicker Park & Bucktown Shopping

The Red Balloon Company. Known for its beautiful handmade children's furniture and stock of colorful Zutano infant wear, this charming store also carries a great selection of classic books and toys, as well as blankets and art work that can be personalized. ⊠ *2060 N. Damen Ave., Bucktown* ☏ *773/489–9800* ⊠ *5407 N. Clark St., Andersonville* ☏ *773/489–9800 or 877/969–9800.*

CLOTHING FOR MEN

Apartment Number 9. Siblings Amy and Sarah Blessing offer sisterly advice to guys born without the metrosexual gene on what styles most suit them. Their store, named for the Tammy Wynette song, carries classic lines like Paul Smith, Marc Jacobs, and Michael Kors. ⊠ *1804 N. Damen Ave., Bucktown* ☏ *773/395–2999.*

Bynum & Bang. Men who want more than ho-hum style come here to shop for fashions by emerging designers like Kent Nielsen. ⊠ *2143 W. Division St., Wicker Park* ☏ *773/384–4546.*

CLOTHING FOR MEN & WOMEN

Eurotrash. Fads from across the Atlantic you won't find; instead, expect an emphasis on vintage and western-inspired fashions. The store is chock-full of pieces by edgy designers you don't often find in Chicago, such as Grail, Krush, and Kowboys. ⊠ *2136 W. Division St., Wicker Park* ☏ *773/828–8298.*

Hejfina. This lifestyle boutique carries everything the mod Wicker Parker needs to get through the day stylishly: clothes by of-the-moment designers from across the globe, custom-made furniture from local designers, and books on modern art and architecture. The store also hosts art installations and speakers on design from time to time. ⊠ *1529 N. Milwaukee Ave., Wicker Park* ☏ *773/772–0002.*

Noir. Set up as a small boutique exclusively selling cutting-edge black clothing, Noir quickly gained a loyal clientele and expanded to include a bold array of colorful clothes and a smaller second storefront for men down the block. Prices are moderate ($25–$150), brand logos are nonexistent, and service is exceptional. ⊠ *1726 W. Division St., Wicker Park* ☏ *773/ 489–1957* ⊠ *1740 W. Division St., Wicker Park* ☏ *773/862–9960.*

Public I. Public I prides itself on paying attention to its customers, offering plenty of helpful suggestions about which of its smart, hip, won't-find-it-down-the-street designs work best. Their inventory includes designs by How & Wen, Joe Michelle, and R. Scott French. ⊠ *1923 W. Division St., Wicker Park* ☏ *773/772–9088.*

Softcore. Club kids go to Softcore for funky styles from Diesel, Miss Sixty, Octopussy (the store's own label), and local designer Geoffrey Mac. ⊠ *1420 N. Milwaukee Ave., Wicker Park* ☏ *773/276–7616.*

The T-Shirt Deli. Order up a made-to-order T-shirt with custom iron-on letters or throwback '70s decals. You'll get your T-shirt served up on the spot, wrapped in paper like a sandwich, and packed with a bag of chips for good measure. ⊠ *1739 N. Damen Ave., Bucktown* ☏ *773/ 276–6266.*

WORD OF MOUTH

"The T-shirt Deli (see www.tshirtdeli.com for more info) was so much fun. You get to pick out your transfer and make the shirt say whatever you want. My girls had a blast here, and the shirts are very cute."

–lacohn

CLOTHING FOR WOMEN

Belly Dance Maternity. The hippest moms-to-be shop here for up-to-the-minute maternity fashions by Japanese Weekend, Cadeau, and Citizens of Humanity. ⊠ *1647 N. Damen Ave., Bucktown* ☎ *773/ 862–1133.*

G Boutique. Here's an all-in-one stop for women planning for a little romance. There's beautiful lingerie from brands like Aubade and Cosabella, plus massage oils, books, videos, and toys. ⊠ *2131 N. Damen Ave., Bucktown* ☎ *773/235– 1234.*

CHIC CLOTHING FOR EXPECTANT MOMS

Krista K Boutique *(3458 N. Southport Ave., Lake View, 773/248–1967).* **Belly Dance Maternity** *(1647 N. Damen Ave., Bucktown, 773/862– 1133).* **Swell** *(1207 W. Webster Ave., Lincoln Park, 773/935–1349).*

Helen Yi. This loftlike, minimalist boutique stocks sophisticated styles from up-and-coming designers, including Shelly Steffen and local handbag maker Susan Fitch. ⊠ *1645 N. Damen Ave., Bucktown* ☎ *773/252– 3838.*

Jade. Former stylist and fashion writer Laura Hagerman's new shop stands out from the crowd of women's boutiques in the neighborhood with a carefully chosen stock of must-have cocktail dresses, tops, jeans, and accessories, all displayed against a calming jade-green backdrop. ⊠ *1557 N. Milwaukee Ave., Wicker Park* ☎ *773/432–0002.*

★ **p. 45.** This store catches attention by showing the most forward styles of a cadre of hip designers like Rebecca Taylor and Ulla Johnson. Customers from all over the city and well beyond come here for adventurous to elegant styles and prices that don't get out of hand. ⊠ *1643 N. Damen Ave., Bucktown* ☎ *773/862–4523.*

Robin Richman. Robin Richman displays her nationally known knitwear in this art gallery–retail store, along with antique goods and wood furniture made by sculptor Floyd Gompf. ⊠ *2108 N. Damen Ave., Bucktown* ☎ *773/278–6150.*

Saffron. Merchandise as indulgent and decadent as the namesake spice lures you into this Bucktown boutique. You'll find fluid, finely finished clothes made of natural fabrics, organically inspired jewelry, and lavish bath products. ⊠ *2064 N. Damen Ave., Bucktown* ☎ *773/486–7753.*

Tangerine. Popular designers, such as Three Dots and Ashley, provide the fun, feminine clothes and accessories here. Keep your eyes open for labels like Built by Wendy that are hard to find elsewhere in town. ⊠ *1719 N. Damen Ave., Bucktown* ☎ *773/772–0505.*

Una Mae's Freak Boutique. This Wicker Park favorite for vintage fashions is bursting at the seams with inventory. The bulk of the bulging stock is from the 1950s through the '80s, but there are also new lines from designers like Hot Sauce and The People Have Spoken. ⊠ *1422 N. Milwaukee Ave., Wicker Park* ☎ *773/276–7002.*

Vive La Femme. The motto is "style beyond size," and the specialty is sexy, exciting clothes for women in sizes 12 to 28 from lines including Anna Scholz, Sizeappeal, and Z. Cavaricci. ⊠ *2115 N. Damen Ave., Bucktown* ☎ *773/772–7429.*

5

Casa Loca. The handsome, rustic pine furniture from Mexico is carved, painted, or fashionably primitive, and the collection is complemented by superb vintage and antique Mexican folk art and tinware from Guanajuato. ☒ *1130 N. Milwaukee Ave., Wicker Park* ☎ *773/278–2972.*

Dubby's Buy the Ounce. Bins are filled with bulk goodies, from candies and chocolates to coffee beans from local favorite Intelligentsia. Create the perfect hostess gift using one of the wicker baskets that line the store. ☒ *2108 W. Division St., Wicker Park* ☎ *773/645–7100.*

Embelezar. The name is Portuguese for "embellish," and after a visit to this airy shop you'll be able to do just that. Everything's geared for gracious living, from the hand-painted, silk-covered, Venetian fixtures to the sumptuous sofas. ☒ *1639 N. Damen Ave., Bucktown* ☎ *773/645–9705.*

For Dog's Sake. Only the finest foods and accessories for pampered pets and their owners are here, from brightly colored toys and bowls by Otis and Claude to the smartly designed beds, baseball hats, and collars by San Francisco's George. ☒ *2257 W. North Ave., Bucktown* ☎ *773/278–4355.*

Jean Alan Upholstered Furniture and Furnishings. The offerings at this design atelier, owned by a former feature-film set decorator, range from Victorian to mid-20th-century modern. There's always a healthy assortment of sofas and chairs recovered in eclectic fabrics, plus pillows made of unusual textiles and refurbished vintage lamps with marvelous shades. ☒ *2134 N. Damen Ave., Bucktown* ☎ *773/278–2345.*

Kachi Bachi. What you'll find here are Claudia Ahuile's visions for home design in the way of custom throw pillows, bedding, and window treatments, even though the name (derived from a Spanish slang term for "junk") might suggest otherwise. ☒ *2041 N. Damen Ave., Bucktown* ☎ *773/645–8640.*

Lille. Hidden behind a low-profile storefront in the middle of a hectic street, Lille sequesters a carefully selected mix of home furnishings and personal accessories by well-known artists (vases from Parisian designer Christian Tortuby) and lesser-known ones (jewelry by Jeanine Payer). ☒ *1923 W. North Ave., Bucktown* ☎ *773/342–0563.*

★ **Orange Skin.** Stock up here on all you need to live stylishly: mod Italian furniture, whimsical kitchen gadgets, even sunglasses. The brand list includes Alessi, Michael Graves, and Tisettanta. ☒ *1429 N. Milwaukee Ave., Wicker Park* ☎ *773/394–4500.*

Stitch. Pottery, jewelry, leather goods, backpacks, briefcases, and bags of every ilk, plus contemporary furniture with a modernist bent, are all displayed in an airy space. ☒ *1723 N. Damen Ave., Bucktown* ☎ *773/782–1570.*

John Fluevog. Fluevog's chunky platforms and bold designs have graced the famous feet of Madonna and throngs of other loyal devotees, and they can house your toes, too, if you shop here. ☒ *1539–41 N. Milwaukee Ave., Wicker Park* ☎ *773/772–1983.*

Pump. High heels are in high supply here, but so are plenty of other shoe styles from well-heeled designers like Dolce Vita, Via Spiga, and Kenneth Cole. ☒ *1659 W. Division St., Wicker Park* ☎ *773/384–6750.*

Ethnic Enclaves

Chicago's ethnic neighborhoods give you the chance to shop the globe without ever leaving the city. **Chinatown** has shops along four blocks of Wentworth Avenue south of Cermak Road selling Far Eastern imports that range from jade to ginseng root to junk. In the **Lincoln Square neighborhood,** a stretch of Lincoln Avenue between Leland and Lawrence avenues on the city's North Side, you'll find German delis and stores that sell European-made health and beauty products, as well as some newer upscale clothing and gift boutiques that attract the hip singles and young families who have started calling this area home. Heading east to **Andersonville,** you'll find a slew of Swedish restaurants, bakeries, and gift shops along Clark Street between Foster and Balmoral avenues, plus specialty boutiques that sell everything from fine chocolates to eclectic home furnishings. Many non-U.S. visitors make the trek to a cluster of dingy but well-stocked electronics stores on **Devon Avenue** (between Western and Washtenaw avenues) in an Indian neighborhood on the city's far North Side. The attraction is a chance to buy electronics that run on 220-volts. Because the United States has no value-added tax, it's often cheaper for international visitors to buy here than at home. ■ TIP→ **The same stretch of Devon Avenue is a great source for spectacularly rich sari fabrics and other Indian and Pakistani goods.**

5

SPORTING GOODS **Shred Shop.** Skaters and snowboarders find their hearts' desires here. The Shred Shop does rentals and servicing, too. ⊠ *2048 W. Division St., Wicker Park* ☎ *773/384–2100.*

Lincoln Park

The upscale residential neighborhood of Lincoln Park entices with its mix of distinctive boutiques and well-known national chain stores. **Armitage Avenue** between Orchard Street and Racine Avenue is a great source for clothing, tableware, jewelry, and gifts. There are also good finds (from lingerie to crafts to maternity clothing) on **Webster Avenue.** On **Halsted Street,** between Armitage Avenue and Fullerton Parkway, new openings include chains geared to the young and thin. The **Clybourn Corridor** section of this neighborhood, which runs along North Avenue and Clybourn Avenue, has become akin to a giant urban strip mall, with standbys like J. Crew (929 W. North Ave.) and Restoration Hardware (938 W. North Ave.) lining the streets. The star of the show, though, is the flagship three-story Crate&Barrel. You'll also find plenty to buy for the little ones, from children's furniture to plush and pricey clothes and gear. The area is easily reached by taking the Ravenswood (Brown) El line to the Armitage stop, or the Howard (Red) line to Clybourn.

Specialty Stores

ACCESSORIES **Fabrice.** The only Fabrice boutique outside of Paris stocks an abundance of French accessories: Herve Chapelier and Longchamp handbags,

Catherine Masson sachets, wonderful floral pins, and other jewelry. ⊠ *1714 N. Wells St., Lincoln Park* ☎ *312/280–0011.*

Isabella Fine Lingerie. Lauren Amerine, a self-confessed lingerie addict who herself has inspired many obsessions among her loyal clientele, runs this jewel of a shop. Look for Cosabella, Parah, and Eberjey, plus bridal pieces and swimwear. ⊠ *1101 W. Webster Ave., Lincoln Park* ☎ *773/ 281–2352.*

The Left Bank. An eclectic mix of antique-style French jewelry brings a touch of Paris chic to Chicago. There's also a beautiful selection of French-theme jewelry boxes, perfume bottles, and other accessories. Owner Susan Jablonski stocks a large assortment of bridal headpieces and tiaras, and she offers wedding planning services as well. ⊠ *1155 W. Webster Ave., Lincoln Park* ☎ *773/929–7422.*

★ **Mint.** Mint is like a craft fair inside a pretty little shop, selling only items—from jewelry and purses to cards and candles—from local designers. The prices are reasonable and the selection is fun and funky, not fuddy-duddy. ⊠ *1450 W. Webster Ave., Lincoln Park* ☎ *773/322–2944.*

★ **1154 Lill Studio.** Creative types design their own handbags and makeup cases from tons of fabric and shape options at this one-of-kind shop. The helpful staff assembles the pieces. Some limited-edition, ready-made bags are available, too. ⊠ *2523 N. Halsted St., Lincoln Park* ☎ *773/ 477–5455.*

BEAUTY **Aroma Workshop.** Customize lotions, massage oils, and bath salts with more than 100 fragrances in this beauty boutique. The workshop makes its own line of facial care products, too. ⊠ *2050 N. Halsted St., Lincoln Park* ☎ *773/871–1985.*

Endo-Exo Apothecary. A DJ sometimes spins for shoppers here, amid vintage pharmacy cabinets mingled with mod furnishings. Sample from a well-chosen stock of such hard-to-find beauty lines as Linda Cantello, Mythic Tribe, and Christy Turlington's Sundari brand. ⊠ *2034 N. Halsted St., Lincoln Park* ☎ *773/ 525–0500.*

BOOK & MUSIC STORES **Gramaphone Records.** Local DJs and club kids go to Gramaphone to find the newest dance releases, from house to hip-hop, and to chat with the in-the-know staff. ⊠ *2663 N. Clark St., Lincoln Park* ☎ *773/472– 3683.*

Transitions Bookplace. Alternative healing, religion, mythology, and folklore are among the subjects stocked at one of the country's top New Age bookstores. There's a lively program of author appearances and

> **TOP SHOPS FOR BEAUTY-PRODUCT JUNKIES**
>
> **Endo-Exo Apothecary** *(2034 N. Halsted St., Lincoln Park, 773/525–0500)* sells the latest makeup lines and offers great advice.
>
> **Bravco Beauty Centre** *(43 E. Oak St., Near North, 312/943–4305)* is a favorite of celebs for its expansive stock (48 types of hair extensions, anyone?), and staff who can explain the differences between them.
>
> **Merz Apothecary** *(4716 N. Lincoln Ave., Lincoln Square, 773/989– 0900)* has been in business since 1875 and specializes in exclusive European lines and holistic and herbal remedies.

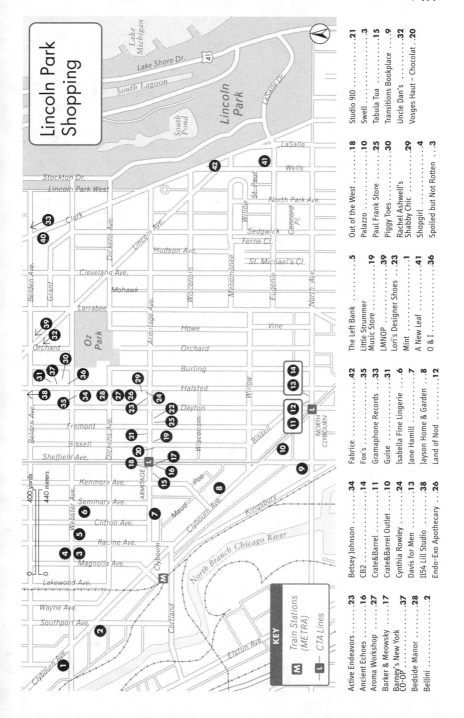

Lincoln Park Shopping

KEY

M Train Stations (METRA)

L CTA Lines

workshops, plus a café. A second location is inside the Unity in Chicago's spiritual center on the city's far north side. ⊠ *1000 W. North Ave., Lincoln Park* ☎ *312/951–7323* ✉ *1925 W. Thome Ave., West Ridge* ☎ *773/338–7323.*

FOR KIDS **Bellini.** Virtually everything a stylish baby will need is here, including high-end clothes, top-of-the-line bedroom furniture, luxury bedding, and accessories. ⊠ *2100 N. Southport Ave., Lincoln Park* ☎ *773/880–5840.*

Land of Nod. Crate&Barrel is next-door neighbor (and business partner) to this quirky-cool children's furniture store. There are plenty of parent-pleasing designs, plus loads of fun accessories, toys, and a great music section, too. ⊠ *900 W. North Ave., Lincoln Park* ☎ *312/475–9903.*

★ **Little Strummer Music Store.** Younger sibling to the Different Strummer store in Lincoln Square, this shop within the Old Town School of Folk Music specializes in children's music and instruments. They have a good selection of new and used instruments, plus violins and guitars for rent. ⊠ *909 W. Armitage Ave., Lincoln Park* ☎ *773/751–3410.*

LMNOP. Designers such as Flora & Henri and Cotton Caboodle create the fun clothes that are sold here for newborns and kids up to size 8. ⊠ *2570 N. Lincoln Ave., Lincoln Park* ☎ *773/975–4055.*

Piggy Toes. This store stocks a good selection of European footwear for well-heeled children. ⊠ *2205 N. Halsted St., Lincoln Park* ☎ *773/281–5583.*

Spoiled. . .but Not Rotten. The owner of Shopgirl and Swell adds to her Webster Avenue dynasty with this shop stocking the latest in hip threads for the preteen set. Lucky small-boned women can score jeans by Miss Sixty and Blue Cult Description here at a fraction of the grown-up prices. ⊠ *1207 W. Webster Ave., Lincoln Park* ☎ *773/935–1399.*

CLOTHING FOR MEN **Davis for Men.** The all-European labels at Chicago's hippest haberdasher run the gamut from business to casual wear, understated to avant-garde. ⊠ *824 W. North Ave., Lincoln Park* ☎ *312/266–9599* ✉ *900 North Michigan Shops, 900 N. Michigan Ave., Near North* ☎ *312/440–0016.*

Guise. For men who want to look good without all the energy it takes to make it happen, Guise is the place to go. This one-stop shop stocks designer clothes from the likes of Theory and Nicole Farhi, offers manicures, shoe shines, haircuts, barbershop-style shaves, and—to make the experience as painless as possible—serves complimentary beer to drink while catching a game on manly sized TVs. ⊠ *2217 N. Halsted St., Lincoln Park* ☎ *73/929–6101.*

CLOTHING FOR MEN & WOMEN **Active Endeavors.** Active Endeavors is where on-the-move types go for the latest brands of high-performance threads, plus the latest après-workout fashions that show off the results. ⊠ *853 W. Armitage Ave., Lincoln Park* ☎ *773/281–8100* ✉ *Shops at North Bridge, 55 E. Grand Ave., Near North* ☎ *312/822–0600.*

Barneys New York CO-OP. The first CO-OP in Chicago opened in 2005 and, like the others, is geared to younger Barneys customers, bucking convention in store design, layout, and inventory. ■ TIP➜ **Look for a huge designer denim inventory that includes brands like Stitch and Rogan for lasses, funky**

shoes, and a too-cool-for-school hipster vibe. ⊠ *2209–11 N. Halsted St., Lincoln Park* ☎ *773/248–0426.*

Out of the West. Whatever your Western style, be it Native American, farmhouse, or log cabin, you'll find a great selection of blue jeans, other clothing, and home furnishings to match here. A tailor visits the store weekly to do custom alterations on jeans. ⊠ *1000 W. Armitage Ave., Lincoln Park* ☎ *773/404–9378.*

Uncle Dan's. This is the place to go for camping equipment and outdoorsy fashions by brands like Marmot and The North Face. ⊠ *2440 N. Lincoln Ave., Lincoln Park* ☎ *773/477–1718.*

CLOTHING FOR WOMEN

Betsey Johnson. All of the bold designer's signature fun and over-the-top styles are here. ⊠ *2120 N. Halsted St., Lincoln Park* ☎ *773/871–3961.*

Cynthia Rowley. Cynthia Rowley is a Chicago-area native, and she fills her Lincoln Park store with the exuberant, well-priced dresses, separates, and accessories that have made her so popular. ⊠ *808 W. Armitage Ave., Lincoln Park* ☎ *773/528–6160.*

Fox's. Snap up canceled and overstocked designer clothes at 40%–70% discounts. New shipments come in several times a week, so there's always something new to try on. ⊠ *2150 N. Halsted, Lincoln Park* ☎ *773/281–0700.*

Jane Hamill. Jane Hamill is a local designer who sells must-have looks at reasonable prices to the Lincoln Park set. Dress Fancy by Jane Hamill is the designer's take on bridesmaid dresses—contemporary and feminine without any frightening frills. ⊠ *1117 W. Armitage Ave., Lincoln Park* ☎ *773/665–1102.*

Palazzo. Chic urban brides who want gowns with beautiful, subtle details, not reams of ruffles, trust designers Jane and Saeed Hamidi for their clean-lined bridal collection. ⊠ *2262 N. Clark St., Lincoln Park* ☎ *773/665–4044.*

Fodor'sChoice
★

Shopgirl. A following of devoted customers come here to find out what to wear next, and fall for pieces by Trina Turk, Ella Moss, and Citizens of Humanity. ⊠ *1206 W. Webster Ave., Lincoln Park* ☎ *773/935–7467.*

Studio 910. A friendly sales staff helps shoppers sort through the classic pieces from Diane von Furstenburg mixed in with funkier styles by labels like Tessuto. ⊠ *910 W. Armitage Ave., Lincoln Park* ☎ *773/929–2400.*

Swell. Hot mamas-to-be with an eye for fashion love Swell, an offspring of Shopgirl across the street. It's where they stock up on maternity clothes and accessories by Japanese Weekend, Blue Cult, and Michael Stars. ⊠ *1207 W. Webster Ave., Lincoln Park* ☎ *773/935–1349.*

GIFTS

Barker & Meowsky. This "paw firm" carries great gifts for dogs, cats, and humans. There are beautiful bowls, plush beds, picture frames, treats, and more—just the things to get tails wagging. ⊠ *1003 W. Armitage Ave., Lincoln Park* ☎ *773/868–0200.*

Paul Frank Store. Young fans of the designer's famous trademarked monkey, Julius, will find his likeness on stickers, slippers, and sunglasses. Scurvy, a skull and crossbones; Ellie, a pink elephant; and the designer's other kitschy characters are well represented here, too. ⊠ *851 W. Armitage Ave., Lincoln Park* ☎ *773/388–3122.*

5

Unpacking Crate&Barrel

GORDON AND CAROLE SEGAL saw a void in the Chicago retail market in 1962, and they set out to fill it by opening the first Crate&Barrel store in an abandoned elevator factory in the then-questionable Old Town neighborhood.

"I was doing the dishes—classic Arzberg dishes we had picked up on our Caribbean honeymoon—and I said to Carole, 'How come nobody is selling this dinnerware in Chicago?'," Gordon Segal recalls. 'I think we should open a store.' "

And, as they say, the rest is history. With "more taste than money," the Segals displayed their unique housewares en masse on the crates and barrels they were shipped in, and, in the process, found a niche and a name.

At a time when gas station give-away glasses were common kitchen table fixtures, shoppers were immediately drawn to the grocery store-style displays of contemporary merchandise at reasonable prices. (So reasonable, in fact, that some of the initial stock was sold below cost because the Segals came up with prices without checking their invoices.) As the business grew, store displays became more sophisticated and the inventory more diverse, but the underlying premise of abundance and affordability remained.

Before the age of home-improvement cable television shows, the Segals brought accessible design into the American home. They added the Finnish fabric line Marimekko to their inventory in the late 1960s, and the bold, colorful prints became a signature style of the era and remain an important part of Crate&Barrel's displays today.

Carole retired to raise their family, but Gordon Segal still runs the Chicago-based company they founded together 43 years ago, now a dominant home furnishings chain with 123 stores across the United States. Always keeping his motto, "Stay humble, stay nervous," in the back of his mind, Segal has continued to fine-tune Crate&Barrel throughout its history, creating shopping environments that engage the senses with striking visuals and inviting music. His goal has been to give the interiors of his stores a bazaarlike atmosphere, with new and different merchandise around every corner. He pays close attention to the exteriors, too, focusing on building stores with architectural merit. Stores in Illinois, Pennsylvania, and Chicago have received awards for their outstanding architectural design.

The home furnishings industry has exploded since Crate&Barrel's humble beginnings, and Segal has kept a keen eye on what interests the buying public. In 2000 Crate&Barrel launched CB2, a new concept store aimed at a young urban market with—again—a single store on Chicago's north side. The bolder colors and materials here have found an audience, and the company soon plans to roll out more stores in other cities. And, so that no one in the family feels left out, in 2001 Crate&Barrel formed a partnership with Land of Nod, a quirky children's furniture catalog company. They opened one store—guess where?—on Chicago's north side to start, and have since expanded to five locations. The Segal empire just keeps growing.

—By Judy Sutton Taylor

Vosges Haut-Chocolat. Local chocolatier Katrina Markoff's exotic truffles, flavored with spices like curry and ancho chili, have fans across the globe. She's recently expanded the Vosges line to include sweet treats in pretty hat boxes and even yogawear and dresses. ⊠ *951 W. Armitage Ave., Lincoln Park* ☎ *773/296–9866* ✉ *520 N. Michigan Ave., Near North* ☎ *312/822–0600.*

FOR THE HOME **Ancient Echoes.** The ornamented home items here, from decorative boxes and vases to chests, often incorporate references to allegorical symbols from cultures all over the world. ⊠ *1022A W. Armitage St., Lincoln Park* ☎ *773/880–1003.*

Bedside Manor. Dreamland is even more inviting with these handcrafted beds and lush designer linens, many of which come in interesting jacquard weaves or are nicely trimmed and finished. ⊠ *2056 N. Halsted St., Lincoln Park* ☎ *773/404–2020.*

Fodor'sChoice **CB2.** A concept store by furniture giant Crate&Barrel, CB2 is unique to
★ Chicago—for now. The idea is stylish, bold basics for trendy urban abodes, all sans big-ticket price tags. ⊠ *800 W. North Ave., Lincoln Park* ☎ *312/787–8329.*

Crate&Barrel. There's plenty to "Oooh" and "Aaah" about throughout the three floors of stylish home furnishings and kitchenware at Crate&Barrel's flagship location. There's plenty of free parking, and you can even take a break from your heavy-duty shopping at the top-floor café. ⊠ *850 W. North Ave., Lincoln Park* ☎ *312/573–9800.*

Crate&Barrel Outlet. Around the corner from the massive flagship store, the outlet carries odds and ends from the company's houseware and kitchen lines. Look for discounts of up to 75% on out-of-season items. ⊠ *1846 N. Clybourn Ave., Lincoln Park* ☎ *312/787–4775.*

Jayson Home & Garden. Loaded with new and vintage European and American furnishings, this decor store carries the Mitchell Gold line. Look for oversize cupboards and armoires and decorative accessories, plus stylish garden furniture and a bevy of beautiful floral arrangements. ⊠ *1885 N. Clybourn Ave., Lincoln Park* ☎ *773/248–8180.*

★ **A New Leaf.** The grande dame of Chicago home and garden shops has one of the best selections of fresh flowers in town. The Wells Street stores stock singular antique and vintage furnishings and accessories as well as a mind-boggling selection of candles, vases, tiles, and pots. ⊠ *1818 N. Wells St., Lincoln Park* ☎ *312/642–8553* ✉ *1645 N. Wells St., Lincoln Park* ☎ *312/642–1576* ✉ *Chicago Place, 700 N. Michigan Ave., Near North* ☎ *773/871–3610.*

Rachel Ashwell's Shabby Chic. A Victorian row house just off Michigan Avenue is one of the six national outposts of this designer of cushy, slip-covered furniture fame. Besides the upholstered pieces there's a complete stock of housewares, including an extraordinary lighting selection and a retro-inspired line of bedding. ⊠ *2146 N. Halsted St., Lincoln Park* ☎ *773/327–9372.*

Tabula Tua. The colorful, contemporary, mix-and-match dishes and tabletop accessories here are worlds away from standard formal china. Other offerings include breathtaking mosaic tables handmade to order, rustic furniture crafted from old barn wood, and sleek, polished pewter pieces. ⊠ *1015 W. Armitage Ave., Lincoln Park* ☎ *773/525–3500.*

Fodor'sChoice
★
SHOES

Lori's Designer Shoes. Owner Lori Andre's obsession with shoes takes her on biannual trips to Europe to scour for styles you won't likely see at department stores. The result is an inventory that many fine-footed women consider to be the best in Chicago. Shoes by designers like Gastone Luciole, janet & janet, and more well-known ones like Steve Madden are sold at competitive prices. Terrific handbags, jewelry, bridal shoes, and other accessories are also available. ⊠ *824 W. Armitage Ave., Lincoln Park* ☎ *773/281–5655.*

O & I. The chic European footwear for babies, kids, and adults sold here is hard to find elsewhere in the city. ⊠ *2203 N. Halsted St., Lincoln Park* ☎ *773/281–5583.*

Lake View

Lake View, a large, diverse neighborhood just north of Lincoln Park, has spawned a number of worthwhile shopping strips, including a wealth of antiques shops around Belmont and Ashland avenues. **Clark Street** between Diversey Avenue and Addison Street has myriad clothing boutiques and specialty stores, as well as Chicago Cubs paraphernalia as you approach Wrigley Field at Addison. Farther north on **Halsted Street** between Belmont Avenue and Addison Street are more gift shops and boutiques—many with a gay orientation—as well as a smattering of vintage-clothing and antiques stores. In West Lake View, the new hot spot is **Southport Avenue** between Belmont Avenue and Grace Street , where a recent onslaught of boutiques with a bent toward trendy upscale fashion have put it on the "must" list. **Broadway** between Diversey Avenue and Addison Street also claims its share of intriguing shops geared to twentysomething hipsters. The **Century Mall,** in a former movie palace at Clark Street, Broadway, and Diversey Parkway, houses stores catering to a young and trendy crowd. To reach this neighborhood from downtown, take the 22 Clark Street bus at Dearborn Street or the 36 Broadway bus at State Street heading north. Or, take the Howard (Red Line) or Ravenswood (Brown Line) El north to the Belmont stop from downtown, which will drop you into the heart of Lake View.

Antiques Districts

BELMONT
AVENUE

Fans of art deco, kitchen collectibles, and bar memorabilia can poke into the shops and malls lining Belmont Avenue, starting a bit west of Ashland Avenue and running to Western Avenue. You may have to scrounge around to unearth treasures in these stores, but the prices are some of the lowest in the city. The shops are usually open weekends but may be closed on one or more weekdays. Call before making a special trip.

WORD OF MOUTH

"There's quite unique shopping in the Lincoln Park area with its small boutiques. Similar shopping areas radiate from Lincoln Park, such as Lake View. Walk north along Halsted to Addison. You'll find some great vintage clothing stores. Then cross over to Broadway and head back south. Broadway has some unusual shops."

–Susie

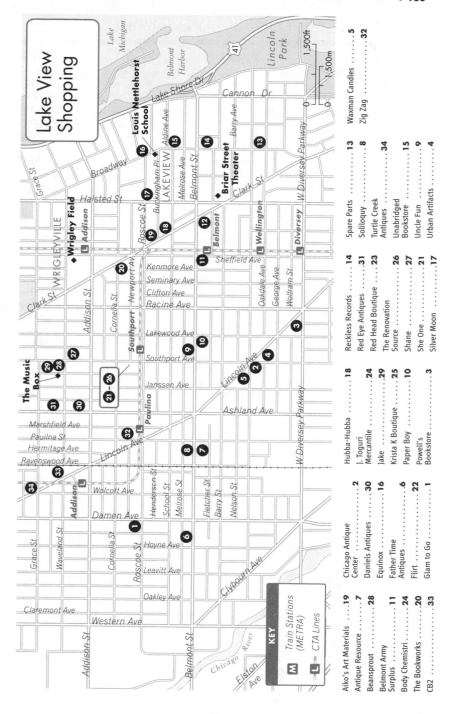

Lake View Shopping

Lake Michigan

Belmont Harbor

Lincoln Park

41

Louis Nettlehorst School

Lake Shore Dr

Cannon Dr

Broadway

LAKEVIEW

Grace St

Wrigley Field

Halsted St

Addison

WRIGLEYVILLE

Clark St

Briar Street Theater

Belmont St

Melrose St

Aldine Ave

Buckingham Pl

Roscoe St

Clark St

Belmont

Wellington

Diversey

W Diversey Parkway

Barry Ave

Sheffield Ave

Kenmore Ave

Seminary Ave

Clifton Ave

Racine Ave

Oakdale Ave

George Ave

Wolfram St

Lakewood Ave

Southport Ave

Janssen Ave

Ashland Ave

Lincoln Ave

The Music Box

Addison St

Cornelia St

Newport Av

Southport

Paulina

W Diversey Parkway

Marshfield Ave

Paulina St

Hermitage Ave

Ravenswood Ave

Lincoln Ave

Wolcott Ave

Damen Ave

Henderson St

School St

Melrose St

Fletcher St

Barry St

Nelson St

Grace St

Waveland St

Cornelia St

Roscoe St

Hoyne Ave

Leavitt Ave

Oakley Ave

Claremont Ave

Western Ave

Addison St

Belmont St

Clybourn Ave

Chicago River

Elston Ave

1,500ft

0

1,500m

0

KEY

Ⓜ Train Stations (METRA)

Ⓛ CTA Lines

Blitz Tour: One-of-a-Kind Finds

Get ready for some serious spending—or at least some serious ogling. This itinerary is geared to the antique lover in you; find exact addresses in the chapter's store listings.

Chicago tempts buyers with antiques, collectibles, and architectural artifacts at prices that generally beat those on either coast. In fact, dealers from both coasts regularly troll these shops, which are clustered mostly in neighborhoods or malls, for stock to resell in their own shops. For a rundown on dealers, buy a copy of *Taylor's Guide to Antique Shops in Illinois & Southern Wisconsin* ($6), which is available in some bookstores and many antiques shops (to order, call ☎ 847/465-3314). Many antiques districts also publish free pamphlets that list dealers in the neighborhood; look for them in the shops.

To catch the maximum number of open dealers, it's best to tackle this route after brunch on a weekend or on a Thursday or Friday. Assuming your interest runs more toward 20th-century collectibles than Biedermeier, this tour focuses mostly on the west Lake View neighborhood (north of Lincoln Park and west of Wrigley Field). Take the 11 Lincoln Avenue bus or a taxi to the **Chicago Antique Centre** to browse through the wares of its 35 dealers. Keep your eyes open for other antiques and vintage-clothing shops along this stretch of Lincoln Avenue. Two superb sources for adventurous, mid-20th-century, modern furnishings and collectibles are **Urban Artifacts** and **Zig Zag.** Venture north on Ashland Avenue to check out the 19th- and 20th-century furnishings at **Daniels Antiques** and **Red Eye Antiques,** crammed to the gills with an eclectic selection of prime furnishings, textiles, and artifacts from different eras that you won't find elsewhere.

There are four other compelling destinations for collectors that are short cab rides away. **Architectural Artifacts** is an amazing repository for statuary, garden ornaments, and the like. **Evanstonia Antiques & Restoration** carries English and Continental furnishings. **Lincoln Antique Mall** stockpiles everything from kitchenware to furniture, mostly post-1920. There's also a huge selection of estate jewelry and photographs. Farthest north on the antiques trail is the **Broadway Antique Market,** with its excellent stash of mid-20th-century pieces that range from art deco and Arts and Crafts to modernism and beyond.

Antique Resources. Choice Georgian antiques are sold at fair prices here. This is an excellent source for stately desks and dignified dining sets, but the true find is a huge trove—numbering more than 300—of antique crystal and gilt chandeliers from France. ⊠ *1741 W. Belmont Ave., Lake View* ☎ *773/871–4242.*

Father Time Antiques. Father Time bills itself as the Midwest's largest restorer of vintage timepieces; it also stocks vintage Victorian and art deco European furniture. ⊠ *2108 W. Belmont Ave., Lake View* ☎ *773/880–5599.*

A 1½-mi stretch of Lincoln Avenue is noted for its funky antiques, collectibles, and vintage clothing. The shops start around the intersection of Lincoln Avenue and Diversey Parkway and continue until Irving Park Road. A car or the 11 Lincoln Avenue bus is the best way to navigate this area. To get the bus from downtown, take the Howard (Red Line) or Ravenswood (Brown Line) El to the Fullerton stop; after exiting the El station, walk ½ block east to the intersection of Fullerton and Lincoln. Then catch the 11 Lincoln Avenue bus to your stop. Most of these shops are open weekends but may be closed early in the week.

Chicago Antique Centre. Open seven days a week, this one-stop spot houses 35 dealers, some with especially good selections of vintage dishes and jewelry. ⊠ *3036 N. Lincoln Ave., Lake View* ☏ *773/929–0200.*

Daniels Antiques. Five blocks north of the six-way Lincoln, Belmont, and Ashland intersection, this cavernous shop shelters a huge stash of Victorian and 20th-century furnishings, especially larger pieces and complete sets. ⊠ *3711 N. Ashland Ave., Lake View* ☏ *773/868–9355.*

Red Eye Antiques. Red Eye begs to be browsed; it's so overloaded with prime furnishings, accessories, and paintings that something catches your eye with every scan of the shop. Items vary widely in age and price; some date back to the 1500s, others are just a few decades old. ⊠ *3715 N Ashland Ave., Lake View* ☏ *773/975–2020.*

The Renovation Source. Home renovators and anyone else looking for cool design finds will have a blast sifting through all kinds of treasures here, from stained-glass windows and reclaimed finials to one-of-a-kind medicine cabinets and door knobs. ⊠ *3512 N. Southport Ave., Lake View* ☏ *773/327–1750.*

Turtle Creek Antiques. Consider this a key source for antique and vintage quilts, tabletop pieces, linens, furniture (mostly Victorian), and estate jewelry. Just about every piece is in mint condition at this shop on the northern tip of the neighborhood. ⊠ *3817 N. Lincoln Ave., Lake View* ☏ *773/327–2630.*

Urban Artifacts. A superb selection of furniture, lighting, and decorative accessories from the 1940s to the '70s emphasizes the industrial designs that are a popular theme in modern furnishings. ⊠ *2928 N. Lincoln Ave., Lake View* ☏ *773/404–1008.*

Zig Zag. Zig Zag displays a well-edited collection of pristine art deco and modern furnishings and jewelry. ⊠ *3419 N. Lincoln Ave., Lake View* ☏ *773/525–1060.*

Specialty Stores

The Bookworks. The stock here includes more than 40,000 titles, most of them used and/or rare. There's an emphasis on sports (for Cubs fans strolling by from nearby Wrigley Field) and contemporary fiction. Check out the vintage vinyl record section. ⊠ *3444 N. Clark St., Lake View* ☏ *773/871–5318.*

Powell's Bookstore. This is one of the oldest and most reliable independent book shops around; the strength here is the section featuring art, architecture, and photography. Also check out the impressive collection of rare books. ⊠ *2850 N. Lincoln Ave., Lake View* ☏ *773/248–1444.*

CHAIN STORES	Women's Apparel	Men's Apparel	Kid's Stuff	Books & Music	Accessories	Furniture & Home	Bath & Beauty	Kitchenware	Notable Outposts	Neighborhood
American Apparel	•	•							46 E. Walton St.	Near North
	•	•							837 W. Armitage Ave.	Lincoln Park
	•	•							1563 N. Milwaukee Ave.	Wicker Park
Anthropologie	•				•	•	•		1120 N. State St.	Near North
Banana Republic	•	•			•				Water Tower Place	Mag Mile
	•	•			•				744 N. Michigan Ave.	Mag Mile
Barnes & Noble				•	•				1130 N. State St.	Near North
				•	•				1441 W. Webster Ave.	Lincoln Park
Borders				•	•				150 N. State St.	Loop
				•	•				830 N. Michigan Ave.	Mag Mile
				•	•				755 W. North Ave.	Lincoln Park
Crate&Barrel						•		•	646 N. Michigan Ave.	Mag Mile
						•		•	850 W. North Ave.	Lincoln Park
Design Within Reach						•			10 E. Ohio St.	River North
						•			1574 N. Kinsbury St.	Lincoln Park
The Gap	•	•	•		•				555 N. Michigan Ave.	Mag Mile
	•	•	•		•				935 W. North Ave.	Lincoln Park
H&M	•	•			•				22 N. State St.	Loop
	•	•			•				840 N. Michigan Ave.	Mag Mile
J.Crew	•	•			•				900 N. Michigan Ave.	Mag Mile
Lush							•		859 W. Armitage Ave.	Lincoln Park
Nordstrom Rack	•	•							24 N. State St.	Loop
L'Occitane en Provence							•		900 N. Michigan Ave.	Mag Mile
Old Navy	•	•	•		•				35 N. State St.	Loop
	•	•	•		•				1596 N. Kinsbury St.	Lincoln Park
Pottery Barn						•		•	734 N. Michigan Ave.	Mag Mile
						•		•	856 W. North Ave.	Lincoln Park
Pottery Barn Kids			•			•			2111 N. Clybourn Ave.	Lincoln Park
Restoration Hardware						•		•	938 W. North Ave.	Lincoln Park
Sephora							•		520 N. Michigan Ave.	Mag Mile
							•		845 N. Michigan Ave.	Mag Mile
Sharper Image					•	•			Water Tower Place	Mag Mile
					•	•			55 W. Monroe St.	Loop
Sur La Table								•	52–54 E. Walton St.	Near North
								•	755 W. North Ave.	Lincoln Park
Tower Records/Videos/Books				•	•				214 S. Wabash Ave.	Loop
				•	•				2301 N. Clark St.	Lincoln Park
T. J. Maxx	•	•	•		•				11 N. State St.	Loop
Urban Outfitters	•	•			•				935 N. Rush St.	Near North
	•	•			•				2352 N. Clark St.	Lincoln Park
Virgin Megastore				•					540 N. Michigan Ave.	Mag Mile
Williams-Sonoma								•	900 N. Michigan Ave.	Mag Mile

Soliloquy. Picking up where the old Act I bookstore left off, Soliloquy has the largest inventory of theater, film, and television materials in the city. ✉ *1724 W. Belmont Ave., Lake View* ☎ *773/348–6757.*

Unabridged Bookstore. This independent bookshop has maintained a loyal clientele for more than 20 years who love its vast selection and dedicated staff. ■ TIP➔ **Known for having one of the most extensive gay and lesbian selections in the city, it also has an impressive children's section and great magazines, too.** ✉ *3251 N. Broadway, Lake View* ☎ *773/883–9119.*

CLOTHING FOR MEN & WOMEN
Belmont Army Surplus. Puma, Diesel, and other funky brands get mixed in with fatigues, flak jackets, and even faux fur coats in this 20,000 square foot store, a neighborhood mainstay. Despite the name, don't expect too many bargains. ✉ *945 W. Belmont Ave., Lake View* ☎ *773/975–0626.*

Flirt. You'll find designs for women by Ben Sherman and Left of Center, plus the latest handbag and jewelry finds at this cute boutique. ✉ *3449 N. Southport Ave., Lake View* ☎ *773/935–4789.*

Hubba-Hubba. Well-chosen vintage clothing mixes smoothly with new clothing with a retro flavor. Jewelry and accessories convey the same period mood. ✉ *3309 N. Clark St., Lake View* ☎ *773/477–1414.*

★ **Jake.** The hip and down-to-earth owners stock men's and women's clothing by up-and-coming designers. An instant favorite from the moment it opened its doors, Jake recently opened a sister store just off the Mag Mile that's not as jeans-and-T-shirt heavy as the original. ✉ *3740 N. Southport Ave., Lake View* ☎ *773/929–5253* ✉ *939 N. Rush St., Near North* ☎ *312/664–5533.*

Krista K Boutique. An inventory of must-haves for women from designers like Citizens of Humanity, Theory, and Helen Wang reflects the style of the neighborhood. The shop has become the go-to spot for the latest denim trends, and a favorite pick for expectant moms with money to burn on the likes of Liz Lange Maternity Wear. ✉ *3458 N. Southport Ave., Lake View* ☎ *773/248–1967.*

Red Head Boutique. This colorful jewel of a shop carries girly clothes with a fun and funky edge, suitable for young trendoids and cool neighborhood moms alike. Look for local labels like Doris Ruth and hard-to-find ones like Beverly & Monika. ✉ *3450 N. Southport Ave., Lake View* ☎ *773/325–9898.*

Shane. This is a great stop for the latest in casual urban duds for guys and girls, including Lawd Knows, Three Dots, and a good selection of vintage T-shirts. ✉ *3657 N. Southport Ave., Lake View* ☎ *773/549–0179.*

She One. A plentiful assortment of bright T-shirts and trendy jewelry dresses the stylish young urban woman. ✉ *3402 N. Southport Ave., Lake View* ☎ *773/549–9698.*

Silver Moon. Vintage wedding gowns and tuxedos are a specialty at Silver Moon, which also showcases less formal vintage clothing and accessories for men and women. ✉ *3337 N. Halsted St., Lake View* ☎ *773/883–0222.*

FOR KIDS
Beansprout. Beansprout carries supercute kids clothes up to size 6x for girls and 6 for boys in fabrics that won't itch, scratch, or (hopefully) become showcases for stains. ✉ *3732 N. Southport Ave., Lake View* ☎ *773/472–4780.*

5

GIFTS & GOODIES **Body Chemistri.** This longtime Evanston favorite for lotions, salves, and aromatherapy goodies recently opened a second location here. You'll find old standbys like Rosebud Salve, in addition to popular bodycare lines like Korres. Alcohol-free essential oils in scents like French lavender and honeysuckle can be mixed into lotions, shampoos, and other bath products. The company has a strict no-animal testing policy for its products. ⊠ *3451 N. Southport Ave., Lake View* ☎ *773/296–4999.*

Glam to Go. The lotions and potions found here will help you stay soft and smelling good, plus there are candles, makeup, and toys for tykes. ⊠ *2002 W. Roscoe St., Lake View* ☎ *773/525–7004.*

Spare Parts. The selection of fine leather goods here draws on a gamut of sources, including Village Tannery, Jack Spade, and local designer Susan Fitch. Jewelry, bath and body products, and home accessories round out the selection. ⊠ *2947 N. Broadway, Lake View* ☎ *773/525–4242.*

Uncle Fun. The astonishing and goofy inventory of new and vintage tricks, gags, party favors, and more, delight young and old—as do the reasonable prices. ■ TIP→ **Think trendy bobblehead dolls and the Official John Travolta Picture/Postcard book.** The store is closed Monday. ⊠ *1338 W. Belmont Ave., Lake View* ☎ *773/477–8223.*

Waxman Candles. The candles sold here are made on the premises and come in countless shapes, colors, and scents. There's an incredible selection of holders for votives and pillars, and incense, too. ⊠ *3044 N. Lincoln Ave., Lake View* ☎ *773/929–3000.*

Fodor'sChoice **CB2.** House-proud locals with tight budgets come to this Crate&Barrel
★ offshoot for kitchenware and accessories that look great but don't break
FOR THE HOME the bank. ⊠ *3757 N. Lincoln Ave., Lake View* ☎ *773/755–3900.*

Equinox. Equinox literally glows from within, thanks to its Tiffany-style lamps, but the true strength here is the selection of Arts and Crafts–style art tiles and reproduction pottery. ⊠ *3401 N. Broadway Ave., Lake View* ☎ *773/281–9151* ⊠ *609 N. State St., River North* ☎ *312/335–8006.*

J. Toguri Mercantile Company. This warehouse-style store carries all things Asian, including tea sets, lacquerware, kimonos, hard-to-find pots, and Japanese music. ⊠ *851 W. Belmont Ave., Lake View* ☎ *773/929–3500.*

MUSIC STORES **Reckless Records.** Reckless Records ranks as one of the city's leading alternative and secondhand record stores. Besides the indie offerings, you can flip through jazz, classical, and soul recordings, or catch a live appearance by an up-and-comer passing through town. ⊠ *3161 N. Broadway, Lake View* ☎ *773/404–5080.*

PAPER **Aiko's Art Materials.** Hundreds of stenciled, marbled, textured, and tie-dyed papers—most from Japan—attract the creatively inclined. You can find bookbinding materials here, too. ⊠ *3347 N. Clark St., Lake View* ☎ *773/404–5600.*

Paper Boy. A hip sensibility informs the cards, gift wrap, and invitations sold here by the people who bring you the quirky goods at Uncle Fun across the street. ⊠ *1351 W. Belmont Ave., Lake View* ☎ *773/388–8811.*

Worth a Special Trip

Antiques & Collectibles

Architectural Artifacts. The selection matches the warehouse proportions here. The mammoth two-story space houses oversize garden ornaments (arbors, benches), statuary, iron grills, fixtures, and decorative tiles. Architectural fragments—marble, metal, wood, terra-cotta—hail from American and European historic buildings. ⊠ *4325 N. Ravenswood Ave., Ravenswood* ☎ *773/348–0622.*

★ **Broadway Antique Market.** More than 75 hand-picked dealers, plus quality that is more carefully monitored than at most malls, make it worth the trek to the Broadway Antique Market, affectionately called BAM! by its loyal fans. Mid-20th century is the primary emphasis, but items range from Arts and Crafts and art deco to Heywood-Wakefield. Display is the market's strong suit—the furniture, jewelry, and bibelots are wonderfully presented. The building itself is a prime example of deco architecture; it's near the Thorndale stop on the Red Line. The Edgewater Antique Mall (6314 N. Broadway), which specializes in 20th-century goods, is a couple of blocks north. ⊠ *6130 N. Broadway, Edgewater* ☎ *773/743–5444.*

Evanstonia Antiques & Restoration. This dealer has a rich collection of fine English and Continental antiques. ⊠ *4555 N. Ravenswood Ave., North Center* ☎ *773/907–0101.*

Lincoln Antique Mall. Dozens of dealers carrying antiques and collectibles share this large space. There's a good selection of French and mid-20th-century modern furniture, plus estate jewelry, oil paintings, and photographs, but you can find virtually anything and everything here. ⊠ *3115 W. Irving Park Rd., North Center* ☎ *773/604–4700.*

★ **Salvage One.** An enormous warehouse chock-full of stained lead glass, garden ornaments, fireplace mantels, bathtubs, bars, and other architectural artifacts draws creative home remodelers and restaurant designers from around the country. ■ TIP→ This is a great place to hunt for all kinds of treasures, from vintage dental chairs to Paris street lamps. ⊠ *1840 W. Hubbard St., Ukrainian Village* ☎ *312/733–0098.*

Apothecary

★ **Merz Apothecary.** Homeopathic and herbal remedies, as well as hard-to-find European toiletries, are available at Merz Apothecary, about 6½ mi northwest of the Loop. It's closed Sunday. There's an outlet in the Macy's on State Street as well. ⊠ *4716 N. Lincoln Ave., Lincoln Square* ☎ *773/989–0900.*

FORTH & TOWNE

Corporate types at the Gap chose the Chicago suburbs as one of two test markets for its latest concept (after the Gap, Banana Republic, and Old Navy), called Forth & Towne. This new chain, launched in fall 2005, is targeted for women 35 and older with fashions that can go from the office to an after-school soccer game. You can visit them in suburban shopping malls at Old Orchard Shopping Center in Skokie, Woodfield Shopping Center in Schaumburg, Algonquin Commons in Algonquin, and Fox Valley Center in Aurora.

5

Auctions

Susanin's Auctioneers and Appraisers. Live, usually themed, sales occur on Saturday mornings in a 35,000-square-foot location in the South Loop. Preview items are also displayed on the floor for immediate sale at a set price. Preview hours are Monday through Saturday from 10 AM to 5 PM. ✉ *900 S. Clinton St., South Loop* ☎ *312/832–9800.*

Book & Music Stores

Afrocentric Bookstore. Owner Desiree Sanders's store is dedicated entirely to African-American literature, though you'll also find some jewelry and gift items. ✉ *4655 S. King Dr., Bronzeville* ☎ *773/924–3966.*

★ **Different Strummer Store.** Musical products of every type—from acoustic and electric instruments to sheet music, books, and CDs can be found here. The Armitage Avenue Little Strummer store stocks kid-size instruments and accessories. ✉ *4544 N. Lincoln Ave., Lincoln Square* ☎ *773/ 751–3398.*

Women & Children First. This feminist bookstore 6½ mi north of the Loop stocks fiction and nonfiction, periodicals, journals, small-press publications, and a strong selection of gay and lesbian titles. The children's section has a great array of books, all politically correct. ✉ *5233 N. Clark St., Andersonville* ☎ *773/769–9299.*

Cameras & Electronics

Helix Camera & Video. Professional photographers buy and rent camera and darkroom equipment at this eight-story warehouse on Racine Avenue just west of Greektown (1½ mi west of the Loop). A good selection of used equipment is available, and underwater photography is a specialty. ✉ *310 S. Racine Ave., Near West Side* ☎ *312/421–6000.*

Factory Outlets & Off-Price Stores

Gap Factory Outlet. Take a detour to net substantial savings on overruns and seconds on Gap men's, women's, and children's clothing. ✉ *2778 N. Milwaukee Ave., Logan Square* ☎ *773/252–0594.*

Mark Shale Outlet. Unsold men's and women's clothing from Mark Shale stores is available here for 30%–70% less than the original retail price. In a strip shopping center about 2¼ mi northwest of the Loop, this outlet stocks corporate and weekend clothing from the likes of Polo and Joseph Abboud. ✉ *2593 N. Elston Ave., Logan Square* ☎ *773/772–9600.*

For Home & Garden

Sprout Home. If your tastes run toward modern furnishings, you'll drool over every nook and cranny of this store, which sells lines like Vessel, Pure, and Thomas Paul for your indoor life, plus unusual plants and gardening products for your outdoor one. ✉ *745 N. Damen Ave., Ukrainian Village* ☎ *312/226–5950.*

Western

Alcala's Western Wear. Alcala stocks more than 10,000 pairs of cowboy boots—many in exotic skins—for men, women, and children. About 2½ mi west of Michigan Avenue, it's a bit out of the way, but the amazing array of Stetson hats and rodeo gear makes this a must-see for cowboys, caballeros, and country-and-western dancers. ✉ *1733 W. Chicago Ave., Ukrainian Village* ☎ *312/226–0152.*

Where to Eat

WORD OF MOUTH

"For breakfast, Orange in Lincoln Park is not to be missed. I had eggs benedict made with filet mignon (instead of Canadian bacon) over brioche, topped with hollandaise sauce and a drizzle of balsamic vinegar."

—sweet_polly

"Alinea is an amazing place. Some bites that you will always remember. I highly recommend that you go once."

—Lightspeed_Chick

www.fodors.com/forums

DINING PLANNER

Reservations

You know the drill: if you want a table at one of the city's hot spots, especially for a weekend, you should have called yesterday. You can call day-of and hope for a cancellation; otherwise, book as far in advance as possible. For everywhere else, you can make reservations as late as a day or two in advance. Lots of places have a limited-reservations policy: half of the available tables are reserved and the rest are first-come, first-served.

Raves & Faves

Favorite Sidekick: *Avec*, next door to *Blackbird*

Square Deal for a Square Meal: Pizza at *Pompeii*

All-American Style: The Supper Club Menu at *RL*

Most Durable Shtick: "Cheezborgers" at the *Billy Goat*

View That Just Won't Quit: The lake as seen from *Spiaggia*

Finest Frugal French: *Bistrot Margot*

What to Wear

For the most part, this is an informal dining town, and neat, casual attire is acceptable in most places. Smart looks—collars for men, trendy threads for women, no denim for either—suffice at the growing spate of upscale but not stuffy restaurants like tru and Alinea. Jackets are appropriate in many formal hotel dining rooms. In the reviews dress is mentioned only when men are required to wear a jacket or jacket and tie.

Local Labels

Goose Island Beer is brewed locally and is featured in many restaurants and stores. Chef Rick Bayless's Frontera Grill line of chips, salsas, and sauces is sold at grocery stores and gourmet shops. Vosges Haut-Chocolate is based in Chicago and sells their truffles at the Peninsula Hotel and other fine retail locales. Eli's Cheesecakes are sold around town and from a kiosk at O'Hare Airport.

Taxes & Tipping

As a rule, you should tip 15% in restaurants in the lower price categories. You can double the 9.5% meal tax (fractionally higher in some parts of town, thanks to special taxing initiatives) when you feel generous. More expensive ($$$ and $$$$) establishments have more service personnel per table, who must divide the tip, so leave 20% (depending on the service, of course). An especially helpful wine steward should be acknowledged with around $5.

Prices

WHAT IT COSTS

	$$$$	$$$	$$	$	¢
Restaurants	over $28	$20–$28	$15–$20	$7–$15	under $7

Restaurant prices are for a main course at dinner.

By Elaine
Glusac

However you judge a city's dining scene—by ethnic diversity, breadth
and depth of high-quality establishments, or nationally prominent
chefs—Chicago ranks as one of the nation's finest restaurant towns.
Chicago's more than 7,000 restaurants range from those ranked among
the best in the country—and priced accordingly—to simple storefront
ethnic places and old-fashioned, unpretentious pubs serving good food
at modest prices.

Chicago's most sophisticated cooking, once clustered neatly downtown,
is increasingly busting the confines of the Loop. Many of the city's most
exciting meals require an outing to Wicker Park (Spring, Mirai Sushi),
nearby West Loop (Nine, Blackbird, Avec), or the north's Lincoln Square
(Bistro Campagne).

There's a rational price-geography correlation in Chicago: the closer you
eat to downtown, the more you pay. But venture into the residential neighborhoods and you not only dine well but reasonably. Bistrot Margot in
the Old Town section of Lincoln Park, for example, upholds downtown
standards but holds the line on prices. Farther afield, you find person-
able places that do not rely on the business crowd to survive, such as
La Petite Folie to the south, Erwin to the north, and plenty of spots in
between—all well worth seeking out.

6

Loop

The Loop rounds up some nostalgic old-timers like Berghoff alongside
tourist hotel cafés and power-eateries specializing in expense-account meals.
Lunches are all about convenience in the city's central business district.
Dinners tend to be slammed with theatergoers before 7:30 PM but fairly
relaxed later (though note that they don't stay open late on weekdays).

Contemporary

$$–$$$$ ✕**Rhapsody.** Attached to the Symphony Center, home of the Chicago
Symphony, Rhapsody is more than a handy spot for a preconcert din-
ner. This restaurant combines fine-dining ambitions with a pleasant
urban greenhouse setting graced by potted palms and picture windows.
Chefs seem to come and go here, but the food is consistently solid. The
handsome bar, pouring an expansive wine-by-the-glass selection, is a per-
fect post-performance hangout. ✉ *65 E. Adams St., Loop* ☎ *312/786–
9911* ▭ *AE, D, DC, MC, V* ☺ *Closed Sun. mid-June–mid-Sept. No lunch
weekends.*

$$–$$$ ✕**Atwood Café.** The Loop can be all business, even after-hours, but we
found an enclave of personality at this spot in the Hotel Burnham. Ma-
hogany columns, cherrywood floors, gold café curtains, and curvy ban-
quettes provide color, and floor-to-ceiling windows provide light. The mostly
American menu includes reliables like chicken potpie and thick pork
chops, peppered by contemporary fare such as duck and manchego que-
sadillas and grilled salmon with charred tomato sauce. ✉ *Hotel Burnham,
1 W. Washington St., Loop* ☎ *312/368–1900* ▭ *AE, D, DC, MC, V.*

$–$$$ ✕**Park Grill.** Location trumps service at Park Grill, where a seat on the
patio in summer, in full view of Millennium Park, is among the best in
the city. Sadly, the waitstaff lapses—grin and bear it with another drink

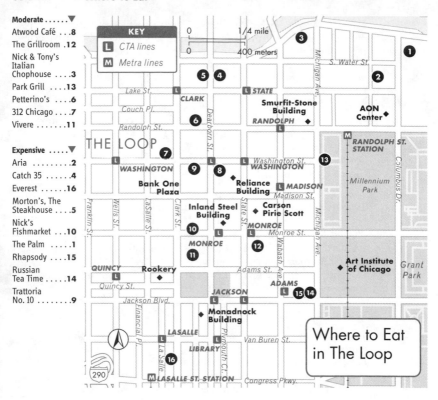

from the outdoor bar. The burgers are first rate, as is the more ambi-tious seasonal fare. A grab-and-go window supplies park picnics. In win-ter the scene moves indoors as indulgent calorie consumers watch ice-skating athletes through picture windows. ✉ *Millennium Park, 11 N. Michigan Ave., Loop* ☎ *312/521–7275* ⊟ *AE, D, DC, MC, V.*

Eclectic

$$$–$$$$ ✗ **Aria.** Can't decide between Moroccan, Asian, or Mediterranean? Take your globe-trotting tastebuds to Aria, which roams the world larder with abandon: sashimi tuna salad from Japan, lamb tagine from Morocco, carpaccio from Italy, soy-glazed cod from Malaysia, duck con-fit from France, and the requisite American steaks. Among generous free-bies, tandoori baked bread with Indian-inspired dipping sauces arrives before the meal and a trio of exotically spiced potatoes comes with the entrées. Art from the Far East visually reinforces Aria's Asian predilec-tions. In the convivial lounge, a small plate menu caters to abbreviated but equally adventurous appetites. ✉ *Fairmont Chicago, 200 N. Colum-bus Dr., Loop* ☎ *312/444–9494* ⊟ *AE, D, DC, MC, V.*

French

$$$–$$$$ ✗ **Everest.** No one expects romance at the top of the Chicago Stock Ex-change, but Everest does its best to throw you a curve wherever and whenever. Consider the trip: two separate elevators whisk you 40 stories up, where you have sweeping views of the city's sprawl westward. Then, there's the food. It's French, but with an Alsatian bent—a nod to Chef Jean Joho's roots. He might just add edible gold leaf to his risotto (and you'll pay handsomely for it). The whole experience, from the tuxedoed waiters to the massive wine list, screams, "Special occasion!" ⊠ *440 S. LaSalle St., Loop* ☎ *312/663–8920* ⌁ *Reservations essential* 🏛 *Jacket required* ⊟ *AE, D, DC, MC, V* ⊗ *Closed Sun. and Mon. No lunch.*

Italian

$$–$$$$ ✕ **Trattoria No. 10.** It's hard to camouflage a basement location, but Trattoria No. 10 gives it a good go with terra-cotta colors, arched entryways, and quarry-tile floors, all of which evoke Italy. Pretheater diners crowd in for the house specialty ravioli filled with seasonal stuffings, classic antipasti selections like prosciutto-wrapped asparagus, and substantial *secondi piatti* like beef tenderloin. Cheap chowsters, meanwhile, elbow into the bar for the $12 nibbles buffet served from 5 to 8 PM weekdays with a $6 drink minimum. ⊠ *10 N. Dearborn St., Loop* ☎ *312/984–1718* ⊟ *AE, D, DC, MC, V* ⊗ *Closed Sun. No lunch Sat.*

$–$$$$ ✕ **Petterino's.** Goodman, Palace, and Oriental theatergoers pack Petterino's (next door to the Goodman lobby) nightly. Not that the Italian supper club with framed caricatures of celebs past and present couldn't stand on its own merits. The deep, red-leather booths make a cozy stage for old-school classics like shrimp *de jonghe* (covered in garlicky bread crumbs then baked) and Bookbinder soup, plus prime steaks, seafood, and the ever-present pasta. ⊠ *150 N. Dearborn St., Loop* ☎ *312/422–0150* ⊟ *AE, D, DC, MC, V* ⊗ *Closed Sun. No lunch Sat.*

$$–$$$ ✕ **312 Chicago.** Part handy hotel restaurant, part Loop power diner, and all Italian down to its second-generation chef, 312 Chicago earns its popularity with well-executed dishes that range from basic rigatoni with meatballs to boffo lamb chops with roast tomatoes and Sicilian olives. We're tempted to carbo-load on the house-baked bread alone. Tables in the bi-level eatery are quieter aloft, though you still may see the occasional hotel guest wander through, looking for the elevator. ⊠ *Hotel Allegro, 136 N. LaSalle St., Loop* ☎ *312/696–2420* ⊟ *AE, D, DC, MC, V* ⊗ *No lunch Sat.*

$–$$$ ✕ **Vivere.** There's no resting on Old World looks at Vivere: think Italian baroque on acid. Cones, swirls, and bright colors guarantee an—ahem—interesting view, should conversation lag. The regional Italian menu includes excellent, beyond-the-norm dishes such as pheasant *agnolotti* (half-moon-shape ravioli) and wild boar over polenta. We love the extensive Italian wine list. ⊠ *71 W.*

WORD OF MOUTH

Trattoria No. 10 is down below ground level and quieter than most [with] a good atmosphere. Trattoria No. 10 is not high end pricing-more mid, but it is not a red sauce spaghetti joint. Most items are à la carte and Northern Italian. They have great salads and good specials of the day both times I've been there this year. One of their specialties is Butternut Squash Ravioli. They also have excellent desserts and a long wine list.

–]]5

Monroe St., Loop ☎ *312/332–7005* ▭ *AE, D, DC, MC, V* ✆ *Closed Sun. No lunch weekends.*

$–$$ ✕ **Nick & Tony's Italian Chophouse.** A Loop locale near offices and theaters plus a patio with views of the Chicago River (from across Wacker) keep the tables turning at this neighborly place. The food breaks no new ground, but fans champion its spinach ravioli, veal Parmesan, and clubby, crowd-friendly vibe. ✉ *1 E. Wacker Dr., Loop* ☎ *312/467–9449* ▭ *AE, D, DC, MC, V* ✆ *No lunch Sun.*

Russian

$$–$$$$ ✕ **Russian Tea Time.** Exotica is on the menu and in the air at this spot that's favored by visitors to the nearby Art Institute and Symphony Center. Mahogany trim, samovars, and balalaika music set the stage for dishes from Russia and neighboring republics (the owners hail from Uzbekistan), including Ukrainian borscht, *blinis* (small, savory pancakes) with salmon caviar, Maldovian meatballs, and game sausages. Chilled vodka flights (three shots) help the herring go down. ✉ *77 E. Adams St., Loop* ☎ *312/ 360–0000* ♙ *Reservations essential* ▭ *AE, D, DC, MC, V.*

Seafood

$$$–$$$$ ✕ **Nick's Fishmarket.** The bold and pricey menu matches the well-paid power lunchers who get down to business over Pacific fish, California abalone, and Maine lobster. If your pursestrings are tight, angle for a spot at the Grill, where the lobster comes in ravioli and windows frame the Marc Chagall mosaic on the plaza outdoors. ✉ *51 S. Clark St., Loop* ☎ *312/621–0200* ♙ *Reservations essential* ▭ *AE, D, DC, MC, V* ✆ *Closed Sun. No lunch Sat.*

$$–$$$$ ✕ **Catch 35.** Eavesdrop on advertising types who do the after-five mix-and-mingle at this spot in the lobby of the Leo Burnett Building. When it comes to food, have it your way: fish or shellfish come grilled, seared, baked, or woked. The multilevel dining room provides plenty of eye candy plus glimpses of the Chicago River beyond. ✉ *35 W. Wacker Dr., Loop* ☎ *312/346–3500* ▭ *AE, D, DC, MC, V* ✆ *No lunch weekends.*

Steak Houses

$$$$ ✕ **The Palm.** If you're somebody in this town, your caricatured mug is hung here on the wood-paneled wall, a practice that feeds the egos of the Palm's power-player regulars. Sizeable steaks and even bigger lobsters sate their appetites. Chicago's soaring skyscrapers and Disney-esque Navy Pier provide distraction on the outdoor patio, making this an all-together handsome link in a national chain. ✉ *Swissôtel, 323 E. Wacker Dr., Loop* ☎ *312/ 616–1000* ♙ *Reservations essential* ▭ *AE, D, DC, MC, V.*

★ $$$–$$$$ ✕ **Morton's, The Steakhouse.** Gibsons on the Gold Coast is more fun, but this is Chicago's best steak house, a spin-off of the Gold Coast original. Excellent service and a good wine list add to the principal attraction: beautiful, hefty steaks cooked to perfection. A kitschy tradition mandates that everything you order, from gargantuan Idahos to massive slabs of beef, is brought to the table for your approval before the chef gets started. White tablecloths and chandeliers create a classy feel. It's no place for the budget conscious, but for steak lovers it's a 16-ounce (or more) taste of heaven. ⊠ *65 E. Wacker Pl., Loop* ☎ *312/201–0410* ⊟ *AE, D, DC, MC, V* ☺ *No lunch weekends.*

$–$$$$ ✗ **The Grillroom.** If you're going to a performance at the Shubert Theatre across the street, you're close enough to dash over here for a drink at intermission (we love the lengthy by-the-glass wine selections). Pre- and post-curtain, the clubby confines fill with showgoers big on beef, though there are also ample raw bar, seafood, and pasta choices. For the most relaxing experience, come after Act I commences. ⊠ *33 W. Monroe St., Loop* ☎ *312/960–0000* ⊟ *AE, D, DC, MC, V* ☺ *No lunch weekends.*

South Loop

Italian immigrants to Chicago originally settled around Taylor Street, which now borders the University of Illinois at Chicago campus. Many families have moved on, but their legacy remains in a string of Italian restaurants lining the street, also known as Little Italy. We recommend it on a summer evening when you can stroll the street with an Italian ice and peruse the menus before settling on a dinner spot.

American–Casual

$$–$$$$ ✗ **Chicago Firehouse Restaurant.** A historic South Side fire station makes a novel setting for this straightforward American restaurant. There's nothing ground-breaking about the menu, which aims to please all with a large list of seafood, pasta, chicken, steak, and gussied-up appetizers like oysters Rockefeller and sautéed frogs' legs. Add sandwiches and burgers to the lunch list. For atmosphere, request a table in the bar area; it has two vintage fire poles. From Soldier Field or Museum Campus, it's walking distance to this group-friendly eatery. ⊠ *1401 S. Michigan Ave., South Loop* ☎ *312/786–1401* ⊟ *AE, D, DC, MC, V* ☺ *No lunch weekends.*

¢–$ ✗ **Manny's Coffee Shop and Deli.** Kibbitzing counter cooks provide commentary as they sling the chow—thick pastrami sandwiches, soul-nurturing matzo-ball soup, and piping-hot potato pancakes—at this classic South Side cafeteria. Though they occasionally bark at dawdlers, it's all in good fun; looking for seating in two teaming, fluorescent lit rooms is not. Don't try to pay the hash-slingers; settle up as you leave. ⊠ *1141 S. Jefferson St., South Loop* ☎ *312/939–2855* ◿ *Reservations not accepted* ⊟ *AE, MC, V* ☺ *Closed Sun. No dinner.*

Chinese

$$–$$$ ✗ **Opera.** Creative Chinese fare and theatrical design share the stage at Opera. Only top-flight ingredients and sparing sauces go into the cooking, distinguishing the five-spice squid, say, or lobster spring roll or crisp snapper from more familiar take-out fare. Former film storage vaults—

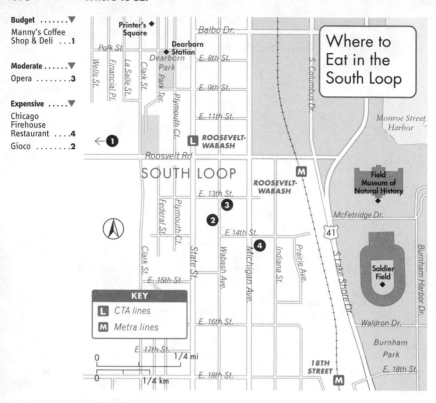

Where to Eat in the South Loop

KEY

L CTA lines

M Metra lines

the building was once used by Paramount Studios—now hold a series of tables for two, providing intimacy for those who want it. Everyone else revels in the eye candy that includes Asian newspaper collages, oversize suspended lamps, and a multicolor-glass-wrapped wine cellar. ✉ *1301 S. Wabash St., South Loop* ☎ *312/461–0161* ☱ *AE, DC, MC, V* ☾ *No lunch.*

Italian

$$–$$$$ ✗ **Gioco.** The name means "game" in Italian, and the restaurant fulfills the promise not with venison, but in the spirit of playing a game. The decor is distressed-urban, with plaster-spattered brick walls and well-worn hardwood floors, but the menu is comfort-Italian, with rustic fare like homemade penne pasta with prosciutto, grilled lamb chops, and sausage with beans. The Speakeasy Room, a private dining space with its own rear-alley entrance, is homage to the building's notorious past under Prohibition. ✉ *1312 S. Wabash Ave., South Loop* ☎ *312/939–3870* ☱ *AE, DC, MC, V* ☾ *No lunch weekends.*

West Loop

Chicago's hottest restaurant district lies, conveniently, just beyond the downtown Loop. Randolph Street, a former wholesale greenmarket, has

Continued on page 203

CHICAGO'S HOLY TRINITY:
Pizza, Hot Dogs & Italian Beef Sandwiches

Long before Chicago's dining scene got all gussied up with boldface-named chefs and swanky hot spots, the City of Big Shoulders perfected hearty, gut-busting food for the Average Joe. Until you've pigged out on deep-dish pizza at Lou Malnati's or Gino's East, sunk your teeth into a loaded hot dog at Superdawg Drive-in, and wiped the grease off your face after devouring an Italian beef sandwich at Al's Italian Beef, you haven't done Chicago. So go on, leave your diet plans at home and get ready to sample the best of the big city.

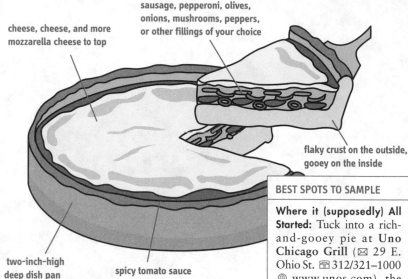

cheese, cheese, and more mozzarella cheese to top

sausage, pepperoni, olives, onions, mushrooms, peppers, or other fillings of your choice

flaky crust on the outside, gooey on the inside

two-inch-high deep dish pan

spicy tomato sauce

TASTE 1 | **DEEP-DISH PIZZA**

A CALORIC HISTORY

Pizza—in one form or another—has been around since the sixth century B.C., but it only gained heft when it settled into this brash, entrepreneurial city. Pizzeria Uno founder Ike Sewell generally gets the credit for turning pizza inside out in 1943. His knife-and-fork creation started with a layer of cheese, followed by the toppings, and then the sauce, all tucked into a doughy crust that he yanked up the sides of a deep pan.

THE CRUST CONTROVERSY

The founders of Lou Malnati's pizzeria worked in Ike's kitchen at Pizzeria Uno and claim that *they* were the ones actually doing the cooking. They broke off and opened up Malnati's in 1971, and a classic Chicago rivalry was born.

BEST SPOTS TO SAMPLE

Where it (supposedly) All Started: Tuck into a rich-and-gooey pie at **Uno Chicago Grill** (✉ 29 E. Ohio St. ☎ 312/321–1000 ⊕ www.unos.com), the former infamous Pizzeria Uno.

Most Authentic: Aficionados of **Lou Malnati's** (✉ 439 N. Wells St. ☎ 312/828–9800 ⊕ www. loumalnatis.com) claim that their favorite pies have more flavor and like that there are fewer tourists to clog up the joint. If you're really feeling indulgent, order yours with a butter crust. Trust us.

Worth the Wait: Join the out-the-door line at **Gino's East** (✉ 633 N. Wells St. ☎ 312/943–1124 ⊕ www. ginoseast.com) for caloric pies and a chance to add to the graffiti on the walls.

Easiest to Find: The ubiquitous **Giordano's** (✉ 730 N. Rush St. ☎ 312/951–0747) has 13 locations throughout the city besides this one.

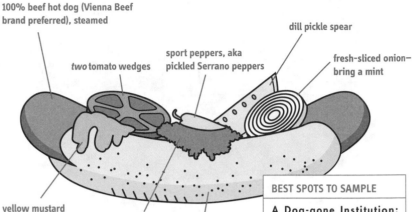

100% beef hot dog (Vienna Beef brand preferred), steamed

dill pickle spear

sport peppers, aka pickled Serrano peppers

two tomato wedges

fresh-sliced onion— bring a mint

yellow mustard

neon green sweet pickle relish

poppy seed bun

6

CHICAGO'S HOLY TRINITY

TASTE 2 | **HOT DOGS**

A DOG IS BORN

The iconic Chicago-style hot dog got its start at the 1893 World's Fair's Columbian Exposition. Two immigrants from Austria and Hungary hawked a beef frankfurter sandwich in a steamed bun piled with mustard, relish, onion, tomato, dill pickle, hot peppers, and celery salt. When the Fair moved on, the cravings persisted, launching an on-going affair with the Chicago-style hot dog.

HOW MUCH GARDEN CAN ONE BUN HOLD?

If you've walked a square block of Chicago, chances are you've passed a hot dog. Dog dealers lodge under El stops, on street corners, and at sports arenas. The one thing they all have in common? Their dogs get "dragged through the garden," or loaded with the aforementioned veggies, unless otherwise specified. Don't forget to grab a fistful of napkins—these dogs are messy.

BEST SPOTS TO SAMPLE

A Dog-gone Institution: Fluky's (✉ 520 N. Michigan Ave. ☎ 312/527–5550 ⊕ www.flukys.com) has been running the goods through the garden since 1929, although it's since moved to a tony Mag Mile address.

Get 'em Retro Style: Look for the boy dog and girl dog topping **Superdawg Drive-In** (✉ 6363 N. Milwaukee Ave. ☎ 773/736–0660 ⊕ www.superdawg. com), where car-hops deliver your chow.

Poshest Pick: For a weiner on a higher plane, check out **Hot Doug's** (✉ 3324 N. California ☎ 773/279–9550 ⊕ www.hotdougs. com). In addition to the classic Chicago beef, encased meats include kangaroo or rabbit.

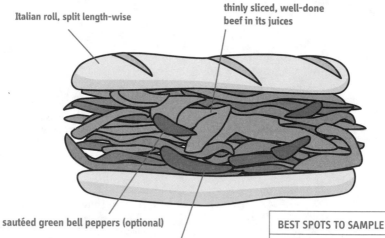

Italian roll, split length-wise

thinly sliced, well-done beef in its juices

sautéed green bell peppers (optional)

hot giardiniera peppers

TASTE 3 | ITALIAN BEEF SANDWICHES

IT'S ALL ABOUT THE BEEF

Italian immigrants in Chicago happily adapted to the locally abundant meat supply to produce the now-classic Italian beef sandwich. Hard hats and desk jockeys crowd beef stands at lunch, joined by the occasional visiting celebrity. Don't expect much in the way of atmosphere: Here it's Formica counters, fluorescent lights, and big shoulder–to–big shoulder intimacy.

GRAB YOUR NAPKINS

The two-fister, a popular lunchtime staple, stuffs an Italian roll, split length-wise, with thin slices of medium beef. Authentic Italian beef sandwiches use sirloin rump, top round, or bottom round that's wet-roasted and dripping in a broth that's spiked with garlic, oregano, and spices. The whole thing is topped with hot giardiniera, a spicy relish of Serrano peppers, diced carrots, cauliflower, celery, and olives in oil. If you've ordered it "wet," it comes with an extra ladle of juice and a stack of napkins; if you order a cheesy beef, they melt a slice or two of mozzarella over the whole mess.

BEST SPOTS TO SAMPLE

Roll up Your Sleeves: Plant your elbows at the window counter or a picnic table in the "elegant dining room" at **Mr. Beef** (✉ 666 N. Orleans St. ☎ 312/337–8500), where famous fans get their mugs on the wall.

Join the Masses: On Little Italy's Taylor Street, standing-room-only crowds of students and local business folk pack **Al's No. 1 Italian Beef** (✉ 1079 W. Taylor St., ☎ 312/226–4017, ⊕ www.alscatering.com).

For Beef and a Breeze: **Al's Italian Beef** (✉ 169 W. Ontario St. ☎ 312/943–3222 ⊕ www.alsbeef.com), no relation to Al's No. 1 Italian Beef, provides canopied eating on a River North outdoor patio, a step up from the typical fast-food setting.

CLOSE UP

The Chain Gang

FOR A QUICK, CONVENIENT BITE, try a nosh from one of these chains with multiple outlets downtown as well as out in the neighborhoods.

Boudin Sourdough Bakery & Cafe: Boudin's luscious sourdough bread is available by the loaf, in deli sandwiches, or accompanying soups and salads at this local minichain.

Briazz: Office workers crowd into downtown Briazz outlets for toasted panini sandwiches, prepackaged heros, leafy salads, and espresso-based drinks.

Burrito Beach: Links of this locally based wrap specialist chain serve tortillas stuffed with everything from Asian chicken to Mexican beans. Local chefs, like Shawn McClain of Spring fame, design wraps for the monthly specials.

Corner Bakery: Fresh-baked breads form the basis of café fare starring deli sandwiches, soups, and salads. Service is cafeteria style, but the bright and woody dining rooms encourage lingering.

Hot Dog Stands: Chicago dogs are a tradition sold at mom-and-pop stands around town. Vienna franks come "dragged through the garden," heaping with onions, tomato, dill pickle, relish, hot peppers, and celery salt, unless you indicate otherwise.

Potbelly Sandwich Works: Superior submarine sandwiches—from classic Italian to chicken salad—are made to order at Potbelly, a local favorite of college students and office workers.

6

emerged as the area's restaurant row, with chockablock trendy ethnic restaurants. Though there are still some good budget spots, this is a prime place to splurge if you're flush. Old-world Greektown provides contrast and comfort just around the corner.

American–Casual

$–$$ ✕ **Ina's.** It's so cozy you almost feel like you're at a diner—there's the loving presence of owner Ina Pinkney, reliable chow, and a regular following. But dishes like vegetable hash and black bean-cheese-eggs-chorizo "scrapple" (a loaded version of scrambled eggs) at breakfast and lamb chops or seared talapia at dinner take this place up several notches. Close to Oprah's studio and loft-dwellers up and down Randolph, Ina's regularly generates a queue, especially on weekends. ✉ *1235 W. Randolph St., West Loop* ☎ *312/226–8227* ⊟ *AE, D, DC, MC, V* ⊘ *No dinner Sun.*

$ ✕ **Lou Mitchell's.** Shelve your calorie and cholesterol concerns; Lou
Fodor$Choice Mitchell's heeds no modern health concerns. The diner, a destination close
★ to Union Station since 1923, specializes in high-fat breakfasts and comfort food lunches. Start the day with double-yolk eggs and homemade hash browns by the skillet (BYO Lipitor). Later break for meat loaf and mashed potatoes. Though you have to deal with out-the-door waits, staffers dole out doughnut holes and Milk Duds to pacify pangs. ✉ *565 W. Jackson Blvd., West Loop* ☎ *312/939–3111* ⊟ *AE, V* ⊘ *No dinner.*

Where to
Eat in the
West Loop

KEY
L CTA lines

Contemporary

$$$–$$$$ ✕ **Blackbird.** Being cramped next to your neighbor has never been as fun
Fodor's Choice as it is at this hot spot run by foodie chef Paul Kahan. Celebs pepper
★ the sleek see-and-be-seen crowd who delve into creative seasonal dishes,
like apple-and-almond-stuffed quail or sturgeon oxtail and corn pan-
cakes. It all plays out against a minimalist backdrop of white walls, mo-
hair banquettes, and aluminum chairs. Reservations aren't required, but
they might as well be; the dining room is typically booked solid on week-
ends. ⊠ *619 W. Randolph St., West Loop* ☏ *312/715–0708* ⌚ *Reser-
vations essential* ⊟ *AE, D, DC, MC, V* ⊘ *Closed Sun. No lunch Sat.*

$$–$$$$ ✕ **one sixtyblue.** Nevermind that former Chicago Bulls superstar Michael
Jordan owns a piece of this place or that the private, cigar-friendly
room has entertained its share of celebs. The real reason to come here
is chef Martial Noguier. His graceful but approachable food balances
challenge-me tastes, like rabbit loin, with standbys like Delmonico steak
with carmelized shallots (Jordan's fave). The leather-sofa lounge makes
a sexy site for nibbles and drinks. ⊠ *1400 W. Randolph St., West Loop*
☏ *312/850–0303* ⊟ *AE, D, DC, MC, V* ⊘ *Closed Sun.*

$$–$$$ ✕ **Rushmore.** The kitchen recasts the classics Mom made in a spiffed-up
loft under the El oozing with urban cache. Mac-and-cheese gets a
makeover with smoked cheddar, and grilled cheese and soup becomes

a grilled Maytag blue cheese sandwich and roast tomato bisque. Bring your bank roll; prices are 10% off when you pay cash. ✉ *1023 W. Lake St., West Loop* ☎ *312/421–8845* ☰ *AE, D, DC, MC, V* ◷ *Closed Sun.*

★ **$–$$$** ✕ **Avec.** Go to this Euro-style wine bar when you're feeling gregarious; the rather stark space only has seating for 55 people, and it's all at communal tables. The results are loud and lively, though happily the shareable fare—a mix of homemade charcuterie, Mediterranean, and American dishes from a wood-burning oven—is reasonably priced. It's as popular as its next-door neighbor Blackbird (and run by the same forces), and only early birds are guaranteed tables. The doors open at—yikes!—3:30 PM. ✉ *615 W. Randolph St., West Loop* ☎ *312/377–2002* ☰ *AE, D, DC, MC, V* ◷ *No lunch.*

$$ ✕ **West Town Tavern.** It's not easy to find this find in a neighborhood bereft of many restaurants, but trust your cabbie to get you here. The handsome wood bar and brick walls may be tavern staples, but the open kitchen and oversize dining room mirror promise more than cheeseburgers. The menu delivers with a mix of upscale comfort foods (try the beer cheese—a cheese ball made with cheddar cheese and spices—and pizza-style flat breads) and gussied-up American classics like pepper-crusted steak in a zinfandel sauce. The focused wine list globe trots for value. ✉ *1329 W. Chicago Ave., West Loop* ☎ *312/666–6175* ☰ *AE, MC, V* ◷ *Closed Sun. No lunch.*

$ ✕ **Flat Top Grill.** Cafeteria meets custom kitchen here: you choose your ingredients from a spread of veggies, meat, fish, and sauces, and the grill man cooks them up. The spacious, converted loft setting masks any similarities to a buffet, and a handy sign gives detailed advice for neophytes. Join the budget-conscious West Loop workers who file in regularly for lunch. It's an extra dollar for unlimited trips to the grill. ✉ *1000 W. Washington Blvd., West Loop* ☎ *312/829–4800* ☰ *AE, D, DC, MC, V.*

French

$$–$$$ ✕ **Marché.** If all the world's a stage, everyone from the waiters to the patrons are players at this theatrical West Loop brasserie. The set: a lively, loftlike room trimmed in collage and paint and furnished with curvaceous metal chairs. The program: classic French onion soup and housemade pâté, braised lamb, and an excellent steak tartare. The finale: one of the largest sweets lists in town. Ovations at your discretion. ✉ *833 W. Randolph St., West Loop* ☎ *312/226–8399* ☰ *AE, DC, MC, V* ◷ *No lunch.*

$$–$$$ ✕ **La Sardine.** We don't know if the sardine reference was meant to telegraph the seating arrangements, but, yes, it's snug here. Still, you'll find it easier to tolerate your neighbors with a solid menu of traditional bistro favorites including leek-bacon tart, bouillabaisse, and mustard-crusted

---

BEST SCENE

Hooked on celeb gossip? Like to look at pretty people? Yeah, us too. Feed your fascinations here: **Blackbird.** You never know who you'll be squeezed in next to here. ✉ *Near West Side* ☎ *312/715–0708.*

Green Zebra. If these veggies are good enough for Gwyneth Paltrow, they're good enough for us. ✉ *Near West Side* ☎ *312/243–7100.*

6

rack of lamb. Across the street from Harpo Studios (where Oprah tapes her talk show), La Sardine seats audiences close to producers. ⊠ *111 N. Carpenter St., West Loop* ☎ *312/421–2800* ⊟ *AE, D, DC, MC, V* ⊗ *Closed Sun. No lunch Sat.*

Greek

$–$$$ ✕ **Costa's.** Greektown is fairly labeled monotonous, cuisine-wise. But Costa's betters its many neighbors in both looks and taste. The multilevel Hellenic interior has terra-cotta tile work and rough-textured white walls and archways. There's a generous assortment of *mezes* (tapaslike Greek appetizers), traditional saltfish, kebobs, and roast leg of lamb. Live piano and the enthusiasm of diners tend to send the decibels soaring. ⊠ *340 S. Halsted St., West Loop* ☎ *312/263–9700* ⊟ *AE, D, DC, MC, V.*

$ ✕ **The Parthenon.** The claim to fame here is the *saganaki*, the Greek flaming cheese dish, which the Parthenon says it invented in the late 1960s, thereby introducing "opa!" to the American vocabulary. They also take credit for being the first to serve gyros stateside. True or not, indulge the legends and stick to these classics. The food is cheap and the atmosphere festive, generating happy campers. ⊠ *314 S. Halsted St., West Loop* ☎ *312/726–2407* ⊟ *AE, D, DC, MC, V.*

Italian

$–$$$ ✕ **Vivo.** Vivo was trendy on this west-of-the-Loop stretch long before Randolph Street's restaurant row got hot. Slightly more about scene— brick walls, black ceiling, open wine racks, and lots of pretty people— than cuisine, Vivo manages reliable Italian fare. You can't go wrong with carpaccio, grilled portobello mushroom salad, seafood linguine, and a thin-sliced veal chop. ⊠ *838 W. Randolph St., West Loop* ☎ *312/733–3379* ⊟ *AE, DC, MC, V* ⊗ *No lunch weekends.*

Japanese

$–$$$ ✕ **Sushi Wabi.** This funky, West Loop sushi restaurant dances to an industrial-pop beat—on weekend evenings, at least, when it employs a DJ (club attitude suffices on weekdays). The urban-chic brick-and-exposed-steel interior draws a young, martini-swilling crowd. Superior sushi and maki rolls along with straightforward entrées such as seared tuna with gingered ponzu sauce, bring substance to the style haunt. ⊠ *842 W. Randolph St., West Loop* ☎ *312/563–1224* ⊟ *AE, D, DC, MC, V* ⊗ *No lunch weekends.*

Pan-Asian

$$–$$$$ ✕ **Red Light.** Sultry, all-red decor and a club soundtrack stoke the high-energy vibe (read: loud) at Red Light. Chinese, Thai, Vietnamese, and Indonesian dishes commingle on the pan-Asian menu, which is heavily weighted with appetizers to encourage nibbling. Standout dishes include foie gras and pork dumplings, jumbo shrimp curry, a coconut seafood stew, and the signature "chocolate bag" dessert filled with white chocolate mousse. ⊠ *820 W. Randolph St., West Loop* ☎ *312/733–8880* ⊟ *AE, D, DC, MC, V* ⊗ *No lunch weekends.*

Seafood

$$–$$$$ ✕ **Blue Point Oyster Bar.** Blue Point is the seafood stop on the around-the-world restaurant row, otherwise known as Randolph Street. Wooden-louvered windows and overstuffed booths impart a slick 1940s aesthetic at this West Looper. Mix and match from a half-dozen oysters featured daily. Fish and shellfish menus depend on the season, but the spicy crab gazpacho is worth a trip in late summer, and the kitchen generally keeps preparations contemporary. Tab watch: the sum also rises here quickly. ⊠ *741 W. Randolph St., West Loop* ☎ *312/207–1222* ▭ *AE, D, DC, MC, V* ⊗ *No lunch weekends.*

Steak Houses

$$–$$$$ ✕ **Carmichael's.** The look here is old-time Chicago—oak and brass, black-and-white photographs, and waiters dressed in suspenders and shirtsleeve garters—though the true vintage is late 1980s. We forgive them the ruse for the well-priced (around $30) Angus steaks, which make this one of the more reasonable top-tier steak houses in town. Planked salmon is a good nonbeef option. Live jazz lures prowling carnivores to the lush garden in summer. ⊠ *1052 W. Monroe St., West Loop* ☎ *312/433–0025* ▭ *AE, D, DC, MC, V* ⊗ *No lunch weekends.*

$$–$$$$ ✕ **Nine.** Nightclub meets steak house in Nine, replete with mirrored columns, futuristic plasma TV screens, and a dramatic, circular cham-pagne-and-caviar bar set smack in the middle of the dining room. Scen-esters and business folk find common ground in the menu: prime steaks and chops complemented by fresh fish and shellfish. If you crave caviar choose from beluga and sevruga by the ounce or cute crispy cones lay-ered with caviar and egg salad. On weekends, dress to thrill—most of the trendy patrons do. ⊠ *440 W. Randolph St., West Loop* ☎ *312/575–9900* ▭ *AE, DC, MC, V* ⊗ *Closed Sun. No lunch Sat.*

Vegetarian

★ **$–$$** ✕ **Green Zebra.** Chef Shawn McClain of Spring fame took the vegetable sidedish and ran it up the marquee. The result gives good-for-you veg-gies the star treatment in a sleek shop suave enough to attract the likes of Gwyneth Paltrow. All dishes are small and change seasonally. You might see roast beets with fiddlehead ferns or poached egg with spinach puree and lentils. One chicken and one fish dish make do for carnivores. ⊠ *1460 W. Chicago Ave., West Loop* ☎ *312/243–7100* ▭ *AE, D, DC, MC, V* ⊗ *Closed Mon.*

Near North

Some of the glitzier dining venues in Chicago cluster in this high-toned district where luxury Mag Mile hotels meet historic Gold Coast brown-stones. You'll pay well for marquee meals like those at Spiaggia or NoMI, but the consensus is that there's good value for the buck here. On the budget beat, you can always find a café serving the thousands of shoppers who descend here daily (the best deals are just off, not on, Michigan Avenue).

American

$–$$$$ ✕ **RL.** Power brokers, moneyed locals, and Michigan Avenue shoppers keep the revolving doors spinning at RL, the initials of designer Ralph Lauren who lent his name and signature soignée style to the eatery that adjoins his Polo Ralph Lauren store. The cozy confines cluster leather banquettes under hunt-club–style art hung on wood-paneled walls. The menu of American classics, including steak tartare, Dover sole in butter, and steak Diane flamed table-side, suits the country-club-in-the-city setting. ⊠ *115 E. Chicago Ave., Near North* ☎ *312/475–1100* ▤ *AE, DC, MC, V.*

American–Casual

¢ ✕ **Billy Goat Tavern.** The late comedian John Belushi immortalized the Goat's

Fodor'sChoice short-order cooks on *Saturday Night Live* for barking, "No Coke!

★ Pepsi!" and "No fries! Cheeps!" at customers. They still do the shtick at this subterranean hole-in-the-wall favored by reporters posted nearby at the *Tribune* and the *Sun-Times.* Griddle-fried "cheezborgers" are the featured chow, and people-watching the favored sport. ⊠ *430 N. Michigan Ave., lower level, Near North* ☎ *312/222–1525* ▤ *No credit cards.*

> **WORD OF MOUTH**
>
> "We ate at the Billy Goat Tavern underneath the Wrigley Building - what a hoot!"
>
> –Spikeit

Barbecue

$–$$ ✕ **Joe's Be-Bop Cafe and Jazz Emporium.** Joe's looks like a classic jazz club with a raised stage but plays like a family restaurant on raucous Navy Pier. Ribs and creole fare are clan-pleasing, and the jazz bands—booked most nights and during Sunday brunches—lift Joe's from merely touristy to actually enjoyable. ⊠ *600 E. Grand Ave., Near North* ☎ *312/595– 5299* ▤ *AE, D, DC, MC, V.*

Cafés

$–$$ ✕ **Pierrot Gourmet.** Despite the legions of shoppers on Michigan Avenue there are few casual cafés to quell their collective hunger, making this bakery-patisserie-café a welcome neighbor. Lunches center on upscale greens like herb salad with olives and Parmesan, along with open-face *tartine* sandwiches on crusty, house-made sourdough. Break mid-afternoon for a *tarte flambé,* an Alsatian flat bread with cheese and cream, and a glass of Riesling. Solos are accommodated at the magazine-strewn communal table. Meals are served 7 AM to 7 PM daily. The upscale Peninsula hotel runs Pierrot, accounting for both the high quality and the high cost. ⊠ *108 E. Superior St., Near North* ☎ *312/573–6749* ▤ *AE, D, DC, MC, V.*

$ ✕ **Fox & Obel Food Market Cafe.** Skip the tourist trap funnel-cake fare at Navy Pier. This riverside gourmet market a block away is a toothsome escape. The prepared fine and organic foodstuffs are treated with reverence, and although service is cafeteria-style, selections are decidedly more sophisticated. We like the entrée salads with duck, tortilla soup with smoked chicken, and steak–blue cheese–caramelized onion sandwiches. ⊠ *401 E. Illinois St., Near North* ☎ *312/379–0112* ▤ *AE, D, MC, V.*

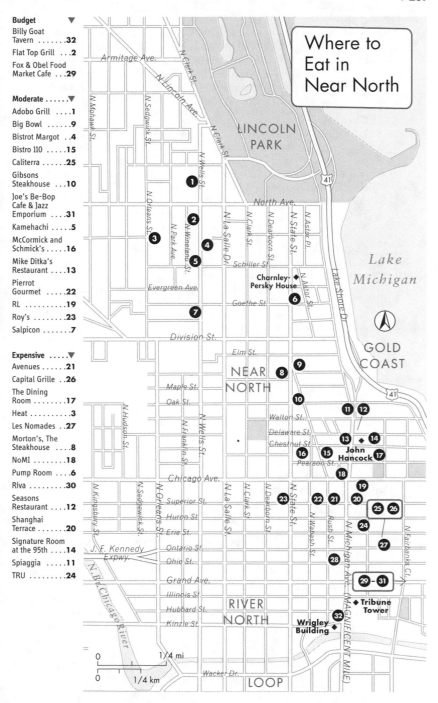

Where to
Eat in
Near North

Cajun

$–$$ ✕ **Heaven on Seven on Rush.** It's Mardi Gras all day, every day here. Look for the infamous "Wall of Fire," a stunning collection of hot sauces, on your way to your table, where a selection of the fiery stuff awaits the intrepid. The food is well-shy of ambrosia, but it's plentiful and filling, with great book ends in cheddar jalapeño biscuits and seven-layer cake. ⊠ *220 E. Chicago Ave., Near North* ☎ *312/280–7774* ▤ *AE, D, DC, MC, V.*

Chinese

$$–$$$$ ✕ **Shanghai Terrace.** As precious as a jewel box, and as pricey, this red, lacquer-trimmed 40-seater hidden away in the Peninsula Hotel reveals the hotelier's Asian roots. Come for upscale dim sum, stylishly presented, and luxury-laden entrées such as steamed fish, Szechuan beef, and wok-fried lobster. A summer patio lets you revel in the skyline, seven stories above the madding crowds of Michigan Avenue. ⊠ *Peninsula Hotel, 108 E. Superior St., Near North* ☎ *312/573–6744* ▤ *AE, D, DC, MC, V* ☉ *Closed Sun.*

Contemporary

$$$$ ✕ **Avenues.** Ever tried foie gras with Pop Rocks? How about seared foie gras with cinnamon ice cream? Neither had we, but somehow chef Graham Elliot Bowles makes this experimental, daring food harmonious. The restaurant is in a hotel (the Peninsula), so some dishes on the three-course prix-fixe menu, such as prime beef, are designed to please hotel guests who want less challenge at dinner. For everyone else, there are truffled frogs' legs. Intermediate six-course menus focus on veggies, seafood, and protein. For the full shock-and-awe experience, go with the 12-course "chefs' presentation." ⊠ *Peninsula Hotel, 108 E. Superior St., Near North* ☎ *312/573–6754* ▤ *AE, D, DC, MC, V* ☉ *Closed Sun. and Mon. No lunch.*

$$$$ ✕ **NoMI.** The expensive linens, Limoges china, and Isamu Noguchi sculpture make NoMI completely luxurious, but the vibe here is casual, as if all this elegance were everyday and not special occasion. This is the place to call if you're celebrating the latter or traveling on a generous expense account—you'll have one of the city's best tables, overlooking the historic Water Tower from a seven-story perch. The menu leans French, with strong Asian and Mediterranean accents. ⊠ *Park Hyatt Hotel, 800 N. Michigan Ave., Near North* ☎ *312/239–4030* ▤ *AE, D, DC, MC, V.*

$$$$ ✕ **Seasons Restaurant.** How the Four Seasons's boîte manages to please business diners and traveling families is a mystery worthy of a hotel-school case study. Service is suave, the room elegant, and the seasonal food refined; altogether, it's an ideal spot for power-dining appointments. At the same time, the hotel makes a big deal about being family friendly, which, if you read between the lines a bit, means there's a children's menu for better behaved clans (it *is* still the Four Seasons). Fixing for a good deal and a quick lunch? There's an affordable three-course daily lunch menu that's served within an hour. Dinner menus include five- and eight-course tasting options. Reservations are essential for Chicago's best (and most expensive) Sunday brunch. ⊠ *Four Seasons Hotel, 120 E. Delaware Pl., Near North* ☎ *312/280–8800* ▤ *AE, D, DC, MC, V.*

$$$$ ✕ **TRU.** Chefs Rick Tramonto and, on pastries, Gale Gand do fine dining with a sense of humor. The quite-serious food is leavened by the presentations: caviar atop a tabletop crystal staircase, between-course sorbets in cones, or dishes served over a mini fishbowl occupied by a live fighting fish. The dining room resembles a gallery, with white walls and carefully chosen art, including an Andy Warhol. The menu starts with a basic three-course prix-fixe, priced at $90, and escalates to 6, 8, and 10 courses. Several of those are dessert, so save space. ✉ *676 N. St. Clair St., Near North* ☎ *312/202–0001* ✍ *Reservations essential* 🏛 *Jacket required* ▤ *AE, D, DC, MC, V* ☉ *Closed Sun. No lunch.*

> **WORD OF MOUTH**
>
> "Loved TRU. It was amazing in every way, and although expensive, it was well worth it."
>
> –cindymal

$$$–$$$$ ✕ **Pump Room.** The Pump Room clings to its 1930s Chicago fame, when celebrities passing through town via rail beat it to the restaurant to see and be seen. The likes of Frank Sinatra, Bette Davis, and Humprey Bogart held court in the storied Booth One, and publicity photos taken there line the entrance to the restaurant. In keeping with tradition, the booth is off-limits to all but A-list celebs who, truthfully, don't show like they used to. Now the regulars are wealthy Gold Coasters, but new management is working hard to lure the next generation, meaning there's seared tuna alongside steak and potatoes. ✉ *1301 N. State Pkwy., Near North* ☎ *312/266–0360* ▤ *AE, D, DC, MC, V.*

$$$–$$$$ ✕ **Signature Room at the 95th.** When you've got the best view in town and a lock on the prom business, do you need to be daring with the food? Signature Room isn't, making a formal affair of dishes such as rack of lamb and salmon in puffed pastry while couples ogle the skyline views from the John Hancock's 95th floor. Avoid the clichés by calling here at lunch: the $18 buffet gets you good and stuffed and the daytime light lets you see Lake Michigan. The appeal of the lavish and pricey Sunday brunch? The abundance of food. Brunch reservations essential. ✉ *John Hancock Center, 875 N. Michigan Ave., Near North* ☎ *312/787–9596* ▤ *AE, D, DC, MC, V.*

$–$$$$ ✕ **Caliterra.** The seasonal orientation of the West Coast merges with old-world Italian recipes in dishes such as goat cheese ravioli, crispy bass with truffled tomato, and prosciutto-wrapped pork medallions. The wood-trimmed dining room flows into a display kitchen and adjacent jazz lounge, so wherever you sit, there's something to look at should the conversation lag. ✉ *Wyndham Chicago Hotel, 633 N. St. Clair St., Near North* ☎ *312/274–4444* ▤ *AE, D, DC, MC, V.*

$ ✕ **Flat Top Grill.** Cafeteria meets custom kitchen at Flat Top Grill where you choose the ingredients—from a spread of veggies, meat, fish, and sauces—and the grill man does the heating. The narrow, brick-walled setting masks any similarities to a buffet. A handy sign gives detailed advice for neophytes (it's an extra dollar for unlimited trips to the grill). Students and other budget-conscious patrons jam the place on weekends. This location is in Old Town, near Second City. ✉ *319 W. North Ave., Near North* ☎ *312/787–7676* ▤ *AE, D, DC, MC, V.*

6

French

★ $$$$ ✕ **The Dining Room.** With walnut paneling, tapestry carpeting, crystal chandeliers, and formal service, the Ritz Carlton's Dining Room is all about celebrations. Toast your occasion over saddle of rabbit with mustard dumplings, escargot from Burgundy, and confit of Tasmanian salmon. The oft-changing menu includes three-to-seven course options. The cheese selection is tops in Chicago, and few restaurants can match the breadth and depth of the wine list. The popular Sunday brunch is among the city's most elaborate and expensive. ⊠ *Ritz-Carlton, 160 E. Pearson St., Near North* ☎ *312/266–1000* ⩜ *Reservations essential* 🏛 *Jacket required* ▤ *AE, D, DC, MC, V* ◷ *No lunch.*

$$$$ ✕ **Les Nomades.** Intimate and elegant don't make headlines, but Les Nomades holds a torch for tender refinements. Wood-burning fireplaces and original art warm the dining rooms of the Streeterville brownstone. A carefully composed menu of contemporary French food includes the usual suspects, such as duck consommé and sautéed foie gras, plus earthy indulgences like veal tenderloin with veal sweetbreads. Compose your own prix-fixe dinner from the menu; four courses cost $90, five go for $105. ⊠ *222 E. Ontario St., Near North* ☎ *312/649–9010* ⩜ *Reservations essential* 🏛 *Jacket required* ▤ *AE, D, DC, MC, V* ◷ *Closed Sun. and Mon. No lunch.*

$$–$$$ ✕ **Bistro 110.** The knock against Bistro 110 is that it can be noisy and chaotic, but we consider that a testament to its popularity. Besides the lively bar scene and Water Tower views, the real draw is the food from the wood-burning oven. The kitchen consistently offers excellent renditions of French classics like roast chicken, and vegetarians praise the roasted-vegetable platter. The Sunday jazz brunch makes things more crowded—and louder—than usual. ⊠ *110 E. Pearson St., Near North* ☎ *312/266–3110* ▤ *AE, D, DC, MC, V.*

★ $–$$ ✕ **Bistrot Margot.** We love this Old Town bistro for its faithfully executed menu, budget-friendly prices, and Parisian art nouveau interior, even if we have to sit a little too close for comfort to our neighbors. Chef-owner Joe Doppes whips up silky chicken liver pâté, succulent *moules mariniere* (mussels in tomato sauce), and soul-satisfying coq au vin. Table spacing is tight and crowds abundant, warranting your best behavior. ⊠ *1437 N. Wells St., Near North* ☎ *312/587–3660* ▤ *AE, D, DC, MC, V.*

Hawaiian

$$–$$$ ✕ **Roy's.** Hawaii's most exported chef, Roy Yamaguchi, raids the island pantry, refining the goods with Asian flourishes. The results are busy, multi-ingredient dishes that seduce with the ease of a trade wind. Roy's signatures include many seafood dishes like blackened ahi in soy mustard and butterfish in ginger wasabi sauce. But honey mustard short ribs, lamb two ways, and other carnivores' options please heartier palates. Though the cozy and warm dining room says contemporary chic, the waiters' greetings and flower-print ties spread a little aloha around the place. ⊠ *720 N. State St., Near North* ☎ *312/787–7599* ▤ *AE, D, DC, MC, V* ◷ *No lunch.*

Italian

$$–$$$$
Fodor'sChoice
★
✕ **Spiaggia.** Refined Italian cooking dished alongside three-story picture window views of Lake Michigan make Spiaggia one of the city's top eateries. The tiered dining room guarantees good sight lines from each table. Chef Tony Mantuano prepares elegant, seasonal dishes such as veal-filled pasta with fennel pollen, roast Guinea hen with truffle sauce, or Mediterranean bass with wild arugula. Oenophiles consider the wine list scholarly. For Spiaggia fare, minus the luxury ingredients, try lunch or dinner at the casual Cafe Spiaggia next door. ☒ *980 N. Michigan Ave., Near North* ☎ *312/280–2750* ⌔ *Reservations essential* 🏛 *Jacket required* ▤ *AE, D, DC, MC, V* ☽ *No lunch.*

Japanese

$$–$$$$
✕ **Heat.** Fans of so-fresh-it's-breathing sushi check into this wee, chic 40-seater for chef Kee Chan's "live kill" menu. Fish tanks discretely tucked below the sushi bar hold flounder, eel, and other selections, which chefs flay alive, delivering the seconds-old sashimi on a plate. In addition to creative nigiri sushi, sashimi, and maki, Heat also specializes in the chef's-choice 11-course *kaiseki* menu. But if it's the sushi you crave, reserve a spot at the sushi bar for a chat with the educational Kee, who freely imparts the dos and don'ts of eating raw fish. ☒ *1507 N. Sedgwick, Near North* ☎ *312/397–9818* ▤ *AE, D, DC, MC, V* ☽ *Closed Sun. No lunch.*

$$–$$$
✕ **Kamehachi.** It seems like there's a sushi spot on practically every corner in Chicago, but when Kamehachi opened in Old Town in 1967, it was the first. Quality fish, updated decor, and eager-to-please hospitality keep fans returning. Behind the busy sushi bar, chefs manage both restaurant orders and the many take-out calls of neighbors. We find combinations, including maki rolls, nigiri sushi, and miso soup, are often a bargain, running from $13 to $30. Pony up to the sushi bar, or take a seat in the upstairs lounge, or the flowering garden (in season). The Streeterville spin-off offers semiprivate tatami rooms ideal for groups. ☒ *1400 N. Wells St., Near North* ☎ *312/664–3663* ▤ *AE, D, DC, MC, V* ☽ *No lunch Sun.* ☒ *240 E. Ontario, Near North* ☎ *312/587–0600* ▤ *AE, D, DC, MC, V* ☽ *No lunch Sun. and Mon.*

Mexican

$$–$$$
✕ **Salpicon.** Anyone who does authentic Mexican in Chicago operates in the shadow of Frontera Grill's Rick Bayless, which makes it easier for those in the know to snag a table at Salpicon. Chef Priscila Satkoff grew up in Mexico City and her renditions of Oaxacan mole pork and grilled fish with "salsa fresca" have unforced flare. Wash 'em down with a belt of one of 100 tequilas or 800 vintage wines. Once you try the Mexican-style Sunday brunch, with dishes like skirt steak and eggs, you'll never go back to eggs benedict. ☒ *1252 N. Wells St., Near North* ☎ *312/988–7811* ▤ *AE, D, DC, MC, V* ☽ *No lunch.*

$–$$$
✕ **Adobo Grill.** Mexico's two greatest crowd-pleasers—guacamole and tequila—star here. Cooks wheel carts tableside to make fresh guacamole in authentic molcajetes (stone mortars). Meanwhile, a tequila sommelier helps you navigate the 100-plus varieties on offer. Margaritas are killer, including a $50 splurge made of tippy-top shelf booze. Pair one with regional fare like grilled chicken in tamarind-chipotle glaze and Ve-

6

racruz-style red snapper topped with tomatoes, capers, and olives. If you needed more jolly reasons to enjoy Second City, this is one—it's right next door. ⊠ *1610 N. Wells St., Near North* ☎ *312/266–7999* ⊟ *AE, D, DC, MC, V* ☺ *No lunch.*

Seafood

$$–$$$$ ✕ **Riva.** Riva's got the lock on upscale dining in the middle of junk-food–central Navy Pier. The restaurant relies a bit too much on the views—which, gazing southward over Lake Michigan, are admittedly fantastic—when it should concentrate on better cooking. Opt for simpler preparations, such as grilled salmon or various pastas, over the menu's more ambitious efforts. Grilled fish, shellfish, and steaks are pricey, though the hordes that crowd the place, especially in summer, don't seem to mind (good service helps). A casual grill downstairs, which spills onto the pier's promenade in summer, is kinder to your wallet. ⊠ *700 E. Grand Ave., Near North* ☎ *312/644–7482* ⊟ *AE, D, DC, MC, V.*

$–$$$$ ✕ **McCormick and Schmick's.** If you're the indecisive type, don't even think about dining here. This link in the Oregon-based chain updates its massive menu twice daily to list the freshest fish available. Expect six varieties of oysters, regional specialities like Louisiana crab cakes and Wisconsin rainbow trout, and several dozen fish, like Barcelona anchovies and Hawaiian marlin. Wood paneling, cozy booths, and high ceilings generate a clubby setting. We love the bar not just for the cheap happy hour nibbles, but because the bartenders squeeze all the juices that go into the fresh and zesty cocktails. ⊠ *41 E. Chestnut St., Near North* ☎ *312/397–9500* ⊟ *AE, D, DC, MC, V.*

Steak Houses

$$$$ ✕ **The Capital Grille.** The Chicago outpost of this steak-house chain manages to hold its own among the local players. You can see prime steaks being dry-aged in a glassed-in room. The menu also includes a strong selection of fresh fish and shellfish. The decor avoids some of the steak-house clichés by mixing mounted deer heads and portraits-in-oil. ⊠ *633 N. St. Clair St., Near North* ☎ *312/337–9400* ⊟ *AE, D, DC, MC, V* ☺ *No lunch weekends.*

★ **$$$–$$$$**   ✕ **Morton's, The Steakhouse.** Gibson's is more fun, but this is Chicago's best steak house, the one that's been replicated around the country. Excellent service and a good wine list add to the principal attraction: beautiful, hefty steaks cooked to perfection. A kitschy tradition mandates that everything you order, from gargantuan Idahos to massive slabs of beef, is brought to the table for your approval before the chef gets started. White tablecloths and chandeliers create a classy feel despite the subterranean locale. It's no place for the budget conscious, but for steak lovers it's a 16-ounce (or more) taste of heaven. ⊠ *1050 N. State St., Near North* ☎ *312/266–4820* ⊟ *AE, D, DC, MC, V* ☺ *No lunch.*

★ **$–$$$$**   ✕ **Gibsons Steakhouse.** Chicago movers and shakers mingle with conventioneers at Gibsons, a lively, home-grown, Gold Coast steak house renowned for overwhelming portions, good service, and celebrity spotting. Generous steaks and chops center the menu, but there are plenty of fish options including planked whitefish and massive Australian lobster tails. One dessert will feed a table of four. Reservations aren't re-

CLASSIC CHICAGO STEAK HOUSES

Chicago's stockyards are gone but its reputation for prime persists. If you've come to town to steak it out, check out these locally raised purveyors:

Carmichael's. Relative newcomer that looks like it's been around forever. Great summer patio. ✉ Near West Side ☎ 312/433–0025.

Gene and Georgetti's. A throwback to old Chicago complete with a location under the El and supper club style. ✉ River North ☎ 312/527–3718.

Gibsons Steakhouse. Clubby with a who's who crowd and massive portions. ✉ Near North ☎ 312/266–8999.

Keefer's. Great steaks complemented by macho-free decor. ✉ River North ☎ 312/467–9525.

Morton's, The Steakhouse. The chain was born here. Best porterhouse in the city. ✉ Near North ☎ 312/266–4820.

Nine. Looks like a nightclub but feeds like a linebacker. ✉ West Loop ☎ 312/575–9900.

quired but are near essential given the hoards of fans. ✉ *1028 N. Rush St., Near North* ☎ *312/266–8999* ♿ *Reservations essential* ▤ *AE, D, DC, MC, V.*

$-$$$$ ✗ **Mike Ditka's Restaurant.** NFL Hall-of-Famer Mike Ditka was the only coach to take the Bears to the Super Bowl. Sure, it was in 1985, but Bears fans have long memories, and they still love "Da Coach" as well as his clubby, sports-themed restaurant. The dark-wood interior, upstairs cigar lounge, and sports memorabilia are predictable, but the menu clearly aims to please large and diverse audiences. Café staples (salads, fish) and bar food (burgers, meat loaf) join steak-house fare (steaks, chops) and a few unexpected indulgences (rack of lamb). ✉ *Tremont Hotel, 100 E. Chestnut St., Near North* ☎ *312/587–8989* ▤ *AE, D, DC, MC, V.*

Thai

$-$$ ✗ **Big Bowl.** Good thing the low-carb craze is over, or it might put Big Bowl out of business. Noodles and rice are the basis of the menu at this gregarious restaurant, serving the starches wok-tossed, peanut-coated, curried, with or without meat, without or without seafood—you name it. Most of the preparations are Thai with some Chinese dishes. Shareable starters like pot stickers, plentiful mains, and a casual vibe make this a strong choice for families and other groups. ✉ *6 E. Cedar St., Near North* ☎ *312/640–8888* ▤ *AE, D, DC, MC, V* ✉ *60 E. Ohio St., Near North* ☎ *312/951–1888.*

River North

Long the restaurant hub of Chicago, River North has seen many of its warehouses, which once charged reasonable rent, demolished to make room for residential high-rises. Some important culinary pioneers such as Rick Bayless still thrive here, but increasingly River North is being colonized by big-box chains like ESPN Zone and Rainforest Café. As you can see from the length of this section, however, you'd be remiss not to spend time eating here, albeit selectively—there are still many spots that have escaped homogenization.

American–Casual

☺ ¢–$ ✕ **Ed Debevic's.** Gum-snapping waiters in garish costumes trade quips and snide remarks with customers at this tongue-in-cheek re-creation of a 1950s diner, but it's all good, clean fun (except perhaps when they dance on the counter without removing their shoes). The menu is deep and cheap with 10 different hamburgers, five chili preparations, four hot dogs, a large sandwich selection, and such "deluxe plates" as meat loaf, pot roast, and chicken-fried steak. The place is crawling with kids. Unlike a real 1950s diner, however, Ed's has a selection of cocktails and wines for their parents. ⊠ *640 N. Wells St., River North* ☎ *312/664–1707* ⚑ *Reservations not accepted* ⊟ *AE, D, DC, MC, V.*

¢–$ ✕ **Mr. Beef.** A Chicago institution for two-fisted Italian beef sandwiches piled with red peppers and provolone cheese (*see* Chicago's Holy Trinity, page 199, for more information on these sandwiches), Mr. Beef garners citywide fans from area hard-hats to restaurateurs and TV personalities. Service and setting—two indoor picnic tables and a dining rail—are fast-food no-nonsense. This working man's favorite is, go figure, located near River North's art galleries. ⊠ *666 N. Orleans St., River North* ☎ *312/337–8500* ⊟ *No credit cards* ⊘ *Closed Sun. No dinner.*

Brazilian

$$$$ ✕ **Fogo de Chao.** Gaucho-clad servers parade through the dining room brandishing carved-to-order skewered and grilled meats in this all-you-can-eat Brazilian churrascaria. Diners warm up with a trip to the lavish salad bar. Then, using a plate-side chip, signal green for "go" to bring on lamb, pork loin, ribs, and several beef cuts, stopped only by flipping the chip to red. You can restart as often as you like. If that's not enough, there are starchy sides and dessert flans included in the $48.50 price as well; only drinks are extra. Compared to traditional steak houses, this carnivorous all-inclusive feast is a bargain. Go on a busy night (Thursday, Friday, or Saturday) to ensure the meat's tender—not dried out from reheating. ⊠ *661 N. LaSalle St., River North* ☎ *312/932–9330* ⊟ *AE, D, DC, MC, V* ⊘ *No lunch weekends.*

Chinese

$–$$$ ✕ **Ben Pao.** Snagging our award for the most Zen Chinese restaurant in town is this spot, with its minimalist black-and-gray decor and soothing water walls. The food livens up the scene, with spicy noodles, Cantonese roast duck, and plenty of the tried-and-true sesame chicken and kung pao chicken. A dozen or so small-plate starters and the Asian hot pot dish—a sort of fondue that uses bubbling broth to cook meat—encourage sharing, making this a good choice for the gang. ⊠ *52 W. Illinois St., River North* ☎ *312/222–1888* ⊟ *AE, D, DC, MC, V* ⊘ *No lunch weekends.*

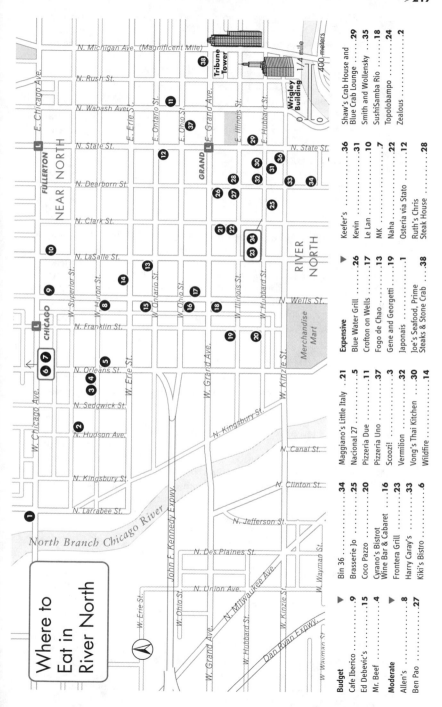

Where to Eat in River North

Budget

▶ Cafe Iberico **9**
Ed Debevic's **15**
Mr. Beef **4**

Moderate

Allen's **8**
Ben Pao **27**

Bin 36 . . . . **34**
Brasserie Jo **25**
Coco Pazzo **20**
Cyrano's Bistrot
Wine Bar & Cabaret . . . **16**
▶ Frontera Grill **23**
Harry Caray's **33**
Kiki's Bistro **6**

Maggiano's Little Italy . . **21**
Nacional 27 . . . . **5**
Pizzeria Due **11**
Pizzeria Uno **37**
Scoozi! **3**
Vermilion **32**
Vong's Thai Kitchen . . . **30**
Wildfire **14**

Expensive

▶ Blue Water Grill **26**
Crofton on Wells **17**
Fogo de Chao **13**
Gene and Georgetti . . . **19**
Japonais **1**
Joe's Seafood, Prime
Steaks & Stone Crab . . . **38**

Keefer's **36**
Kevin **31**
Le Lan **10**
MK **7**
Naha **22**
Osteria via Stato **12**
Ruth's Chris
Steak House **28**

Shaw's Crab House and
Blue Crab Lounge **29**
Smith and Wollensky . . **35**
SushiSamba Rio **18**
Topolobampo **24**
Zealous **2**

Treats for Kids

CLOSE UP

DON'T BE AFRAID to take the kids to dinner at some of the more upscale downtown eateries, particularly those that thrive on volume such as Maggiano's, Scoozi!, and Frontera Grill. But for those spots that the kids will love try one of these.

Big Bowl: Endless varieties of Asian noodles please the mac-and-cheese set. There's even a kid's menu for timid tastes. ⊠ *6 E. Cedar St., Gold Coast* ☎ *312/640-8888.*

Foodlife: The teeming food court at Water Tower Place shopping center suits families with kids age six and up (littler ones tend to get overwhelmed here). Loads of choices ensure something for every member of the clan. ⊠ *Water Tower Place, 835 N. Michigan Ave., Near North* ☎ *312/ 335-3663.*

Pizzeria Uno: Cracker Jacks, malted-milk shakes, and Twinkies were all

invented in Chicago, but no junk food is more allied with the city than deep-dish pizza. ⊠ *Uno, 29 E. Ohio St., River North* ☎ *312/321-1000.*

R. J. Grunts: Opposite the Lincoln Park Zoo, Grunts is accustomed to family traffic and has a terrific salad bar instantly gratifying those hunger pangs. Be forewarned that long waits can overwhelm cranky kids. ⊠ *2056 Lincoln Park W, Lincoln Park* ☎ *773/ 929-5636.*

Wishbone: Two locations—one in the West Loop and another in Lake View—are thronged by families. Kids get crayons, adults can get booze, and everyone gets shareable creole fare at breakfast, lunch, or dinner. ⊠ *1001 W. Washington Blvd., Near West Side* ☎ *312/850-2663* ⊠ *3300 N. Lincoln Ave., Lake View* ☎ *773/549-4105.*

Contemporary

$$$$ ✗ **Kevin.** Harmony reigns at chef-owner Kevin Shikami's namesake, where an understated, soothing setting puts the focus squarely on the kitchen's French-Asian fusion. Fans come for Shikami's tuna tartare alone. The menu changes frequently but typical dishes might include pistachio-crusted red snapper or duck breast in orange-star anise sauce. If price is a problem, try lunching here—entrées drop by almost half. ⊠ *9 W. Hubbard St., River North* ☎ *312/595-0055* ▤ *AE, DC, MC, V* ⊙ *Closed Sun. No lunch Sat.*

★ **$$$-$$$$** ✗ **MK.** Foodies and fashionistas favor owner-chef Michael Kornick's ultrahip spot for its sleek look and elegant menu. Occupying a renovated warehouse, MK weights brick walls and soaring ceilings with fine linens, expensive flatware, and designer wine stems. Menus change with the season and hew to two or three dominant flavors à la halibut with sweet corn and fava beans, and lamb loin with cucumber and mint yogurt. It's not cheap, but it is special. ⊠ *868 N. Franklin St., River North* ☎ *312/ 482-9179* ⚏ *Reservations essential* ▤ *AE, DC, MC, V* ⊙ *No lunch.*

$$$-$$$$ ✗ **Naha.** Carrie Nahabedian lends her name (well, the first two syllables, anyway) and considerable culinary skills to this upscale venture. In a clean space done in shades of cream and sage, Nahabedian presents eye-catching dishes such as a tower of tuna and salmon tartare, vanilla-scented roasted sea scallops, or wild bass in saffron broth. Wine is treated with reverence, from the well-chosen selection of vintages to the high-quality stemware. Solos and social-seekers can sit at the convivial bar and order from the main menu. ✉ *500 N. Clark St., River North* ☎ *312/321–6242* ▭ *AE, D, DC, MC, V* ☾ *Closed Sun. No lunch Sat.*

$$–$$$$ ✕ **Crofton on Wells.** We like this place because it's really good and still manages to be rather low-key. Chef–owner Suzy Crofton breaks a few contemporary-dining rules: she doesn't pack tables too closely together in the small space, and she keeps the noise level down. Her food is similarly short on clichés but gratifyingly long on flavor. Dig into gutsy chipotle roasted Amish chicken or grilled venison with gnocchi and cherries. ✉ *535 N. Wells St., River North* ☎ *312/755–1790* ⚘ *Reservations essential* ▭ *AE, D, DC, MC, V* ☾ *Closed Sun. No lunch.*

$$–$$$$ ✕ **SushiSamba Rio.** *Sex in the City* made SushiSamba a star in New York, and look-alike hotties make the Chicago version a scene. The trendy Brazilian–Japanese hot spot combines a nightclub vibe—dramatic multilevel design, freely flowing cocktails, male servers in eye makeup—with an inventive menu. All the usual sushi suspects are here, as well as offbeat sashimi choices, Brazilian-style marinated fish, and fusion rolls that don't always work. For best results sample the menu with an adventurous, party-hardy crowd on Wednesday when there's a band and samba dancers. An all-weather rooftop lounge, popular with the late-night crowd, serves cocktails (try the sparkling sake) and some sushi. ✉ *504 N. Wells St., River North* ☎ *312/595–2300* ▭ *AE, D, DC, MC, V.*

$$–$$$$ ✕ **Zealous.** We love the look of Zealous: skylights, bamboo plants, curvy metallic half walls, and a two-story glassed-in wine room. Granted, the effect is slightly cold, but the food compensates. Charlie Trotter protégé Michael Taus runs the haute-cuisine kitchen, serving edgy dishes that change seasonally but are typified by mango pancakes with foie gras and freshwater prawns with purple yam puree and coconut-hickory nut sauce. The menu centers around an $85, five-course prix-fixe meal, but those in the mood to splurge may indulge in even grander multicourse degustations, each off-the-menu course selected by the chef. ✉ *419 W. Superior St., River North* ☎ *312/475–9112* ▭ *AE, D, DC, MC, V* ☾ *Closed Sun. and Mon. No lunch.*

$$–$$$ ✕ **Allen's.** Distinguishing himself from the pack of contemporary cooks, chef Allen Sternweiler goes boldly with wild game. Think roast rabbit stuffed with rabbit sausage and grilled duck in port wine. If you're less adventurous, there are plenty of more familiar options in the meat and sea departments. The biggest treat here, though, is the massive collection of fine spirits, like armagnacs, ports, and small-batch bourbons. Our favorite is the 16-year-old Hirsch Reserve bourbon. ✉ *217 W. Huron St., River North* ☎ *312/587–9600* ▭ *AE, D, DC, MC, V* ☾ *Closed Sun. No lunch Sat.*

$$–$$$ ✕ **Wildfire.** This is as close as you can get to the grill without staying home and firing up the barbie. A triple hearth of roaring fires runs along the back wall of the supper club–style joint that plays a soundtrack of vintage jazz. No culinary innovations here, just exceptional aged prime rib, barbecued ribs, and roasted fish, along with wood-fired pizzas and skillet-roasted mussels. Top taste: the horseradish-crusted filet mignon.

UP-AND-COMING

On the horizon at press time, these new restaurants promise big things:

Francesca's Forno from the owners of the popular Mia Francesca promises more hearth-baked dishes. ⊠ *1576 N. Milwaukee Ave., Wicker Park* ☎ *773/770-0184.*

Landmark will open down the street from Boka with whom it shares owners, dishing grilled meats and wood-oven pizzas. ⊠ *1633 N. Halsted St., Lincoln Park* ☎ *312/587-1600.*

Chef Shawn McClain of Spring and Green Zebra will open **Custom**

House, his ode to meat—not steak, but braised rabbit, pork bellies, etc. ⊠ *500 S. Dearborn, Near South* ☎ *312/523-0200.*

Del Toro promises Spanish tapas in Wicker Park. ⊠ *1520 N. Damen.*

Bin 36 will spin off **Bin Wine Café** in Wicker Park with cheeses and wine, wine, wine. ⊠ *1559 N. Milwaukee Ave.*

Building on his fame with Zealous, chef Michael Taus plans to open the less-expensive **Saltaus.** ⊠ *1350 W. Randolph St., Near West Side* ☎ *312/455-1919.*

⊠ *159 W. Erie St., River North* ☎ *312/787-9000* ▭ *AE, D, DC, MC, V* ⊘ *No lunch.*

★ **$-$$$** ✕ **Bin 36.** This hip hybrid—fine-dining establishment, lively wine bar, and wine shop—serves wine anyway you want it: by the bottle, glass, half-glass, and as "flights" of multiple 1½-ounce tastings. The menu similarly encourages sampling, with lots of small-plate grazing choices. Contemporary entrées, such as grilled lamb sirloin and peppercorn-crusted swordfish, are helpfully listed with wine recommendations. An all-glass west wall and 35-foot ceilings lend loft looks to the sprawling space, which can be noisy. Nonetheless, it's a good choice for group gatherings and, since it's open all day, between-standard-mealtime nibbles. ⊠ *339 N. Dearborn St., River North* ☎ *312/755-9463* ▭ *AE, D, DC, MC, V.*

French

$-$$$$ ✕ **Brasserie Jo.** Come for the frites alone at Jean Joho's fun and more affordable brasserie (he of Everest fame). It's authentic down to its zinc-topped bar proffering complimentary hard-boiled eggs. Stay for the *choucroute* (a crock full of pork cuts with Alsatian sauerkraut), phyllo-wrapped shrimp, classic coq au vin, and steak tartare. It's most charming when it's bustling, though peak hours will force you to wait for a table. ⊠ *59 W. Hubbard St., River North* ☎ *312/595-0800* ▭ *AE, D, DC, MC, V* ⊘ *No lunch.*

$$-$$$ ✕ **Kiki's Bistro.** Owner Georges "Kiki" Cuisance hails from France and proudly touts his allegiance with a menu of classic, robust French fare in an urban loft space dressed to look country French. Snails in butter and duck pâté precede entrées of steak frites and veal liver. The early bird's $25, three-course prix fixe is a good buy if you're willing to dine before 6:30 PM. ⊠ *900 N. Franklin St., River North* ☎ *312/335-5454* ▭ *AE, D, DC, MC, V* ⊘ *Closed Sun. No lunch Sat.*

$–$$$ ✕ **Cyrano's Bistrot Wine Bar & Cabaret.** Cyrano's flies under the radar in restaurant-rich River North, which works to your advantage if you want a spontaneous meal. Chef and owner Didier Durand presents the food of his birthplace, Bergerac, in this cheerful restaurant. Traditional starters such as onion tart and bouillabaisse lead into mains of rotisserie chicken, rabbit, and duck. The wine list includes many vintages from lesser-known producers in southern France. The basement cabaret doles out free nibbles with drinks at happy hour. ⊠ *546 N. Wells St., River North* ☎ *312/467–0546* ⊟ *AE, D, DC, MC, V* ☺ *Closed Sun. and Mon. No lunch weekends.*

Fusion

$$$–$$$$ ✕ **Le Lan.** Top toques Roland Liccioni of Le Francais and Arun Sampan-thavivat of Arun's teamed up to create this elegant French-Vietnamese boîte. We like the sophisticated-without-being-stuffy vibe—sharply dressed (yes, don your black to fit in here) foodies fill the exposed brick room that has green accents and orchids on the tables. The menu manages the same balance: the rich flavors of France are piqued by Asian notes. Look for the stuffed squash blossom and the crispy skinned duck. ⊠ *749 N. Clark St., River North* ☎ *312/280–9100* ⊟ *AE, D, DC, MC, V* ☺ *Closed Sun. No lunch.*

Indian

$$–$$$ ✕ **Vermilion.** Vermilion touts itself as a Latin–Indian fusion restaurant, but its best dishes are strictly Eastern. Skip the Latin-salute seviche and empanadas in favor of the Coca-Cola–marinated baby back ribs, traditional vindaloos, and curries. Lots of small-plate options—led by the lamb chops and lentil salad—encourage sampling. Despite cool fashion photography on the walls and techno music in the air, the welcome here is warm. Late-night dining hours draw a club-going crowd. ⊠ *10 W. Hubbard St., River North* ☎ *312/527–4060* ⊟ *AE, D, DC, MC, V* ☺ *No lunch Sat.*

Italian

$$$$ ✕ **Osteria via Stato.** It's no-brainer Italian here, where the schtick is to feed you without asking too many questions. You pick an entrée from the $35.95 prix fixe, and waiters do the rest, working the room with several rounds of communal platters of antipasti, then pasta, followed by your entrée, and dessert. There's even a "just bring me wine" program that delivers preselected vino to your table throughout your meal. The results are savory enough, but Osteria shines brightest at making you feel comfortable. If conversation is important, make a reservation here. You won't spend but a precious minute reading the menu. ⊠ *620 N. State St., River North* ☎ *312/642–8450* ⊟ *AE, D, DC, MC, V* ☺ *No lunch Sun.*

$–$$$$ ✕ **Coco Pazzo.** This Chicago branch of a very successful Manhattan restaurant focuses on Tuscan cuisine—lusty, aggressively seasoned fare, such as homemade pasta with rabbit ragu, rotisserie leg of lamb, and wood-grilled Florentine steaks. Stop in at lunch for pizzas fresh from the wood-fired oven. Swagged draperies and discreet but professional service work hard to soften the open loft setting of exposed brick walls and

6

wood floors. ⊠ *300 W. Hubbard St., River North* ☎ *312/836–0900* ♨ *Reservations essential* ⊟ *AE, DC, MC, V* ⊗ *No lunch weekends.*

$–$$$$ ✕ **Harry Caray's.** Famed Cubs announcer Harry Caray died in 1998, but his legend lives on as fans continue to pour into the namesake restaurant where Harry frequently held court. Italian-American specialties including pastas and chicken Vesuvio share menu space with top-quality prime steaks and chops. The

> ### WORD OF MOUTH
>
> "We ate at Harry Caray's. Food was good–a little pricey but worth it to see all of the Cubs memorabilia."
>
> –vickymc

wine list has won a number of national awards. If you're looking for a classic Chicago spot to catch a game, the generally thronged bar serves classic bar food and televised sports. Holy cow! ⊠ *33 W. Kinzie St., River North* ☎ *312/828–0966* ⊟ *AE, D, DC, MC, V.*

$–$$$ ✕ **Maggiano's Little Italy.** Large portions generate large followings. Maggiano's has followed this mantra, dishing up enormous servings of red-sauced Italian food in this homage to Little Italy and doggie bags. Expect hearty, stereotypical Italian-American fare—brick-size lasagna, chicken Vesuvio, and veal scaloppini. Order two entrées for every three diners in your party and you'll be as happy as the other cheerfully loud patrons in the wide-open dining room. ⊠ *516 N. Clark St., River North* ☎ *312/644–7700* ⊟ *AE, D, DC, MC, V.*

$–$$ ✕ **Pizzeria Due.** This is where everyone goes when they've found out that Uno, the original home of Chicago's deep-dish pizza up the street, has an hour-plus wait. The caveat is that Due quickly builds its own waiting list. The best strategy for dining out at either spot is to arrive early or opt to come at lunch. ⊠ *619 N. Wabash Ave., River North* ☎ *312/943–2400* ⊟ *AE, D, DC, MC, V.*

$–$$ ✕ **Pizzeria Uno.** Chicago deep-dish pizza got its start here in 1943, and **FodorsChoice** both local and out-of-town fans continue to pack in for filling pies. Housed ★ in a Victorian brownstone, Uno offers a slice of old Chicago in dim paneled rooms with reproduction light fixtures. Spin-off Due down the street handles the overflow. Plan on two thick, cheesy slices or less as a full meal. This is no quick-to-your-table pie, so do order salads and be prepared to entertain the kids during the inevitable wait. ⊠ *29 E. Ohio St., River North* ☎ *312/321–1000.*

$–$$ ✕ **Scoozi!** This ever-popular trattoria continues to attract a yuppie crowd after five and plenty of wandering suburbanites on the weekend. You'll recognize it by the gigantic tomato over the front door; inside, a sprawling, two-level dining room sports loft-chic looks of exposed brick walls, open truss ceiling, and steel garage doors. This place is nothing if not chameleon; groups love the shareable antipasti and pizzas, families with kids meld right into the cacophony, and couples find the energy relieves the focus on a boring date. ⊠ *410 W. Huron St., River North* ☎ *312/943–5900* ⊟ *AE, D, DC, MC, V* ⊗ *No lunch.*

Japanese

★ **$$–$$$$** ✕ **Japonais.** Style and substance come together at sleek and chic Japonais. Don't be intimidated by the lengthy menu. Trust servers to direct you to savories such as breaded oysters, white tuna and arugula salad, and a raft of winning maki roll combinations including octopus with spicy tuna. Traditional tables are supplemented by a couch-filled lounge also serving the entire menu. Downstairs an indoor-outdoor bar provides seasonal seating along the Chicago River—don't attempt it on weekends unless you have sharp elbows. ⊠ *606 W. Chicago Ave., River North* ☎ *312/822–9600* ▱ *AE, D, DC, MC, V* ☺ *No lunch weekends.*

Latin

$$–$$$ ✕ **Nacional 27.** Here's a bit of trivia to spring on fellow diners: there are 27 nations south of the U.S. border, and it's the cuisine of those 27 that supposedly comprise the Pan-Latin menu here. That may be an exaggeration, but the menu does offer variety. Try the barbecued pork *arepas* (corn-bread pancakes) appetizer and follow with the pork tenderloin smeared with chili paste. The circular bar draws a following independent of the food. After 11 PM on weekend nights, the floor in the middle of the dining room is cleared for salsa and merengue dancing. ⊠ *325 W. Huron St., River North* ☎ *312/664–2727* ▱ *AE, D, DC, MC, V* ☺ *Closed Sun. No lunch.*

Mexican

$$$–$$$$ ✕ **Topolobampo.** The name is a mouthful; do like a local and call it **Fodor'sChoice** "Topolo." Chef-owner Rick Bayless wrote the book on regional Mexican cuisine—several books, actually—and here he takes his faithfully ★ regional food upscale. Next door to the more casual Frontera Grill (see review below), Topolo is the higher-end room, with a more subdued mood and luxury menu, though it shares Frontera's address, phone, and dedication to quality. The ever-changing offerings showcase game, seasonal fruits and vegetables, and exotic preparations: tequila-cured salmon and pheasant roasted in banana leaves are two examples. ⊠ *445 N. Clark St., River North* ☎ *312/661–1434* ⌁ *Reservations essential* ▱ *AE, D, DC, MC, V* ☺ *Closed Sun. and Mon. No lunch Sat.*

$$–$$$ ✕ **Frontera Grill.** Devotees of chef-owner Rick Bayless queue up for his **Fodor'sChoice** distinct fare at this casual restaurant, brightly trimmed in Mexican folk ★ art. Bayless annually visits Mexico with the entire staff in tow. Servers, consequently, are encyclopedic on the food, typified by salmon in pumpkin-seed mole, pork in a pasilla-pepper sauce, and chiles rellenos. The reservation policy is tricky: they're accepted for parties of five or more, though smaller groups can phone in the same day. Otherwise, make like most and endure the two-margarita wait. ⊠ *445 N. Clark St., River North* ☎ *312/661–1434* ▱ *AE, D, DC, MC, V* ☺ *Closed Sun. and Mon.*

Seafood

$$–$$$$ ✕ **Blue Water Grill.** This isn't your standard seafood restaurant. Nightcrawlers love this spot for its sleek design, chic amenities (like farewell chocolates in a small gift box), and a menu that fishes from Maine to Tokyo. The sexy L-shape interior spans a sushi bar, a cocktail lounge with low sofas, and two dining rooms with dark tables and throw pillows on the banquettes. There's the usual raw bar oysters and steamed lobster, but the kitchen goes to work on creative maki rolls (try the spicy Baja), tempura calamari, and buttery bass. Upstairs the jazz lounge hosts pre- and post-prandial entertainment. ⊠ *520 N. Dearborn St., River North* ☎ *312/777–1400* ▱ *AE, D, DC, MC, V* ☺ *No lunch Sat.*

$$–$$$$ ✕ **Joe's Seafood, Prime Steaks & Stone Crab.** You might wonder what a South Floridian like Joe's is doing so far from the ocean. Apparently, raking it in. Unlike its parent, Joe's Stone Crab in Miami Beach, this outlet doesn't close when the Florida crabs are out of season in summer. Which explains the extra emphasis on other denizens of the deep and prime steaks. One thing this restaurant does share with the Miami original is its popularity—people line up before the restaurant opens to be sure they get a table. ⊠ *60 E. Grand Ave., River North* ☎ *312/379–5637* ⊟ *AE, D, DC, MC, V* ⊙ *No lunch Sun.*

★ **$$–$$$$** ✕ **Shaw's Crab House and Blue Crab Lounge.** Hands down, this is the city's best seafood spot. Though it's held the position a long time, it doesn't rest on its laurels. The kitchen stays on track, turning out famed classics like silky crab cakes and rich halibut while updating the menu with sushi, maki, and fresh tartare selections. The seafood salad served at lunch is loaded and big enough for two. (Lunch, by the way, is a good bargain, with well-priced entrées and $1 desserts). The city's chief specialist in bivalves nurtures a split personality, spanning a clubby main dining room in nautically themed loft digs and a lively exposed-brick bar where shell shuckers work harder than the barkeeps. ⊠ *21 E. Hubbard St., River North* ☎ *312/527–2722* ⊟ *AE, D, DC, MC, V.*

Spanish

$ ✕ **Cafe Iberico.** A Spanish expat from the province of Galicia runs this tapas place hailed by a range of fans from visiting Spaniards (including the national soccer team and guitarist Paco de Lucia) to family clans, dating couples, and cheap chowhounds. You can easily build a meal from the many $2–$7 small plates on offer such as tuna-stuffed cannelloni, Spanish ham, grilled squid, and skewered beef. Think tapas; there are only five entrées on the menu. When it's busy it's loud and boisterous, which is only annoying on weekends when the wait stretches to hours. Only parties of six or more may make reservations for Sunday through Thursday. ⊠ *739 N. LaSalle St., River North* ☎ *312/573–1510* ⊟ *AE, D, DC, MC, V.*

Steak Houses

$$$–$$$$ ✕ **Smith and Wollensky.** Aged-on-the-premises prime beef and an extensive wine cellar are hallmarks of this riverfront steak house, part of a New York–based chain. United by remarkable river views, the dining area is divided into several spaces, one of which is Wollensky's Grill, a more casual room with a compact menu and later serving hours. Steaks and chops are the big draw, but deep-fried pork shank and pepper-dusted "angry lobster" are customer favorites, too. ⊠ *318 N. State St., River North* ☎ *312/670–9900* ⊟ *AE, D, DC, MC, V.*

$$–$$$$ ✕ **Gene and Georgetti.** This old-school steak house thrives on the buddy network of high-powered regulars who pop into the historic

> ### WORD OF MOUTH
>
> "You should try some place with local flavor rather than a place you can go to in almost any city, which is why I recommended the Chop House and G&G."
>
> –almesq

River North joint to carve up massive steaks, good chops, and the famed "garbage salad"—a kitchen-sink creation of greens with vegetables and meats. Service can be brusque if you're not connected, but the vibe is Chicago to the core. ✉ *500 N. Franklin St., River North* ☎ *312/527–3718* ▭ *AE, DC, MC, V* ⊘ *Closed Sun.*

$$–$$$$ ✕ **Keefer's.** Few steak houses advertise their broiler men, but the barrier-busting Keefer's hired acclaimed chef John Hogan to run the kitchen. Hogan's definition of a steak-house menu breaks all conventions by including his signature bistro fare, inventive daily specials (pray for the seafood-rich bouillabaisse), and plenty of fish offerings as well as New York strips and hefty porterhouses. The circular room drops the he-man pose, too. All of which explains why Keefer's pulls the most diverse and gender-balanced crowd of the meat market. ✉ *20 W. Kinzie St., River North* ☎ *312/467–9525* ▭ *AE, D, DC, MC, V* ⊘ *Closed Sun. No lunch Sat.*

$$–$$$$ ✕ **Ruth's Chris Steak House.** With excellent steaks and outstanding service, the Chicago outpost of this fine-dining chain holds its own in this definitive steak town. The lobster is good, although expensive, and there are more appetizer and side-dish options than at most other steak houses. Woody surrounds and low lighting lend a masculine character and draw a clientele of business diners. ✉ *431 N. Dearborn St., River North* ☎ *312/321–2725* ▭ *AE, D, DC, MC, V* ⊘ *No lunch weekends.*

Thai

$–$$$ ✕ **Vong's Thai Kitchen.** This casual spin-off of chef Jean-Georges Vongerichten's New York Thai–French fusion Vong concentrates solely on Thai fare with upmarket accents and pretty presentations. Look for tuna sashimi rolls, sliced New York strip steak over noodles, and a laundry list of curries ranging from mild to "jungle" hot. Candles and palms boost the romance quotient by night, but this is also a strong candidate for a working lunch. ✉ *6 W. Hubbard St., River North* ☎ *312/644–8664* ▭ *AE, D, DC, MC, V* ⊘ *No lunch weekends.*

Lincoln Park

Charlie Trotter put the well-off, lake-bordering residential district of Lincoln Park on the culinary map, bringing foodies from around the world to his brownstone's doors. Beyond Trotter's, you'll find lots of bar food and average fare mucking up North Halsted Street's theater district (which is anchored by the Steppenwolf Theatre), but the neighborhood is adequately salted with restaurants worth seeking out. Especially of note are North Pond in the park and, if you're interested in the future of food, Alinea.

Contemporary

$$$$ ✕ **Alinea.** Though it's smack in the middle of the North Halsted theaters, don't expect to grab a precurtain meal here: the experience is theater itself. Avant-garde chef Grant Achatz specializes in deconstructing and rebuilding food in a way that's playful and modern—and not for everyone. Serious foodies with venturesome tastebuds appreciate distinctive touches like dishes that come on lavender-scented pillows (they enhance the aroma) or a ginger centerpiece that gets shaved into course

Fodor'sChoice
★

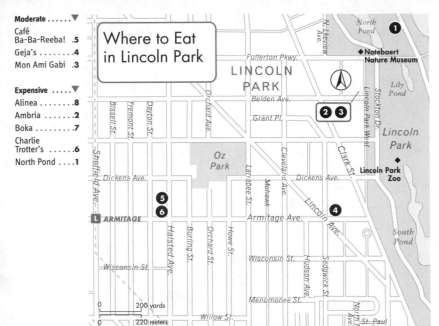

Where to Eat
in Lincoln Park

KEY

L CTA lines

six. Menus change frequently and come in 8-, 12-, and 26-courses. Fortunately, the portions are balanced and the chairs comfortable. For best results, opt for the wine-pairing program. ✉ *1723 N. Halsted St., Lincoln Park* ☎ *773/867–0110* ⌛ *Reservations essential* ▤ *AE, D, DC, MC, V* ✆ *Closed Mon. and Tues. No lunch.*

$$$$ ✕ **Charlie Trotter's.** Plan well in advance to dine at top toque Charlie Trot-
Fodor'sChoice ter's namesake (or call the day of and hope for a cancellation). One of
★ the nation's most experimental chefs, Trotter prepares his menus daily from the best of what's available globally. The results are daring, multi-ingredient dishes that look like art on a dinner plate. Menus follow a multicourse, $135 degustation format ($115 for the vegetarian version). For a worthwhile splurge order the wines-to-match option. This temple of haute cuisine occupies a stately Lincoln Park town house. ✉ *816 W. Armitage Ave., Lincoln Park* ☎ *773/248–6228* ⌛ *Reservations essential* 🎩 *Jacket required* ▤ *AE, DC, MC, V* ✆ *Closed Sun. No lunch.*

$$$–$$$$ ✕ **North Pond.** A former Arts and Crafts–style warming house for ice-
Fodor'sChoice skaters at Lincoln Park's North Pond, this gem-in-the-woods fittingly
★ champions an uncluttered culinary style. Talented chef Bruce Sherman emphasizes organic ingredients, wild-caught fish, and artisan farm products. Menus change seasonally, but order the midwestern favorite wall-

eye pike if available. Like the food, the wine list seeks out small American craft producers. The food remains top-notch at lunch but the scene, dense with strollers and highchairs, is far from serene. ⊠ *2610 N. Cannon Dr., Lincoln Park* ☎ *773/477–5845* ⊟ *AE, D, DC, MC, V* ⊗ *Closed Mon. No lunch Oct.–May.*

$$–$$$$ ✕ **Boka.** If you're doing Steppenwolf pretheater dinner on North Halsted, this unpretentious spot gets foodies' stamp of approval. A seasonally driven menu with standouts such as seared foie gras, salmon tartare, Mediterranean-style snapper, and roast venison loin hint at the chef's former gig working for Wolfgang Puck. The slick lounge and bar, both serving food, draw a following independent of curtain time. ⊠ *1729 N. Halsted St., Lincoln Park* ☎ *312/337–6070* ⊟ *AE, MC, V* ⊗ *No lunch.*

French

★ **$$$–$$$$** ✕ **Ambria.** Romance-inclined couples and suits on expense accounts seem to agree on Ambria. The lush, art nouveau decor sets a sensual stage for updated French food, which might include the likes of blackberry-sauced venison, lobster gazpacho, and rosemary-infused lamb loin. If the à la carte offerings are too much to contemplate, simplify your decision with one of several multicourse dinners. The wine list is encyclopedic, but celebrated sommelier Bob Bansberg is an unintimidating and sensitive guide. ⊠ *2300 N. Lincoln Park W, Lincoln Park* ☎ *773/472–5959* ⊟ *AE, D, DC, MC, V* ⊗ *Closed Sun. No lunch.*

$–$$$$ ✕ **Geja's.** For every course there's a fondue at this Lincoln Park longtimer. Start with the cheese fondue, then progress to the sampler plate of shellfish, chicken, beef, and vegetables cooked in a kettle of hot oil (the tables are riveted to the floor to avoid disaster). Finish by dunking fruits and sweets in liquid chocolate, if you've got room. Candlelight, cozy dining nooks, walls filled with empty wine bottles, and strumming guitarists mean this place is packed on Valentine's Day. ⊠ *340 W. Armitage Ave., Lincoln Park* ☎ *773/281–9101* ⊟ *AE, D, DC, MC, V* ⊗ *No lunch.*

$–$$$ ✕ **Mon Ami Gabi.** This little piece of Paris recreates a classic bistro with views of Lincoln Park that could pass—with the help of a couple of glasses of *vin* from the rolling wine cart—for the Tuileries. Park-front windows let in ample natural light, warming the wood-trimmed interior. Best bites include several versions of steak frites, as well as such bistro essentials as bouillabaisse and *coquilles St. Jacques* (scallops). The casual Gabi offers big savings over its older sibling Ambria (which just happens to be across the hall of the apartment building they're both housed in). ⊠ *2300 N. Lincoln Park W, Lincoln Park* ☎ *773/348–8886* ⊟ *AE, D, DC, MC, V* ⊗ *No lunch.*

Spanish

$–$$ ✕ **Café Ba-Ba-Reeba!** It has a kitschy name and is jammed with partying Lincoln Parkers, so at first you don't expect much food-wise here, but expat Spaniards swear it's the best in town. Colorful interiors filled with folk art encourage the fiesta feel. The large assortment of cold and warm tapas ranges from manchego cheese with Serrano ham to grilled squid. It's worth visiting the entrée menu for paella and skewered meats. In warm weather the sangria flows freely on the outdoor patio. ⊠ *2024 N. Halsted St., Lincoln Park* ☎ *773/935–5000* ⊟ *AE, D, DC, MC, V* ☺ *No lunch weekdays.*

Wicker Park & Bucktown

The art-centric Wicker Park and its more gentrified neighbor Bucktown have emerged with a critical mass of hip restaurants to warrant a feed here. The eateries have followed the cluster of music clubs and shops to the intersection of Damen, North, and Milwaukee Avenues and again at Damen and Division. With Spring, the neighborhoods have their first real destination draw. The rest is gravy and it's pretty good.

Barbecue

$–$$ ✕ **Smoke Daddy.** A rib and blues emporium in a funky Wicker Park corner bar, Smoke Daddy serves tangy barbecued ribs with generously supplied paper towels for swabbing stray sauce. Fans pack bar stools and booths for the chow, which includes richly flavored smoked pork and homemade fries, as well as for the no-cover R&B bands that play nightly after 9:30. ⊠ *1804 W. Division St., Wicker Park* ☎ *773/772–6656* ⊟ *AE, D, MC, V.*

Cafés

$–$$ ✕ **Hot Chocolate.** The city's most celebrated pastry chef, Mindy Segal, strikes out solo at Hot Chocolate, a hit with, as you might expect, a really great dessert selection. For the big finish, there's chocolate mousse, baked pear, buttermilk cake, apple pot pie, and a myriad of milk shakes and hot chocolate flavors with homemade marshmallows. How sweet, and how swamped, it is. PS: the menu also has upscale café fare like pork chops with polenta or a Kobe beef sandwich with carmelized onions. But who came here for the real food? ⊠ *1747 N. Damen Ave., Wicker Park* ☎ *773/489–1747* ⊟ *AE, MC, V* ☺ *Closed Mon.*

¢–$ ✕ **Milk & Honey Café.** Wicker Park's Division Street has long been a prowl of night owls. But with the advent of spas and boutiques in the area, not to mention the many work-from-home locals, the boho neighborhood needed a good breakfast and lunch spot. Milk & Honey exceeds expectations with hearty (eggs) and healthy (granola) breakfasts, and creative sandwiches (grilled salmon with arugula) and salads (smoked shrimp) at lunch. Choice seats change with the season: out on the sidewalk café in warm weather, in near the fireplace in cooler temps. ⊠ *1920 W. Division St., Wicker Park* ☎ *773/395–9434* ⊟ *AE, MC, V* ☺ *No dinner.*

Contemporary

$$–$$$$ ✕ **Meritage Café and Wine Bar.** Locals come here for downtown caliber fare in the neighborhood. The menu dabbles in French (duck breast with dates and brie pudding) and Pacific Northwest (seared halibut with oxtail ragout) flavors. The digs are warmly lighted and romantic, but in season opt for the lovely outdoor dining patio. Meritage's namesake

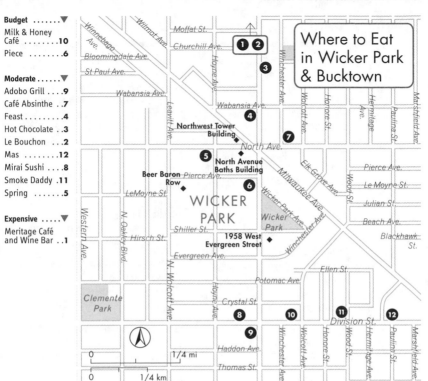

Where to Eat in Wicker Park & Bucktown

6

blended wines and other American vintages center the wine list. ✉ *2118 N. Damen Ave., Bucktown* ☎ *773/235–6434* ▭ *AE, MC, V* ⊗ *No lunch.*

$$–$$$ ✕ **Café Absinthe.** It's hip to be obscure. What else could explain Absinthe's move to put its sign out front but its entrance on an alley? Once you find the door, you'll enter a funky, theatrical restaurant well suited to the Bucktown neighborhood. Dishes like pork tenderloin with apple bread pudding and maple jus and pancetta-wrapped monkfish with basil-cream orzo have some luxuries and a little edge—the better to accessorize the look. ✉ *1954 W. North Ave., Bucktown* ☎ *773/278–4488* ▭ *AE, D, DC, MC, V* ⊗ *No lunch.*

$$–$$$ ✕ **Spring.** Leave pretense downtown. Chef Shawn McClain's artistic but unfussy fish preparations—from tuna tartare with quail egg to cod in crab and sweet pea sauce—distinguish the sophisticated Spring from the seasonal restaurant. Like McClain's cooking, the restaurant's interior design faces east for inspiration, beginning with a rock garden in the foyer. Original white glazed-tile walls hearken back to the space's former life as a bathhouse. ✉ *2039 W. North Ave., Wicker Park* ☎ *773/ 395–7100* ▭ *AE, DC, MC, V* ⊗ *Closed Mon. No lunch.*

FodorsChoice

★

$–$$$ ✕ **Feast.** The gregarious communal table, cozy fireplace, and sofa-filled lounge create a fittingly social setting for the arty Bucktown locals who dine here regularly. If you can't find something to eat here, you're not

Neighborhood Noshes

THE SUM OF CHICAGO is greater than the Mag Mile and Pizzeria Uno. It's Lincoln Square and Bistro Campagne, Devon Avenue and curry, Maxwell Street Market and tacos—reasons both edible and entertaining to venture beyond the usual tourist norms into Chicago's 198 neighborhoods. For those who like to sample a city by literally tasting it, Chicago encourages progressive feasting in food-centric enclaves.

Come to West Randolph Street, near downtown in the West Loop when dithering. This restaurant row for the stylish offers more tempting options than you can stomach and is a good place to graze at the restaurants' bars (tables are oft reserved).

Farther west is Wicker Park, a part Hispanic, part Ukrainian, mostly hipster 'hood of gentrifying Victorians, throbbing nightclubs, edgy boutiques, and hip eateries. Troll three blocks in any direction of the Damen/North/Milwaukee intersection for cafés and shops by day; music and meals at Hot Chocolate or Spring by night.

To the far north the former German settlement of Lincoln Square feeds new urbanites a street full of solid eateries from the new Bistro Campagne to the old school Chicago Brauhaus. Farther north yet, Chicago's Indian community inhabits Devon Avenue, a colorful Saturday-afternoon stop for sari shops, Bollywood videos and curries, samosas and nan.

Early Sunday morning make for Maxwell Street Market in Pilsen—not for the tube socks and hardware of questionable origin, but for the Mexican vendors serving homemade tortillas, tacos, and stews.

Three of Chicago's better known ethnic neighborhoods hunger for attention: Greektown, at night when the Halsted Street strip is lively; Chinatown, by day when both the restaurants and the exotic import shops are open; and Little Italy on Taylor Street, in summer when fans line up for Mario's Italian ice and stroll the old neighborhood in search of dinner.

Buon appetito, early and often.

–Elaine Glusac

---

hungry. World cuisines from Cuba to India mingle freely on an expansive, bold menu; try the ancho chili and maple-glazed pork chop, shrimp over spicy noodles, or chimichurri skirt steak. ⊠ *1616 N. Damen Ave., Bucktown* ☎ *773/772–7100* ▭ *AE, DC, MC, V.*

French

$$ ✕ **Le Bouchon.** The French comfort food at this charming-but-cramped bistro in Bucktown is in a league of its own. Onion tart has been a signature dish of owner Jean-Claude Poilevey for years; he also does a succulent sautéed rabbit and a definitive *salade Lyonnaise* (mixed greens topped with a creamy vinaigrette and a poached egg). Save room for the fruit tarts. Don't attempt Le Bouchon on weekends without a reservation. ⊠ *1958 N. Damen Ave., Bucktown* ☎ *773/862–6600* ▭ *AE, D, DC, MC, V* ☺ *Closed Sun. No lunch.*

Japanese

\$\$–\$\$\$ ✕ **Mirai Sushi.** This Japanese hipster helped turn Wicker Park's Division Street into a foodie destination. Make the trek for top-quality classic sushi and sashimi dishes, as well as lesser-known varieties, such as monkfish, horse mackerel, and rockfish. Display tanks keep a fresh supply of fish on hand. Don't know your toro from your hirame? Knowledgeable servers can guide you through the menu. For the full monty, sit at the sushi bar and put yourself into the hands of the inventive sushi chefs. The upstairs sake lounge is more about the scene and less about cuisine. ⊠ *2020 W. Division St., Wicker Park* ☎ *773/862–8500* ▭ *AE, D, DC, MC, V* ☺ *No lunch.*

Latin

★ **\$\$–\$\$\$** ✕ **Mas.** Inventive nuevo Latino fare, creative pan-Latin cocktails, and intimate 74-seat confines generate a significant buzz (and, some complain, noise) at Mas. We love perusing the menu over Chilean pisco sours or Cuban mojitos. The flavors here are nothing if not bold: tequila cured duck, jerked grouper, herbed lamb loin, and tuna-and-papaya tacos. Phone ahead for a table on weekends. ⊠ *1670 W. Division St., Wicker Park* ☎ *773/276–8700* ▭ *AE, D, DC, MC, V* ☺ *No lunch.*

Mexican

\$–\$\$ ✕ **Adobo Grill.** Mexico's two greatest crowd-pleasers—guacamole and tequila—star at Adobo Grill. Cooks wheels carts tableside to make fresh guacamole to taste in authentic molcajetes (stone mortars). Meanwhile a tequila sommelier helps gringos navigate the 100-plus varieties on offer (margaritas are killer, including a $50 splurge made of tippytop shelf booze). The Wicker Park location isn't as daring in the kitchen as the Old Town Adobo, topping out with standard fare like adobo-marinated tilapia and chicken mole enchiladas. ⊠ *2005 W. Division St., Wicker Park* ☎ *773/252–9990* ▭ *AE, D, DC, MC, V* ☺ *No lunch Mon.–Sat.*

Pizza

\$ ✕ **Piece.** The antithesis of Chicago-style deep-dish pizza, Piece's flat pies mimic those made famous in New Haven, Connecticut. The somewhat free-form, eat-off-the-baking-sheet pizzas come in plain (tomato sauce, Parmesan, and garlic), white (olive oil, garlic, and mozzarella) or traditional red, with lots of topping options. Salads like the greens with Gorgonzola and pears are more stylish than expected, and housebrewed beers pair perfectly with the chow. It's good enough that multipierced Wicker Parkers are willing to risk dining alongside local families (with kids in tow) in this former garage space. ⊠ *1927 W. North Ave., Wicker Park* ☎ *773/772–4422* ▭ *AE, D, DC, MC, V.*

Lake View

The mood relaxes and the prices deflate as you move north in Lake View, and it's not because you're settling for bar fare at the corner tap (though there's plenty of that around if you're craving it). Complementing good ethnic food are stars like Erwin and Brett's—they could make it downtown but choose not to.

American–Casual

¢–$　✕ **Kitsch'n on Roscoe.** If you love all things seventies, you'll love Kitsch'n like the regulars. It's a diner in retro garb, with lava lamps and vintage toasters–turned–table-lamps. Dine, with tongue firmly in cheek, on pesto-dyed "green eggs and ham" and Twinkies tiramisu. Or play it straight with hefty tuna and grilled cheese sandwiches and Mexican burritos. Weekends are jammed; midweek is better for slacking. ⊠ *2005 W. Roscoe St., Lake View* ☎ *773/248–7372* ▭ *AE, MC, V.*

¢–$　✕ **Orange.** Follow Wrigleyville's weekend crowds to the cheerful Orange for inventive, and thronged, breakfasts. If you think breakfast has to be dull, try the fruit sushi, kebab-style skewered French toast, or jam-filled pancakes. Standard stuff is done right, too: the fruit's juiced on-site and the omelets are big enough to take you through lunch. Arrive early or prepare to wait for tables, especially on game days. If you're here for lunch, don't miss the steak and Spanish blue cheese sandwich. ⊠ *3231 N. Clark St., Lake View* ☎ *773/549–4400* ▭ *D, MC, V* ⊗ *No dinner.*

¢　✕ **Hot Doug's.** Don't tell the zealots who have made Hot Doug's famous that these are *just* hot dogs—these "encased meats" go beyond your standard Vienna weiner. The gourmet purveyor wraps buns around mint-garlic lamb sausage, bacon sausage with avocado mayo, and even rabbit sausage. Make the trek on a Friday or Saturday, when the artery-clogging duck fat fries are available. The clientele is a curious mix of hungry hard-hats and serious foodies, neither of which care about the lack of frills. ⊠ *3325 N. California Ave., Lake View* ☎ *773/751–1500* ▭ *No credit cards* ⊗ *Closed Sun.*

Cafés

¢–$　✕ **Julius Meinl Cafe.** Viennese coffee roaster Julius Meinl operates this very European café in an unexpected location at the intersection of Addison and Southport, just a few blocks from Wrigley Field. Comfortable banquettes and a well-stocked supply of international newspapers bid coffee sippers to stick around. Smoked salmon and pear and brie sandwiches, strawberry and goat cheese salads, mushroom soup, and loads of European pastries feed the peckish. We love the Austrian breakfast of poached egg, ham, and Emmentaler cheese—this is the only place in the city that serves it. Classical and jazz combos entertain Friday and Saturday evenings. ⊠*3601 N. Southport Ave., Lake View* ☎*773/ 868–1857* ▭ *AE, D, MC, V.*

Cajun

$–$$　✕ **Heaven on Seven on Clark.** Every day is Mardi Gras at Heaven on Seven, which pursues a good time all the time—and even more so during Cubs season. Tables are centered with a daring collection of hot sauces, and the food, though it's well shy of ambrosia, is plentiful and filling. Cheddar jalapeño biscuits and seven-layer cake are great menu book ends. ⊠*3478 N. Clark St., Lake View* ☎ *773/477–7818* ▭ *AE, D, DC, MC, V.*

Where to Eat in Lake View

KEY

L CTA lines

6

Contemporary

$$$–$$$$ ✕ **Green Dolphin Street.** It's hard to pass up this one-stop dinner-and-music spot. There are globally influenced American dishes in the main dining room, a burgers-and-salads bar menu in the jazz club, a cigar-friendly bar, and a seasonal outdoor patio overlooking a relatively quiet stretch of the Chicago River. Dinner in the main room gets you into the handsome club, though you'll pay half the cover charge on weekends. ✉ *2200 N. Ashland Ave., Lake View* ☎ *773/395–0066* ▭ *AE, D, DC, MC, V* ⊗ *Closed Sun. Nov.–May and Mon. year-round. No lunch.*

$$–$$$ ✕ **Yoshi's Cafe.** Decades ago Yoshi's launched as a pricey fine-dining restaurant in the 'hood. We offer this history lesson to say that while the atmosphere went jeans-casual and the prices south, the cooking quality remained, and remains, high. Yoshi Katsumura turns out informal French-Asian, like duck breast and leg confit with honey-sesame sauce or grilled tofu with ginger-soy sauce (it's good enough to convert a carnivore). Sunday brunch includes the expected eggs along with a Japanese-inspired breakfast (rice, tofu, and seaweed). ✉ *3257*

N. Halsted St., Lake View ☎ 773/248–6160 ▭ *AE, D, DC, MC, V* ⊙ *Closed Mon.*

$–$$$ ✕ **Erwin.** Striking a pose between friendly and refined, this spot has comforting food, a cozy setting, and polished service. Chef Erwin Dreschsler often patrols the dining room of his namesake restaurant, greeting regulars. The straightforward, seasonal menu may look ordinary—roasted chicken with lemon-garlic sauce and one of the city's best burgers—but the skillful cooking and vibrant flavors gives you new respect for simplicity. The booths by the front windows are the best for views of neighborhood comings and goings, but as they're also in the smoking section, consider yourself warned. ☒ *2925 N. Halsted St., Lake View* ☎ 773/528–7200 ▭ *AE, D, DC, MC, V* ⊙ *Closed Mon. No lunch.*

$$ ✕ **Brett's.** This storefront charmer in Roscoe Village has soft lighting, classical music, and the kind of serious food you'd only expect downtown. Creative surprises spice the oft-changing menu: potato tacos with poblano chili sauce, Thai-style salmon, jerk pork chops. Soups are a particular strength. Don't miss the homemade bread, fresh from the steam-injected oven. Neighborhood fans line the sidewalk for a seat at brunch, served both Saturday and Sunday. ☒ *2011 W. Roscoe St., Lake View* ☎ 773/248–0999 ▭ *AE, D, DC, MC, V* ⊙ *Closed Mon. and Tues.*

$ ✕ **Flat Top Grill.** Cafeteria meets custom kitchen at Flat Top Grill where you choose the ingredients—from a spread of veggies, meat, fish, and sauces—and the grill man does the heating. The convivial storefront setting masks any similarities to a buffet. A handy sign gives detailed advice for neophytes (it's an extra dollar for unlimited trips to the grill). Students and other budget-conscious patrons consider Flat Top home meal replacement. ☒ *3200 N. Southport Ave., Lake View* ☎ 773/665–8100 ▭ *AE, D, DC, MC, V.*

Ethiopian

¢–$ ✕ **Mama Desta's Red Sea.** Mama told you to use a fork. But eating with your hands isn't just acceptable at Mama Desta's—it's expected. Tear off a hunk of spongy, slightly sour flat bread to scoop up generously herby dishes such as spicy chicken, lamb stew, or pureed lentils. Flavors, like the dining style, are earthy and simple. ☒ *3216 N. Clark St., Lake View* ☎ 773/935–7561 ▭ *AE, DC, MC, V* ⊙ *No lunch.*

French

★ $–$$ ✕ **Bistro Campagne.** This is the place to dine on the North Side for rustic French fare: crispy roast chicken, steak piled with frites, duck confit salads, and ale-steamed mussels. The lovely, wood-trimmed Arts and Crafts interior provides instant attitude adjustment; in warmer weather, aim to get a table in the torch-lit garden. Prices are reasonable, including those for the French-centric wine list. ☒ *4518 N. Lincoln Ave., Lake View* ☎ 773/271–6100 ▭ *AE, MC, V* ⊙ *No lunch.*

Italian

$–$$$ ✕ **Mia Francesca.** Moderate prices and a smart, urbane style drive ceaseless crowds to this Wrigleyville storefront. Enlightened Italian dishes like classic bruschetta, *quattro formaggi* (four cheese) pizza, sausage and wild mushroom pasta, and roast chicken are made with fresh ingredients and avoid stereotypical heaviness. With the exception of one pricey veal dish, the limited meat options keep the prices low here. While you wait for one of the small, tightly spaced tables—and you *will* wait—you can have a drink at the bar. ⊠ *3311 N. Clark St., Lake View* ☎ *773/281–3310* ⊟ *AE, D, DC, MC, V* ☺ *No lunch weekdays.*

$ ✕ **Pompeii.** Cheap, cheerful, and fast—what's not to love about Pompeii? The house specialty is square slices of pizza—each under $3 with toppings ranging from shredded onions and sausage to bread crumbs and tomato. One to two easily make a meal. Pompeii also sells first-rate homemade pasta, generous sandwiches, and salads. Illinois-Masonic hospital workers drive the busy lunch trade. If you can tolerate the self-serve system at dinner, the evening hours are more relaxing. ⊠ *2955 N. Sheffield Ave., Lake View* ☎ *773/325–1900* ⊟ *AE, D, DC, MC, V.*

Latin

$–$$$ ✕ **Coobah.** Loud and lively Coobah loves a good party and encourages reveling to the wee hours by serving dinner until 1 AM most nights, 2 AM on Saturday. Unlike lots of lounge-restaurants, however, this one doesn't rely on the mojitos and sangria to distract you from so-so food. Indeed, dishes such as blue corn–crusted talapia, Serrano ham–stuffed mussels, and spicy pork tamales distinguish the kitchen. Weekend brunches, held 10 AM to 3 PM, lend a Latin accent to eggs and sandwiches. ⊠ *3423 N. Southport Ave., Lake View* ☎ *773/528–2220* ⊟ *AE, D, DC, MC, V* ☺ *No lunch weekdays.*

Mexican

$–$$$ ✕ **Platiyo.** The folks behind the wildly successful Mia Francesca next door run Platiyo, another Wrigleyville hit, this time for Mexican food. Colorful artwork, Mexican tiles, and piñatalike sculptures conjure a fiesta-ready setting for marlin seviche, *carne asada* (marinated strip steak), and double-cut pork chops in pineapple mole. A selection of tacos and enchiladas placate Tex-Mex fans. ⊠ *3313 N. Clark St., Lake View* ☎ *773/477–6700* ⊟ *AE, D, DC, MC, V.*

Swedish

$–$$ ✕ **Ann Sather.** The aroma of fresh cinnamon rolls put this place on the map, and it still draws a mob that lines up down the block for weekend breakfasts. Dinner is a sensory journey to Sweden via duck breast with lingonberry glaze, Swedish meatballs, potato sausage, dumplings, and sauerkraut. Lunches offer similar Scandinavian specialties as well as standard café sandwiches and salads. ⊠ *929 W. Belmont Ave., Lake View* ☎ *773/348–2378* ⊟ *AE, D, DC, MC, V* ☺ *No dinner Mon. and Tues.*

> ### WORD OF MOUTH
>
> "For breakfast on Saturday, Ann Sather's is a don't miss."
>
> –Susan

Thai

$ ✕ **Arun's.** The finest Thai restaurant in Chicago—some say in the country—is also the most expensive, featuring only 12-course tasting menus for a flat $85. That said, the kitchen readily adjusts its offerings to food preferences and, of course, distastes. The kitchen artfully composes six appetizers, four entrées, and two desserts using the freshest ingredients. Results might include shrimp-filled golden pastry baskets, whole tamarind snapper, and veal medallions with ginger-lemongrass sauce. Arun's out-of-the-way location in a residential neighborhood on the northwest side doesn't discourage a strong following among locals and visiting foodies. ✉ *4156 N. Kedzie Ave., Irving Park* ☎ *773/539–1909* ⚑ *Reservations essential* ▭ *AE, D, DC, MC, V* ⊘ *Closed Mon. No lunch.*

¢–$ ✕ **Thai Classic.** With apologies to Chinatown, Chicago is really a Thai town when it comes to outstanding Asian food. The assets here include a prime location three blocks south of Wrigley Field, good service, and even better dishes. Not only are prices low, but there is no liquor license (pick up a six-pack of Singha beer from the liquor store down the street), saving you the mark-up. Bargain hunters should hit the $10.95 buffet, available Saturday afternoon and all day Sunday. Come on foot during Cubs games when parking is near impossible. ✉ *3332 N. Clark St., Lake View* ☎ *773/404–2000* ▭ *AE, D, DC, MC, V* ⍢ *BYOB.*

Turkish

$–$$$ ✕ **Turquoise Cafe.** The bustling Turkish-owned café attempts to please every palate with a mixed menu of continental and Turkish foods, but it's the latter that stars here. Don't-miss items include lamb kebabs, *sogurme* (a smoked eggplant, yogurt, and walnut dip), and homemade noodles with feta and dill. Vested waiters, a martini menu, and wood-trimmed surroundings out-class the neighborhood lot. ✉ *2147 W. Roscoe St., Lake View* ☎ *773/549–3523* ▭ *AE, D, DC, MC, V.*

Far North Side

Pockets of great food throughout the North Side include Argyle Street off Broadway for Vietnamese fare, and Devon Street west of Western Avenue for Indian food. Two neighborhoods, however, stand out for their variety and high standards: the Swede-settled Andersonville and the former German enclave of Lincoln Square.

American–Casual

$–$$ ✕ **Square Kitchen.** Families crowd this popular Lincoln Square weekend brunch option for better-than-expected casual fare. Kitchen ambitions include a seared ahi tuna niçoise salad or wild mushroom ravioli at lunch and ginger-sesame tilapia and wine-sauced pork tenderloin at dinner. Deluxe omelets, oversize pancakes, and burgers satisfy simpler tastes. ✉ *4600 N. Lincoln Ave., Far North Side* ☎ *773/751–1500* ▭ *AE, D, DC, MC, V* ⊘ *No lunch weekdays.*

Café

$–$$ ✕ **Café Selmarie.** For a light meal in Lincoln Square, line up at this bakery-turned-café, a long-standing favorite among locals. Breakfast gets you croissant French toast and corned beef hash with eggs; lunch ranges

Where to Eat on the Far North Side

from goat cheese salads to smoked salmon baguettes; and dinner runs to quiche and roast chicken. Don't miss the sink-your-teeth-in pastries (you can also buy them to-go at the front counter). Pass summer waits pleasantly in the neighboring plaza; during other seasons, you're out in the cold. ⊠ *4729 N. Lincoln Ave., Far North Side* ☎ *773/989–5595* ▭ *MC, V.*

Contemporary

$$–$$$ ✕ **Tomboy.** Here's your spot for great people-watching. A bohemian crowd mingles in this funky, brick-walled storefront that plates food with a playful presentation. There's a fanciful "porcupine" shrimp coated with splayed-out spikes of phyllo dough and a crème brûlée served in a cookie cone inside a martini glass. ⊠ *5402 N. Clark St., Far North Side* ☎ *773/907–0636* ▭ *AE, D, DC, MC, V* ☉ *Closed Sun. No lunch.*

French

$$–$$$ ✕ **La Tache.** Warm, wood-paneled interiors, a classic bistro menu, and reasonable prices sum the charms of the 45-seat La Tache. You could make a meal of appetizers from toasted ham *croque monsieur* sandwiches to egg-topped Lyonnaise salads. But save room for steak frites, braised rabbit leg, and fish specials. The popular Sunday brunch features French toast, French-style eggs with leeks and truffle oil, and savory salads.

✉ *1475 W. Balmoral St., Andersonville* ☎ *773/334–7168* ⟁ *Reservations not accepted* ⊟ *AE, D, DC, MC, V.*

German

$–$$ ✕ **Chicago Brauhaus.** The German immigrants who settled in Lincoln Square have mostly moved on, making room for a new generation of urban hipsters. But they leave behind the Brauhaus, an Oktoberfest of a restaurant featuring a *lederhosen*-clad duo playing nightly polkas and waltzes that bring old-timers and new converts to the dance floor. Though the atmosphere is the draw over the food, you can't go wrong with the bratwurst and sauerkraut or the schnitzel. Large tables easily accommodate groups. The spacious bar and a good selection of German beers draws oompah-loving drinkers. ✉ *4732 N. Lincoln Ave., Far North Side* ☎ *773/784–4444* ⊟ *AE, D, DC, MC, V* ⊙ *Closed Tues.*

Italian

$–$$$ ✕ **La Donna.** We deem this Andersonville's best Italian because of its excellent pastas—try the pumpkin ravioli in creamy balsamic sauce or the fine penne *arrabiata* (spicy tomato sauce)—and good, cracker-crust pizzas. The generally crowded storefront dining room either makes you feel like part of a very large party or just trapped. The wine list is well chosen and fairly priced, and there's a bargain-price Sunday brunch. ✉ *5146 N. Clark St., Far North Side* ☎ *773/561–9400* ⊟ *AE, D, DC, MC, V.*

Swedish

$ ✕ **Ann Sather.** A link in the locally treasured Swedish restaurant minichain, Ann Sather specializes in breakfast, home-style food, and friendly service. Go for the homemade cinnamon rolls alone—giant, gooey confections that made the place famous—and the unusual combo of Swedish pancakes with Swedish meatballs. Lunches are much more American though you can still get the Swedish meatball, at this hour in a sandwich. ✉ *5207 N. Clark St., Far North Side* ☎ *773/271–6677* ⊟ *AE, D, DC, MC, V* ⊙ *No dinner.*

¢–$ ✕ **Svea.** The North Side's Andersonville neighborhood, once a haven for Swedes, plays host to the humble Svea, a Swedish version of an American diner. There are Swedish pancakes with lingonberries and Swedish rye *limpa* bread with eggs in the morning, Swedish meatball heroes and open-face roast beef sandwiches at lunch. The digs are no-frill, but the service is friendly. ✉ *5236 N. Clark St., Far North Side* ☎ *773/275–7738* ⊟ *No credit cards* ⊙ *No dinner.*

Pilsen, Little Italy, University Village & Chinatown

Ready for dim sum? Though Chicago's Chinatown is small, you can still dine well. And nearby, in Pilsen, Little Italy, and University Village, are all kinds of tasty ethnic eats.

Chinese

$–$$$$ ✕ **Phoenix.** Phoenix softens you up with second-floor picture window views that frame the Loop skyline. Just when you're most vulnerable, it develops the food punch—and it's a pretty good one, too. The dim sum, dispensed from rolling carts daily from 8 AM to 3 PM, is a big draw (servers often don't speak English; just smile and point at what you want).

Arrive before noon on the weekends or stew as you wait . . . and wait. ✉ *2131 S. Archer Ave., Chinatown* ☎ *312/328–0848* ▭ *AE, D, DC, MC, V.*

$–$$$ ✕ **Emperor's Choice.** This sophisticate sets out to prove that Chinese seafood specialties can go well beyond deep-fried prawns. It succeeds with dishes such as steamed oysters and Peking-style lobster. A separate menu includes such "delicacies" as rattlesnake soup and pork bellies. Seating is cramped and not for serenity-seekers. Discounted parking (with validation) is available in the Cermak/Wentworth lot. ✉ *2238 S. Wentworth Ave., Chinatown* ☎ *312/225–8800* ▭ *AE, D, MC, V.*

$ ✕ **Lao Sze Chuan.** If you're looking for spice, filling food, and great prices in Chinatown, check out this Szechuan kitchen. Chilies, garlic, and ginger seem to go into every dish, whether it's chicken, eggplant, or dumplings. The digs are nothing to write a postcard home about, but you'll feel smug for choosing it once the feast is finished. ✉ *2172 S. Archer Ave., Chinatown* ☎ *312/326–5040* ▭ *AE, D, DC, MC, V.*

French

$$–$$$ ✕ **Chez Joel.** Breaking Taylor Street's Italian allegiance, Chez Joel waves the flag for France. The sunny bistro serves well-prepared classics like steak frites, coq au vin, and bouillabaisse. It's a good pasta-free date choice, and a favorite of locals. ✉ *1119 W. Taylor St., South Loop* ☎ *312/ 226–6479* ▭ *AE, D, DC, MC, V* ☾ *No lunch weekends.*

Italian

$–$$$$ ✕ **New Rosebud Cafe.** For *Sopranos*–style food and scene, crowd in here with half of Chicago. What's all the fuss about? Truthfully, the food breaks no new ground: there's the typical roasted peppers, homemade sausage, and pastas, and most of them are red-sauced. But the old neighborhood vibe is authentic—and extremely loud. Come prepared for a three-cocktail wait. ✉ *1500 W. Taylor St., South Loop* ☎ *312/942–1117* ▭ *AE, D, DC, MC, V* ☾ *No lunch weekends.*

$–$$$$ ✕ **Tuscany.** Under the Tuscan Sun fans, Italo-philes, and University of Illinois Chicago staffers head to Tuscany for the rustic but celebrated fare of the Tuscan countryside. Recommended: rotisserie-grilled chicken, thin-crust pizzas, and, for splurgers, the rack of lamb Vesuvio. Not recommended: carbo-loading at lunch. ✉ *1014 W. Taylor St., South Loop* ☎ *312/829–1990* ▭ *AE, D, DC, MC, V* ☾ *No lunch weekends.*

$–$$$ ✕ **Francesca's on Taylor.** Among the molto, molto Italianos on the block, Francesca's one-ups 'em with good cooking and a modern menu. You might find ravioli stuffed with a spinach and artichoke mix or blue marlin with sea scallops and roasted peppers. There's not a lot of meat on the menu, ergo you won't break the bank. Early birds flock here before heading to the United Center for a Bulls game, Blackhawks game, or special event. ✉ *1400 W. Taylor St., South Loop* ☎ *312/829–2828* ▭ *AE, DC, MC, V* ☾ *No lunch weekends.*

¢–$ ✕ **Pompeii.** Cheap, cheerful, and fast—what's not to love about Pompeii? Little Italy's only casual café with a strong kitchen specializes in square slices of pizza, each under $3 with toppings ranging from shredded onions and sausage to bread crumbs and tomato. One to two easily makes a meal. Between University of Illinois Chicago students and

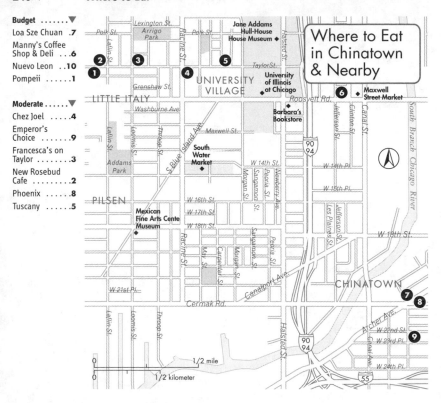

Rush-Presbyterian hospital workers, Pompeii is jammed at lunch. If you can tolerate the self-serve system at dinner, the evening hours are more relaxing. If pizza's not your thing, salad, generous sandwiches, and homemade pastas are also on the menu. ⊠ *1531 W. Taylor St., South Loop* ☎ *312/421–5179* ▭ *AE, D, DC, MC, V.*

Mexican

$ ✕ **Nuevo Leon.** Fill up on the exotic (tripe soup) or the familiar (tacos) at this bustling, family-run restaurant in the heart of Pilsen, Chicago's Mexican neighborhood. Big tables accommodate big families, lending a fiesta feel to the scene. Meals run from breakfast chilaquiles (eggs scrambled with tortillas) to dinners of beef stew. Brush up your Spanglish; not all servers are fluent in English. ⊠ *1515 W. 18th St., Pilsen* ☎ *312/421–1517* ⌚ *Reservations not accepted* ▭ *No credit cards.*

Worth a Special Trip

French

$$$$ ✕ **Carlos'.** One of Chicago's best French restaurants is actually in its suburbs. Service runs smoothly thanks to owner Carlos Nieto's dining room presence. Dishes are mainly contemporary French: you might find hot and cold foie gras (together), or roast, poached, and confit duck

in a seven-spice sauce. The substantial wine list includes some magnificent vintages, often at eye-popping prices. The main dining room is dark, woody, and serious, though mismatched antique china plates lend character. ✉ *429 Temple Ave., 26 mi north of downtown Chicago, Highland Park* ☎ *847/432–0770* ⤳ *Reservations essential* 🏛 *Jacket required* 🍽 *AE, D, DC, MC, V* ⊘ *Closed Tues. No lunch.*

$$$$ ✕ **Le Français.** Greater Chicago's landmark French restaurant has emerged from a recent revolving-door phase with Roland Liccioni, Le Français' chef in the 1990s, back at the stoves. Even better news is that the prices have been reduced ($90 is relatively reasonable for the seven-course degustation). Raised in France and trained in Paris, Liccioni has a deft hand at balancing dishes such as poached veal with dry-aged beef, braised cabbage, and porcini sauce. The menu is peppered, of course, with luxuries like lobster, truffles, and foie gras that entice special-occasion diners. A picture window in the contemporary-style dining room lets you peek into the kitchen. ✉ *269 S. Milwaukee Ave., 30 mi northwest of downtown Chicago, Wheeling* ☎ *847/541–7470* ⤳ *Reservations essential* 🏛 *Jacket required* 🍽 *AE, D, DC, MC, V* ⊘ *Closed Sun. No lunch Sat.–Mon.*

$–$$$ ✕ **Trio Atelier.** Trio owner Henry Adaniya has a reputation for nurturing young chefs who refine their talents at Trio and then leave to open their own restaurants. Alumni include Rick Tramonto and Gale Gand (both of Tru), Shawn McClain (Spring, Green Zebra), and Grant Achatz (Alinea). Now Dale Levitski is in charge, turning out savory French in small (pomme frites with wasabi-caviar dip), medium (white truffle quiche), and large plates (braised veal cheeks), allowing diners ample freedom to compose their meals. Unlike the special-occasion fare of incarnations past, you could eat here once a week. ✉ *1625 Hinman Ave., 14 mi north of downtown Chicago, Evanston* ☎ *847/733–8746* 🍽 *AE, D, DC, MC, V* ⊘ *Closed Mon. and Tues. No lunch.*

Southern

$–$$ ✕ **Army and Lou's.** First-rate home-cooked soul food banners this far South Side institution. The fried chicken is arguably the city's best, but leave room for outstanding corn bread, chicken gumbo, mustard greens, and sweet potato pie. The setting is surprisingly genteel for such down-home fare: waiters in bow ties, tables with starched white cloths, and African and Haitian art on the walls. On Sunday dress up and join the after-church crowds. ✉ *422 E. 75th St., South Side* ☎ *773/483–3100* 🍽 *AE, D, DC, MC, V* ⊘ *Closed Tues.*

$ ✕ **Soul Queen.** Since 1971, Soul Queen has been sating the famished with one of the most generous buffets in town. For $7.75, help yourself to fried chicken, chicken and dumplings, ham hocks, turkey wings, black-eyed peas, succotash, peach cobbler, and more. The spread gets even more elaborate on Sunday when the price goes up $2. ✉ *9031 S. Stony Island Ave., South Shore* ☎ *773/731–3366* ⤳ *Reservations not accepted* 🍽 *No credit cards.*

6

Entertainment

WORD OF MOUTH

"The Green Mill was frequented by Al Capone. Great place, one of the true must sees in the city."

—exiledprincess

ENTERTAINMENT PLANNER

Find Out What's Going On

To find out what's happening in the Windy City, check out the following: the *Chicago Tribune*'s Metromix.com, *Time Out Chicago* magazine or Web site (www.timeout.com/chicago), the *Chicago Reader*, an alternative newsweekly and Web site (www. chicagoreader.com), and Centerstage. net, which has a calendar of music and theater events.

Getting There

Parking in North Side neighborhoods, particularly Lincoln Park and Lake View, is increasingly scarce, even on weeknights. If you're going out in these areas, take a cab or public transportation. If you do decide to drive, use the curbside valet service available at many restaurants and clubs for about $6–$7. If you're headed to the South Side, be cautious about public transportation late at night. It's best to drive or cab it here.

Get Tickets

You can save money on seats at **Hot Tix** (⊕ www. hottix.org, for listings and booth information only), where unsold tickets are available, usually at half price (plus a service charge) on the day of perform-ance; you won't know what's available until that day. On Friday, however, you can buy tickets for Saturday and Sunday. Hot Tix booths are at the Chicago Tourism Center at 72 East Randolph Street; the Chicago Water Works Visitor Center at the southeast corner of Michigan Avenue and Pearson Street; the North Shore Center for the Performing Arts at 9501 Skokie Boulevard, in suburban Skokie; and at Chicago-area Tower Records stores. Hot Tix also func-tions as a Ticketmaster outlet, selling advance, full-price, cash-only tickets.

You can charge full-price tickets over the phone or on-line at **Ticketmaster** (☎ 312/559–1212 for rock con-certs and general interest events, 312/902–1500 arts line ⊕ www.ticketmaster.com).

For hot, sold-out shows, such as performances by the Chicago Symphony Orchestra or the Lyric Opera of Chicago, call a day or two before the show to see if there are any subscriber returns. Another option is to show up at the box office on concert day—a surpris-ing number of people strike it lucky with on-the-spot tickets due to cancellations.

Small fees can have big payoffs! Many of the smaller neighborhood street festivals (there are hundreds in summer) request $5–$10 donations upon entry, but it's often worth the expense: big-name bands are known to take the stage of even the most under-publi-cized festivals. For moment-to-moment festival cover-age, check out ⊕ www.metromix.com.

Festivals

For the first two weeks in October, the **Chicago International Film Festival** (☎ 312/332–3456 ⊕ www.chicagofilmfestival.org) screens more than 100 films, including premieres of Hollywood films, international releases, documentaries, short subjects, animation, videos, and student films. Movie stars usually make appearances at the opening events.

Grant Park Music Festival (☎ 312/742–7638 ⊕ www.grantparkmusicfestival.com), a program of the Chicago Park District, gives free concerts June–August in the spectacular new Frank Gehry–designed Jay Pritzker Pavilion in Millennium Park. Tote along dinner and make a full night of the performance by the superb Grant Park Orchestra and Chorus. Concerts are usually Wednesday–Sunday evenings.

In summer you can enjoy the Chicago Symphony at the **Ravinia Festival** (☎ 847/266–5100 ⊕ www.ravinia.org) in Highland Park, a 25-mi train trip from Chicago. The park is lovely, and lawn seats are always available even when those in the pavilion are sold out. Ravinia also draws crowds with jazz, pop, and dance concerts.

In early June, the **Chicago Blues Festival** (☎ 312/744–3370), the largest free blues festival in the world, rocks the city. Blues legends such as B. B. King, Koko Taylor, and Buddy Guy have all headlined the festival, and blues lovers from around the world—most notably Chuck Berry and Keith Richards—have been known to attend (and sometimes take the stage).

Labor Day weekend blasts off with the unmistakable sounds of the **Chicago Jazz Festival.** (☎ 312/744–3370) Set in Grant Park, the four-day festival offers not only a prime lakefront locale, but also free performances by local, national, and international musicians and special tributes to jazz legends.

Raves & Faves

Pointe of Pride: Joffrey Ballet of Chicago

Most Wanted Tickets: Lyric Opera of Chicago

Hits Closest to Home: Victory Gardens Theater

Chicest Sidewalk Café: Cru Café and Wine Bar

Sharpest Wits: The Second City

Hours

Live music starts around 9 PM at bars around town.

Bars close at 2 AM Friday and 3 AM Saturday.

Curtain calls for performances are usually at 7:30 or 8 PM.

7

Updated by
Jessica Volpe

Chicago's arts and nightlife scene is as vivacious and diverse as its neighborhoods. Sing along with a biographical musical at Black Ensemble Theater to the north or zip southwest to Wicker Park's renowned Steppenwolf Theatre, where you just might run into longtime ensemble member John Malkovich. Head for the Loop where renowned companies such as the Lyric Opera and the Joffrey Ballet hold court. And remember that this is the city that gave birth to the often raucous "poetry slam" at the Green Mill jazz club.

Nighttime entertainment options before and after hours are infinite—as long as you're willing to explore. Sip an imported Belgian beer at Hopleaf, a cozy North Side tavern, or tap into your wild side at a downtown dance club such as Le Passage. And we wouldn't forget to mention comedy: Second City Club has been unleashing top comedic talents, including John Belushi and Bill Murray, for decades.

GREAT PERFORMANCES

If you're even mildly interested in the performing arts, Chicago has the means to put you in your seat—be it floor, mezzanine, or balcony. Just pick your preference (theater, dance, or symphony/orchestra), and let Chicago's impressive body of artists do the rest. From critically acclaimed big names to fringe groups that specialize in experimental work, there truly is a performance art for everyone.

Ticket prices vary wildly depending on whether you're seeing a high-profile group or venturing into more obscure territory. Chicago Symphony tickets range from $15 to $200, the Lyric Opera from $30 to $175 (if you can get them). Smaller choruses and orchestras charge from $10 to $30; watch the listings for free performances. Commercial theater ranges from $15 to $75; smaller experimental ensembles might charge $5, $10, or pay-what-you-can. Movie prices range from $9 for first-run houses to as low as $1.50 at some suburban second-run houses.

■ TIP→ For free, live music in summer, head downtown to the Grant Park Music Fest (a classical music series) and the jam-packed Chicago Blues and Chicago Jazz Festivals. Held at the visually stunning Millennium Park and Grant Park, there's no cheaper way to experience some of the best sites and sounds Chicago has to offer. See the Festivals section in the Planner for more information.

Top 5 Performances

Joffrey Ballet. Fine-tuned performances, such as the glittering production of *The Nutcracker,* make this Chicago's premier classical dance company. Treat yourself to one of several annual performances at the Auditorium Theatre and help celebrate more than 50 seasons of superb ballet. ☎ *312/739–0120* ⊕ *www.joffrey.com.*

Lookingglass Theatre Company. Gawk at offbeat and fantastical acrobatic performances inside the belly of the Chicago Water Works building. The company's physically and artistically daring works incorporate theater, dance, music, and circus arts. ☎ *312/337–0665* ⊕ *www. lookingglasstheatre.org.*

FodorsChoice ★ **Steppenwolf.** The alumni roster speaks for itself: John Malkovich, Gary Sinise, Joan Allen, and Laurie Metcalf all honed their chops with this troupe. The company's trademark cutting-edge acting style and consistently successful productions have won national acclaim. ☎ *312/335–1650* ⊕ *www.steppenwolf.org.*

> ## WORD OF MOUTH
>
> "Among the locals, Steppenwolf is usually the hottest ticket in town, and since it's located on a nice street next to several restaurants, I think it's a great option for a special night out."
>
> –Chgogal

☺ **Chicago Symphony Orchestra.** Three internationally celebrated conductors, one in-house award-winning composer, and 200 magnificent performances a year make the Chicago Symphony Orchestra a musical tour de force. The impressive annual roster offers regular concerts and special theme series including classical, chamber, and children's concerts. Tickets are sometimes scarce, but they do become available; call or check the Web site for status updates. If you buy your tickets online, click on the "Know Your Seats" section, where you can see photos of the views of the stage from different seats. ☉ *Sept.–June* ☎ *312/294–3000 or 800/223–7114* ⊕ *www.cso.org.*

★ **Lyric Opera of Chicago.** The big voices of the opera world star in these top-flight productions. This is one of the top two opera companies in America today. Don't worry about understanding German or Italian; English translations are projected above the stage. All of the superb performances have sold out for more than a dozen years, and close to 90% of all Lyric tickets go to subscribers—the key to getting in is to call the Lyric in early August when individual tickets first go on sale. ☉ *Sept.–Mar.* ☎ *312/332–2244* ⊕ *www.lyricopera.org.*

Beautiful Voices: Highly Recommended Vocal Performances

From a capella to opera, the City of Big Shoulders has some of the nation's top vocal groups. Treat the kids to a sprightly concert by the Chicago Children's Choir or hear the sacred sounds of Bella Voce reverberate from the walls of a gorgeous area church. The following are our picks for the most beautiful voices in the city.

Choral & Chamber Groups

Apollo Chorus of Chicago (☎ 312/427–5620 ⊕ www.apollochorus.org), formed in 1872, is one of the country's oldest oratorio societies. Don't miss the annual Handel's *Messiah* if you're here in December. Otherwise, they perform various choral classics throughout the year at area churches.

Bella Voce. (☎ 847/866–7464 ⊕ www.bellavoce.org) "Beautiful voices," indeed. Formerly known as His Majestie's Clerkes, the 16-person a cappella group performs a variety of sacred and secular music, including everything from early music to works by living composers. Concerts are often held in churches throughout the city, providing a powerful acoustical and visual accompaniment to the music. The season runs October through May.

7

VENUES WORTH CHECKING OUT

The following host various productions. Call or check their schedules online to see who will be on stage.

The **Athenaeum Theatre** (✉ 2936 N. Southport Ave., Lake View ☎ 773/935-6860 ⊕ www. athenaeumtheatre.com) hosts innovative, small dance companies, and the fall series Dance Chicago, which features all forms of dance from Chicago dance companies.

The **Dance Center of Columbia College Chicago** (✉ 1306 S. Michigan Ave., South Loop ☎ 312/344-8300 ⊕ www.dancecenter.org) presents thought-provoking fare with leading international and national contemporary dance artists.

☙ A performance by the **Chicago Children's Choir** (☎ 312/849-8300 ⊕ www. ccchoir.org) is the closest thing we can imagine to hearing angels sing. Its members—ages 8–18—are culled from a broad spectrum of racial, ethnic, and economic groups. Performances, culled from an international music base, are given each year during the holiday season and in May. Other concerts are scheduled periodically, sometimes in the Chicago Cultural Center's Preston Bradley Hall.

Take a step back in time with **Music of the Baroque** (☎ 312/551-1414 ⊕ www.baroque.org), one of the Midwest's leading music ensembles specializing in Baroque and early classical music. See one of seven yearly programs at either Millennium Park's Harris Theater or one of several beautiful Chicago-area churches. Performances run from September to May.

The small but mighty **Oriana Singers** (☎ 773/262-4558 ⊕ www.oriana. org) are an outstanding a cappella sextet with an eclectic early, classical, and jazz repertoire. The close-knit traveling group performs from September to June, periodically in conjunction with Joffrey Ballet and other Chicago area groups.

Opera

Chicago Opera Theater (☎ 312/704-8414 ⊕ www.chicagooperatheater. org) shrugs off esoteric notions of opera, preferring to make productions that are accessible to aficionados and novices alike. The production of "Nixon in China," a contemporary American opera detailing conversations between the former U.S. President and Henry Kissinger (among others), is a shining example of the company's open-mindedness toward the operatic canon. From innovative versions of traditional favorites to important lesser-known works, the emphasis is on both theatrical and musical aspects. Fear not—performances are sung in English, or in Italian with English supertitles projected above the stage. They're held at the Harris Theater for Music and Dance.

Light Opera Works (☎ 847/869-6300 ⊕ www.light-opera-works.org) favors the satirical tones of the distinctly British Gilbert and Sullivan operettas, but takes on frothy Viennese, French, and other light operettas and American musicals from June to early January.

CINEMATHEQUE

Brew and View. Watch a cult fave or a late-night show with a rowdy crowd who come for cheap flicks and beer specials. ⊠ *Vic Theatre* ☎ *773/929-6713* ⊕ *www.brewview.com.*

Facets Cinematheque shows rare and exotic films in its cinema and video theater. ☎ *773/281-4114.*

Gene Siskel Film Center screens unusual current films and revivals of rare classics; the best part is that filmmakers sometimes give lectures to accompany the movie. ☎ *312/846-2600.*

Music Box Theatre. If you love old theaters, old movies, and ghosts

(rumor has it the theater is haunted by the spirit of its original manager) don't miss a trip here. ☎ *773/871-6604.*

For **IMAX and OMNIMAX theaters** go to Navy Pier (☎ 312/595-5629) or the Museum of Science and Industry (☎ 773/684-1414).

For a change of scenery, watch classic films under the stars at the **Chicago Outdoor Film Festival,** which runs July through August in Grant Park on Tuesday nights. ☎ 312/742-7529.

Trouping Around: Highly Recommended Dance & Theater Troupes

Chicago's reputation as a dance and theatrical powerhouse was born from its small, independent companies that produce a roster of works, from jazz-inflected ballets to biographical musicals. The groups listed do consistently interesting work, and a few have gained national attention. Be open-minded when you're choosing a show; even a group you've never heard of may be harboring one or two underpaid geniuses. *The Reader* carries complete dance and theater listings, plus reviews of the more avant-garde shows.

Dance

Hubbard Street Dance Chicago (☎ 312/850-9744 ⊕ www.hubbardstreetdance.com), Chicago's most notable success story in dance, exudes a jazzy vitality that has made it extremely popular. The style mixes classical ballet techniques, theatrical jazz, and contemporary dance.

Muntu Dance Theatre of Chicago (☎ 773/602-1135 ⊕ www.muntu.com) showcases dynamic interpretations of contemporary and traditional African and African-American dance. Artistic director Amaniyea Payne travels to Africa to learn traditional dances and adapts them for the stage.

Trinity Irish Dance Co. (☎ 773/549-6135 ⊕ www.trinityirishdancecompany.org), founded long before *Riverdance,* promotes traditional and progressive Irish dancing. In addition to the world-champion professional group, you can also catch performances by younger dancers enrolled in the Trinity Academy of Irish Dance.

CHECK OUT

For complete music and theater listings, check two weeklies, *The Reader* and *Time Out Chicago*, both published midweek; the Friday and Sunday editions of the *Chicago Tribune* and *Chicago Sun-Times*; and the monthly *Chicago* magazine.

If you're interested in Broadway-scale shows, contact the following theaters to see what's playing while you're in town.

Auditorium Theatre (☎ 312/922-2110 ⊕ www.auditoriumtheatre.org)

Chicago Theatre (☎ 312/462-6300 ⊕ www.thechicagotheatre.com)

Goodman Theatre (☎ 312/443-3800 ⊕ www.goodman-theatre.org)

Oriental Theatre (☎ 312/782-2004 or 312/902-1400 ⊕ www.broadwayinchicago.com)

LaSalle Bank Theatre (formerly the Shubert Theatre) (☎ 312/902-1400 or 312/977-1700 ⊕ www.broadwayinchicago.com)

For other performances, check out:

Cadillac Palace Theatre (☎ 312/977-1700 ⊕ www.broadwayinchicago.com)

Joan W. and Irving B. Harris Theater for Music and Dance (☎ 312/334-7777 ⊕ www.harristheaterchicago.org)

Storefront Theater (☎ 312/742-8497 ⊕ www.storefronttheater.org)

Athenaeum Theatre (☎ 773/935-6860 ⊕ www.athenaeumtheatre.com)

Briar Street Theatre (☎ 773/348-4000 or 800/258-3626)

Drury Lane Theatre Water Tower Place (☎ 312/642-2000 ⊕ www.drurylanewatertower.com)

Royal George Theatre Center (☎ 312/988-9000 ⊕ www.theroyalgeorgetheatre.com)

Theatre Building (☎ 773/327-5252 ⊕ www.theatrebuildingchicago.org)

Theatre on the Lake (☎ 312/742-7994)

For concerts, try the following halls:

Chicago Cultural Center (☎ 312/346-3278 or 312/744-6630 ⊕ www.cityofchicago.org)

Mandel Hall (☎ 773/702-8511 or 773/702-7300)

Newberry Library (☎ 312/943-9090 ⊕ www.newberry.org)

Orchestra Hall (☎ 312/294-3000)

Three Arts Club (☎ 312/944-6250 ⊕ www.threearts.org)

Theater

About Face Theatre (☎ 773/784-8565 ⊕ www.aboutfacetheatre.com) is the city's best-known gay and lesbian performing group, which in its short history has garnered awards for original works, world premieres, and adaptations presented in larger theaters like the Steppenwolf and the Goodman.

Bailiwick Repertory Theatre (⊠ 1229 W. Belmont Ave., Lake View ☎ 773/883–1090 ⊕ www.bailiwick.org) stages new and classical material at its namesake Arts Center. Its Pride Performance series, held every summer, focuses on plays by gays and lesbians.

★ **Black Ensemble Theater** (⊠ 4520 N. Beacon St., Ravenswood ☎ 773/769–4451 ⊕ www.blackensembletheater.org) has a penchant for long-running musicals based on popular African-American icons. Founder and executive producer Jackie Taylor has written and directed such hits as *The Jackie Wilson Story* and *The Other Cinderella*.

Collaboraction (⊠ 437 N. Wolcott Ave., Ukrainian Village ☎ 312/226–9633 ⊕ www.collaboraction.org) lets actors, artists, and musicians share the stage together in an experimental free-for-all that puts the "fun" in dysfunctional. Of its several performances a year, we recommend Sketchbook—a series of 16 seven-minute long plays—for its color and energy.

★ **Chicago Shakespeare Theater** (⊠ 800 E. Grand Ave., Near North ☎ 312/595–5600 ⊕ www.chicagoshakes.com) devotes its considerable talents to keeping the Bard's flame alive in the Chicago area, with at least three plays a year. The best part? The Courtyard Theater, on Navy Pier, has sparkling views of the city, and seats are never farther than 30 feet from the thrust stage.

ETA Creative Arts Foundation (⊠ 7558 S. South Chicago Ave., Grand Crossing ☎ 773/752–3955 ⊕ www.etacreativearts.org), a South Side performing arts center, has established a strong presence for African-American theater, with six plays each year. It also hosts black cultural presentations. Tip: enjoy your trip to the South Side, but be aware that some areas are sketchier than others. To ensure your safety, avoid public transportation and opt for a cab instead.

Neo-Futurists (⊠ 5153 N. Ashland Ave., Uptown ☎ 773/275–5255 ⊕ www.neofuturists.org) perform their long-running, late-night hit *Too Much Light Makes the Baby Go Blind* in a space—oddly enough—above a funeral home. The piece is a series of 30 ever-changing plays performed in 60 minutes; the order of the plays is chosen by the audience. In keeping with the spirit of randomness, the admission price is set by the roll of a die, plus $7.

Fodor'sChoice
★ **Redmoon Theater** (☎ 312/850–8440 ⊕ www.redmoon.org) tells imaginative, seasonal stories with the magically creative use of puppets, sets, and live actors. The company's annual outdoor spectacle series presents madcap theater in unlikely places, including undiscovered parks and even on water. The series usually takes place in the fall, but experimental theater would be nothing if not unpredictable, so be sure to call for confirmation. Nonseries performances are held everywhere, from grassroots neighborhood events to Redmoon Central.

★ **Victory Gardens Theater** (⊠ 2257 N. Lincoln Ave., Lincoln Park ☎ 773/871–3000 ⊕ www.victorygardens.org), winner of the 2001 Regional Tony Award, is known for its workshops and Chicago premieres. The theater sponsors works mainly by local playwrights on four stages.

AFTER DARK

Chicago's entertainment varies from loud and loose to sophisticated and sedate. You'll find classic Chicago corner bars in most neighborhoods, along with trendier alternatives like wine bars. The strains of blues and jazz provide much of the backbeat to the city's groove, and an alternative country scene is flourishing. As far as dancing is concerned, the action has switched from cavernous clubs to smaller spots with DJs spinning dance tunes; there's everything from hip-hop to swing. Wicker Park and Bucktown have the hottest nightlife, but prime spots such as Sound-Bar and Le Passage are spread throughout the city.

The Reader (distributed midweek in bookstores, record shops, and other city establishments) is your best guide to the entertainment scene. This free weekly has comprehensive, timely listings and reviews. Another reliable weekly is *Time Out Chicago* magazine. The Friday editions of the *Chicago Tribune* and *Chicago Sun-Times* are also good sources of information. Daily updates on happenings around town are listed in the *Chicago Tribune's* sister paper, *RedEye,* or on the Web at ⊕ www. metromix.com.

Shows usually begin at 9 PM; cover charges generally range from $3 to $20, depending on the day of the week (Friday and Saturday nights are the most expensive). Most bars stay open until 2 AM Friday night and 3 AM Saturday, except for a few after-hours spots and some larger dance clubs, which are often open until 4 AM Friday night and 5 AM Saturday (Berlin, Crobar, and Transit are very popular). Outdoor beer gardens such as Sheffield's and John Barleycorn are the exception; these close at 11 PM on weekdays and midnight on weekends. Some bars are not open seven days a week, so call before you go.

The list of blues and jazz clubs includes several South Side locations: be cautious about transportation here late at night because some of these neighborhoods can be unsafe. Drive your own car or ask the bartender to call you a cab.

Bars

Chicago bars—whether they're sports bars, wine bars, neighborhood bars, or even trendy bars—are surprisingly accessible. With few exceptions, snobbishness and exclusivity are not tolerated throughout the scene, so bring your ID (most places card at the door), pocket some cash, and join the party!

■ TIP→ **If you're sticking to downtown and North Side bars, it's relatively safe to take public transportation. But if you're planning on staying out past midnight, we suggest taking a cab home.**

Loop, South Loop, and West Loop
Sleek and sexy wine bars and lounges light up Chicago's core business district after work and on weekends. Beware: downtown bars are seldom budget-friendly (but often worth the money).

BARS WITH VIEWS

Vertigo is a small price to pay for these stellar views.

Castaways (✉ 1603 N. Lakeshore Dr., River North ☎ 773/281–1200) puts you so close to Lake Michigan, you might consider wearing a swimsuit. Perched atop the North Avenue Beach Boathouse, the breezy, casual bar and grill creates the perfect setup for lazy, summertime sipping.

When it comes to heights, **Signature Lounge** (✉ 875 N. Michigan Ave., Near North ☎ 312/787–7230)–set on the 96th floor of the John Hancock Center–is in a category all its own. Drinks and appetizers are pricey, but well-worth it: the cityscape views are simply unmatched.

Glittering panoramic views of Lake Michigan and the city draw visitors worldwide to **Whiskey Sky** (✉ 644 N. Lakeshore Dr., Near North ☎ 312/943–9200). The W Hotel-Lakeshore's plush, low-lit lounge also offers tasty cocktails, a cool vibe, and owner Rande Gerber's seal of approval.

Encore (✉ 171 W. Randolph St., Loop ☎ 312/338–3788) is a jazzed-up hotel lounge sandwiched between the Cadillac Palace Theatre and the Hotel Allegro. Clubby seating and a classic cocktail menu make it an appealing downtown destination for post-dinner or -theater drinks, a light bite, and conversation.

Ghost Bar (✉ 440 W. Randolph St., West Loop ☎ 312/575–9900) is a sexy downtown space perched above the restaurant Nine. Cool and futuristic with cushy vinyl banquettes and designer-looking seating, the bar is white as a, well, you know what, and the muted lighting casts the fashion-conscious crowd in silhouette.

Kitty O'Shea's (✉ Chicago Hilton and Towers, 720 S. Michigan Ave., South Loop ☎ 312/922–4400), a handsome room in the Chicago Hilton and Towers, re-creates an Irish pub with all things Irish, including live music six nights a week, beer, food, and bar staff.

The **Tasting Room** (✉ 1415 W. Randolph St., Loop ☎ 312/942–1313) makes the short list of nightspots where Chicagoans take guests they want to impress. This two-story wine bar has casual, loft-chic looks and sweeping skyline views. More than 100 wines are poured by the glass and twice as many by the bottle. Cheese, caviar, and other light bites are the perfect complement. If you love the vintage you taste here, buy a bottle to take home at the adjacent wine shop, Randolph Wine Cellars.

Near North & River North

The famous Chicago bar scene known as **Rush Street** has faded into the mists of time, although the street has found resurgent energy with the opening of a string of upscale restaurants and outdoor cafés. For the vestiges of the old Rush Street, continue north to trendy **Division Street** between Clark and State streets. The crowd here consists mostly of suburbanites and out-of-towners on the make. The bars are crowded and noisy. Among the better-known singles bars are **Butch McGuire's** (✉ 20 W. Division St., Near North ☎ 312/337–9080), the **Lodge** (✉ 21 W. Division St., Near North ☎ 312/642–4406), and **Original Mother's** (✉ 26 W. Division St., Near North ☎ 312/642–7251), which was featured in the motion picture *About Last Night.*

Reprieve from the bustling Division Street scene is only a few blocks south, in the Near North and River North neighborhoods. Hunker down in a low-key lounge or sip a hearty pint of Guinness at an authentic Irish pub. Whatever your preference, plenty of conversation-friendly bars are a brief cab ride away.

Cru Café and Wine Bar (✉ 888 N. Wabash Ave., Near North ☎ 312/337–4078) is a swank Gold Coast wine bar that embraces the living-large ethos—from the oversize chandeliers to the extensive wine list to the international set that roosts here. In warmer months, a Euro-style sidewalk café extends the seating options.

Fado (✉ 100 W. Grand Ave., River North ☎ 312/836–0066) uses imported wood, stone, and glasswork to create its Irish look. The second floor—its bar was imported from Dublin—feels more like the real thing than the first. There's expertly drawn Guinness, a fine selection of Irish whiskeys, live Irish music on weekends, and a menu of traditional Irish food.

Oprah's pet designer Nate Berkus assembled **Rockit's** (✉ 22 W. Hubbard St., River North ☎ 312/645–6000) hunter-lodge look: wood plank–framed plasma TVs, antler chandeliers, and brown leather booths. The crowd, much like the beer list, is diverse and tasteful, and despite the masculine vibe, there's a good mix of men and women. Dress to impress.

★ The **Signature Room at the 95th** (✉ 875 N. Michigan Ave., Near North ☎ 312/787–9596) has no competition when it comes to views. Perched on the 96th floor of the John Hancock Center—above even the tower's observation deck—the bar offers stunning vistas of the skyline and lake for only the cost of a pricey drink.

Wicker Park & Bucktown

Hip cats, artists, and yuppies converge on the famed six corners of North, Milwaukee, and Damen avenues, where the cast of *Real World Chicago* once resided. Previously scruffy and edgy, the area is now dotted with pricey, upscale bars, though the occasional honky-tonk still exists.

★ **California Clipper** (✉ 1002 N. California Ave., Wicker Park ☎ 773/384–2547), in Humboldt Park, just to the west of Wicker Park, has a 1940s vintage look, including a curving 60-foot-long Brunswick bar and tiny booths lining the long room back to back like seats on a train. Alternative country acts and soul-gospel DJs are part of the eccentric musical lineup.

The **Map Room** (✉ 1949 N. Hoyne Ave., Bucktown ☎ 773/252–7636) might help you find your way around Chicago, if not the world. Maps and travel books decorate the walls of this self-described "travelers' tavern," and the beers represent much of the world. Tuesday is international night, with a free buffet of cuisines from different countries.

Northside Bar & Grill (✉ 1635 N. Damen Ave., Wicker Park ☎ 773/384–3555) was one of the first anchors of the now-teeming Wicker Park nightlife scene. Arty (and sometimes slightly yuppie) types come to drink, eat, shoot pool, and see and be seen. The enclosed indoor-outdoor patio lets you get the best out of the chancy Chicago weather.

Silver Cloud Bar & Grill (✉ 1700 N. Damen Ave., Bucktown ☎ 773/489–6212) might be the only place in the city where you can order a champagne cocktail alongside sloppy Joes and Tater Tots and not open yourself up to a citizen's arrest. For us, that's reason enough to go. Spacious red-leather booths, retro-fringed lamps, friendly service, and an upbeat, neighborhood crowd round out the good points.

★ **Sonotheque** (✉ 1444 W. Chicago Ave., Wicker Park ☎ 312/226–7600), with its tasteful, modern design and sparse, podlike seating, is one of the more visually progressive lounges in Chicago. A thoughtful Scotch list, high-profile DJs, and down-to-earth service bring heavy crowds to West Town, a few blocks south of Wicker Park, on weekends.

> **WORD OF MOUTH**
>
> "I am a big fan of Sonotheque on Chicago Ave. Easy to get to via cab from downtown. Great space, great music, great crowd. Sometimes there's a cover, but its minimal and the drinks are reasonable."
>
> –superk

Vintage Wine Bar (✉ 1942 W. Division St., Wicker Park ☎ 773/772–3400) offers affordable vino (several bottles clock in for under $20) in an attitude-free atmosphere. You won't find many wine snobs here; just people looking to sip in a hip environment. Choose a seat at the glowing lipstick red bar, or relax in the lounge up front, where there's a working fireplace. Hungry? A serious menu lists everything from bisques to entrées to cheese platters.

Lincoln Park

One of the most beautiful (and bustling) neighborhoods on the north side of Chicago, Lincoln Park is largely defined by the DePaul students who inhabit the area. Irish pubs and sports bars line the streets with college students, but intimate wine bars attract an older, more sophisticated set.

John Barleycorn (✉ 658 W. Belden Ave., Lincoln Park ☎ 773/348–8899), a historic pub with a long wooden bar, can get somewhat rowdy despite the classical music (played until 8 PM) and the art slides shown on video screens. It has a spacious summer beer garden, a good pub menu, and a wide selection of beers. A second location at 3524 North Clark Street brings the fun to Wrigleyville.

There are two reasons to go to **Red Lion** (✉ 2446 N. Lincoln Ave., Lincoln Park ☎ 773/348–2695). The first is the British kitsch: check out the London Metro maps that line the walls, duck into the hulking red phone booth, and feast on fish-and-chips and Guinness or bangers-and-mash and hard cider. The second is the legend: a bookie joint in the 1930s, it's said to be one of America's most haunted places.

Webster's Wine Bar (✉ 1480 W. Webster Ave., Lincoln Park ☎ 773/868–0608), a romantic place for a date, stocks more than 450 types of wine, with at least 30 by the glass, as well as ports, sherries, single-malt Scotches, a few microbrews, and a menu of small tasting entrées at reasonable prices.

Clybar (✉ 2417 N. Clybourn Ave., Lincoln Park ☎ 773/338–1877) is one of the few Lincoln Park bars not filled to the brim with frat boys. Inside, sophisticates of all ages gather round to sip a stiff drink and carry on conversation. Booths and a roomy backroom couch are perfect for groups of four or more. Singles and smaller parties tend to stick to the bar, where chatty bartenders keep the conversation as frothy as the shaken martinis. Twinkling lights, dark-wood furniture, and a cherrywood fireplace add a touch of romance for those in the mood.

Lake View & Far North Side

Lake View and Uptown and Andersonville, both on the Far North Side, have one thing in common: affordability. Unbelievable as it sounds, there are places in the city where $20 stretches beyond the price of admission and a martini. Drink deals are frequently offered at many bars.

Gingerman Tavern (✉ 3740 N. Clark St., Lake View ☎ 773/549–2050), up the street from Wrigley Field, deftly manages to avoid being pigeonholed as a sports bar. Folks here take their beer and billiards seriously, with three pool tables and—our favorite part—a list of more than 100 bottles of beer. New and vintage tunes crank out of the jukebox all night long.

Holiday Club (✉ 4000 N. Sheridan Rd., Far North Side ☎ 773/348–9600) bills itself as "a swinger's mecca." It attracts goodfellas with its 1950s decor and well-stocked CD jukebox with selections ranging from Dean Martin and Frank Sinatra to early punk. Down a pint of good beer (or even bad beer in cans) and scan the typical (but tasty) bar menu.

★ **Hopleaf** (✉ 5148 N. Clark St., Far North Side ☎ 773/334–9851), an anchor in the Andersonville corridor, continues the tradition of the classic Chicago bar hospitable to conversation (not a TV in sight). Pick one of the too-many-to-choose-from beers on the menu, with special offerings of Belgian beers and regional microbrews. A menu of Belgian bar fare usurps typical bar food options.

Sheffield's (✉ 3258 N. Sheffield Ave., Lake View ☎ 773/281–4989) spans the seasons with a shaded beer garden in summer and a roaring fireplace in winter. This laid-back neighborhood pub has billiards and more than 100 kinds of bottled beer that change seasonally, including regional microbrews, the bartender's "bad beer of the month"—a cheap can of beer (think PBR)—as well as 18 brands on tap.

Space is so limited at **Joie de Vine** (✉ 1744 W. Balmoral Ave., Lake View ☎ 773/989–6846), the wine barely has room to breathe. Good

NEW SPOTS TO WATCH

The buzz is strong on these new hot spots.

The super-white, fashionably cramped interior of **Jet Vodka Lounge** (✉ 1551 N. Sheffield Ave., Lincoln Park ☎ 312/730-4395) has the look and feel of a sleekly designed aircraft. Ease your way through the 130-strong international vodka list by trying a (uh-hem) test flight of four tastings.

Finally, a hotel bar worth its weight in Johnnie Walker Gold. **Hard Drive,** (✉ 151 E. Wacker Dr. ☎ 312/239-4544) set inside the Hyatt

Regency's newly restructured atrium, specializes in premium bottle service, flashy VIP rooms, and late-night hours. The dance floor—open until 4 AM on weekends—sits inside a fountain.

Motel (✉ 600 W. Chicago Ave., River North ☎ 312/822-2900) has all the comforts of a real, honest-to-goodness motel bar (TVs tuned to sports, classic cocktails, and a retro color scheme), but the whole ordeal is amped-up with sexy, low-rise furniture, and a "room service" menu of upscale bites.

design (and sidewalk tables in summer months) saves the space from feeling claustrophobic. Sit at the long wooden bar or opposing banquette and enjoy the real focal point of the room, a glass brick wall lit up in multicolors. All sorts of tasty delights, including wine, olives, or cheese, come in reasonably priced flights. Try stopping by on a weeknight when the neighborhood regulars are least likely to crowd the slender bar.

Cafés

High-maintenance ("half-caff-double-foam-soy-latte-to-go") and low-maintenance ("cup 'a joe, black") coffee drinkers feel at home in the diverse range of cafés dotting the streets of Chicago's busiest North Side neighborhoods. Expect to spend anywhere from $2 to $6 (depending on your order) for a caffeinated beverage.

Near North, Wicker Park & Bucktown

Caffe de Luca (✉ 1721 N. Damen Ave., Bucktown ☎ 773/342–6000) is the place to go when you crave air and light with your caffeine and calories. This sophisticated Bucktown spot hints at Tuscany with richly colored walls and a fine selection of Italian sandwiches, salads, and sorbets.

Earwax (✉ 1561 N. Milwaukee Ave., Wicker Park ☎ 773/772–4019) is a mecca for local vegans and vegetarians looking to order scrambled tofu alongside their ordinary cup of coffee. Well-worn, comfy furniture and a quirky staff go hand-in-hand with the relaxed atmosphere. A small selection of second-hand videos is for sale. Stop by for coffee, sweets, or a light meal.

Third Coast Café (✉ 1260 N. Dearborn St., Near North ☎ 312/649–0730), the oldest coffeehouse in the Gold Coast, lets you indulge your need for caffeine until the wee hours (until 2 AM on weeknights, 3 AM on weekends) with a full liquor, coffee, and food menu.

★ **Café Ballou's** (✉ 939 N. Western Ave., Wicker Park ☎ 773/342–2909) European charm lies in details like pretty lace curtains, a squishy couch, a preserved tin ceiling, and smooth marble tables. The inviting atmosphere at this café nestled in the Ukranian Village, near Wicker Park, is a far cry from Starbucks, and you won't find many grab-and-go caffeine addicts here. Choose from a menu of international sippers that are served according to tradition, like Turkish coffee brewed on a hot plate inside a mound of sand, or Russian tea drizzled with cherry compote. The friendly owner speaks fluent Polish and Ukranian, most often to her customers, many of whom are local neighborhood immigrants.

Lake View & Far North Side

Intelligentsia (✉ 3123 N. Broadway, Lake View ☎ 773/348–8058) was named to invoke the prechain days when cafés were forums for discussion, but the long, broad farmer's tables and handsome couches are usually occupied by students and other serious types who treat the café like their office. The store does all of its own coffee roasting and sells its custom blends to local restaurants.

Kopi, a Traveler's Cafe (✉ 5317 N. Clark St., Far North Side ☎ 773/989–5674) is a study in opposites, with healthy vegetarian options as well as decadent desserts. In the Andersonville district, a 20-minute cab ride from downtown, this café has a selection of travel books (for sale), foreign artifacts, and artfully painted tables.

The **Pick Me Up Café** (✉ 3408 N. Clark St., Lake View ☎ 773/248–6613) combines the charm of a quirky, neighborhood café with the late-night hours of those chain diners. The thrift-store treasures hanging on the walls are as eclectic as the crowd that comes at all hours of the day and night to drink bottomless cups of coffee or dine on sandwiches, appetizers, and desserts.

Uncommon Ground's (✉ 3800 N. Clark St., Lake View ☎ 773/929–3680) expanded Lake View location is roomier and smoke-free. It continues to deliver the goods with bowls of coffee, hot chocolate, a full bar, and a hearty, all-day food menu. Fun perks include two fireplaces, a sidewalk café, and a steady lineup of acoustic musical acts.

Comedy & Improv Clubs

Improvisation has long had a successful following in Chicago; stand-up comedy hasn't fared as well. Most comedy clubs have a cover charge ($5–$20); many have a two-drink minimum on top of that. In the stand-up circuit, keep an eye out for performances by Steve Harvey, star of his own WB television series.

Barrel of Laughs (✉ 10345 S. Central Ave., Oaklawn ☎ 708/499–2969), in the city's southwest suburbs (a 30-minute drive from downtown), spotlights local and national comics. The dinner package includes a meal at

Looking for Laughs? Try Improv

MIKE MYERS, TINA FEY, BILL MURRAY, John Belushi, Dan Aykroyd, Alan Alda, Shelley Long, Ed Asner, John Candy, Andy Dick. These are just a few of the comic actors who, were they to attempt to trace their path to stardom, might credit nights spent improvising on Chicago stages.

Chicago was the birthplace of the improvisational comedy form some 50-odd years ago, and the city remains the country's primary breeding ground for this challenging art form. Performers, usually working in an ensemble, ask the audience for a suggestion, then launch into short, long, silly, serious, or surreal scenes loosely related to that original audience input. All without any advance preparation. It's just the performers and their own creativity and confident ability to take risks in front of an audience that keep the evening entertaining.

Second City (☎ 312/337-3992) is the anchor of Chicago improv. The revues on the company's main stage and in its smaller e.t.c. space next door are actually sketch comedy shows, but the scripts in these prerehearsed scenes have been developed through improvisation and there's usually a little time set aside in each show for the performers to demonstrate their quick wit. Most nights there is a free improv set after the late show featuring cast members and invited guests (sometimes famous, sometimes not, never announced in advance). It's in Donny's Skybox upstairs that you're more likely to see one of Chicago's many fledgling improv comedy troupes making their first appearance working together on freshly penned material in public. Often these are groups of students in the Second City's performance or writing programs strutting their stuff for audiences in an ongoing quest to make it big, be discovered, and get called up to *Saturday Night Live* or *MadTV.*

But Second City isn't the only place in Chicago churning out improvising talent. **I.O.** (☎ 773/880-0199) (formerly called ImprovOlympic) is the city's home of long-form improvisation. The signature piece is "The Harold," in which a team of improvisers explores a single audience suggestion throughout a series of stories and characters until they all eventually weave back together to fit with the original audience idea. At **ComedySportz Chicago** (☎ 773/549-8080), teams of professional improvisers perform songs and scenes all based on your suggestions in an audience-interactive competition. The itinerant **Annoyance** was constructing a new home in Uptown at 4840 North Broadway at this writing. *Coed Prison Sluts* and *Splatter Theatre*—titles of past hits for the company—give a good idea of the Annoyance edge.

Scope out the hordes of up-and-comers at neighborhood stages such as the **Playground Theater** (☎ 773/871-3793) and **Frankie J's on Broadway/Methadome Theater** (☎ 773/769-2959), where improv and sketch comedy is king.

The springtime **Chicago Improv Festival** (☎ 773/935-9810), the nation's largest festival for improvisers, has stages devoted to group, pair, and single improv and sketch comedy and more.

the adjacent Senese's restaurant and reserved seats at the show.

ComedySportz (✉ 2851 N. Halsted St., Lake View ☎ 773/549–8080) specializes in "competitive improv," in which two teams vie for the audience's favor.

I.O. (✉ 3541 N. Clark St., Lake View ☎ 773/880–0199) (formerly called ImprovOlympic) has shows with student and professional improvisation in two intimate spaces every night of the week. Team members present long-form comedic improvisations drawn on audience suggestions, including an improvised musical and a Monday-night alumni show. No drink or age minimum.

★ **Second City** (✉ 1616 N. Wells St., Near North ☎ 312/337–3992), an institution since 1959, has served as a launching pad for some of the hottest comedians around. Alumni include Dan Aykroyd and the late John Belushi. Funny, loony skit comedy is presented on two stages, with a free improv set after the show every night but Friday.

Zanies (✉ 1548 N. Wells St., Near North ☎ 312/337–4027) books outstanding national talent and is Chicago's best stand-up comedy spot. Jay Leno, Jerry Seinfeld, and Jackie Mason have all performed at this intimate venue.

Dance Clubs

Most clubs don't get crowded until 11 or 12, and they remain open into the early-morning hours. Cover charges range from $5 to $20. A few dance clubs have dress codes that don't allow jeans, gym shoes, or baseball caps.

To avoid the exhausting lines and cover charges at most nightclubs, chat with your hotel concierge or even your server at dinner. Admission into the VIP lounges of Chicago's hottest clubs is often a conversation-with-the-right-person away from becoming a reality.

Great news for those who like to club hop: most of Chicago's best dance clubs (Sound-Bar, Transit, and Le Passage, to name a few) are within the Near North and River North neighborhoods, just north of downtown. The close proximity makes it relatively easy (and cheap) to cab it from one club to another. Wicker Park and Lakeview are also good 'hoods for when you feel like dancing.

Fodor'sChoice **Berlin** (✉ 954 W. Belmont Ave., Lake View ☎ 773/348–4975), a mul-
★ ticultural, pansexual dance club near the Belmont El station, has progressive electronic dance music and fun theme nights—Madonna and Prince are celebrated on the first and last Sunday of the month, and

Wednesday is devoted to disco. The crowd tends to be predominantly gay on weeknights, mixed on weekends.

Crobar—The Nightclub (✉ 1543 N. Kingsbury St., Near North ☎ 312/266–1900), the reigning Chicago nightclub, has scrapped its scruffy, Goth-like decor for a sprawling South Beach makeover complete with a glass-enclosed VIP lounge and booth-lined balcony. Top DJs spin house and techno over the enormous dance floor, which draws a mostly gay crowd, especially on themed Sundays.

Excalibur (✉ 632 N. Dearborn St., River North ☎ 312/266–1944) won't win any prizes for breaking new ground, but this River North nightclub complex, carved out of the Romanesque fortress that was the original home of the Chicago Historical Society, has been going strong for years with its mix of dancing, dining, and posing. At the same address and phone number but with a separate entrance is the smaller, alternative dance club **Vision**.

■ TIP➔ Deejays and music styles change regularly (consequently, so does the club's vibe), so be sure to call ahead for information on the night's selections.

Funky is the operative word for the **Funky Buddha Lounge** (✉ 728 W. Grand Ave., Wicker Park ☎ 312/666–1695), with its diverse crowd, seductive dance music, and a big metal Buddha guarding the front door. It has an intimate bar and dark dance floor, where patrons groove as DJs spin dance hall, hip-hop, R&B, funk, and old-school house. The VIP room in back can be declared no-smoking upon request.

Le Passage (✉ 937 N. Rush St., Near North ☎ 312/255–0022) is in the Gold Coast area, but it feels like an underground Parisian nightclub, complete with low ceilings, dim lighting, and French colonial furniture. Stop in for an early-evening cocktail and plate of French-inspired cuisine and stay for late night dancing. DJs spin house and hip-hop most nights except Wednesday, when audience choice rules.

Spy Bar (✉ 646 N. Franklin St., River North ☎ 312/587-8779) pulls some smooth moves. Image is everything at this subterranean spot with a brushed stainless-steel bar and exposed brick walls. The slick, stylish crowd hits the tight dance floor for house, underground, and DJ remixes.

Fodor'sChoice ★ **Sound-Bar** (✉ 226 W. Ontario St., River North ☎ 312/787–4480) reigns supreme as Chicago's trendiest and busiest dance club. Weave your way through a bi-level labyrinth of nine bars, each with a unique design and color scheme (some even serve matching colored cocktails), or nestle into one of four sleek boutique lounges. Feel like dancing? Join the pulse of Chicago's best-dressed on the huge dance floor.

Transit (✉ 1431 W. Lake St., West Loop ☎ 312/491–8600 or 312/491–9729), despite being hidden away underneath the El tracks in a spooky stretch west of downtown, is wildly popular with young club goers. Inside, the multiroom space has a crisp design, earthy colors, and sumptuous VIP area.

Gay & Lesbian Nightlife

Chicago's gay bars appeal to mixed crowds and tastes. Most are on North Halsted Street from Belmont Avenue to Irving Park Road, an area nicknamed Boys Town. Bars generally stay open until 2 AM weekends, but a few keep the lights on until 5 AM Sunday morning. The *Chicago Free Press, Windy City Times,* and *Gay Chicago* list nightspots, events, and gay and lesbian resources; all three are free and can be picked up at bookstores, bars, and some supermarkets, especially those in Boys Town.

Big Chicks (✉ 5024 N. Sheridan Rd., Far North Side ☎ 773/728–5511), in the Uptown area of the Far North Side, is a striking alternative to the Halsted strip, with a funky crowd that appreciates the owner's art collection hanging on the walls. The fun-loving staff and their self-selected eclectic music are the payoffs for the hike to get here. Special attractions include weekend dancing, midnight shots, and free Sunday-afternoon buffets.

Charlie's (✉ 3726 N. Broadway, Lake View ☎ 773/871–8887), a country-and-western dance club, lets you two-step nightly to achy-breaky tunes, though dance music is played every night from 2 AM to 4 AM. It's mostly a boots-and-denim crowd on weekends.

Circuit (✉ 3641 N. Halsted St., Lake View ☎ 773/325–2233), the biggest dance club in Boys Town, is a stripped-down dance hall energized by flashing lights, booming sounds, and a partying crowd. Take a break in the up-front martini bar, Rehab.

The **Closet** (✉ 3325 N. Broadway, Lake View ☎ 773/477–8533) is a basic Chicago tavern with a gay twist. This compact bar—one of the few that caters to lesbians, though it draws gay men, too—can be especially lively after 2 AM when most other bars close. Stop by Sunday afternoons when bartenders serve up what are hailed as the best Bloody Marys in town.

Gentry (✉ 440 N. State St., River North ☎ 312/836–0933), one of the few gay bars downtown, is a premier piano bar/cabaret, featuring local and national talent. Sophisticates linger at the upscale piano bar; the video bar downstairs attracts a younger group. A smaller, Boys Town branch is at 3320 North Halsted Street.

Roscoe's Tavern (✉ 3356 N. Halsted St., Lake View ☎ 773/281–3355), in the heart of Boys Town, is a longtime favorite with a mix of amenities sure to please its peppy patrons, including a jam-packed front bar, a dance floor, a pool table, an outdoor garden, and lively music. The sidewalk café serves May–September.

The video bar **Sidetrack** (✉ 3349 N. Halsted St., Lake View ☎ 773/477–9189) is tuned into a different theme every night of the week, from show tunes on Monday to comedy on Thursday—all broadcast on TV screens that never leave your sight. The sprawling stand-and-pose bar and rooftop deck are always busy with a good-looking, professional crowd, and the vodka slushies are a house specialty.

At **Hydrate** (✉ 3458 N. Halsted St., Lake View ☎ 773/975–9244), sip a slushy in the blue-tinged front room, or head to the flashy mirror-banked dance floor, where an international roster of deejays spins nightly.

Music

Country
There are slim pickin's for country music clubs in Chicago, even though country radio continues to draw wide audiences.

★ **Carol's Pub** (✉ 4659 N. Clark St., Far North Side ☎ 773/334–2402), in the Uptown area of the Far North Side, showcased country before it was ever cool. The house band at this urban honky-tonk plays country and country-rock tunes on weekends, and the popular karaoke night on Thursday draws all walks of life, from preppie to punk.

The Hideout (✉ 1354 W. Wabansia, Bucktown ☎ 773/227–4433), which is literally hidden away in a North Side industrial zone, has managed to make country music hip in Chicago. Players on the city's alternative country scene have adopted the friendly hole-in-the-wall, and bands ranging from the obscure to the semi-famous take the stage. The bluegrass band Devil in a Woodpile plays on Tuesday.

Eclectic
Clubs in this category don't limit themselves to a single type of music. Call ahead to find out what's playing.

At **Baton** (✉ 436 N. Clark St., River North ☎ 312/644–5269), boys will be girls. The lip-synching revues with female impersonators have catered to curious out-of-towners and bachelorette parties since 1969. Some of the regular performers, such

> **WORD OF MOUTH**
>
> The Baton's female impersonator show is a hoot.
> –Kris

as Chili Pepper and Mimi Marks, have become Chicago cult figures. The more the audience tips, the better the show gets, so bring your bills.

Beat Kitchen (✉ 2100 W. Belmont Ave., Lake View ☎ 773/281–4444) brings in the crowds because of its good sound system and local and touring rock, alternative rock, country, and rockabilly acts. It also serves soups, salads, sandwiches, pizzas, and desserts.

Elbo Room (✉ 2871 N. Lincoln Ave., Lincoln Park ☎ 773/549–5549), a multilevel space in an elbow-shape corner building, has a basement rec-room feel. The bar plays host to talented live bands seven days a week, with a strong dose of acid jazz, funk, soul, pop, and rock.

FitzGerald's (✉ 6615 W. Roosevelt Rd., Berwyn ☎ 708/788–2118), though a 30-minute schlep west of Chicago, draws crowds from all over the city and suburbs with its mix of folk, jazz, blues, zydeco, and rock. This early 1900s roadhouse has great sound and sight lines for its roots music.

Fodor's Choice ★ **HotHouse** (✉ 31 E. Balbo Ave., South Loop ☎ 312/362–9707) bills itself as "the center for international performance and exhibition," and delivers globe-spanning musical offerings—Spanish guitar one night, mambo the next—in a spacious venue that can be counted on to draw an interesting crowd.

★ **House of Blues** (✉ 329 N. Dearborn St., River North ☎ 312/923–2000), though its name implies otherwise, attracts big-name performers of all genres, from jazz, roots, blues, and gospel to alternative rock, hip-hop, world, and R&B. The interior is an elaborate cross between blues bar and ornate opera house. Its restaurant has live blues every night on a "second stage," as well as a satisfying Sunday gospel brunch. Part of the Marina City complex, the entrance is on State Street.

Folk & Ethnic

Old Town School of Folk Music (✉ 4544 N. Lincoln Ave., Far North Side ☎ 773/728–6000), Chicago's first and oldest folk music school, has served as folk central in the city since 1957. This friendly spot in Lincoln Square hosts outstanding performances by national and local acts in a 420-seat concert hall.

Wild Hare (✉ 3530 N. Clark St., Lake View ☎ 773/327–4273), with a wide-open dance floor, is the place for infectious live reggae and world-beat music seven nights a week.

Jazz

Jazz thrives all around town. For a recorded listing of upcoming live performances, call the **Jazz Institute Hot Line** (☎ 312/427–3300).

Andy's (✉ 11 E. Hubbard St., River North ☎ 312/642–6805), a favorite after-work watering hole with a substantial bar menu, has live, local jazz daily. In addition to the evening performances, there's a jazz program at noon on weekdays—a boon for music lovers who aren't night owls.

Cotton Club (✉ 1710 S. Michigan Ave., South Loop ☎ 312/341–9787) draws big, diverse crowds and good bands. There's an open mike every Monday and live jazz by candlelight in the elegant Cab Calloway Room on weekends, as well as dancing to hip-hop and R&B in the Gray Room.

Green Dolphin Street (✉ 2200 N. Ashland Ave., Lake View ☎ 773/395–0066), a stylish, upscale club-restaurant with the glamour of the 1940s (in a converted auto-body shop, no less), attracts tight ensembles and smooth-voiced jazz divas for big band, bebop, Latin, and world jazz.

★ **Green Mill** (✉ 4802 N. Broadway, Far North Side ☎ 773/878–5552), a Chicago institution off the beaten track in untrendy Uptown, has been around since 1907. Deep leather banquettes and ornate wood paneling line the walls, and a photo of Al Capone occupies a place of honor on the piano behind the bar. The jazz entertainment is both excellent and contemporary—the club launched the careers of Kurt Elling and Patricia Barber—and the Uptown Poetry Slam, a competitive poetry reading, takes center stage on Sunday.

Jazz Showcase (✉ 59 W. Grand Ave., River North ☎ 312/670–2473), the second-oldest jazz club in the country, presents national and international names in jazz, and mostly acoustic groups. This serious, no-

Continued on page 271

CHICAGO STILL SINGS THE BLUES

The cool, electric, urban blues are the soundtrack of the Windy City. The blues traveled up the Mississippi River with the Delta sharecroppers during the Great Migration, settled down on Maxwell Street and South Side clubs, and gave birth to such big-name talent as Muddy Waters, Howlin' Wolf, Willie Dixon, and, later, Koko Taylor. Today, you can still hear the blues in a few South Side clubs where it all began, or check out the current scene on the North Side.

THE BIRTH OF THE CHICAGO BLUES

CHESS RECORDS

Founded by Philip and Leonard Chess, Polish immigrant brothers, in 1947. For the first two years, the label was called Aristocrat.

Its famous address, 2120 S. Michigan Avenue, was the nucleus of the blues scene. Up-and-comers performed on the sidewalk out front in hopes of being discovered. Even today, locals and visitors peek through the windows of the restored studio (now the Blues Heaven Foundation) looking for glimpses of past glory.

The label's first hit record was Muddy Waters' *I Can't Be Satisfied*.

The brothers were criticized for having a paternalistic relationship with their artists. They reportedly bought Muddy Waters a car off the lot when he wasn't able to finance it himself.

The label was sold in 1969 after Leonard's death.

Did you know? When the Rolling Stones recorded the track "2120 South Michigan Avenue" (off the *12 x 5* album) at the Chess Records studio in June 1964, the young Brits were reportedly so nervous about singing in front of Willie Dixon (Buddy Guy and Muddy Waters were also hanging around the studio that day) that they literally became tongue-tied. As a result, the song is purely instrumental.

WILLIE DIXON (7/1915–1/1992)

Chess Record's leading A & R (artist and repertoire) man, bass player, and composer. Founded the Blues Heaven Foundation, Chess Records' restored office and studio. *See Blues Heaven Foundation review next page.*

Famous compositions: "Hoochie Coochie Man" (recorded by Muddy Waters), "My Babe" (recorded by Little Walter), and "Wang Dang Doodle" (recorded by Koko Taylor)

MUDDY WATERS: KING OF ELECTRIC BLUES (4/1915–4/1983)

When Muddy Waters gave his guitar an electric jolt, he didn't just revolutionize the blues. His electric guitar became a magic wand: Its jive talk (and cry) turned country-blues into city-blues, and it gave birth to rock and roll. Waters' signature sound has been firmly imprinted on nearly all subsequent musical genres.

Best known for: Riveting vocals, a swooping pompadour, and, of course, plugging in the guitar

Biggest break: Leonard Chess, one of the Chess brothers of Chess Records, let Waters record two of his own songs. The record sold out in two days, and stores issued a dictum of "one per customer"

Biggest song: "Hoochie Coochie Man"

Lyrics: *Y'know I'm here / Everybody knows I'm here / And I'm the hoochie-coochie man*

Awards: 3 Grammies, Lifetime Achievement induction into the Rock and Roll Hall of Fame

Local honor: A strip of 43rd Street in Chicago is renamed Muddy Waters Drive

HOWLIN' WOLF (6/1910–1/1976)

In 1951, at the age of 41, Wolf recorded with Sun Studios in Memphis, TN. Shortly thereafter, Sun sold Wolf's only two songs, "Moanin' At Midnight" and "How Many More Years," to Chess Records, kicking off his prolific recording career with Chess.

Most popular songs: "Backdoor Man" and "Little Red Rooster"

Instruments: Electric guitar and harmonica

Dedication to his craft: Wolf was still taking guitar lessons even a year before his death, even though he was long recognized as one of the two greatest blues musicians in the world.

THE CHICAGO BLUES TODAY

KOKO TAYLOR:
Queen of the Blues

Blessed with neither Bessie Smith's beauty nor Billie Holiday's power of seduction, Taylor offers grit; a been-there-done-that wisdom that personified urban-blues by the 1970s.

Best known for: Slam-bang stage presence and powerhouse vocals

Big break: It wasn't until Chess Records blues producer Willie Dixon saw her singing at a South Side club one night in the early 1960s that her career really took off. Dixon reportedly said, "My God, I've never heard a woman sing the blues like you," and signed her up to record

Biggest song: "Wang Dang Doodle" sold a staggering one million copies in six weeks

Lyrics: *We gonna jump and shout 'til daylight / We gonna pitch a wang dang doodle / All night long*

Most significant hardship: Gettin' paid. Though Taylor was a star, she barely saw a penny of the profits while working with Chess Records and Willie Dixon

Awards: 25 W.C. Handy Awards (more than any other recording artist, male or female); a Grammy for *Blues Explosion*, 1984; Legend of the Year by Mayor Daley in 1993

Local honor: March 3rd is Koko Taylor Day in Chicago

Catch her act: Upcoming tour information is available at www.kokotaylor.com

BEST PLACES TO HEAR THE BLUES

Checkerboard Lounge (✉ 5201 S. Harper Ct., Hyde Park ☎ 773/684–1472) has reopened in Hyde Park! It was a sad day for blues fans when the world-famous Bronzeville location, owned by Buddy Guy in the 1970s and early 1980s, closed in 2003. Though the new location's in a shopping center—a far cry from its former gritty digs—it has the same diverse selection of local and big-name blues and jazz talent. Kudos on retaining some of the old picnic tables (used inside) from the first location. Note: Call ahead for information on the cover charge, which ranges from $3 to $20 depending on who's playing.

Chicago Blues Festival (☎ 312/744–3370) There's no doubt about it; Chicago still loves to sing the blues. Each June, the city pulses with sounds from the largest free blues festival in the world, which takes place over four days and on six stages in both Grant Park and Millennium Park. The always-packed open air festival has been headlined by blues legends such as B.B. King, Koko Taylor, and Buddy Guy.

Set in an upscale part of downtown, **Blue Chicago** (✉ 536 N. Clark St., River North ☎ 312/661–0100 ✉ 736 N. Clark St., River North ☎ 312/642–6261) has none of the trademark grit or edginess of the older South Side blues clubs. It does have two bars within two blocks of each other.

7

BUDDY GUY

Though he recorded his first album in 1958, Guy didn't really take off until he recorded with Vanguard in 1968 and was sent on tour with blues harmonica legend Junior Wells and the Rolling Stones.

Instrument: Electric guitar

Influenced: His stinging guitar playing had strong influences on Jimi Hendrix and Eric Clapton

Catch his act: Guy is still impressing fans with his sizzling guitar and vocals both on tour and in his Chicago-based club, Buddy Guy's Legends

Honors: 2005 inductee to the Rock and Roll Hall of Fame

DON'T MISS ACTS:

If these acts are playing when you're in town, don't miss them. For contact information for the venues mentioned below, see the club reviews on this page.

Classic slide-guitar and hard-driving blues beats mixed with jazz and even rock 'n' roll influences makes **Melvin Taylor & The Slack Band** a must-see. Call Rosa's Lounge for details. **Gloria Shannon Blues Band** plays everything from Delta blues to electric blues to Chicago blues. Catch their all-ages act every Saturday "Down in the Basement" at the Blue Chicago Store. **Billy Branch and the Sons Of Blues** frequently bring their forward-thinking sounds (steeped in blues tradition) to Rosa's Lounge and Kingston Mines, though they have been known to make rousing on-stage appearances at the Chicago Blues Festival.

Both have good sound systems, regularly book female vocalists, and attract a cosmopolitan audience that's a tad more diverse than some of the baseball-capped crowds at Lincoln Park blues clubs. We like that one cover gets you into both bars.

The **Blue Chicago Store** (✉ 534 N. Clark St., River North ☎ 312/661–1003) sells CDs and other merchandise, but the real attraction is "Down in the Basement." Bring the kids to the only all-ages blues program in Chicago, which has live music every Saturday night. It's smoke- and alcohol-free.

★ The best part about **B.L.U.E.S.** (✉ 2519 N. Halsted St., Lincoln Park ☎ 773/

528–1012) is that there isn't a bad seat in the smoky joint. The worst part? The smoke (stay away if you can't stand cigarettes). Narrow and intimate, the jam-packed North Side club has attracted the best in local talent since it opened in 1979. Big names such as Son Seals, Otis Rush, Jimmy Johnson, and Magic Slim have all played here.

★ **Fodor's Choice** **Buddy Guy's Legends** (✉ 754 S. Wabash Ave., South Loop ☎ 312/427–0333) serves up Louisiana-style barbecue along with the blues. The big club has good sound, good sight lines, and pool tables if you get restless in between sets. Look for local blues acts during the week and larger-scale touring

A MODERN HISTORY LESSON:

The Blues Heaven Foundation (✉ 2120 S. Michigan Ave., South Loop ☎ 312/808–1286)

Breathe the same rarefied air as blues (and rock 'n' roll) legends Muddy Waters, Howlin' Wolf, Chuck Berry, and the Rolling Stones, all of whom recorded here. Check out the Chess brothers' private offices, the recording studio, and the back stairway used only by signed musicians. Don't miss the eerie "Life Cast Portraits" wall showcasing the plaster heads of the Chess recording artists.

Note: Make a phone reservation before stopping by—the Foundation keeps irregular hours.

acts on weekends. Don't miss Grammy Award winning blues performer/owner Buddy Guy in January, when he performs a month-long home stand of shows (tickets go on sale one month in advance).

In 1968, **Kingston Mines** (✉ 2548 N. Halsted St., Lincoln Park ☎ 773/477–4646) went down in Chicago history as the first blues club to open on the North Side. Though it's since moved to bigger digs, it still offers the same traditional sounds and late-night hours as the orig-

inal club. Swarms of blues lovers and partying singles take in the good blues and tasty barbecue.

★ **Fodor's Choice** **Lee's Unleaded Blues** (✉ 7401 S. South Chicago Ave., Grand Crossing ☎ 773/493–3477) has been a South Side favorite since it opened in the early 1970's. Locals come decked out in their showiest threads and University of Chicago students often pop in for a round. The cramped, triangular bar may inhibit free movement, but that doesn't seem to bother the crowd that comes for powerhouse blues and jazz. Note: the club can be difficult to find if you don't know the area, so be sure to take a cab or study a map before making the trip.

★ **Fodor's Choice** On a given night at **Rosa's Lounge,** (✉ 3420 W. Armitage Ave., Bucktown in Logan Square ☎ 773/342–0452) near Bucktown, you'll find Tony, the owner, working the crowd, and his mother, Rosa, behind the bar. What makes the club extra special is that the duo moved here from Italy out of a pure love for the blues. Stop by and partake in Rosa's winning mixture of big-name and local talent, stiff drinks, and friendly service—the same since it opened in 1984.

CLASSIC CHICAGO SPOTS

Imbibe your way through a history lesson at these Chicago institutions.

The Omni Ambassador East's glamorous **Pump Room** (✉ 1301 N. State Pkwy., Old Town ☎ 312/943-9200) is the spot for anyone interested in the Golden Age of Hollywood. Booth One alone has played host to more celebrities than Oprah Winfrey's couch like Humphrey Bogart, Lauren Bacall, Irv "Kup" Kupcinet, and Judy Garland.

The **Green Mill** (✉ 4802 N. Broadway, Far North Side ☎ 773/878-5552), opened in 1914 in Uptown, has undergone quite a few makeovers and owners (including Al Capone). We like its current incarnation: dark-wood carvings, passionate jazz, and smoke-filled booths.

Since the 1960s, **Original Mother's** (✉ 26 W. Division St., Near North ☎ 312/642-7251) has been a local favorite for cutting-edge music and dance-'til-you-drop partying. The subterranean singles destination was immortalized by Demi Moore, Jim Belushi, and Rob Lowe in the film *About Last Night.*

---

smoking club, bedecked with photos of all the jazz greats who have played it, is one of the best places to hear jazz in Chicago. Children under 12 are admitted free for the Sunday matinee.

Pops for Champagne (✉ 2934 N. Sheffield Ave., Lake View ☎ 773/472-1000), despite the incongruous name, is a good spot for serious jazz fans, who come for the instrumental ensembles and jazz vocalists. A 140-strong champagne bar and a selection of tasty appetizers and desserts enhance the scene.

Rock

Chicago has an active rock scene with many local favorites, some of which—including Smashing Pumpkins, Wilco, and Liz Phair—have won national acclaim. Bone up on Chicago's rock scene by tuning into 93.1 WXRT's Sound Opinions, a weekly radio show hosted by *Chicago Tribune* and *Chicago Sun-Times* rock critics, Greg Kot and Jim DeRogatis. The program airs Tuesday from 10 PM to midnight.

The Abbey (✉ 3420 W. Grace St., Far North Side ☎ 773/478-4408), about 15 minutes northwest of downtown in the Irving Park neighborhood, showcases rock, as well as some Irish, Celtic, and country music, in a large concert hall with a separate, busy, smoky pub. By day, the hall is used to show soccer and rugby games from the United Kingdom and Ireland.

Double Door (✉ 1572 N. Milwaukee Ave., Wicker Park ☎ 773/489-3160) is a hotbed for music in hip Wicker Park. The large bar books up-and-coming local and national acts from rock to acid jazz. Unannounced Rolling Stones shows have been held here. The entrance is on Damen Avenue.

BEST DIVE BARS

Plunge head-first into Chicago's most modest bars.

Matchbox (✉ 770 N. Milwaukee Ave., Wicker Park ☎ 312/666–9292), in West Town near Wicker Park, isn't much bigger than a you-know-what, but the hodgepodge of regulars don't seem to mind. In fact, many claim it's the dark, cramped quarters (and dirty martinis) that keep them coming back. The crowd spills outside in summer, when iron rod tables dot the sidewalk.

Rainbo Club (✉ 1150 N. Damen Ave., Wicker Park ☎ 773/489–5999) is the unofficial meeting place for Chicago hipsters and Indie-rockers. Apart from the working photo booth wedged into a corner, the stripped-down hang is pretty barren, but drinks are dirt cheap and the bartenders are upbeat–and willing–conversationalists.

Cans (yes, cans) of beer, dingy decor (think wood paneling and Christmas lights), and a loyal crowd of regulars makes **Lakeview Lounge** (✉ 5110 N. Broadway, Far North Side ☎ 773/769–0994), in Uptown, the quintessential dive bar. The house band belts out everything from blues to old-time rock-and-roll to a rowdy crowd on weekends; weekdays are low-key excuses for dart-playing and beer-slamming.

Empty Bottle (✉ 1035 N. Western Ave., Wicker Park ☎ 773/276–3600), in the Ukranian Village near Wicker Park, may have toys and knick-knacks around the bar (including a case of macabre baby doll heads), but when it comes to booking rock, punk, and jazz bands from the indie scene, it's a serious place with no pretensions.

Martyrs' (✉ 3855 N. Lincoln Ave., Far North Side ☎ 773/404–9869) brings local and major-label rock bands to this small, North Side neighborhood sandwiched between Lincoln Square and Roscoe Village. Music fans can see the stage from just about any corner of the bar, while the more rhythmically inclined gyrate in the large standing-room area. A mural opposite the stage memorializes late rock greats.

Metro (✉ 3730 N. Clark St., Lake View ☎ 773/549–0203) brings in progressive, nationally known artists and the cream of the local crop. A former movie palace, it's an excellent place to see live bands, whether you're moshing on the main floor or above the fray in the balcony. In the basement is **Smart Bar,** a late-night dance club that starts hopping after midnight.

Schubas Tavern (✉ 3159 N. Southport Ave., Lake View ☎ 773/525–2508) favors local and national power pop and indie rock bands. The wood-paneled back room has good seating and is laid-back. The bar was built in 1900 by the Schlitz Brewing Company, and it still sells Schlitz beer—a bargain at $2 a bottle.

Piano Bars

Coq d'Or (✉ 140 E. Walton St., Near North ☎ 312/787–2200) is a dark, wood-paneled room where Chicago legend Buddy Charles held court before retiring. Fine music and cocktails served in blown-glass goblets draw hotel guests as well as neighborhood regulars.

Davenport's (✉ 1383 N. Milwaukee Ave., Wicker Park ☎ 773/278–1830), a sophisticated cabaret booking both local and touring acts, brings a grown-up presence to the Wicker Park club scene. The piano lounge is set up for casual listening, while the cabaret room is a no-chat zone that requires your full attention—as well as reservations and a two-drink minimum.

> **WORD OF MOUTH**
>
> "My new favorite place is Howl at the Moon. It is a dueling piano bar that has fun music, sing alongs, and great people watching. It can be a little loud, but I had a blast there with a group aged 25-62. It was a weeknight and there wasn't a cover charge."
>
> –reynms

The dueling pianists at **Howl at the Moon** (✉ 26 W. Hubbard St., Near North ☎ 312/863–7427) attract a rowdy crowd who delight in belting out popular tunes along with the pianos. Reservations aren't accepted, but for a hefty sum ($75–$150), you can "buy out" a four-top table for the evening (the price includes no waiting in line, no cover, and a free round of drinks).

★ **Pump Room** (✉ Omni Ambassador East Hotel, 1301 N. State Pkwy., Near North ☎ 312/266–0360) shows off its storied past with photos of celebrities covering the walls. The bar at this restaurant has live piano music and a small dance floor that calls out for dancing cheek to cheek, especially on weekends.

Zebra Lounge (✉ 1220 N. State St., Near North ☎ 312/642–5140), small and funky with a striped motif, attracts a good crowd of dressed-up and dressed-down regulars who come to sing along to the pianist on duty.

Sports Bars

Gamekeepers (✉ 1971 N. Lincoln Ave., Lincoln Park ☎ 773/549–0400) is full of former frat boys and sports fans. With more than 40 TVs, three projection screens, and complete satellite sports coverage, there's barely a game Gamekeepers doesn't get.

Hi-Tops (✉ 3551 N. Sheffield Ave., Lake View ☎ 773/348–0009), within a ball's toss of Wrigley Field, may be the ultimate sports bar. Big-screen TVs, a lively crowd, and good bar food keep the Cubs fans coming. A dozen satellites and 65 TV monitors ensure that the place gets packed for a good game.

North Beach Chicago (✉ 1551 N. Sheffield Ave., Lincoln Park ☎ 312/266–7842) has multiple large-screen TVs plus two sand-filled indoor volleyball courts, pool tables, and four bowling lanes in this huge former warehouse.

Sluggers (✉ 3540 N. Clark St., Lake View ☎ 773/248–0055) is packed after Cubs games in the nearby stadium, and the ballplayers make occasional appearances in summer. Check out the fast- and slow-pitch batting cages on the second floor, as well as the pool tables, air hockey tables, and trampoline basketball.

Where to Stay

WORD OF MOUTH

"Chicago has a fantastic mass transit system, so you can stay just about anywhere and have fairly rapid access to both Wrigley Field and O'Hare Airport."

—Paul Rabe

"Chicago can be very hot in July and August. The city also gets crowded in the summer, and there are festivals all summer long, so plan ahead on hotels. The 4th of July is always busy."

—Kris

LODGING PLANNER

Hotel Prices

Hotel price categories in this chapter are based on the standard weekday rate for one room, double occupancy. These are the rack rates—the highest price at which the rooms are rented. However, although standard rates are quoted *per room*, package rates are often quoted *per person, double occupancy*. Be warned that many Chicago hotels quote rates based on single occupancy, with a second person adding $10–$20 to the nightly rate.

The lodgings we list are the cream of the crop in each price category. We always list the facilities that are available–but we don't specify whether they cost extra: when pricing accommodations, always ask what's included and what costs extra. Properties are assigned price categories based on the range between their least and most expensive standard double rooms at high season (excluding holidays).

Assume that hotels operate on the European Plan (EP, with no meals) unless we specify that they use the Continental Plan (CP, with a continental breakfast) or Breakfast Plan (BP, with a full breakfast).

A Note on Conventions

Proximity to **McCormick Place**, where most of Chicago's huge trade shows hunker down, is often a conventioneer's top priority, so most wind up staying in the Loop or South Loop, where hotels are just a five-minute cab ride away from the mammoth venue. In these neighborhoods, accommodations tend to be older and somewhat less expensive—although there are certainly a few exceptions. Expect somewhat quiet nights in these parts; while the Loop boasts a revitalized theater district, come sundown, there's a lot more revelry north of the Chicago River in the neighborhoods surrounding the Mag Mile. Vibrant Rush Street is the site of many bars, while River North has a high concentration of restaurants and nightclubs.

A meeting or convention in Rosemont or a tight flight schedule should be the only reasons to consider an airport hotel. Prices at these properties are a bit lower, but the O'Hare area is drab. Plus, trips from there to downtown may take an hour during rush hour, bad weather, or periods of heavy construction on the Kennedy Expressway.

WHAT IT COSTS				
FOR 2 PEOPLE				
$$$$	$$$	$$	$	¢
over $350	$225–$350	$150–$225	$100–$150	under $100

All prices are for a standard double room, excluding service charges and Chicago's 14.9% room tax. The tax is slightly lower at suburban hotels.

Lodging Know-How

Hotels are in the business of making guests happy. So, should you have a request or a special need, bring it to the attention of the concierge or hotel manager. Ordering room service? Make sure to vocalize any dietary needs; hotels generally have entrées at the ready that aren't printed on their menus. Have allergies? More and more properties these days are rolling out hypoallergenic rooms; if you can book them. Other hotels have trended toward using all allergy-sensitive bedding and pillows.

If a super-quiet stay is important to you, ask in advance about the hotel's sound proofing. Some properties have triangular layouts, which alleviate echoes, while others have improved wall insulation.

Don't walk away from your stay without vocalizing concerns to the appropriate person and, if you get home and are still uncomfortable with the outcome, put your thoughts down in writing. Hotels are usually responsive to letters from guests.

Raves and Faves

Most Innovative Use of a Hotel Lobby . . .
Hard Drive dance club in the atrium foyer of Hyatt Regency Chicago (151 E. Wacker Dr., Loop, 312/565–1234)

Cheap Lodging, Cool Location . . .
Red Roof Inn (162 E. Ontario St., Near North, 312/787–3580)

Best Beach-y Oasis in the City . . .
Hotel Indigo (1244 N. Dearborn Pkwy., Near North, 312/787–4980)

Coolest Amenity . . .
Hotel Burnham's "pillow library" (1 W. Washington St., Loop, 312/782–1111)

Hotel Restaurant Where the Locals Hang . . .
Aria restaurant at Fairmont (200 N. Columbus Dr., Loop, 312/565–8000)

Antiques Lover's Paradise . . .
Margarita European Inn (1566 Oak Ave., Evanston, Lake View & North, 847/869–2273)

Reservations

When making reservations, be sure to get a confirmation number and keep it with you for check-in. It's courtesy—and sometimes mandatory—to notify the hotel if you are arriving later than 5 PM. If you need to cancel your reservation, call as soon as possible (be sure to find out cancellation policies in advance). An alternative to reserving a room through a hotel is to contact a booking service. These agencies book excess rooms at major hotels, often at a discount. The no-fee hotel-reservation service Hot Rooms (773/468-7666; www.hotrooms.com) is one such service.

WHEN NOT TO GO TO CHICAGO

■ Many leisure travelers are fazed by Chicago's **frigid winters.**

■ Also be aware of the **more than 1,000 conventions and trade shows** scheduled throughout the year.

■ Contact the **Chicago Convention and Tourism Bureau** at (877/244-2246) for more information.

8

Revised by
Kelly Aiglon

The Loop

Chicago's business district, laced with overhead train tracks, is a desirable—if slightly noisy—place to stay. Hotels here tend to be moderately priced; many are housed in historic buildings, giving them a charm you won't find along glitzier North Michigan Avenue. Easy access to the Art Institute and Millennium Park is a plus.

$$$$ 🏨 **Palmer House Hilton.** The *grand palais* feel of this historic property is conveyed through the huge lobby ceiling mural, which gets touched up every four years by the same Florentine gentleman who restores the art in the Sistine Chapel. Rooms—reached via a winding maze of corridors—are adequately sized and have a robust green-and-red color

> **WORD OF MOUTH**
>
> "We nearly always stay at the Palmer House Hilton. The location for sightseeing, walking, restaurants, and shopping can't be beat."
>
> –lscott

scheme. With more than 1,600 rooms, the property can seem overwhelming; luckily two executive levels, nabbed for $80 above standard rates, have their own lobbies and concierges, providing a hotel-within-a-hotel feel. ⊠ *17 E. Monroe St., Loop, 60603* ☎ *312/726–7500 or 800/445–8667* 📠 *312/263–2556* ⊕ *www.hilton.com* 🛏 *1,639 rooms, 88 suites* ♿ *5 restaurants, room service, minibars, coffeemakers, hair dryers, irons, cable TV, in-room data ports and broadband, Wi-Fi in public spaces, indoor pool, fitness center, hair salon, spa, bar, shops, dry cleaning, laundry service, concierge, business center, meeting rooms, parking (fee), some pets allowed, no-smoking floor* ⊟ *AE, D, DC, MC, V.*

$$$–$$$$ 🏨 **Fairmont.** On a quiet block near the Loop, this 45-story pink-granite tower fluctuates between the understated and the opulent, with a huge, glistening chandelier in the foyer and guest rooms bedecked in less-than-brilliant shades of beige. Good thing that it caters to the chatty; there are three telephones per room (including one hanging conspicuously on the bathroom wall). Suites offer stunning views of Lake Michigan and feature dining rooms. Coveted whirlpools are only available in grand suites, which, housed on the top floor, also boast fireplaces, libraries, and kitchenettes. **Aria,** an upscale restaurant within the Fairmont, attracts plenty of locals; it's a global-cuisine gem, featuring American food with Indian, Greek, Asian, and Turkish influences. ⊠ *200 N. Columbus Dr., Loop, 60601* ☎ *312/565–8000 or 800/526–2008* 📠 *312/856–1032* ⊕ *www.fairmont.com* 🛏 *692 rooms, 66 suites* ♿ *Restaurant, room service, minibars, coffeemakers, hair dryers, irons, cable TV, in-room data ports and broadband, Wi-Fi in public spaces, 2 bars, babysitting, dry cleaning, laundry service, concierge, business services, meeting rooms, parking (fee), some pets allowed, no-smoking rooms* ⊟ *AE, D, DC, MC, V.*

$$$–$$$$ 🏨 **Hard Rock Hotel.** We're not huge fans of the ubiquitous restaurant chain, but the hotel—flashy, loud, and packed with plasma TVs—has our approval. Set within the 40-story Carbide & Carbon Building, it touts modern rooms adorned with rock-and-roll paraphernalia and a brilliant dining concept called **China Grill.** Ask for a tower room, which offers striking

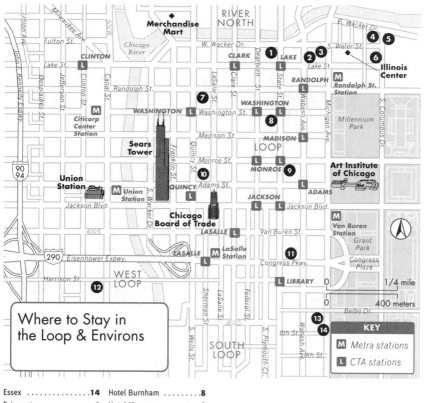

Where to Stay in
the Loop & Environs

KEY

M Metra stations

L CTA stations

views of Michigan Avenue, Millennium Park, and the Chicago River. ✉ *230 N. Michigan Ave., Loop, 60601* ☎ *312/345–1000* 🖷 *312/345–1012* ⊕ *www.hardrockhotelchicago.com* ✏ *368 rooms, 11 suites* ♨ *Restaurant, room service, coffeemakers, hair dryers, irons, minibars, cable TV, in-room VCRs, in-room data ports and broadband, Wi-Fi in public spaces, gym, bar, shop, concierge, business center, meeting rooms, parking (fee), no-smoking rooms* ⊟ *AE, D, DC, MC, V.*

★ **$$$–$$$$** 🏨 **Renaissance Chicago Hotel.** The cosmopolitan Renaissance Chicago, situated on the south bank of the Chicago River, puts a premium on a good night's sleep: there's no missing the six—yep, six—fluffy white pillows on each bed. Cushiness carries through to the lobby, where guests are treated to live music Thursday through Sunday. Stay on the hotel's slightly pricier "club levels" for a more exclusive feel and access to a private business center. ✉ *1 W. Wacker Dr., Loop, 60601* ☎ *312/372–7200 or 800/468–3571* 🖷 *312/372–0093* ⊕ *www.renaissancehotels.com* ✏ *513 rooms, 40 suites* ♨ *2 restaurants, room service, minibars, refrigerators, coffeemakers, hair dryers, irons, cable TV, in-room data ports, broadband and Wi-Fi in public spaces, indoor pool, gym, spa, bar, dry cleaning, laundry service, concierge, business services, meeting rooms, parking (fee), some pets allowed, no-smoking floors* ⊟ *AE, D, DC, MC, V.*

> ## WORD OF MOUTH
>
> "This is a great hotel at a great price in a great location. It's an easy walk to shopping, but its location on the river is quieter and the river view rooms are charming. Service is always top-notch and the rooms are in good repair and nicely appointed." —PJ

$$$–$$$$ 🏨 **W Chicago City Center.** Bellhops in slick black pants and T-shirts, plus a welcome mat imprinted with "Well, Hello There," are early indicators that this hotel is hip. The couch-filled lobby (nicknamed the Living Room) is seemingly always dark (during our visit, candles were flickering at noon), and kaleidoscopic-looking film projections complement ambient music. Rooms cater to the business traveler, with desks, WebTV, and cordless phones. **Whiskey Blue,** the hotel bar, is frequented by celebs passing through town. ✉ *172 W. Adams St., Loop, 60603* ☎ *312/332–1200 or 800/621–2360* 🖷 *312/917–5771* ⊕ *www.starwood.com* ✏ *365 rooms, 6 suites* ♨ *Restaurant, bar, room service, in-room safes, hair dryers, irons, minibars, cable TV, WebTV, in-room data ports and broadband, Wi-Fi in public spaces, gym, spa, dry cleaning, laundry service, concierge, business services, meeting rooms, parking (fee), some pets allowed, no-smoking floors* ⊟ *AE, D, DC, MC, V.*

$$–$$$$ 🏨 **Hotel Burnham.** Making creative use of a city landmark, this hotel is **Fodor'sChoice** housed in the famed 13-story Reliance Building, which D. H. Burnham ★ & Company built in 1895. The refurbished interior retains such original details as Carrara marble wainscoting and ceilings, terrazzo floors, and mahogany trim. Guest rooms, which were once the building's offices, are compact. But we'll overlook the lack of wiggle room thanks to perks like the "pillow library," which offers anything from firm to hypo-allergenic pillows. On the ground floor, the intimate **Atwood Café**

has a stylish mahogany bar and serves contemporary American fare, including its popular potpies. ☒ *1 W. Washington St., Loop, 60602* ☎ *312/782–1111 or 877/294–9712* 🖶 *312/782–0899* ⊕ *www.burnhamhotel.com* ☜ *103 rooms, 19 suites* ⚐ *Restaurant, room service, in-room fax, minibars, coffeemakers, hair dryers, irons, cable TV, in-room data ports, Wi-Fi in public spaces, gym, bar, dry cleaning, concierge, business services, parking (fee), some pets allowed, no-smoking floor* ▱ *AE, D, DC, MC, V.*

$$$ ▦ **Hotel Allegro Chicago.** The Cadillac Palace Theater is an appropriate neighbor for this music-themed hotel: witness the clefs on the shower curtains, a music room off the lobby, and the *High Society*–inspired watercolor mural by the lobby stairs at the entrance. While the standard rooms—lusciously decorated with chocolate browns and grapefruit pinks—are charming, they're outshined by premium rooms, which have whirlpool tubs, complimentary bottles of Mr. Bubble, and zebra-print robes. Suites have themes; the surprisingly un-kitschy

> ### WORD OF MOUTH
>
> "We have always enjoyed being right downtown near shopping, museums, and theatres. Our newest hotel of choice is the Allegro, which is a wonderful, funky, young-energetic-staff kind of place. Have fun!"   –maaria

Lion King suite, for example, emits an African wilderness vibe, with wicker furniture and netting hanging over the bed. ☒ *171 W. Randolph St., Loop, 60601* ☎ *312/236–0123 or 800/643–1500* 🖶 *312/236–3440* ⊕ *www.allegrochicago.com* ☜ *451 rooms, 32 suites* ⚐ *2 restaurants, room service, minibars, coffeemakers, hair dryers, irons, cable TV with movies, in-room data ports and Wi-Fi, health club, hair salon, bar, shop, concierge, business services, meeting rooms, parking (fee), some pets allowed, no-smoking rooms* ▱ *AE, D, DC, MC, V.*

★ $$–$$$ ▦ **Hotel Monaco.** A registration desk, fashioned after a classic steamer trunk, and meeting rooms named for international destinations such as Tokyo and Paris inspire wanderlust here. Besides the bellhops dressed in safari gear, we love each room's bay windows (the Monaco is the only hotel in the city with 'em) and the pet-goldfish-in-a-bowl, provided on request. It's clear this hotel has humor: look to the honor bars stocked with wax lips, Etch-A-Sketches, and hand buzzers. ☒ *225 N. Wabash Ave., Loop, 60601* ☎ *312/960–8500 or 800/397–7661* 🖶 *312/960–1883* ⊕ *www.monaco-chicago.com* ☜ *170 rooms, 22 suites* ⚐ *Restaurant, 24-hour room service, in-room safes, minibars, coffeemakers, hair dryers, irons, cable TV, in-room data ports and Wi-Fi, gym, bar, dry cleaning, laundry service, concierge, business services, meeting rooms, parking (fee), some pets allowed, no-smoking floors* ▱ *AE, D, DC, MC, V.*

$$–$$$ ▦ **Swissôtel.** The Swissôtel's triangular Harry Weese design allows for panoramic vistas of the city, lake, or river. The comfortable, contemporary rooms have a condo feel, with two-line phones and marble bathrooms. A 42nd-floor fitness center, pool, and spa manage to draw even the most exercise-reticent, thanks to the bird's-eye views. ☒ *323 E. Wacker*

HISTORIC HOTELS

Palmer House Hilton (*17 E. Monroe St., Loop, 312/726-7500*) opened on September 26, 1871, and, 13 days later, was obliterated by the Great Chicago Fire. The current hotel was built in 1873 and is where the brownie was invented. Check out the amazing lobby.

Hotel Burnham (*1 W. Washington St., Loop, 312/782-1111*), designed by Daniel Burnham, Charles Atwood, and John Root in 1894, preserves the building's history with reconstructed mosaic-tile floors and ornamental metal elevator grills.

Drake Hotel (*140 E. Walton Pl., Near North, 312/787-2200*), around since 1920, is known for its rich velvet furnishings and afternoon tea service.

Hotel Inter-Continental Chicago (*505 N. Michigan Ave., Near North, 312/944-4100*), built in 1929 as a private men's club, is where "Tarzan" TV star Johnny Weissmuller took a dip in the Olympic-size swimming pool, an attraction to this day.

Dr., Loop, 60601 ☎ *312/565-0565 or 888/737-9477* 🖷 *312/565-0540* ⊕ *www.swissotel.com* ⬦ *596 rooms, 36 suites* ⬦ *2 restaurants, café, room service, some in-room faxes, minibars, coffeemakers, hair dryers, irons, cable TV, some in-room VCRs, in-room data ports, indoor pool, gym, spa, 2 bars, dry cleaning, laundry service, concierge, business services, meeting rooms, parking (fee), no-smoking floor* ▭ *AE, DC, MC, V.*

$-$$$ 🖭 **Hyatt Regency Chicago.** Ficus trees, palms, and gushing fountains fill the two-story greenhouse lobby, but it's hardly an oasis of tranquility when, after dark, the space is transformed into a mega dance club called Hard Drive. This is one of the largest hotels in the world, with illuminated signs that guide you through the labyrinth of halls. In the comfortably sized guest rooms, black-and-white photographs of Chicago landmarks give things an authentic spin. ⬦ *151 E. Wacker Dr., Loop, 60601* ☎ *312/565-1234 or 800/233-1234* 🖷 *312/239-4414* ⊕ *www.chicagohyatt.com* ⬦ *1,900 rooms, 119 suites* ⬦ *6 restaurants, room service, in-room safes, coffeemakers, hair dryers, irons, minibars, cable TV with movies, in-room broadband and Wi-Fi, gym, nightclub (Fri. and Sat. nights only), spa, shop, dry cleaning, laundry service, concierge, car rental, business services, convention center, meeting rooms, parking (fee), no-smoking rooms,* ▭ *AE, D, DC, MC, V.*

South Loop & West Loop

Rapid gentrification, most apparent in the new restaurants popping up along South Michigan Avenue, has made this area increasingly popular. A hotel boom has not occurred here yet, so lodging choices are limited to a few old and reliable standards. Many hotels offer package deals with the nearby Museum Campus.

A Beautiful Stay in the Neighborhood

CHICAGO IS, FAMOUSLY, a city of neighborhoods. Chicagoans like to define themselves by where they hang their hat, with attendant pride, snobbery, or aspirations to street cred (of all kinds). For visitors, setting up a temporary base in one of the neighborhoods offers many advantages. This is especially true for leisure travelers. Without an expense account to ease downtown's hotel bills and menu shock, staying right downtown can get very costly very quickly.

When choosing accommodations, it pays to look beyond the Loop and the Magnificent Mile.

A walk up Clark Street or Lincoln Avenue in Lincoln Park opens up miles of reasonably priced dining possibilities. Along one short stretch of the former you'll pass an excellent fusion restaurant, a take-out crepes place, a grocery store, and a couple of diners where the waitress might call you "hon." Remember that the next time you're called something else in the Loop.

There's also better and cheaper parking. Downtown you'll usually pay at least $30 a day. Rates at garages in outlying neighborhoods run less. There's even a chance, albeit rather remote, of finding street parking. Some days that's like saying there's a chance of a Republican mayor, but it happens.

The best reason to stay in a neighborhood is the chance to immerse yourself in the rhythms of the city. You get a chance to live as most Chicagoans live. In the neighborhoods you'll see the sky. You'll have countless independently owned shops and restaurants to browse.

If you'd like to be somewhat near downtown, the happening Lincoln Park and Lake View neighborhoods offer a handful of hotels. As a bonus, accommodations are relatively near the lakefront. Most also have relatively easy access to public transportation or routes well traveled by cabs. A determined walker can even get from Lincoln Park to the Magnificent Mile in a half hour.

Getting to downtown sights from farther afield may sound like too much trouble. But keep in mind thousands upon thousands of Chicagoans make the trip every day. And, like them, you'll come home to something vital and intriguing at night. Much of the Loop, on the other hand, turns into a ghost town after rush hour. In places like Lake View, the starting gun goes off at 7 PM.

The neighborhood experience isn't for everyone. Those determined to "see it all" may find the journey in from such outposts takes too much time. And small hotels and B&Bs cannot offer the same pampering and facilities typical at the luxury digs downtown.

It's a search for small moments, for random encounters, for something indefinable—the vibe, you might say—that most appeals to visitors who stay in outer neighborhoods. Each district's rhythm is different. And it's easier to hear the city's songs away from the bustle and tall buildings.

–by Kevin Cunningham

8

$$–$$$ 🏨 **Holiday Inn & Suites Downtown Chicago.** Thanks to its proximity to the financial district, this hotel welcomes hoards of business travelers. But leisure seekers have an added incentive to visit in the summer months: the rooftop pool. Take advantage of the Buddy Guy's Legends package, which scores you a room, hot breakfast, parking, and passes to the popular blues club. The on-site **Aurelio's,** part of a popular pizza chain, serves breakfast, lunch, and dinner. ✉ *506 W. Harrison St., West Loop, 60607* ☎ *312/957–9100* 🖶 *312/583–4463* ⊕ *www.hidowntown. com* ⇨ *145 rooms, 27 suites* ♨ *Restaurant, room service, some microwaves, some refrigerators, cable TV with video games, in-room broadband and Wi-Fi, pool, gym, bar, video game room, dry cleaning, laundry facilities, business center, meeting rooms, parking (fee), no-smoking floors* ⊟ *AE, D, DC, MC, V.*

$–$$$ 🏨 **Hilton Chicago.** On a busy day the lobby of this Hilton might be mistaken for a terminal at O'Hare Airport; it's a bustling convention hotel, but one that retains its distinguished 1920s heritage in a Renaissance-inspired entrance hall and gold-and-gilt Grand Ballroom. We're fans of its gym, which, at 28,000 square feet, includes an indoor track and swimming pool. Tip for families: ask for a room with two double beds and two baths (if you nab one with a view of Lake Michigan and the Museum Campus, all the better). ✉ *720 S. Michigan Ave., South Loop, 60605* ☎ *312/922–4400 or 800/445–8667* 🖶 *312/922–5240* ⊕ *www. hiltonchicagosales.com* ⇨ *1,477 rooms, 67 suites* ♨ *3 restaurants, bar, room service, minibars, coffeemakers, hair dryers, irons, cable TV with movies and video games, in-room broadband and Wi-Fi, indoor pool, gym, hair salon, spa, shop, pub, dry cleaning, laundry service, concierge, business center, meeting rooms, parking (fee), some pets allowed, no-smoking floors* ⊟ *AE, D, DC, MC, V.*

¢–$$ 🏨 **Essex.** A budget-friendly alternative to the area's bigger properties, Essex doesn't rank among the most glamorous places to stay. But it serves its function: convenience to the Museum Campus and Grant Park. A number of the basic rooms have nice views of Grant Park, and facilities include a rooftop pool. Prices edge a bit higher on weekends the Bears are in town. ✉ *800 S. Michigan Ave., South Loop, 60605* ☎ *312/939–2800 or 800/621–6909* 🖶 *312/922–6153* ⊕ *www.essexinn.com* ⇨ *231 rooms, 23 suites* ♨ *Restaurant, room service, cable TV with movies, coffeemakers, hair dryers, irons, in-room data ports and Wi-Fi, some in-room refrigerators, some kitchenettes, indoor pool, gym, dry cleaning, laundry facilities, business center, meeting rooms, parking (fee), no-smoking rooms* ⊟ *AE, D, MC, V.*

Near North

With a cluster of accommodations around North Michigan Avenue ("The Mag Mile"), this area is where new hotels are springing up—or reinventing themselves, thanks to multimillion-dollar renovations. Prices hover at the high end, but there are a few deals to be found if you're willing to forego a pool or concierge service. Consider the wealth of shopping in easy reach part of the bargain.

$$$$ 🏨 **Drake Hotel.** Built in 1920, the grande dame of Chicago hotels presides over the northernmost end of Michigan Avenue. The lobby, inspired

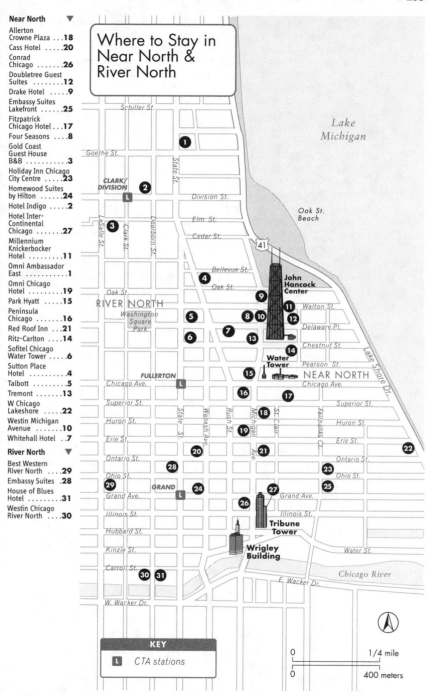

Where to Stay in Near North & River North

Lake
Michigan

Schiller St.

Goethe St.

**CLARK/
DIVISION**

Division St.

Elm St.

Cedar St.

Oak St.
Beach

41

Bellevue St.

Oak St.

**John
Hancock
Center**

Walton St.

Delaware Pl.

Chestnut St.

**Water
Tower**

Pearson St.

NEAR NORTH

FULLERTON

Chicago Ave.

Chicago Ave.

Superior St.

Superior St.

Huron St.

Huron St.

Erie St.

Erie St.

Ontario St.

Ontario St.

Ohio St.

Ohio St.

GRAND

Grand Ave.

Grand Ave.

Illinois St.

Illinois St.

**Tribune
Tower**

Hubbard St.

Kinzie St.

**Wrigley
Building**

Water St.

Carroll St.

Chicago River

E. Wacker Dr.

W. Wacker Dr.

Oak St.

RIVER NORTH

Washington
Square
Park

LaSalle St.

Clark St.

Dearborn St.

State St.

Wabash Ave.

State St.

Rush St.

Michigan
Ave.

St. Clair

Fairbanks Ct.

Lake Shore Dr.

KEY

🄻 CTA stations

0   1/4 mile
0   400 meters

by an Italian Renaissance palace, is all deep-red walls and glimmering crystal. The sounds of a fountain and harpist beckon at Palm Court, a traditional setting for afternoon tea. There's live jazz in the **Coq d'Or** most nights and the **Cape Cod Room** serves to-die-for crab cakes. The downsides? No swimming pool (a bummer for the price you're paying) and some rooms are tiny. ✉ *140 E. Walton Pl., Near North, 60611* ☎ *312/787–2200 or 800/553–7253* 🖷 *312/787–1431* ⊕ *www. thedrakehotel.com* ⇝ *537 rooms, 55 suites* 🖒 *4 restaurants, room service, in-room safes, some minibars, hair dryers, irons, cable TV, in-room data ports and broadband, Wi-Fi in public spaces, gym, bar, shops, dry cleaning, laundry service, concierge, business services, meeting rooms, parking (fee), no-smoking floors* ⊟ *AE, D, DC, MC, V.*

$$$$
Fodor'sChoice
★

🖸 **Peninsula Chicago.** This property—one of only three Peninsula hotels in the United States—has cornered the market on cool electronics. Look for high-tech bells and whistles like the "beside panel," featuring buttons to control just about anything in the room, including the flat-screen TV, temperature, and radio. Bathrooms are made to linger in, with hands-free telephones and TVs positioned above huge soaking tubs. Peninsula "pages" (personal valets) can be seen scurrying about the lobby or running errands for guests across town. ◼ TIP➔ On weekend nights, the lobby offers soft jazz and "Chocolate at the Pen," an elaborate buffet of candies, cookies, and—no kidding–chocolate soup. ✉ *108 E. Superior St., Near North, 60611* ☎ *312/337–2888 or 866/288–8889* 🖷 *312/751–2888* ⊕ *www.chicago. peninsula.com* ⇝ *291 rooms, 48 suites* 🖒 *4 restaurants, bar, room service, in-room fax, in-room safes, minibars, cable TV with movies and video games, DVDs, in-room Wi-Fi and broadband, hair dryers, irons, indoor pool, health club, massage, spa, dry cleaning, laundry service, concierge, business services, shop, meeting rooms, parking (fee), no-smoking rooms, pets allowed* ⊟ *AE, D, DC, MC, V.*

★ **$$$$**

🖸 **Ritz-Carlton.** Perched over Water Tower Place, Michigan Avenue's best-known shopping mall, the Ritz-Carlton specializes in showering guests with attention. Amenities aren't for wont: rooms are spacious, with walk-in closets and separate dressing areas, plus little luxuries like Anichini bed throws. The two-story, flower-filled greenhouse lobby serves afternoon tea, and the **Dining Room**'s chef, Kevin Hickey, has earned a top-notch reputation. ✉ *160 E. Pearson St., Near North, 60611* ☎ *312/266–1000, 800/621–6906 outside Illinois* 🖷 *312/266–1194* ⊕ *www.fourseasons. com* ⇝ *344 rooms, 91 suites* 🖒 *3 restaurants, 24-hour room service, in-room safes, hair dryers, irons, minibars, cable TV with movies and video games, WebTV, in-room data ports, Wi-Fi and broadband in public spaces, indoor pool, gym, health club, spa, bar, shop, dry cleaning, laundry service, concierge, business services, meeting rooms, parking (fee), some pets allowed, no-smoking floors* ⊟ *AE, D, DC, MC, V.*

$$$$

🖸 **Sutton Place Hotel.** Talk about art in unexpected places: the largest single collection of original Robert Mapplethorpe floral photographs grace the walls in rooms and common spaces at this hotel. Rooms—decorated in calming sage and periwinkle tones—have sound-resistant walls, down duvets, and three phones. Splurge for a loft suite, with terraces overlooking bustling Rush Street. Rande Gerber (Cindy Crawford's husband) owns the **Whiskey Bar and Grill,** serving seasonal selections for breakfast, lunch, and dinner. ✉ *21 E. Bellevue Pl., Near North, 60611* ☎ *312/266–2100 or 800/606–8188* 🖷 *312/266–2141* ⊕ *www.suttonplace.com* ⬠ *206 rooms, 40 suites* ⎔ *Restaurant, outdoor café, 24-hour room service, some in-room safes, hair dryers, irons, minibars, cable TV, in-room data ports and Wi-Fi, gym, bar, dry cleaning, laundry service, concierge, Internet café, business services, meeting rooms, parking (fee), some pets allowed (fee), no-smoking floors* ⊟ *AE, D, DC, MC, V.*

\$\$\$–\$\$\$\$ 🏨 **Conrad Chicago.** Formerly Le Meridien hotel, this hotel's art-deco-inspired lobby has a residential feel, with clean-lined furniture and a large mural. Rooms—featuring European duvets, oversize pillows, plush bathrobes, and slippers—aim to pamper. Don't leave without checking out the building's limestone facade, cut from the same quarries as the Empire State Building and Tribune Tower, and depicting figures from ancient mythology and the zodiac. ✉ *521 N. Rush St., Near North, 60611* ☎*312/645–1500* 🖷*312/645–1550* ⊕*www.conradhotels.com* ⬠*278 rooms, 33 suites* ⎔*2 restaurants, bar, room service, in-room safes, minibars, hair dryers, irons, cable TV, in-room data ports and broadband, Wi-Fi in public spaces, gym, shop, dry cleaning, laundry service, concierge, business services, business center, meeting rooms, some suites with balconies, parking (fee), some pets allowed, no-smoking rooms* ⊟*AE, D, DC, MC, V.*

\$\$\$–\$\$\$\$
Fodor's Choice
★
🏨 **Four Seasons.** At the ultrarefined Four Seasons, guest rooms begin on the 30th floor (the hotel sits atop the tony 900 North Michigan Shops), so there's a distinct feeling of seclusion—and great views, to boot. The rooms look English manor–like, with Italian marble, handcrafted woodwork, and botanical prints. To get the most out of the experience, buy a package, such as one called "Girls Just Wanna Have Fun," in which a handsome gent who makes custom martinis shows up at your room door. ✉ *120 E. Delaware Pl., Near North, 60611* ☎ *312/280–8800 or 800/332–3442* 🖷 *312/280–1748* ⊕ *www.fourseasons.com* ⬠ *174 rooms, 169 suites* ⎔ *3 restaurants, room service, in-room safes, hair dryers, irons, minibars, cable TV with movies, in-room data ports and broadband, Wi-Fi in public spaces, pool, gym, spa, bar, shop, dry cleaning, laundry service, concierge, business center, business services, meeting rooms, parking (fee), some pets allowed, no-smoking floors* ⊟ *AE, D, DC, MC, V.*

\$\$\$–\$\$\$\$
Fodor's Choice
★
🏨 **Park Hyatt.** Thanks to unique partnerships with the Art Institute, this hotel is full of blue-chip art—and even boasts its own gallery. (Check out the 1968 masterpiece *Piazza del Duomo* by German painter Ger-

---

COCKTAIL FEVER

Book the "Girls Just Want to Have Fun" package at **Four Seasons** (*120 E. Delaware Pl., Near North, 312/280–8800*), and the "Martini Man" will visit your room to shake up one of four choice martinis.

Knickerbocker (*163 E. Walton St., Near North, 312/751–8100*) has 50 martini variations, each one dreamed up at a different Knickerbocker property from around the world.

Hotel Monaco (*225 N. Wabash Ave., Loop, 312/960–8500*) hosts a complimentary manager's wine reception every evening–a little perk before you go out on the town.

8

hard Richter, which hangs prominently in the lobby.) Rooms have mellow bamboo colors and, with a nod to the minimalist and mod, come with Eames chairs. Cherrywood doors between bedrooms and bathrooms glide open, making rooms appear more spacious. ⊠ *800 N. Michigan Ave., Near North, 60611* ☎ *312/335–1234 or 800/778–7477* 🖷 *312/239–4000* ⊕ *www.parkhyatt.com* 🛏 *193 rooms, 9 suites* ♿ *Restaurant, 24-hour room service, in-room safes, minibars, hair dryers, irons, refrigerators, cable TV with movies and video games, DVDs, in-room broadband and Wi-Fi, indoor pool, gym, hair salon, spa, bar, dry cleaning, laundry service, concierge, business services, meeting rooms, parking (fee), no-smoking rooms, no-smoking floor* ▭ *AE, D, DC, MC, V.*

$$$–$$$$
Fodor's Choice
★
▫ **Sofitel Chicago Water Tower.** A wonder of modern architecture, this French-owned gem is a prism-shaped structure that juts over the street. Design sensibility shines in guest rooms, too, with beechwood furnishings, Barcelona chairs, and marble bathrooms bedecked with bamboo (think feng shui). The sophisticated **Café des Architectes** is notable for its lunchtime soups, while **Le Bar** is a homey den of sorts, replete with books about architecture and a rack of international newspapers. The hotel's on-site boutique, **Petit Bijou,** is a far cry from the typical souvenir shop, carrying handcrafted jewelry, paper goods, and more. ⊠ *20 E. Chestnut St., Near North, 60611* ☎ *312/324–4000 or 800/763–4835* 🖷 *312/324–4026* ⊕ *www.sofitel.com* 🛏 *383 rooms, 32 suites* ♿ *Restaurant, 2 bars, shop, 24-hour room service, in-room safes, hair dryers, irons, minibars, cable TV with movies and video games, WebTV, in-room data ports, broadband and Wi-Fi, gym, massage, bar, dry cleaning, laundry service, concierge, business services, meeting rooms, parking (fee), some pets allowed, no-smoking floors* ▭ *AE, D, DC, MC, V.*

★ **$$$–$$$$**
▫ **Talbott.** The Talbott has a large European following, thanks to its intimacy and multilingual staff. Rooms are moderately sized and boast granite-and-marble bathrooms and Victorian furnishings. Coffee, tea, and chocolate turtle brownies are served fireside in the lobby on winter nights—a lovely touch. Another bonus? Guests get free admission to the nearby Multiplex gym. ⊠ *20 E. Delaware Pl., Near North, 60611* ☎ *312/944–4970 or 800/825–2688* 🖷 *312/944–7241* ⊕ *www.talbotthotel.com* 🛏 *120 rooms, 29 suites* ♿ *Restaurant, 24-hour room service, in-room safes, hair dryers, irons, minibars, cable TV, in-room data ports and Wi-Fi, bar, dry cleaning, laundry service, concierge, business services, meeting rooms, parking (fee), some pets allowed, no-smoking floors* ▭ *AE, D, DC, MC, V.*

> **WORD OF MOUTH**
>
> "The location is great–the heart of the city. The entrance to the hotel was warm and inviting with two fireplaces blazing."   —Debra

$$$–$$$$
▫ **Whitehall Hotel.** There's a woodland-lodge feel in this hotel's lobby, where oil paintings of hunting dogs and horses hang in gilt frames. The old-world-style rooms, many with four-poster beds, include modern luxuries such as Anichini bedding, marble bathrooms, and broadband. **Fornetto Mei** is a new Pan-Italian dining concept that deserves more attention than it gets. ⊠ *105 E. Delaware*

Pl., Near North, 60611 ☏ *312/944–6300 or 800/948–4255* 🖷 *312/944–8552* 📠 *213 rooms, 8 suites* ⚲ *Restaurant, bar, room service, in-room safes, hair dryers, irons, some minibars, cable TV with video games, in-room data ports and broadband, Wi-Fi in public spaces, gym, dry cleaning, laundry service, concierge, business services, meeting rooms, parking (fee), no-smoking floor* 🚭 *AE, D, DC, MC, V.*

$$–$$$$ 🏨 **Allerton Crowne Plaza.** Named a national historic landmark in 1998, this limestone building was a residential "club hotel" for men when it opened in 1924. A welcome 1999 renovation restored the limestone facade and overhauled the interior. The small rooms have unique layouts with classic wood furnishings, dramatic floral bedspreads, and marble baths. The bar adjoining the second-floor restaurant **Taps on Two**—Parisian in setting with its tiny tables and piped-in jazz music—will make you want to linger over cappuccino on blustery days. ✉ *701 N. Michigan Ave., Near North, 60611* ☏ *312/440–1500 or 800/227–6963* 🖷 *312/440–1819* ⊕ *www.allertonchi.crowneplaza.com* 📠 *383 rooms, 60 suites* ⚲ *Restaurant, room service, in-room safes, hair dryers, irons, minibars, refrigerators, cable TV, in-room data ports and broadband, gym, bar, dry cleaning, laundry facilities, laundry service, concierge, business services, meeting rooms, parking (fee), no-smoking floors* 🚭 *AE, D, DC, MC, V.*

★ **$$–$$$$** 🏨 **Doubletree Guest Suites.** Two simple reasons to love this place: the homemade chocolate chip cookies at check-in and the always-fresh flowers in the lobby. The striking postmodern lobby owes its character to Prairie School architecture. Business traffic rules the roost during the week, especially in winter, but the weekends are flooded with families who appreciate the two-minute walk to Michigan Avenue entertainment. ✉ *198 E. Delaware Pl., Near North, 60611* ☏ *312/664–1100 or 800/222–8733* 🖷 *312/664–8627* ⊕ *www.doubletreehotels.com* 📠 *345 suites* ⚲ *2 restaurants, room service, minibars, hair dryers, irons, refrigerators, cable TV, in-room data ports and broadband, indoor pool, gym, hair salon, spa, 2 bars, dry cleaning, laundry service, concierge, business services, meeting rooms, parking (fee), no-smoking floors* 🚭 *AE, D, DC, MC, V.*

★ **$$–$$$$** 🏨 **W Chicago Lakeshore.** Once a dreary Days Inn, a complete renovation transformed this space into a sleek, high-energy hotel—and the only in Chicago directly overlooking Lake Michigan. The lobby is part lounge, part club scene, with velvety couches and DJs on weekends. The hotel's "whatever, whenever" desk—its version of a concierge service—is on call 24 hours a day. ✉ *644 N. Lake Shore Dr., Near North, 60611* ☏ *312/943–9200 or 888/627–9034* 🖷 *312/255–4411* ⊕ *www.whotels.com* 📠 *525 rooms, 27 suites* ⚲ *Restaurant, room service, in-room safes, hair dryers, irons, minibars, cable TV with movies and video games, DVDs, in-room data ports and broadband, Wi-Fi in public spaces, indoor pool, gym, spa, bar, dry cleaning, laundry service, concierge, business services, meeting rooms, airport shuttle, parking (fee), some pets allowed (fee), no-smoking floors* 🚭 *AE, D, DC, MC, V.*

★ **$$$** 🏨 **Hotel Inter-Continental Chicago.** The Shriner greeting "Es Salamu Aleikum" ("Peace Be To God") that's etched on foyer columns and the marble lions throughout remind us of the building's past as the Medi-

8

nah Health Club, a private men's club. Lodging is found in two adjoining buildings. We love the contemporary air of the main building's guest rooms, featuring mahogany furniture and rich red-and-gold fabrics. The historic tower rooms, however, are more matronly, with floral bedspreads and russet colors. The pinnacle of the whole place is the junior Olympic swimming pool, which "Tarzan" TV show star Johnny Weissmuller took a dip in. ✉ *505 N. Michigan Ave., Near North, 60611* 🕾 *312/944–4100 or 800/628–2112* 🖷 *312/944–1320* ⊕ *www. chicago.intercontinental.com* ↩ *735 rooms, 72 suites* ♿ *3 restaurants, room service, in-room safes, coffeemakers, hair dryers, irons, minibars, cable TV with movies and games, in-room data ports, broadband and Wi-Fi in public spaces, indoor pool, fitness center, spa, bar, shop, dry cleaning, laundry service, concierge, business services, Internet café, convention center, parking (fee), some pets allowed, no-smoking floors* ☰ *AE, D, DC, MC, V.*

$$$ 🖫 **Omni Ambassador East.** One of the few hotels tucked in the residential Gold Coast neighborhood, this small 1920s property is a 10- to 15-minute cab ride from the Loop. The secluded setting makes it popular with celebs and literary figures, and the world-famous **Pump Room** still attracts a loyal following (Humphrey Bogart and Lauren Bacall celebrated their wedding in Booth One). Rooms have a certain amount of glitz, with jewel tones and cherrywood furniture. Bookworms, take heed: the "author" suite has held book signings by the likes of John Grisham and Maya Angelou. ✉ *1301 N. State Pkwy., Near North, 60610* 🕾 *312/ 787–7200 or 800/843–6664* 🖷 *312/787–4760* ⊕ *www.omnihotels. com* ↩ *239 rooms, 46 suites* ♿ *Restaurant, room service, minibars, hair dryers, irons, some microwaves, cable TV, in-room data ports and broadband, gym, hair salon, bar, dry cleaning, laundry service, concierge, business services, parking (fee), some pets allowed (fee), no-smoking floors* ☰ *AE, D, DC, MC, V.*

$$$ 🖫 **Westin Michigan Avenue.** The lobby of the Westin reminds us of an airport hangar—long, narrow, and full of folks tapping on laptops. Location-wise, the hotel scores big, as major malls and flagship shops are within steps of the hotel's front door. Rooms are furnished with specially designed Simmons Heavenly Beds with quilted mattresses—which guests have raved about and even purchased—as well as foam, feather, and rolled pillows. The lobby restaurant, the **Grill on the Alley,** is a steakhouse with a clubby atmosphere. ✉ *909 N. Michigan Ave., Near North, 60611* 🕾 *312/943–7200 or 800/937–8461* 🖷 *312/943–9347* ⊕ *www. westin.com/michiganave* ↩ *728 rooms, 23 suites* ♿ *Restaurant, room service, minibars, cable TV, in-room data ports and broadband, Wi-Fi in public spaces, gym, spa, bar, dry cleaning, laundry service, concierge, business services, meeting rooms, parking (fee), some pets allowed, no-smoking floor* ☰ *AE, D, DC, MC, V.*

$$–$$$ 🖫 **Embassy Suites Lakefront.** Every guest in this all-suites hotel has views of either Lake Michigan or the Chicago skyscrapers. And they also have room to roam, thanks to the spacious layout (rooms have separate bedrooms and living rooms). The sleek glass atrium bustles in the morning for complimentary breakfast buffet and in the evening for complimentary happy hour. A bonus for families on vacation is the location: within

WORD OF MOUTH: TEA TIME

"We had tea at the Drake and I highly recommend it. The harpist provided relaxing background music, the tea & goodies were tasty and ample, and we were not rushed at all. (And the ladies room is very nice!)"

—Margie

"My family loves tea time. We have tried almost all of the places in Chicago. The Ritz-Carlton and Peninsula have the best selection

for tea sandwiches and pastries, although the Ritz is nicer about refills. Sometimes, in the winter, the Ritz has chocolate fondue—you should call and check. The Four Seasons has the best atmosphere, especially if you get a spot by the fireplace. You must make a reservation, no matter where you choose. All of these places fill up quickly."

—Rine1967

walking distance of Navy Pier and North Michigan Avenue. ☒ *511 N. Columbus Dr., Near North, 60611* ☏ *312/836–5900 or 800/362–2779* 🖷 *312/836–5901* ⊕ *www.chicagoembassy.com* ↪ *455 suites* ⚓ *Restaurant, room service, kitchenettes, minibars, coffeemakers, hair dryers, irons, microwaves, refrigerators, cable TV with movies, in-room data ports and broadband, indoor pool, gym, bar, dry cleaning, laundry facilities, concierge, business services, meeting rooms, airport shuttle, parking (fee), no-smoking rooms* ⊟ *AE, D, DC, MC, V* ⏏ *BP.*

\$\$–\$\$\$ 🖷 **Fitzpatrick Chicago Hotel.** Irish warmth prevails at this all-suites hotel, from the brogue of the front-desk staff to the Irish stew served at the lower-level pub. Sunny suites come with canopy beds and a rooftop pool keeps children entertained in summer. ☒ *166 E. Superior St., Near North, 60611* ☏ *312/787–6000 or 800/367–7701* 🖷 *312/787–6133* ⊕ *www.fitzpatrickhotels.com* ↪ *140 suites* ⚓ *Restaurant, room service, refrigerators, hair dryers, irons, cable TV, in-room data ports and broadband, outdoor pool, gym, bar, dry cleaning, concierge, business services, meeting rooms, parking (fee), no-smoking floor* ⊟ *AE, D, DC, MC, V.*

☼ **\$\$–\$\$\$** 🖷 **Holiday Inn Chicago City Centre.** In winter, weekend rates can drop to \$150 or less at this family-friendly chain. That's a real bargain, considering the hotel is just two blocks east of North Michigan Avenue. Guests get complimentary access to an on-site health club with tennis courts and an indoor pool. Unless you have business at the Merchandise Mart, this location is preferable to the Holiday Inn Mart Plaza. ☒ *300 E. Ohio St., Near North, 60611* ☏ *312/787–6100 or 800/465–4329* 🖷 *312/787– 6259* ⊕ *www.chicc.com* ↪ *496 rooms, 4 suites* ⚓ *Restaurant, café, room service, coffeemakers, hair dryers, irons, cable TV, in-room data ports and broadband, Wi-Fi in public spaces, 3 tennis courts, 2 pools (1 indoor), gym, bar, dry cleaning, laundry facilities, laundry service, concierge, business services, meeting rooms, parking (fee), no-smoking floor* ⊟ *AE, D, DC, MC, V.*

★ **\$\$–\$\$\$** 🖷 **Hotel Indigo.** Formerly the Claridge Hotel, this renovated space bucks norms by featuring hardwood floors in all guest rooms. The whole place has a beachy, summer-in-Nantucket vibe, with a cool blue color scheme, shell motifs on the lobby floor, and guest-room walls covered with enlarged photos of sea glass. The front-of-the-house bar, replete with chairs shaped like pineapples, can whip up daiquiris on demand. ⊠ *1244 N. Dearborn Pkwy., Near North, 60610* 🕾 *312/787–4980 or 866/246–3446* 🖷 *312/787–4069* ⊕ *www.hotelindigo.com* ⤴ *163 rooms, 2 suites* ⟁ *Restaurant, room service, cable TV with movies and video games, WebTV, in-room broadband and Wi-Fi, coffeemakers, hair dryers, irons, gym, spa, bar, dry cleaning, laundry service, business services, meeting rooms, parking (fee), no-smoking floor* ⊟ *AE, D, DC, MC, V* ⏐◎⏐ *CP.*

$$–$$$ 🖳 **Millennium Knickerbocker Hotel.** This 1927 hotel has had a number of identities in its time—including a 1970s stint as the Playboy Hotel & Towers under owner Hugh Hefner. Chinoiserie wallpaper pattern and dark-wood armoires lend an Asian feel to guest rooms. We love the complimentary shoeshine service; hang your kicks on the door at night and they'll be spiffed up by morning. Your downtime is well spent in the lobby bar, which features 50 different kinds of martinis. ⊠ *163 E. Walton St., Near North, 60611* 🕾 *312/751–8100 or 866/866–8086* 🖷 *312/ 751–9205* ⊕ *www.millenniumhotels.com* ⤴ *279 rooms, 26 suites* ⟁ *Restaurant, room service, minibars, hair dryers, irons, cable TV with video games, in-room data ports and broadband, Wi-Fi in public spaces, gym, bar, dry cleaning, laundry service, concierge, business services, business center, meeting rooms, parking (fee), no-smoking floors* ⊟ *AE, D, DC, MC, V* ⏐◎⏐ *CP.*

$$–$$$ 🖳 **Omni Chicago Hotel.** The only all-suites hotel on Michigan Avenue has another thing going for it: every room has a plasma TV. French doors separate each suite's parlor from the bedroom, giving it a residential atmosphere. Its **Cielo** restaurant serves American bistro fare with views overlooking North Michigan Avenue. ⊠ *676 N. Michigan Ave., Near North, 60611* 🕾 *312/944–6664 or 800/843–6664* 🖷 *312/266–3015* ⊕ *www.omnihotels.com* ⤴ *347 suites* ⟁ *Restaurant, room service, in-room safes, hair dryers, coffeemakers, irons, minibars, cable TV with movies and video games, in-room broadband and Wi-Fi, indoor pool, gym, hot tub, sauna, bar, dry cleaning, laundry service, concierge, business services, meeting rooms, parking (fee), some pets allowed (fee), no-smoking floors* ⊟ *AE, D, DC, MC, V.*

$$–$$$ 🖳 **Tremont.** Just off North Michigan Avenue, this hotel's restaurant, **Mike Ditka's,** gets infinitely more attention than the rooms do (we love Ditka's "Da Pork Chop" dish). Standard guest rooms—with yellow walls and white molding—are on the small side. Need more space? Book a suite, which are equipped with kitchens. ⊠ *100 E. Chestnut St., Near North, 60611* 🕾 *312/751–1900 or 800/621–8133* 🖷 *312/751–8691* ⊕ *www.tremontchicago.com* ⤴ *118 rooms, 12 suites* ⟁ *Restaurant, in-room safes, hair dryers, irons, cable TV with movies, in-room data ports, broadband in public spaces, bar, dry cleaning, laundry service, concierge, business services, meeting rooms, parking (fee), no-smoking floor* ⊟ *AE, D, DC, MC, V.*

$–$$$ 🖳 **Homewood Suites by Hilton.** Suites here seem custom-designed for families, with sleeper sofas, separate bedrooms, and fully equipped kitchens with dishwashers. Free food isn't lacking; indulge in a complimentary breakfast buffet seven days a week, and an evening reception with drinks and a light meal Monday through Thursday. Another bonus? Work out for free at the Gorilla Sports facility in the basement. ✉ *40 E. Grand Ave., Near North, 60611* ☎ *312/644–2222 or 800/225–5466* 🖷 *312/644–7777* ⊕ *www.homewoodsuiteschicago.com* ⟿ *233 suites* ♿ *Room service, kitchens, microwaves, coffeemakers, hair dryers, irons, refrigerators, cable TV, in-room data ports and broadband, indoor pool, gym, laundry facilities, business services, meeting rooms, parking (fee), no-smoking rooms, no-smoking floors* ☰ *AE, D, DC, MC, V* ⧓ *BP.*

$–$$ 🏨 **Gold Coast Guest House B&B.** A five-minute walk to Michigan Avenue, this 1873 brick row house–turned–bed-and-breakfast has a 20-foot-tall window looking out onto a lush private garden with patio seating. Rooms contain a mix of antiques and contemporary furnishings, and all have individual air-conditioning units. Hospitality baskets with items such as shampoo, razors, and sunscreen are pluses, as are the discounted admissions offered to the Chicago's First Lady architectural boat tours in spring, summer, and fall. ✉ *113 W. Elm St., Near North, 60610* ☎ *312/337–0361* 🖷 *312/337–0362* ⊕ *www.bbchicago.com* ⟿ *4 rooms* ♿ *Cable TV, DVDs, laundry facilities, in-room broadband, business services, parking (fee); no smoking* ☰ *AE, D, MC, V* ⧓ *CP.*

★ **¢–$$** 🏨 **Red Roof Inn.** Sure, the accommodations are cookie-cutter (the chain's red-and-purple color scheme is a bit uninspired), but there's no beating the low rates for the right-off-the-Mag-Mile location. There's history here, too; the hotel was formerly the Richmont, which from 1987 to 1990 was the holder of one of the largest collections of French art outside of France. Some of the gems remain on view. ✉ *162 E. Ontario St., Near North, 60611* ☎ *312/787–3580* 🖷 *312/787–2354* ⊕ *www. redroof-chicago-downtown.com* ⟿ *195 rooms, 13 suites* ♿ *Cable TV with video games and movies, hair dryers, irons, some refrigerators, in-*

WHERE THE STARS STAYED

Hotels keep it hush-hush when they're hosting celebrity guests, but after the celebs leave—or if they're visible during their stay—the word leaks out. Here are some buzz-worthy reported celebrity sightings:

Sandra Bullock at Sofitel Chicago Water Tower (*20 E. Chestnut St., Near North, 312/324-4000*)

Jennifer Aniston at Peninsula Chicago (*108 E. Superior St., Near North, 312/337-2888*)

Matt Damon at Peninsula Chicago (*108 E. Superior St., Near North, 312/337-2888*)

Jaime Foxx at W Chicago Lakeshore (*644 N. Lake Shore Dr., Near North, 312/943-9200*)

Queen Latifah at Sutton Place Hotel (*21 E. Bellevue Pl., Near North, 312/266-2100*)

BEST VIEWS

At **Hilton Chicago** (*720 S. Michigan Ave., South Loop/Near South Side, 312/922-4400*), book an east-facing room for views of Lake Michigan and Grant Park. Presidents and celebs favor its top-floor Presidential Suite.
Park Hyatt's restaurant, NoMI (*800 N. Michigan Ave., Near North, 312/335-1234*), looks out over the brilliantly lit original Chicago Water Tower, one of the only structures to survive the Great Chicago Fire.

Fairmont (*200 N. Columbus Dr., Loop, 312/565-8000*), a pink-granite marvel of a building, has sweeping views of the lake, which can be best enjoyed from a top-floor whirlpool suite.
The outdoor terrace at **Conrad Chicago** (*521 N. Rush St., Near North, 312/645-1500*) might not have lake views, but it's a great place to watch the buzz of Michigan Avenue traffic and skim the Chicago skyline from the heart of downtown.

room data ports, dry cleaning, laundry service, parking (fee), some pets allowed, no-smoking floors ☱ AE, D, DC, MC, V.

¢–$ 🖥 **Cass Hotel.** This spot's cheap, but not so chic (built in 1927, it hasn't undergone the overhaul that many other area hotels have enjoyed). Guest rooms are small, but have modern bathrooms with vanities and soaking tubs. King and double rooms are equipped with refrigerators. The lobby coffee shop offers budget breakfast and lunch fare, and the **Sea of Happiness Lounge** has a charmingly dive-y atmosphere. ☒ *640 N. Wabash Ave., Near North, 60611* ☎ *312/787-4030 or 800/227-7850* 🖨 *312/787-8544* ⊕ *www.casshotel.com* 📞 *150 rooms* ♦ *Restaurant, coffee shop, some refrigerators, cable TV, in-room data ports, Wi-Fi in public spaces, laundry facilities, parking (fee), no-smoking rooms* ☱ *AE, D, DC, MC, V.*

River North

Besides the concentration of independently owned galleries, commerce around these parts tends to be of a national-chain nature (note the Hard Rock Cafe and Red Lobster). The same can be said of the hotels. But while boutique-lodging charm is harder to find, good prices are not; you'll find plenty of competitive rates from familiar names.

★ $$$–$$$$ 🖥 **House of Blues Hotel.** Despite the loud music that usually blares in the lobby, there's a certain degree of calm here, thanks to the gold Burmese Buddha statue at the door and the blue-glass panels behind the bar brought from an ancient East Indian meditation temple. Rooms are a dizzying variety of patterns, and feature original southern folk art. ⚠ **Request a room away from the elevators, where crowds tend to congregate.** The adjacent **House of Blues** bar-restaurant serves casual fare and hosts live musical acts in a separate concert hall. ☒ *333 N. Dearborn St., River North, 60610* ☎ *312/245-0333 or 800/235-6397* 🖨 *312/923-2444* ⊕ *www.loewshotels.com* 📞 *344 rooms, 21 suites* ♦ *2 restaurants, bowling alley, room service, minibars, hair dryers, irons, cable TV, in-*

CLOSE UP

Lodging Alternatives

APARTMENT RENTALS

Furnished rentals can save you money, especially if you're traveling with a group. Home-exchange directories sometimes list rentals as well as exchanges.

Rental apartments are available in the Loop for temporary business lodging. Try Bridgestreet Corporate Housing.

International Agents: Hideaways International (✉ 767 Islington St., Portsmouth, NH 03801 ☎ 603/430-4433 or 800/843-4433 🖷 603/430-4444 ⊕ www.hideaways.com); annual membership $145.

Local Agents: Bridgestreet Corporate Housing (✉ 10 E. Ontario St. ☎ 847/564-3000).

BED-AND-BREAKFASTS

Reservation Services: At Home Inn Chicago (✇ Box 14088, 60614 ☎ 773/394-2000 or 800/375-7084 🖷 773/394-2002 ⊕ www.athomeinnchicago.com).

HOME EXCHANGES

Exchange Clubs: HomeLink International (✇ Box 47747, Tampa, FL 33647 ☎ 813/975-9825 or 800/638-3841 🖷 813/910-8144 ⊕ www.homelink.org); $110 yearly for a listing, online access, and catalog; $70 without catalog. Intervac U.S. (✉ 30 Corte San Fernando, Tiburon, CA 94920 ☎ 800/756-4663 🖷 415/435-7440 ⊕ www.intervacus.com); $125 yearly for a listing, online access, and a catalog; $65 without catalog.

HOSTELS

No matter what your age, you can save on lodging costs by staying at hostels. In some 4,500 locations in more than 70 countries around the world, **Hostelling International (HI)**, the umbrella group for a number of national youth-hostel associations, offers single-sex, dorm-style beds and, at many hostels, rooms for couples and family accommodations. Membership in any HI national hostel association, open to travelers of all ages, allows you to stay in HI-affiliated hostels at member rates; one-year membership is about $28 for adults; hostels charge about $10-$30 per night. Members have priority if the hostel is full; they're also eligible for discounts around the world, even on rail and bus travel in some countries.

Organizations: Hostelling International-USA (✉ 8401 Colesville Rd., Suite 600, Silver Spring, MD 20910 ☎ 301/495-1240 🖷 301/495-6697 ⊕ www.hiusa.org).

Hostelling International-Canada (✉ 205 Catherine St., Suite 400, Ottawa, Ontario K2P 1C3 ☎ 613/237-7884 or 800/663-5777 🖷 613/237-7868 ⊕ www.hihostels.ca).

8

room data ports, Wi-Fi in public spaces, gym, sauna, steam room, 2 bars, concert hall, dry cleaning, laundry service, concierge, business services, meeting rooms, parking (fee), some pets allowed, no-smoking rooms ▭ *AE, D, DC, MC, V.*

$$–$$$$ 🏨 **Embassy Suites.** Fully equipped suites are arranged around an 11-story, plant-filled atrium lobby, where bubbling fountains and birds keep noise levels relatively high. Bright rooms use space efficiently, with sensible separate living rooms with a pullout sofa, four-person dining table, and extra television. A complimentary full breakfast each morning and cocktails each evening are especially appealing to business travelers. ✉ *600 N. State St., River North, 60610* 🕾 *312/943–3800 or 800/362–2779* 🖷 *312/943–7629* ⊕ *www.embassysuites.com* 🗲 *358 suites* ♿ *Restaurant, room service, kitchenettes, minibars, microwaves, refrigerators, coffeemakers, hair dryers, irons, cable TV with video games, in-room data ports and broadband, indoor pool, gym, hot tub, sauna, bar, dry cleaning, laundry facilities, laundry service, concierge, business services, meeting rooms, parking (fee), no-smoking rooms* ▭ *AE, D, DC, MC, V* ℐℴℓ *BP.*

$$–$$$ 🏨 **Westin Chicago River North.** Gym rats don't need to hoof it to the on-site fitness center, thanks to two Westin Workout Guest Rooms that come equipped with either a bicycle or a treadmill. Standard rooms—some with views of the Chicago River—have all the basics, including high-speed Internet. Nab a Deluxe Room for more square footage. ✉ *320 N. Dearborn St., River North, 60610* 🕾 *312/744–1900 or 800/937–8461* 🖷 *312/527–2650* ⊕ *www.westinchicago.com* 🗲 *407 rooms, 17 suites* ♿ *Restaurant, room service, minibars, hair dryers, irons, cable TV, in-room data ports and broadband, gym, spa, bar, dry cleaning, laundry service, concierge, business services, meeting rooms, parking (fee), some pets allowed, no-smoking rooms* ▭ *AE, D, DC, MC, V.*

$–$$ 🏨 **Best Western River North.** Partially housed in a turn-of-the-last-century freezer building, this hotel retains a loft-like air. The somewhat forgettable lobby decor is offset by large and reasonably priced guest rooms featuring black-and-white tiled bathrooms. Parking is free, a cost-saving rarity downtown. Families convene at the on-site **Pizzeria Oro** for Chicago-style deep-dish pies. ✉ *125 W. Ohio St., River North, 60610* 🕾 *312/467–0800 or 800/727–0800* 🖷 *312/467–1665* ⊕ *www.rivernorthhotel.com* 🗲 *125 rooms, 25 suites* ♿ *Restaurant, room service, in-room safes, coffeemakers, hair dryers, irons, some refrigerators, cable TV, in-room data ports and Wi-Fi, indoor pool, gym, sauna, bar, dry cleaning, laundry service, business services, free parking, no-smoking floor* ▭ *AE, D, DC, MC, V.*

Lincoln Park

Three miles of lakefront parkland draw people to this neighborhood—and most hotels here are just blocks away. Room rates are decidedly lower than those downtown, with the downside being that you'll invest more in transportation to hit top sites. Parking is easier, but never a snap; plan on using the valet.

$–$$ 🏨 **Belden-Stratford.** A magnificent 1920s facade beckons you to this primarily upscale apartment building. Most tenants have long-term leases here, but management keeps some attractively priced studios and suites for overnight stays. Hand-painted clouds grace the ceiling of the elegant lobby, which houses two popular French restaurants: **Ambria** and **Mon Ami Gabi.** The Lincoln Park Zoo is across the street. And the lakefront? A mere three blocks away. ⊠ *2300 N. Lincoln Park W, Lincoln Park, 60614* ☎ *773/281–2900 or 800/800–8301* 🖨 *773/880–2039* ⊕ *www. beldenstratford.com* ⇆ *24 rooms, 5 suites* ♿ *2 restaurants, snack bar, kitchenettes, microwaves, cable TV, in-room broadband and Wi-Fi, gym, hair salon, bar, dry cleaning, laundry facilities, laundry service, business services, parking (fee)* ▤ *AE, D, DC, MC, V.*

¢–$$ 🏨 **Days Inn Lincoln Park North.** This award-winning Days Inn is one of
Fodor'sChoice   the more luxurious in the sometimes so-so chain, featuring a lobby
★   with a pressed-tin ceiling and brass chandeliers. The updated look of its guest rooms is one of cheery mixed patterns and dark-wood furniture. All guests have free use of the nearby Bally's health club. ⊠ *644 W. Diversey Pkwy., Lincoln Park, 60614* ☎ *773/525–7010 or 888/576–3297* 🖨 *773/525–6998* ⊕ *www.lpndaysinn.com* ⇆ *129 rooms, 4 suites* ♿ *In-room safes, coffeemakers, hair dryers, irons, some microwaves, some refrigerators, cable TV, in-room data ports and Wi-Fi, dry cleaning, laundry facilities, laundry service, business services, meeting room, parking (fee), no-smoking rooms* ▤ *AE, D, DC, MC, V* ⊺⊙⊺ *CP.*

Lake View & North of the City

Seemingly light years away from the downtown buzz, Lake View hotels entice with their proximity to Wrigley Field and the summertime street festivals for which the neighborhood is known. As you venture farther north, accommodations tend to be quainter; spaces more intimate; and guests much quieter. Another bustling pocket of activity is found just beyond Chicago, in the cheery university town of Evanston.

★ $–$$$ 🏨 **Majestic Hotel.** In cool weather, a welcoming fire burns in the Majestic's library-style lobby. Pleasant touches are the freshly brewed coffee and

---

THREE HOTEL SHOPS THAT GO BEYOND SOUVENIRS

Le Petit Bijou at Sofitel Chicago Water Tower (*20 E. Chestnut St., Near North, 312/324–4000*) lives up to its name, which, in French, means "the little jewel." Find ambient-music CDs, watches, hand-crafted jewelry, home decor, and more.

W The Store (*at W Chicago City Center, 172 W. Adams St., Loop, 312/332–1200 & W Chicago Lakeshore, 644 N. Lake Shore Dr., Near North, 312/943–9200*) sells the pillows fea-

tured in guest rooms, along with a range of high-design items, like compass cuff links and ballet-style shoes.

The Shop at the Ritz-Carlton (*160 E. Pearson St., Near North, 312/266–1000*) is as classy as its namesake hotel, offering crystal, porcelain, jewelry, and plenty of other splurge-worthy items that rival those sold at the luxury boutiques of Michigan Avenue.

abundant dried-flower arrangements. Rooms are quaint with Prairie-style furnishings. The Lake View location puts you three blocks from Wrigley Field and close to the lakefront jogging paths, restaurants, nightlife, and transportation downtown. ⊠ *528 W. Brompton Ave., Lake View, 60657* ☏ *773/404–3499 or 800/727–5108* 🖷 *773/404–3495* ⊕ *www.cityinns. com* ⇋ *31 rooms, 21 suites* ♿ *Some microwaves, some refrigerators, hair dryers, irons, cable TV, in-room data ports, dry cleaning, laundry facilities, concierge, parking (fee)* ═ *AE, D, DC, MC, V* ⵌ *CP.*

$–$$ 🖼 **Best Western Hawthorne Terrace.** The hotel's front terrace becomes a place to see and be seen in the summer months, especially when street festivals roar into town. There's little room to relax in the American Colonial–style lobby, but rooms are inviting enough; deluxe rooms come with whirlpool tubs. ⚠ **Proximity to Wrigley Field is a plus.** ⊠ *3434 N. Broadway, Lake View, 60657* ☏ *773/244–3434 or 888/675–2378* 🖷 *773/244–3435* ⊕ *www.hawthorneterrace.com* ⇋ *46 rooms, 13 suites* ♿ *Some microwaves, some refrigerators, hair dryers, irons, cable TV, in-room data ports and Wi-Fi, gym, dry cleaning, laundry facilities, business services, parking (fee)* ═ *AE, D, DC, MC, V* ⵌ *CP.*

$–$$ 🖼 **The Willows.** The lobby of this 1920s boutique hotel, designed in 19th-century French Provincial style, opens onto a tree-lined street just three blocks from the lake and central to stores, restaurants, and movie theaters. The complimentary continental breakfast makes it an inviting alternative to area bed-and-breakfasts. ⊠ *555 W. Surf St., Lake View, 60657* ☏ *773/528–8400 or 800/787–3108* 🖷 *773/528–8483* ⊕ *www.cityinns. com* ⇋ *51 rooms, 4 suites* ♿ *Cable TV, hair dryers, irons, in-room data ports, dry cleaning, laundry facilities, concierge, parking (fee)* ═ *AE, D, DC, MC, V* ⵌ *CP.*

¢–$$ 🖼 **Margarita European Inn.** Just north of Chicago in the suburb of Evanston, the Margarita (two blocks from both the train and bus) is full of history: it began as an all-girls residence club in 1915 and retains the original elevator shaft. Rooms range in size from monklike cells to comfortable minisuites and are furnished with old-time photographs and antiques. Complimentary continental breakfast is served in an antiques-filled parlor lined with a wall of arched windows. Downstairs, **Va Pensiero** serves some of the area's best regional Italian cooking. ⊠ *1566 Oak Ave., Evanston, 60201* ☏ *847/869–2273* 🖷 *847/869–2353* ⊕ *www. margaritainn.com* ⇋ *42 rooms, 22 with bath* ♿ *Restaurant, in-room data ports, Wi-Fi and broadband in public spaces, library, business services, meeting rooms, parking (fee)* ═ *AE, D, DC, MC, V* ⵌ *CP.*

$ 🖼 **City Suites Hotel.** Two-thirds of this affordable art deco hotel consists of suites, each of which has a separate sitting room and pull-out couch. A free continental breakfast, afternoon cookies, and newspapers are available daily. The hotel is on a busy street in Lake View, so if noise is a concern, request a room on the east side of the building. ⊠ *933 W. Belmont Ave., Lake View, 60657* ☏ *773/404–3400 or 800/248–9108* 🖷 *773/404–3405* ⊕ *www.cityinns.com* ⇋ *16 rooms, 29 suites* ♿ *Some refrigerators, hair dryers, irons, cable TV, in-room data ports, concierge, parking (fee)* ═ *AE, D, DC, MC, V* ⵌ *CP.*

UNDERSTANDING
CHICAGO

CHICAGO SLANG

Like New Yorkers and New Englanders, Chicagoans put their own unique twist on the English language. Here's a quick primer to help you talk like a native while you're visiting.

Beef—Short for Italian beef sandwiches, a Chicago staple made of thinly sliced roast beef served on a long crusty Italian roll. Beefs are ordered "wet" (dipped in the meat juices), "hot" (with giardiniera, an Italian relish containing jalapeños), and/or "sweet" (with roasted sweet peppers).

Bleacher Bums—Regulars who sit in the bleachers at the "Friendly Confines" (see below).

The Blizzard of Oz—Nickname for Ozzie Guillen, the charismatic and often foul-mouthed manager of the 2005 World Champion Chicago White Sox.

The Boot—Short for the Denver Boot, a contraption the city uses to lock the wheels of cars with unpaid traffic and parking tickets. Often heard around town: "My car just got booted."

Boul Mich—Tongue-in-cheek nickname for the high-end Magnificent Mile.

Brat—Short for bratwurst, a staple at sporting events and tailgating parties (pronounced "braht").

The Cell—What White Sox fans affectionately call U.S. Cellular Field, formerly known as Comiskey Park.

Cheesehead—What the locals call people from Wisconsin.

Chicagoland—Chicago and the surrounding suburbs.

The Curse—A local legend that says that a Chicago barkeep, whose pet goat was denied entry into the 1945 Chicago Cubs–Detroit Tigers World Series, put a curse on the team. The Cubs lost, and have not been to a World Series since. Their last championship was in 1908.

Da Mare—"The Mayor," pronounced like a dyed-in-the-wool native.

The El—The nickname for the city's public train system, short for "elevated." Even though most of the system is above ground, the term is used even when the train goes underground.

Friendly Confines—This means Wrigley Field, home of the Chicago Cubs. A sign inside the ballpark says "Welcome to the Friendly Confines of Wrigley Field."

Gapers—Drivers who slow down traffic to look at an accident. You'll hear about "gapers blocks" or "gapers delays" on traffic reports.

Pop—A soft drink, like Coca-Cola. Don't use the word "soda" here.

Reversibles—The express lanes on the Kennedy Expressway, which reverse direction depending upon the time of day.

Sammitch—A sandwich, of course!

Trixies—A jabbing nickname for the young, ex-sorority types who live in and around the Lincoln Park neighborhood.

CHICAGO AT A GLANCE

Fast Facts

Nickname: Second City, Windy City, City of the Big Shoulders, Gem of the Prairie, Hog Butcher to the World, "I Will" City, Packingtown, City in a Garden (the city's motto)
Type of government: Mayor elected every four years; 50 aldermen, one from each of the city's wards; city clerk and treasurer also elected to citywide positions
Population: 2.8 million (city); 8.3 million (metro)
Population Density: 12,281 people per square mi
Median age: 34
Crime rate: Down 6% for the beginning of 2004; Chicago led the nation in homicides in 2003
Literacy: 37% have trouble with basic reading; 27% speak a language other than English at home, usually Spanish.

Ethnic groups: White 57%; Latino 19%; black 18%; Asian 5%; other 1%

Chicago seems a big city instead of merely a large place.
—A. J. Liebling

Things are so tough in Chicago that at Easter time, for bunnies the little kids use porcupines.
—Fred Allen

Chicago is not the most corrupt American city, it's the most theatrically corrupt.
—Studs Terkel

Chicago is a city of contradictions, of private visions haphazardly overlaid and linked together.
—Pat Colander

Geography & Environment

Latitude: 41° N (same as Barcelona, Spain; Istanbul, Turkey)
Longitude: 87° W (same as San Salvador, El Salvador)
Elevation: 579 feet
Land area: 228 square mi
Parkland: 7,337 acres
Terrain: Flat lakefront, extending inland to the west
Natural hazards: Extreme winter storms, tornadoes

Environmental issues: Toxic pollution, invasive species, habitat destruction, and contamination on Lake Michigan; air pollution from coal-fired power plants and diesel engines; wastewater treatment plants have exceeded pollution limits for effluents often

I miss everything about Chicago, except January and February.
—Gary Cole

Economy

Per capita income: $35,583
Unemployment: 6.5%
Workforce: 4.2 million; trade, transportation, and utilities 21%; professional and business services 15%; other 14%; government 13%; manufacturing 12%; educational and

health services 12%; leisure and hospitality 8%; construction 5%
Major industries: Aircraft, business services, chemicals, electronics, food processing, insurance, iron, machinery, manufacturing, meatpacking, retail, shipping, steel fabricators, trade

Did You Know?

• The nickname "the Windy City" doesn't come from Chicago's bitter winter conditions. Promoters of the city went to the East Coast boasting of Chicago's greatness, in hopes of securing the World's Fair of 1893. *New York Sun* editor Charles Dana tired of the bragging and bestowed the "windy" nickname.

• Chicago's name comes from a Potawatomi Indian word meaning "wild onion" or "skunk." When Indians first arrived, the future home of America's third-largest city was a patch of rotting marshland onions.

• Chicago's sports teams hold many distinctions, among them: the highest points scoring average in NBA playoff games (Michael Jordan, 33.4 points), the most home runs hit in one month (Sammy Sosa, 20), and the most touchdowns in an NFL game (Ernie Nevers, 6).

• Chicago produced the first roller skates (1884), steel-framed skyscraper (1885), elevated railway (1892), pinball game (1930), and blood bank (1937), among other things.

• The last concert that the perennial tour band the Grateful Dead ever played was at Soldier Field in Chicago, on July 9, 1995.

• In April 2000, the northwest corner of Walton Street and Michigan Avenue was named Hugh Hefner Way. The Chicago native, raised as a strict Methodist, went on to found *Playboy,* a magazine some credited with helping Americans talk about sex and others said popularized demeaning pornography.

• Only 29% of Chicago sushi chefs are of Japanese descent.

• Chicago counts the world's largest sewage tunnel among its many architectural and engineering distinctions. The Chicago Tunnels and Reservoir Plan (TARP) has 93 mi of machine-bored sewer tunnels 9 to 33 feet in diameter.

• Rudolph the Red-Nosed Reindeer is a Chicago native. A copywriter for Montgomery Ward department store created the character as part of a Christmas promotion in 1939.

• O'Hare Airport used to be a military airport named Orchard Place. That's the reason your luggage tags read ORD today.

ISN'T THAT THE CORNICHE?

THIS IS A SHORT AND YET EMBLEMATIC TALE about Chicago. At its center is a man who was so in love with his city's architecture that he decided to find a way to have it captured on film for posterity. In the course of one year, he managed to accumulate more than half a million photographs, but in the end, few of them were of buildings, and even fewer have remained on display in the city itself, instead ending up in the unlikeliest places.

In 1963 Gary Comer, an unassuming man who had grown up in Chicago and who had a comfortable position in advertising, quit his job to pursue his passion: sailing. He and a friend opened a small mail-order company that sold hardware for sailboats, and the firm did okay until the oil embargo of the early 1970s, when powerboat stores, faced with the decline in sales of their usual wares, muscled in on their sailboat business. So Comer diversified and began selling other things—first big-brimmed hats, and then clothing in general. His business took off, in time morphing into what we know today as Lands' End. It became the nation's largest catalogue clothing company, and Comer eventually sold the firm to Sears for $1.9 billion.

Not long ago, in a survey conducted by the American Institute of Architects, its members declared Chicago home to the finest architecture in the country, and Comer and his wife, Francie, would agree; every Sunday they used to take a drive around the city, mostly to admire its older buildings. On one of these drives, in 1999, Comer was approaching the Loop from the south and he suddenly understood that he was watching a city shedding its skin: "I saw this magnificent facade of buildings, and I realized that what I was looking at was temporary. There isn't much over one hundred twenty years old in the city. Most buildings last eighty to a hundred years. I realized the city was really in transition. New buildings going up. Old ones coming down." And in that instant, Comer had

a notion. "The city was being rebuilt from the center out. I thought, 'Gee, let's lock it into place at the end of the millennium.'" He decided to hire some photographers to capture the city as it was right at this moment in its history; then he might create a kind of time capsule, perhaps bury it in a canister beneath a new park under construction downtown.

Comer approached Richard Cahan to head up the project. Cahan was a likely candidate for the job because he'd written a book about a local architectural photographer, Richard Nickel, who was among the first preservationists to fight for buildings because of their architectural rather than their historical significance. (In 1972, Nickel died doing what he loved: While he was combing through Chicago's old Stock Exchange, bulldozers bore through the building and buried him.) Cahan, who was also the picture editor at the *Chicago Sun-Times*, told Comer, "If you're going to capture the city you ought to capture its people, its life, not the architecture. That's what people will care about a thousand years from now." Besides, he added, "Human lives are more interesting than buildings." Comer gradually came to agree, and so Cahan left his job at the *Sun-Times* to direct the project, which they christened CITY 2000.

Two hundred local photographers were hired, most of them on a part-time basis, to take pictures around the city over the next year. Comer didn't set a budget; he just told Cahan and the photographers he assembled to make it as good as possible. "I don't want to hear any excuses," he told them. Initially, Cahan skimped. When they needed aerial shots, for instance, he rented an old Piper airplane that cost seventy-five dollars an hour, but the resulting photographs were distant and out of focus. Comer heard of the problem and suggested they hire a turbo helicopter at five hundred twenty-five dollars an hour.

In the end, Comer spent roughly two million dollars on the project.

Photographers were given free rein and told to do whatever they'd long dreamed of doing. Leah Missbach asked women throughout the city to empty the contents of their purses, and then shot the contents along with the owners. Lloyd DeGrane took photos of people in uniform, from players for the Chicago Cubs to maids at the Hilton Hotel. Scott Strazzante documented the last days of a tire store where his father worked. Kevin Horan set up a makeshift studio at ten locations around the city, including outside the Criminal Courts building, by the lakefront, and on the streets of the immigrant community Albany Park, and asked passersby if he might photograph them against a white sheet. The result is an arresting collection of everyday people out of context. The subjects' faces, their clothes, their postures reveal all, almost as if you'd caught them in a state of undress: two elderly women in matching pink bathing suits; a bulging defense attorney in a mustard-stained shirt; a musician with his trumpet. Horan asked each subject two questions. The first was, "Why are you here?" The second was, "What would you like people to know about that they wouldn't know from looking at your picture?"—to which one woman, a young model, replied, "That I am really a nice person because everyone thinks I'm a bitch."

So, what to do with all these photographs? For two and a half months they were shown at the city's Cultural Center in the Loop, where they were visited by twenty-five thousand people, a respectable number for exhibitions there. Then the five hundred thousand negatives were collected for storage at the library of the University of Illinois at Chicago. The collection has never found its rightful place in the city.

Both Comer and Cahan have moved on. Comer grew up on the South Side—his father was a conductor for the Illinois Central Railroad—and during the CITY 2000 year, he visited the elementary school he'd attended. The students are now all African-American, and mostly poor. He asked the principal, "How are they treating you?"

"Beg your pardon?" the principal replied.

"Are you getting everything you need?"

In fact, the principal told Comer, they had new computers that were sitting idle because the school wasn't properly wired. Comer paid to have that done, and he has since made the well-being of the Paul Revere Elementary School an ongoing priority. He has also provided funding for the South Shore Drill Team, whose director is the school's disciplinarian; two hundred fifty kids participate, and there are another hundred on the waiting list. They're a crowd favorite at the Bud Billiken Day Parade, the country's largest parade, which is held on the city's predominantly African-American South Side on the second Saturday each August. As for Cahan, he opened a store in Evanston, the suburb just north of the city. It's called CityFile, and it sells rare books on Chicago as well as photographs, memorabilia, and original art. Cahan's running out of money, though, and when I last saw him he told me he would probably close soon. But one of his final gestures was to hold an exhibition, the first in the city, of Robert Guinan's work. (For nearly thirty years, Guinan painted portraits of prostitutes and junkies, recent immigrants and blues singers, in taverns around the city; his work—all oils—is immensely popular in France, where he exhibits at a gallery and in museums, but is virtually ignored in his hometown, Chicago.) In Paris, there's a tradition that on weekends artists will drop by their galleries to meet with art-seekers, and so, for a month, Guinan visited Cahan's store each Saturday afternoon and held court. A number of visitors, thinking Guinan lived in Paris, asked him how often he visited Chicago. Another began speaking to him in French. "All I could say is 'Où est le téléphone?'" he said. "It's the only French I know."

Guinan would undoubtedly identify with the fate of CITY 2000, for the project has resurfaced far from Chicago. In September 2001, the city entered one hundred thirty-five of the photographs in the International Photography Festival in Aleppo, Syria, and the show opened on September 11—the day the world's axis shifted. Valentine Judge, who works for the city and was traveling with the exhibition, told the Syrians that "in these pictures you see the faces of the fathers, mothers, sisters, and brothers of the people killed in the World Trade Center. This is what America looks like." People were drawn to the photographs, which were the hit of the festival, and so the U.S. State Department chose to take these images of Chicago around the world—more precisely, to the places where America is viewed with some hostility. So far they have been exhibited in India, Lebanon, Egypt, Morocco, Tunisia, South Africa, Brazil, Jordan, Thailand, and Malaysia. The pictures continue to make their way around the globe.

People, after all, like looking at people, and peeking in at American life. A photograph of a rather large woman in a body-clinging dress often gets puzzled looks, presumably because obesity is not a common sight in most Third World countries. Passersby look on in amusement at a diptych of a woman in a North Side bar called Slow Down Life's Too Short and the emptied contents of her purse, which include a disposable camera, an address book, a pack of Marlboro Lights, a cell phone, a makeup case, a wallet, keys (to her motorcycle, car, bike lock, and apartment), a credit card, and sunglasses—the daily accoutrements of life in America. There are portraits of two waitresses, one with a nose ring, at the South Side restaurant Soul Queen; a group of Ethiopian Jews celebrating the Sabbath; two Mexican-Americans dancing at a rodeo in Pilsen; four Knights of Columbus members dressed in feathered fezzes, capes, and sashes; and

Rex, a toothless, smiling homeless man in a Laborers' Union baseball cap.

But people also see themselves in these photos: an entire world reflected in one place, in one city. In Beirut, a woman looking at an image of two veiled Muslim women standing by Lake Michigan asked, "Isn't that the Corniche?" In Bombay, a cleaning woman in her sari took Judge's hand and walked her over to a picture of a nine-year-old girl about to be baptized at the Unity of Love Missionary Baptist Church on the city's South Side; she pointed first to the shower-cap-clad girl, and then to herself. An Indian diplomat translated: "She's trying to tell you she's Christian. That she was baptized." In Tunis, a middle-aged man looking at an image of a young Puerto Rican man with his wife's name, Natalie, shaved into his hair, mumbled, "Oh, I hope my son doesn't see that." One of the favorites is from Horan's collection, a portrait of two teenage friends on their way home from school: One girl is a Somali, wearing a traditional head scarf, and the other is from Thailand.

For Cahan, the project had from the beginning seemed like an opportunity to freeze-frame America, and what better place to do that than in Chicago. Ordered and bedraggled. Excessive and austere. Familiar and foreign. An imperfect city, a city of quixotic quests and of reluctant resignation. A city that was, Nelson Algren once wrote, the product "of Man's endless war against himself." These are Chicago's truths but they are also, after all, America's truths, and they always have been.

I've heard it suggested that Chicago is passé. The steel mills have closed. Public housing is coming down. The mob has been dismantled. And, Chicago is no longer hog butcher to the world. Even the city's one claim to edginess, *Playboy* magazine, has picked up shop and moved. "I love Chicago," the magazine's new editor who's now based in New York told a reporter.

"It's my second favorite city." The city, though, always finds a way to move on: Now, for example, with more than a hundred sweets manufacturers, it has become the world's candy capital. (As I write, two large confectioners have announced their closing; it is, indeed, a city in motion.)

When Comer first considered his project, it was because he'd been struck by the vast physical changes here, but in the end, what he captured was a people—a people evolving, a people shifting and changing, a people finding their way. I asked Comer why he thought the photographs of Chicago had become such an attraction abroad. "Because," he replied simply, "the place is real."

–Alex Kotlowitz

From *Never a City So Real: A Walk in Chicago* by Alex Kotlowitz. Copyright 2004 by Alex Kotlowitz. Published by Crown Journeys, member of the Crown Publishing Group, a division of Random House, Inc.

BOOKS & MOVIES

Books

Chicago has been celebrated and vilified in fiction and nonfiction, as well as on film. For the flavor of the city a century ago, pick up a copy of Theodore Dreiser's *Sister Carrie*, the story of a country innocent who falls from grace in Chicago. Upton Sinclair's portrayal in *The Jungle* of the meatpacking industry's squalor and employee exploitation raised a public outcry. *The Pit*, Frank Norris's muckraking 1903 novel, captures the frenzy (yes, even then) of futures speculation on the Board of Trade.

More recently, native Chicagoan Saul Bellow set many novels in the city, most notably *Humboldt's Gift* and *The Adventures of Augie March*. Richard Wright's explosive *Native Son* and James T. Farrell's *Studs Lonigan* depict racial clashes in Chicago from the black and white sides, respectively. The works of longtime resident Nelson Algren—*The Man with the Golden Arm, A Walk on the Wild Side,* and *Chicago: City on the Make*—show the city at its grittiest, as does playwright David Mamet's *American Buffalo*. On a lighter but still revealing note, two series of detective novels use a current-day Chicago backdrop: Sara Paretsky's excellent V. I. Warshawski novels (the 1991 movie *V. I. Warshawski* starred Kathleen Turner) and the Monsignor Ryan mysteries of Andrew Greeley. Greeley has set other novels in Chicago as well, including *Lord of the Dance.*

Chicago was once the quintessential newspaper town; the play *The Front Page*, by Ben Hecht and Charles MacArthur, is set here. Local reporters have penned some excellent chronicles, including *Fabulous Chicago*, by Emmett Dedmon; and *Boss,* a portrait of the late mayor Richard J. Daley, by the late Mike Royko. For a selection of Royko's award-winning columns, check out *One More Time: The Best of Mike Royko*. Lois Wille's *Forever Open, Clear and Free* is a superb history of the fight to save Chicago's lakefront parks. Books by Studs Terkel, a great chronicler of Chicago, include *Division Street: America* and *Chicago*. Erik Larson traces two men, architect Daniel Burnham and serial killer Henry H. Holmes, through the Chicago World's Fair of 1893 in *The Devil in the White City. Never a City So Real,* a collection of essays by Alex Kotlowitz, profiles the heart of the city and its people. Jack Schnedler's *Chicago* (Compass American Guides) provides a fine overview of the city as well as practical travel information.

Architecture buffs can choose from a number of excellent guidebooks. Ira J. Bach, former Director of City Development, is the author of *A Guide to Chicago's Public Sculpture*; this is currently out of print but worth looking for in a library. James Cornelius revised *Chicago on Foot,* by Ira J. Bach and Susan Wolfson; the book contains dozens of walking tours that concentrate on architecture. Franz Schulze and Kevin Harrington edited the fourth edition of *Chicago's Famous Buildings,* a pocket guide to the city's most important landmarks and notable buildings. The *A. I. A. Guide to Chicago,* edited by Alice Sinkevitch, is an exhaustive source of information about local architecture. The pocket-size *Chicago: A Guide to Recent Architecture,* by Susanna Sirefman, covers everything from office buildings to the new airport terminal. Finally, David Garrad Lowe's *Lost Chicago* is a fascinating and heartbreaking history of vanished buildings; it has some terrific, rare photographs.

Movies

Chicago has been the setting for films about everything from gangsters to restless suburbanites. Classic early gangster flicks include *Little Caesar* (1930), with Edward G. Robinson, and *Scarface* (1932), starring Paul Muni and George Raft. The theme is carried out on a lighter note in *The Sting* (1973), George Roy Hill's charming Scott Joplin–scored movie that stars Paul Newman and Robert Redford as suave con men. *Carrie* is the 1952 adaptation of Dreiser's novel about a country girl who loses her innocence in the city; Laurence Olivier and Jennifer Jones are the stars. Lorraine Hansberry's drama about a black Chicago family, *A Raisin in the Sun*, became a film with Sidney Poitier in 1961.

As Elwood and Jake, respectively, Dan Aykroyd and the late John Belushi brought wild energy and cool music to the screen in *The Blues Brothers* (1980). *Ordinary People*, the Oscar-winning 1980 film, starred Mary Tyler Moore in a drama about an affluent and agonized North Shore family. John Hughes directed 1986's *Ferris Bueller's Day Off*, in which Matthew Broderick and a couple of his high-school friends play hooky and tour Chicago for a day, taking in everything from the Board of Trade and a Cubs game to a parade in the Loop; the film has wonderful scenes of the city. In *About Last Night* (1986), which is based on the David Mamet play *Sexual Perversity in Chicago*, Demi Moore and Rob Lowe go through realistic modern dating games with the help (and hindrance) of hilarious friends played by Elizabeth Perkins and Jim Belushi. Brian De Palma's *The Untouchables* (1987) stars Kevin Costner as Eliot Ness and Robert De Niro as Al Capone in a gangster tale with a 1920s Chicago background. *Eight Men Out* (1988)— with John Cusack, John Mahoney, and Charlie Sheen—depicts baseball's infamous Black Sox scandal, when members of the Chicago White Sox took bribes to throw the 1919 World Series against the Cincinnati Reds.

Kurt Russell and William Baldwin play firefighter brothers in *Backdraft* (1991). In the action thriller *The Fugitive* (1993), Harrison Ford pulls off one narrow escape in Chicago's St. Patrick's Day parade. Steve James's *Hoop Dreams* (1994) is a powerful documentary about a couple of inner-city teens who dream that basketball will be their ticket out. In the romantic comedy *While You Were Sleeping* (1995), Sandra Bullock plays a CTA clerk who saves a man from death on the El. *My Best Friend's Wedding* (1997) is a romantic comedy starring Julia Roberts, who tries to break up the wedding of Dermot Mulroney and Cameron Diaz. Roberts and Mulroney dance on an architectural boat tour in the Loop.

In *High Fidelity* (2000), John Cusack is a record-store owner struggling with his past and present romantic life. In *Save the Last Dance* (2001), suburban ballerina Julia Stiles learns hip-hop from Sean Patrick Thomas on Chicago's South Side. Second City alum Nia Vardalos adapted the screenplay for the wildly popular *My Big Fat Greek Wedding* (2002) from her one-woman play. The comedy about marriage, family, and Windex is set in Chicago, though it was filmed in Toronto. *Chicago* (2002) razzle-dazzled its way to six Oscars, helping to bring back the movie musical. *The Road to Perdition* (2002) stars Tom Hanks and Paul Newman in a 1930s gangster drama. *Barbershop* (2002) chronicles a day in the life of a South Side barbershop. Director Robert Altman and star Neve Campbell go behind the scenes with the Joffrey Ballet of Chicago in *The Company* (2003). Will Smith visits the Lake Michigan Landfill in the 2035 Chicago created in the sci-fi thriller *I, Robot* (2004). Josh Harnett plays a young ad exec in Chicago in *Wicker Park* (2004). Jennifer Aniston, still recovering from a very public divorce from Brad Pitt, spent some quality time in the Windy City while filming *Derailed* (2005; co-starring Clive Owen); then she was rumored to fall in love with Vince Vaughn while filming *The Break Up* (2006), a movie about a couple who break up but keep living together in an increasingly cramped condo.

SMART TRAVEL TIPS

Finding out about your destination before you leave home means you won't spend time organizing everyday minutiae once you've arrived. You'll be more streetwise when you hit the ground as well, better prepared to explore the aspects of Chicago that drew you here in the first place. The organizations in this section can provide information to supplement this guide; contact them for up-to-the-minute details. Happy landings!

ADDRESSES

Chicago streets generally follow a grid pattern, running north–south or east–west and radiating from a center point at State and Madison streets in the Loop. East and west street numbers go up as you move away from State Street; north and south street numbers rise as you move away from Madison Street. Each block is represented by a hundred number.

AIR TRAVEL TO & FROM CHICAGO

There are no direct flights from Chicago to Australia or New Zealand. There are several daily direct flights to the U.K. by British Midland, United, and American.

BOOKING

When you book, look for nonstop flights and remember that "direct" flights stop at least once. Try to avoid connecting flights, which require a change of plane. Two airlines may operate a connecting flight jointly, so ask whether your airline operates every segment of the trip; you may find that the carrier you prefer flies you only part of the way. To find more booking tips and to check prices and make online flight reservations, log on to www.fodors.com.

CARRIERS

🛪 Major Airlines Aer Lingus ☎ 888/474-7424 ⊕ www.aerlingus.com. Air Canada ☎ 888/247-2262 ⊕ www.aircanada.ca. Alaska Airlines ☎ 800/426-0333 ⊕ www.alaskaair.com. American ☎ 800/433-7300 ⊕ www.aa.com. British Airways ☎ 800/247-9297 ⊕ www.britishairways.com. BMI British Midland ☎ 800/788-0555 ⊕ www.flybmi.com. Continental ☎ 800/525-0280 ⊕ www.continental.com. Delta ☎ 800/221-1212 ⊕ www.

delta.com. **Mexicana** ☎ 800/531-7921 ⊕ www.
mexicana.com. **Northwest** ☎ 800/225-2525
⊕ www.nwa.com. **TACA Airlines** ☎ 888/337-8466
⊕ www.taca.com. **United** ☎ 800/241-6522
⊕ www.united.com. **US Airways** ☎ 800/428-4322
⊕ www.usairways.com.
🗗 **Smaller Airlines America Trans Air (ATA)**
☎ 800/225-2995 ⊕ www.ata.com. **America West**
☎ 800/235-9292 ⊕ www.americawest.com. **Co-
mair** ☎ 800/927-0927 ⊕ www.comair.com. **Frontier Airlines** ☎ 800/432-1359 ⊕ www.
frontierairlines.com. **Independence Air** ☎ 800/
359-3594 ⊕ www.flyi.com. **JetBlue** ☎ 800/538-
2583 ⊕ www.jetblue.com. **Southwest Airlines**
☎ 800/435-9792 ⊕ www.southwest.com. **Spirit
Airlines** ☎ 800/772-7177 ⊕ www.spiritair.com.
USA 3000 ☎ 877/872-3000 ⊕ www.
usa3000airlines.com/.

CHECK-IN & BOARDING

Always **find out your carrier's check-in
policy.** Plan to arrive at the airport about
two hours before your scheduled departure time for domestic flights and 2½ to 3
hours before international flights. You
may need to arrive earlier if you're flying
from one of the busier airports or during
peak air-traffic times. In Chicago, the general rule is to arrive at the airport two
hours before an international flight; for a
domestic flight, plan to arrive 90 minutes
early if you're checking luggage and 60
minutes if you're not.

To avoid delays at airport-security check-
points, try not to wear any metal. Jewelry,
belt and other buckles, steel-toe shoes,
barrettes, and underwire bras are among
the items that can set off detectors.

Assuming that not everyone with a ticket
will show up, airlines routinely overbook
planes. When everyone does, airlines ask
for volunteers to give up their seats. In return, these volunteers usually get a several-
hundred-dollar flight voucher, which can
be used toward the purchase of another
ticket, and are rebooked on the next available flight out. If there are not enough volunteers, the airline must choose who will
be denied boarding. The first to get
bumped are passengers who checked in
late and those flying on discounted tickets,
so get to the gate and check in as early as
possible, especially during peak periods.

Always **bring a government-issued photo
ID** to the airport; even when it's not required, a passport is best.

CUTTING COSTS

The least expensive airfares to Chicago are
often priced for round-trip travel and must
usually be purchased in advance. Flights to
Midway Airport are generally slightly
cheaper than those that land at O'Hare.
Airlines generally allow you to change
your return date for a fee; most low-fare
tickets, however, are nonrefundable. It's
smart to call a number of airlines and
check the Internet; when you are quoted a
good price, book it on the spot—the same
fare may not be available the next day, or
even the next hour. Always check different
routings and look into using alternate airports. Also, price off-peak flights and redeye, which may be significantly less
expensive than others. Travel agents, especially low-fare specialists (⇨ Discounts &
Deals), are helpful.

Consolidators are another good source.
They buy tickets for scheduled flights at
reduced rates from the airlines, then sell
them at prices that beat the best fare available directly from the airlines. (Many also
offer reduced car-rental and hotel rates.)
Sometimes you can even get your money
back if you need to return the ticket. Carefully read the fine print detailing penalties
for changes and cancellations, purchase
the ticket with a credit card, and confirm
your consolidator reservation with the airline.

When you fly as a courier, you trade your
checked-luggage space for a ticket deeply
subsidized by a courier service. There are
restrictions on when you can book and
how long you can stay. Some courier companies list with membership organizations,
such as the Air Courier Association and
the International Association of Air Travel
Couriers; these require you to become a
member before you can book a flight.
🗗 **Consolidators AirlineConsolidator.com** ☎ 888/
468-5385 ⊕ www.airlineconsolidator.com; for international tickets. **Best Fares** ☎ 800/880-1234
⊕ www.bestfares.com; $59.90 annual membership.
Cheap Tickets ☎ 800/377-1000 or 800/652-4327
⊕ www.cheaptickets.com. **Expedia** ☎ 800/397-

3342 or 404/728-8787 ⊕ www.expedia.com.
Hotwire 🖃 866/468-9473 or 920/330-9418
⊕ www.hotwire.com. **Now Voyager Travel** 🖃 212/
459-1616 ⊕ www.nowvoyagertravel.com. **Onetravel.
com** ⊕ www.onetravel.com. **Orbitz** 🖃 888/656-
4546 ⊕ www.orbitz.com. **Priceline.com** ⊕ www.
priceline.com. **Travelocity** 🖃 888/709-5983, 877/
282-2925 in Canada, 0870/111-7061 in U.K. ⊕ www.
travelocity.com.

**🖪 Courier Resources Air Courier Association/
Cheaptrips.com** 🖃 800/211-5119 ⊕ www.aircourier.
org or www.cheaptrips.com; $49 annual member-
ship. **Courier Travel** 🖃 303/570-7586 ⊕ www.
couriertravel.org; $50 annual membership. **Interna-
tional Association of Air Travel Couriers** 🖃 515/
292-2458 ⊕ www.courier.org; $45 annual member-
ship. **Now Voyager Travel** 🖃 212/459-1616.

ENJOYING THE FLIGHT

State your seat preference when purchasing your ticket, and then repeat it when
you confirm and when you check in. For
more legroom, you can request one of the
few emergency-aisle seats at check-in, if
you're capable of moving obstacles com-
parable in weight to an airplane exit door
(usually between 35 pounds and 60
pounds)—a Federal Aviation Administration requirement of passengers in these
seats. Seats behind a bulkhead also offer
more legroom, but they don't have under-
seat storage. Don't sit in the row in front
of the emergency aisle or in front of a
bulkhead, where seats may not recline.
SeatGuru.com has more information
about specific seat configurations, which
vary by aircraft.

Ask the airline whether a snack or meal is
served on the flight. In economy class,
many cheaper U.S. carriers like JetBlue
and ATA offer little more than pretzels or
nuts, even on long flights. Check before
leaving to find out if a meal will be
served on your flight; if not, it's a good
idea to bring a small (plastic) bottle of
water, a healthful snack, or a meal on
board. If a meal is being served and you
have dietary concerns, request special
meals when booking. These can be vegetarian, low-cholesterol, or kosher, for example. On long flights, try to maintain a
normal routine, to help fight jet lag. At
night, get some sleep. By day, eat light

meals, drink water (not alcohol), and
move around the cabin to stretch your
legs. For additional jet-lag tips consult
Fodor's FYI: Travel Fit & Healthy (available at bookstores everywhere).

Smoking policies vary from carrier to carrier. U.S. airlines prohibit smoking on all
flights.

FLYING TIMES

To Chicago: From New York, 2 hours;
from San Francisco, 4 hours; from Los Angeles, 4 hours; from Dallas, 2½ hours;
from London, 7 hours; from Sydney, 17
hours.

HOW TO COMPLAIN

If your baggage goes astray or your flight
goes awry, complain right away. Most carriers require that you **file a claim immediately.** The Aviation Consumer Protection
Division of the Department of Transportation publishes *Fly-Rights,* which discusses
airlines and consumer issues and is available online. You can also find articles and
information on mytravelrights.com, the
Web site of the nonprofit Consumer Travel
Rights Center.

**🖪 Airline Complaints Aviation Consumer Protec-
tion Division** 🖃 202/366-2220 ⊕ airconsumer.ost.
dot.gov. **Federal Aviation Administration Consumer Hotline** 🖃 800/322-7873 ⊕ www.faa.gov.

RECONFIRMING

Check the status of your flight before you
leave for the airport. You can do this on
your carrier's Web site, by linking to a
flight-status checker (many Web booking
services offer these), or by calling your carrier or travel agent. Always confirm international flights at least 72 hours ahead of
the scheduled departure time.

AIRPORTS & TRANSFERS

The major gateway to Chicago is **O'Hare
International Airport** (ORD). One of the
world's busiest airports, it's 19 mi from
downtown, in the far northwest corner of
the city. **Midway Airport (MDW),** which is
about 11 mi southwest from downtown,
primarily serves budget airlines. Both airports are served by the CTA, the city's
public transportation system of buses and
trains. Security screenings at both airports

are fairly quick (it takes about 15 minutes or less to get through security lines); however, during peak holiday travel, you should arrive about two hours before your flight.

🛪 **Airport Information Midway Airport** ☎ 773/838-0600 ⊕ www.ohare.com/midway/home.asp. **O'Hare International Airport** ☎ 773/686-2200 or 800/832-6352 ⊕ www.ohare.com.

AIRPORT TRANSFERS

If you're traveling to or from the airport by bus or car during morning or afternoon rush hours, factor in some extra time— ground transport to or from both O'Hare and Midway airports can be slow.

BY BUS: Shuttle buses run between O'Hare and Midway airports and to and from either airport and various points in the city. When taking an airport shuttle bus to O'Hare or Midway to catch a departing flight, be sure to allow at least 1½ hours. When going to either airport, it's a good idea to make a reservation 24 hours in advance. Though some shuttles make regular stops at the major hotels and don't require reservations, it's best to check. Reservations are not necessary from the airports. Omega Airport Shuttle runs an hourly shuttle between the two airports for approximately $16 per person. Travel time is approximately one hour. Omega Airport Shuttle also provides an hourly service from the two airports and Hyde Park. The fare is $25 from O'Hare to Hyde Park and $16 from Midway to Hyde Park. Continental Airport Express coaches provide service from both airports to major downtown and Near North locations and the northern suburbs. The trip downtown from O'Hare takes at least 45 minutes, depending on traffic conditions; the fare is $24, $44 round-trip. The trip downtown from Midway takes at least a half hour; the fare is $19, $34 round-trip. Call to find out times, and prices for other destinations.

BY CAR: Depending on traffic and the time of day, driving to and from O'Hare takes about an hour, and driving to and from Midway takes at least 45 minutes. From O'Hare, follow the signs to I–90 east (Kennedy Expressway), which merges with

I–94 (Edens Expressway). Take the eastbound exit at Ohio Street for Near North locations, the Washington or Monroe Street exit for downtown. After you exit, continue east about a mile to get to Michigan Avenue. From Midway, follow the signs to I–55 east, which leads to I–90.

BY TAXI: Metered taxicab service is available at both O'Hare and Midway airports. Trips to and from O'Hare may incur a $1 surcharge to compensate for changing fuel costs. Expect to pay about $40–$45 plus tip from O'Hare to Near North and downtown locations, about $30–$35 plus tip from Midway. Some cabs, such as Checker Taxi and Yellow Cab, participate in a share-a-ride program in which each cab carries up to four individual passengers going from the airport to downtown. The cost per person is substantially lower than the full rate, which is approximately $50.

BY TRAIN: Chicago Transit Authority (CTA) trains are the cheapest way to and from the airports; they can also be the most convenient transfer. TRAINS TO CITY signs will guide you to the subway or elevated train line. In O'Hare Airport the Blue Line station is in the underground concourse between terminals. Travel time to the city is about 45 minutes. Get off at the station closest to your hotel, or from the first stop in the Loop (Washington and Dearborn streets) you can take a taxi to your hotel or change to other transit lines. At Midway Airport the Orange Line El runs to the Loop. The stop at Adams Street and Wabash Avenue is the closest to the hotels on South Michigan Avenue; for others, the simplest strategy is to get off anywhere in the Loop and hail a cab to your final destination. Train fare is $1.75, which you'll need in dollar bills (turnstiles don't give change) and/or coins. A fare card is another option. Pick up brochures outside the entrances to the platforms that detail the stops of the train lines; the "Downtown Transit Sightseeing Guide" is also helpful.

🛪 **Taxis & Shuttles American United Cab Co.** ☎ 773/248-7600. **Continental Airport Express** ☎ 312/454-7800 or 800/654-7871 ⊕ www.

airportexpress.com. **Checker Taxi** ☎ 312/243-2537. **Flash Cab** ☎ 773/561-1444. **Omega Airport Shuttle** ☎ 773/483-6634 ⊕ www.omegashuttle.com. **Yellow Cab Co.** ☎ 312/829-4222.
🚹 **Public Transit Information CTA** ☎ 312/836-7000 ⊕ www.transitchicago.com.

BIKE TRAVEL

Mayor Daley's goal is to make Chicago the most bike-friendly city in the United States, and he's well on his way. One-hundred-twenty miles of designated bike routes run throughout the city, through historic areas, beautiful parks, and along city streets (look for the words "bike lane"). Bicycling on busy city streets can be a challenge and is not for the faint of heart—cars come within inches of riders, and the doors of parked cars can swing open at any time. The best bet for a scenic ride is the lakefront, which has a traffic-free 18-mi asphalt trail affording scenic views of the skyline. When your bike is unattended, always lock it; there are bike racks throughout the city. In Millennium Park at Michigan Avenue and Randolph Street (⊕ www.chicagobikestation.com), there are 300 free indoor bike spaces plus showers, lockers, and bike-rental facilities. Bike rentals are also readily available at Bike Chicago, which has five locations, two downtown and three along the lakefront (⊕ www.bikechicago.com). Both carry a good selection of mountain and cross bikes. Rates start at $8.75 per hour. The Chicago Department of Tourism publishes free route maps. Chicagoland Bicycle Federation maps cost $6.95 plus a membership fee of $5. Maps are updated every few years. From April through October, Bobby's Bike Hike takes guests on cycling tours of Chicago. The three-hour tours begin at the Water Tower on the Magnificent Mile and cycle through historic neighborhoods, shopping areas, and the lakefront. A $30 fee includes bikes, helmuts, and guides.
🚹 **Bike Maps Bobby's Bike Hike** ☎ 312/933-2980 ⊕ www.bobbysbikehike.com. **Chicago Department of Tourism (CDOT)** ☎ 312/742-2453 ⊕ www. cityofchicago.org/Transportation publishes free route maps. **Chicagoland Bicycle Federation** ☎ 312/427-33254 ⊕ www.chibikefed.org.

BIKES IN FLIGHT

Most airlines accommodate bikes as luggage, provided they are dismantled and boxed; check with individual airlines about packing requirements. Some airlines sell bike boxes, which are often free at bike shops, for about $20 (bike bags can be considerably more expensive). International travelers often can substitute a bike for a piece of checked luggage at no charge; otherwise, the cost is about $100. Most U.S. and Canadian airlines charge $40–$80 each way.

BUSINESS HOURS

Neighborhood business hours are generally 9–6 Friday–Wednesday, and 9–9 on Thursday. When holidays fall on a weekend, businesses usually close around four on the preceding Friday. On a Monday following a weekend holiday, retail businesses are rarely closed but regular businesses often are. Most stores close for Christmas, New Year's, and Easter Sunday.

MUSEUMS & SIGHTS

Chicagoland museums are generally open daily 9–5, closing only on major holidays; some larger attractions keep later hours (until about 8 PM) one weeknight per week. A number of smaller museums keep limited hours; it's always advisable to phone ahead for details.

PHARMACIES

Most pharmacies are open regular business hours, starting as early as 8 AM. Some close as early as 5 PM, but many stay open later, anywhere from 6 to 10 PM.
🚹 **24-Hour Pharmacies Osco** ☎ 800/539-3561 for nearest location ⊕ www.jewelosco.com. **Walgreens** ✉ 757 N. Michigan Ave., at Chicago Ave. ☎ 312/664-8686 ⊕ www.walgreens.com.

SHOPS

Most businesses in Chicago are open 9–5 Monday through Saturday; many are open Sunday, too, but often with shorter hours (for example, noon to 4 or 5).

BUS TRAVEL TO & FROM CHICAGO

Greyhound has nationwide service to its main terminal in the Loop and to neighborhood stations, at the 95th Street and Dan Ryan Expressway CTA station and at the Cumberland CTA station, near O'Hare Airport. The Harrison Street terminal is far from most hotels, so plan on another bus or a cab to your hotel.

🛈 **Greyhound Lines** ☎ 800/231-2222 or 312/408-5970 ⊕ www.greyhound.com.

BUS TRAVEL WITHIN CHICAGO

For information on bus travel within Chicago, *see* Public Transportation.

CAMERAS & PHOTOGRAPHY

With its striking architectural landscape, Chicago is a great city to photograph. Take a trip up to a skyscraper's observatory deck for a panoramic shot of the city. Or point your lens back at the unique skyline seen only from a trip out on Lake Michigan. You may also want to check with the Chicago Architecture Foundation; it occasionally leads special photographers' tours of the Loop.

The *Kodak Guide to Shooting Great Travel Pictures* (available at bookstores everywhere) is loaded with tips.

🛈 **Photo Help Kodak Information Center** ☎ 800/242-2424 ⊕ www.kodak.com.

EQUIPMENT PRECAUTIONS

Don't pack film or equipment in checked luggage, where it is much more susceptible to damage. X-ray machines used to view checked luggage are extremely powerful and therefore are likely to ruin your film. Try to ask for hand inspection of film, which becomes clouded after repeated exposure to airport X-ray machines, and keep videotapes and computer disks away from metal detectors. Always keep film, tape, and computer disks out of the sun. Carry an extra supply of batteries, and be prepared to turn on your camera, camcorder, or laptop to prove to airport security personnel that the device is real.

CAR RENTAL

Rates in Chicago begin at $77 a day, $188 a week or $35 a weekend for an economy car with air-conditioning, automatic transmission, and unlimited mileage. This does not include the car-rental tax of 18% plus a $2.75 surcharge per rental. If you rent

from the airport, it's slightly more expensive because of airport taxes.

🛈 **Major Agencies Alamo** ☎ 800/327-9633 ⊕ www.alamo.com. **Avis** ☎ 800/331-1212, 800/879-2847 or 800/272-5871 in Canada, 0870/606-0100 in U.K., 02/9353-9000 in Australia, 09/526-2847 in New Zealand ⊕ www.avis.com. **Budget** ☎ 800/527-0700 ⊕ www.budget.com. **Dollar** ☎ 800/800-4000, 0800/085-4578 in U.K. ⊕ www.dollar.com. **Hertz** ☎ 800/654-3131, 800/263-0600 in Canada, 0870/844-8844 in U.K., 02/9669-2444 in Australia, 09/256-8690 in New Zealand ⊕ www.hertz.com. **National Car Rental** ☎ 800/227-7368 ⊕ www.nationalcar.com.

CUTTING COSTS

For a good deal, book through a travel agent who will shop around. Also, price local car-rental companies—whose prices may be lower still, although their service and maintenance may not be as good as those of major rental agencies—and research rates on the Internet. Paragon Auto Leasing Co. rents cars that are four years old with 30,000 or more miles; you save $10 per day compared to newer cars. Rates for older cars start at $20 per day plus $10 mandatory liability coverage. Rent A Wreck's cars are three to five years old with 50,000 to 100,000 mi; rates start at $25 per day. Consolidators that specialize in air travel can offer good rates on cars as well (⇨ Air Travel). Remember to ask about required deposits, cancellation penalties, and drop-off charges if you're planning to pick up the car in one city and leave it in another. If you're traveling during a holiday period, also make sure that a confirmed reservation guarantees you a car.

🛈 **Local Agencies Enterprise** ✉ 303 W. Lake St. ☎ 312/332-7783 ⊕ www.enterprise.com. **Paragon Auto Leasing Co.** ✉ 2550 N. Cicero Ave. ☎ 773/622-7660. **Rent A Wreck** ✉ Lincoln Park ☎ 773/281-1111 ⊕ www.rentawreck.com.

INSURANCE

When driving a rented car you are generally responsible for any damage to or loss of the vehicle. You also may be liable for any property damage or personal injury that you may cause while driving. Before you rent, see what coverage you already have under the terms of your personal auto-insurance policy and credit cards.

For about $9 to $25 a day, rental companies sell protection, known as a collision- or loss-damage waiver (CDW or LDW), that eliminates your liability for damage to the car; it's always optional and should never be automatically added to your bill. In most states you don't need a CDW if you have personal auto insurance or other liability insurance. Some states, including Illinois, have capped the price of the CDW and LDW. However, **make sure you have enough coverage to pay for the car.** If you do not have auto insurance or an umbrella policy that covers damage to third parties, purchasing liability insurance and a CDW or LDW is highly recommended.

REQUIREMENTS & RESTRICTIONS

In Chicago you must be at least 21 to rent a car. Rates are much higher if you're under 25. Children under 8 are required to use child safety seats.

SURCHARGES

Before you pick up a car in one city and leave it in another, ask about drop-off charges or one-way service fees, which can be substantial. Also inquire about early-return policies; some rental agencies charge extra if you return the car before the time specified in your contract while others give you a refund for the days not used. Most agencies note the tank's fuel level on your contract; to avoid a hefty refueling fee, return the car with the same tank level. If the tank was full, refill it just before you turn in the car, but be aware that gas stations near the rental outlet may overcharge. It's almost never a deal to buy a tank of gas with the car when you rent it; the understanding is that you'll return it empty, but some fuel usually remains. Surcharges may apply if you're under 25 or if you take the car outside the area approved by the rental agency. You'll pay extra for child seats (about $8 a day), which are compulsory for children under five, and usually for additional drivers (up to $25 a day, depending on location).

CAR TRAVEL

Chicago's network of buses and rapid transit rail is extensive, and taxis and limousines are readily available (the latter often priced competitively with metered cabs), so **rent a car only to visit the outlying suburbs that are not accessible by public transportation.** Chicago traffic is often heavy, on-street parking is nearly impossible to find, parking lots are expensive, congestion creates frustrating delays, and other drivers may be impatient with those who are unfamiliar with the city and its roads. **Expect snarled traffic during rush hours.** In these circumstances you may find a car to be a liability rather than an asset. The Illinois Department of Transportation gives information on expressway congestion, travel times, and lane closures and directions on state roadways.

The Illinois tollways snake around the outskirts of the city. I–294 runs north and south between Wisconsin and Indiana. I–90 runs northwest to western Wisconsin, including Madison and Wisconsin Dells. I–88 runs east–west and goes from Eisenhower to I–55. Traffic on all is sometimes just as congested as on the regular expressways. Most toll gates are unmanned, so bring lots of change if you don't have an I-Pass, which are sometimes included with rental cars. Even though tolls are double without the I-Pass, it's not cost effective to purchase one for a couple of days.

EMERGENCY SERVICES

Dial 911 in an emergency to reach police, fire, or ambulance services. AAA Chicago provides roadside assistance to members. Emergency Locksmith Service will unlock as well as tow your vehicle 24 hours a day. **AAA Chicago** ☎ 800/AAA-HELP. **Emergency Locksmith Service** ☎ 312/666-2929.

PARKING

Most of Chicago's streets have metered parking, but during peak hours it's hard to find a spot. Most meters take quarters, buying as little as 5 minutes in high-traffic areas, up to an hour in less crowded neighborhoods. Parking lots and garages are plentiful downtown, but they're expensive. You could pay anywhere from $13 for the day in a municipal lot to $24 for three hours in a private lot. Some neighborhoods, such as the area of Lake View known as Wrigleyville, enforce restricted parking and will tow cars without permits. You won't really find parking lots in the neighborhoods. Many major thoroughfares restrict parking during peak travel hours, generally 9–11 AM heading toward downtown and 4–6 PM heading away. **Read street signs carefully** to determine whether a parking spot is legal. During the winter snow days, cars parked in designated "snow route areas" will be towed. There's a $30 fine plus the cost of towing the car. In sum, Chicago isn't the most car-friendly place for visitors. Unless it's a necessity, it's best to forget renting a car and use public transportation.

ROAD CONDITIONS

Chicago drivers can be reckless, zipping through red lights and breaking posted speed limits. **Check both ways after a light turns green** to make sure that the cross traffic has stopped.

Rush hours are 6:30–9:30 AM and 4–7 PM. There are always bottlenecks on the expressways, particularly where the Edens and Kennedy merge, and downtown on the Dan Ryan from 22nd Street into the Loop. Sometimes anything around the airport is rough. There are electronic signs on the expressways that post updates on the congestion. Additionally, summertime is high time for construction on highways and inner-city roads. Drive with patience.

RULES OF THE ROAD

Speed limits in Chicago vary, but on most city roads it's 35 mph. Most interstate highways, except in congested areas, have a speed limit of 65 mph. In Chicago, you may turn right at a red light after stopping if there's no oncoming traffic and no posted restrictions. When in doubt, wait for the green. Cameras have been installed at certain intersections in the city to catch drivers who run red lights. There are many one-way streets in Chicago, particularly in and around the Loop, so be alert to signs and other cars. Illinois drunk-driving laws are quite strict. Anyone caught driving with a blood-alcohol content of .08 will automatically have his or her license seized and be issued a ticket, and authorities in home states will be notified. Those with Illinois drivers' licenses can have their li-

censes suspended for three months on the very first offense.

Passengers are required to wear seat belts. Always strap children under age eight into approved child-safety seats.

It's illegal to use hand-held cellular phones in the city, but there aren't any restrictions in the suburbs. Headlights are compulsory if you're using windshield wipers. Radar detectors are legal in Illinois.

CHILDREN IN CHICAGO

There's no need to hire a babysitter on this trip—Chicago offers plenty of diversion for youngsters, so be sure to plan ahead and **involve your kids** as you outline your trip. Museums have special rates for children, and Navy Pier—with its games, IMAX movies, and Ferris wheel—is like an amusement park in the middle of the city. Many restaurants provide children's menus. When packing, include items that will keep your children busy en route. On sightseeing days try to schedule activities of special interest to your children. When you arrive, pick up a copy of *Chicago Parent,* a monthly publication with event and resource listings, available free at locations throughout the city. The Web site, www. chicagoparent.com, has an online calendar of children's activities in and around the city. *Fodor's Around Chicago with Kids* (available in bookstores everywhere) can help you plan your days together. If you're renting a car, don't forget to arrange for a car seat when you reserve.

🚩 Local Information *Chicago Parent* ✉ 139 S. Oak Park Ave., Oak Park 60302 ☎ 708/386–5555 ⊕ www.chicagoparent.com.

BABYSITTING

Sitters from the American Registry for Nannies and Sitters range from 18 years of age on up to grandmotherly. Advance reservations are recommended, especially during holidays.

🚩 Agencies American Registry for Nannies and Sitters ☎ 866/626–6939 or 312/475–1515 ⊕ www. american-registry.com.

FLYING

Experts agree that it's a good idea to use safety seats aloft for children weighing less than 40 pounds. Airlines set their own policies: if you use a safety seat, U.S. carriers usually require that the child be ticketed, even if he or she is young enough to ride free, because the seats must be strapped into regular seats. And even if you pay the full adult fare for the seat, it may be worth it, especially on longer trips. Do **check your airline's policy about using safety seats during takeoff and landing.** Safety seats are not allowed everywhere in the plane, so get your seat assignments as early as possible.

When reserving, request children's meals or a freestanding bassinet (not available at all airlines) if you need them. But note that bulkhead seats, where you must sit to use the bassinet, may lack an overhead bin or storage space on the floor.

LODGING

Most hotels in Chicago allow children under a certain age to stay in their parents' room at no extra charge, but others charge for them as extra adults; be sure to find out the cutoff age for children's discounts. Many hotels feature an indoor heated pool, have pay-as-you-go in-room video game rentals, and are near popular kid-friendly restaurants. Embassy Suites Downtown Lakefront is steps away from Navy Pier. Amenities include complimentary made-to-order breakfasts, and each suite has two televisions and Nintendo. The Four Seasons and the Ritz Carlton offer free extra beds and cribs, complimentary use of the swimming pool and, upon check-in, kids get a free gift.
🏠 Best Choices **Best Western River North** ✉ 125 W. Ohio St., 60610 ☏ 800/727-0800 or 312/467-0800. **Embassy Suites Downtown Lakefront** ✉ 511 N. Columbus Dr., 60611 ☏ 888/903-8884 or 312/836-5900. **Four Seasons Hotel Chicago** ✉ 120 E. Delaware Pl., 60611 ☏ 312/280-8800. **The Ritz-Carlton Chicago** ✉ 160 E. Pearson St., 60611 ☏ 312/266-1000.

SIGHTS & ATTRACTIONS

Places that are especially appealing to children are indicated by a rubber-duckie icon (🐤) in the margin.

The top five visitor attractions for kids are Navy Pier (which has a Ferris wheel, merry-go-round, the Chicago Children's

Museum, and other rides), Millennium Park, the Art Institute, the Sears Tower or the John Hancock building, and Chicago's architecture. The Sears Tower has a kids' scavenger hunt.

CONCIERGES

Concierges, found in many hotels, can help you with theater tickets and dinner reservations: a good one with connections may be able to get you seats for a hot show or prime-time dinner reservations at the restaurant of the moment. You can also turn to your hotel's concierge for help with travel arrangements, sightseeing plans, services ranging from aromatherapy to zipper repair, and emergencies. **Always tip** a concierge who has been of assistance (⇨ Tipping).

CONSUMER PROTECTION

If you have any trouble with any shopping scams, contact the Illinois Bureau of Consumer Fraud.

Whether you're shopping for gifts or purchasing travel services, **pay with a major credit card** whenever possible, so you can cancel payment or get reimbursed if there's a problem (and you can provide documentation). If you're doing business with a particular company for the first time, contact your local Better Business Bureau and the attorney general's offices in your state and (for U.S. businesses) the company's home state as well. Have any complaints been filed? Finally, if you're buying a package or tour, always consider travel insurance that includes default coverage (⇨ Insurance).
🏠 BBBs **Better Business Bureau Chicago** ✉ 330 N. Wabash Ave., Suite 2006, Chicago, IL 60611 ☏ 312/832-0500 🖷 312/832-9985 ⊕ www.chicago. bbb.org. **Council of Better Business Bureaus** ✉ 4200 Wilson Blvd., Suite 800, Arlington, VA 22203 ☏ 703/276-0100 🖷 703/525-8277 ⊕ www. bbb.org. **Illinois Bureau of Fraud** ☏ 800/386-5438 ⊕ www.ag.state.il.us/about/hotlines.html.

CUSTOMS & DUTIES

IN AUSTRALIA

Australian residents who are 18 or older may bring home A$900 worth of souvenirs and gifts (including jewelry), 250 cigarettes or 250 grams of cigars or other tobacco products, and 2.25 liters of alcohol (including wine, beer, and spirits). Residents under 18 may bring back A$450 worth of goods. If any of these individual allowances are exceeded, you must pay duty for the entire amount (of the group of products in which the allowance was exceeded). Members of the same family traveling together may pool their allowances. Prohibited items include meat products. Seeds, plants, and fruits need to be declared upon arrival.

🛂 **Australian Customs Service** ⌁ Customs House, 10 Cooks River Dr., Sydney International Airport, Sydney, NSW 2020 ☎ 02/6275-6666 or 1300/363263, 02/8334-7444 or 1800/020-504 quarantine-inquiry line 📠 02/8339-6714 ⊕ www.customs.gov.au.

IN CANADA

Canadian residents who have been out of Canada for at least seven days may bring in C$750 worth of goods duty-free. If you've been away fewer than seven days but more than 48 hours, the duty-free allowance drops to C$200. If your trip lasts 24 to 48 hours, the allowance is C$50; if the goods are worth more than C$50, you must pay full duty on all of the goods. You may not pool allowances with family members. Goods claimed under the C$750 exemption may follow you by mail; those claimed under the lesser exemptions must accompany you. Alcohol and tobacco products may be included in the seven-day and 48-hour exemptions but not in the 24-hour exemption. If you meet the age requirements of the province or territory through which you reenter Canada, you may bring in, duty-free, 1.5 liters of wine *or* 1.14 liters (40 imperial ounces) of liquor *or* 24 12-ounce cans or bottles of beer or ale. Also, if you meet the local age requirement for tobacco products, you may bring in, duty-free, 200 cigarettes, 50 cigars or cigarillos, and 200 grams of tobacco. You may have to pay a minimum duty on tobacco products, regardless of whether or not you exceed your personal exemption. Check ahead of time with the Canada Border Services Agency or the Department of

Agriculture for policies regarding meat products, seeds, plants, and fruits.

You may send an unlimited number of gifts (only one gift per recipient, however) worth up to C$60 each duty-free to Canada. Label the package UNSOLICITED GIFT—VALUE UNDER $60. Alcohol and tobacco are excluded.

🛂 **Canada Border Services Agency** ⌁ Customs Information Services, 191 Laurier Ave. W, 15th fl., Ottawa, Ontario K1A 0L5 ☎ 800/461-9999 in Canada, 204/983-3500, 506/636-5064 ⊕ www.cbsa.gc.ca.

IN NEW ZEALAND

All homeward-bound residents may bring back NZ$700 worth of souvenirs and gifts; passengers may not pool their allowances, and children can claim only the concession on goods intended for their own use. For those 17 or older, the duty-free allowance also includes 4.5 liters of wine or beer; one 1,125-ml bottle of spirits; and either 200 cigarettes, 250 grams of tobacco, 50 cigars, *or* a combination of the three up to 250 grams. Meat products, seeds, plants, and fruits must be declared upon arrival to the Agricultural Services Department.

🛂 **New Zealand Customs** ⌁ Head office: The Customhouse, 17–21 Whitmore St., Box 2218, Wellington ☎ 09/300-5399 or 0800/428-786 ⊕ www.customs.govt.nz.

IN THE U.K.

From countries outside the European Union, including the United States, you may bring home, duty-free, 200 cigarettes, 50 cigars, 100 cigarillos, or 250 grams of tobacco; 1 liter of spirits or 2 liters of fortified or sparkling wine or liqueurs; 2 liters of still table wine; 60 ml of perfume; 250 ml of toilet water; plus £145 worth of other goods, including gifts and souvenirs. Prohibited items include meat and dairy products, seeds, plants, and fruits.

🛂 **HM Customs and Excise** ⌁ Portcullis House, 21 Cowbridge Rd. E, Cardiff CF11 9SS ☎ 0845/010-9000 or 0208/929-0152 advice service, 0208/929-6731 or 0208/910-3602 complaints ⊕ www.hmce.gov.uk.

DISABILITIES & ACCESSIBILITY

The Chicago Mayor's Office for People with Disabilities maintains an information and referral service for disability resources. The office publishes guides, including *Access Chicago,* which contains more than 200 pages of detailed information about Chicago's airports, accessible ground transportation, hotels, restaurants, sights, shopping, and resources regarding medical equipment and supplies.

🖫 **Local Resources Mayor's Office for People with Disabilities** ⊠ 121 N. LaSalle St., Room 1104 ☎ 312/744-7050, 312/744-4964 TTY ⊕ http://egov. cityofchicago.org.

LODGING

Despite the Americans with Disabilities Act, the definition of accessibility seems to differ from hotel to hotel. Some properties may be accessible by ADA standards for people with mobility problems but not for people with hearing or vision impairments, for example.

If you have mobility problems, ask for the lowest floor on which accessible services are offered. If you have a hearing impairment, check whether the hotel has devices to alert you visually to the ring of the telephone, a knock at the door, and a fire/ emergency alarm. Some hotels provide these devices without charge. Discuss your needs with hotel personnel if this equipment isn't available, so that a staff member can personally alert you in the event of an emergency.

If you're bringing a guide dog, get authorization ahead of time and write down the name of the person with whom you spoke.

Hotels in every price range offer special facilities for people who use wheelchairs, including ramps and specially designed rooms with roll-in showers. Hotels of all price ranges offer these amenities, including **Four Seasons Hotel Chicago, Hilton Chicago, Hampton Inn & Suites Chicago Downtown,** and **Days Inn Lincoln Park North.**

RESERVATIONS

When discussing accessibility with an operator or reservations agent, ask hard questions. Are there any stairs, inside *or* out? Are there grab bars next to the toilet *and* in the shower/tub? How wide is the doorway to the room? To the bathroom?

For the most extensive facilities meeting the latest legal specifications, opt for newer accommodations. If you reserve through a toll-free number, consider also calling the hotel's local number to confirm the information from the central reservations office. Get confirmation in writing when you can.

SIGHTS & ATTRACTIONS

Chicago's major sights and attractions all provide accessibility to people using wheelchairs, including ramps and bathrooms. Most stores and restaurants also welcome disabled visitors by providing access.

TRANSPORTATION

The U.S. Department of Transportation Aviation Consumer Protection Division's online publication *New Horizons: Information for the Air Traveler with a Disability* offers advice for travelers with a disability, and outlines basic rights. Visit DisabilityInfo.gov for general information.

Although some subway stations might be difficult to reach, many Chicago Transit Authority (CTA) buses are specially equipped to handle the specific needs of customers who are physically challenged.

At O'Hare Airport, American and United airlines have specially designated lounges to provide assistance to travelers with disabilities. If needed, **ask for a wheelchair escort,** available from all airlines at O'Hare. O'Hare's CTA Blue Line train station is equipped with an elevator; downtown stops with elevators are at Clark/Lake and Jackson Boulevard.

The RTA Travel Information Center's Chicago Transit Map includes information on more than 70 lift-equipped bus routes and accessible subway and El stations. The CTA offers a paratransit program with curb-to-curb service for those unable to use conventional mainline bus or rail services. To use this service, out-of-town visitors must make travel arrangements at least one week in advance.

If you're renting a car, Alamo, Avis, Hertz, and National all rent cars with hand controls, but they require advance notice.

Handicap parking cards are valid from state to state.

⚡ Information & Complaints Aviation Consumer Protection Division (⇨ Air Travel) for airline-related problems; ⊕ airconsumer.ost.dot.gov/publications/horizons.htm for airline travel advice and rights. **Departmental Office of Civil Rights** ✉ For general inquiries, U.S. Department of Transportation, S-30, 400 7th St. SW, Room 10215, Washington, DC 20590 🖷 202/366-4648, 202/366-8538 TTY 🖶 202/366-9371 ⊕ www.dotcr.ost.dot.gov. **Disability Rights Section** ✉ NYAV, U.S. Department of Justice, Civil Rights Division, 950 Pennsylvania Ave. NW, Washington, DC 20530 🖷 ADA information line 202/514-0301, 800/514-0301, 202/514-0383 TTY, 800/514-0383 TTY ⊕ www.ada.gov. **U.S. Department of Transportation Hotline** 🖷 For disability-related air-travel problems, 800/778-4838 or 800/455-9880 TTY.

⚡ Transportation Information Chicago Transit Authority paratransit program 🖷 312/432-7025, 312/432-7140, 312/836-4949 TTY. **RTA Travel Information Center** 🖷 312/836-7000, 312/432-7025 TTY ⊕ www.transitchicago.com/maps/accessible.html.

TRAVEL AGENCIES

In the United States, the Americans with Disabilities Act requires that travel firms serve the needs of all travelers. Some agencies specialize in working with people with disabilities.

⚡ Travelers with Mobility Problems Access Adventures/B. Roberts Travel ✉ 1876 East Ave., Rochester, NY 14610 🖷 800/444-6540 ⊕ www.brobertstravel.com, run by a former physical-rehabilitation counselor. **Accessible Vans of America** ✉ 37 Daniel Rd. W, Fairfield, NJ 07004 🖷 877/282-8267, 888/282-8267, 973/808-9709 reservations 🖶 973/808-9713 ⊕ www.accessiblevans.com. **CareVacations** ✉ No. 5, 5110-50 Ave., Leduc, Alberta, Canada, T9E 6V4 🖷 780/986-6404 or 877/478-7827 🖶 780/986-8332 ⊕ www.carevacations.com, for group tours and cruise vacations. **Flying Wheels Travel** ✉ 143 W. Bridge St., Box 382, Owatonna, MN 55060 🖷 507/451-5005 🖶 507/451-1685 ⊕ www.flyingwheelstravel.com.

DISCOUNTS & DEALS

Be a smart shopper and compare all your options before making decisions. A plane ticket bought with a promotional coupon from travel clubs, coupon books, and direct-mail offers or purchased on the Internet may not be cheaper than the least expensive fare from a discount ticket agency. And always keep in mind that what you get is just as important as what you save.

To save money on sightseeing, **buy a Chicago CityPass** (⊕ citypass.com/city/chicago), which costs $49.50. The passes are good for nine days from the day of first use and include admission to the Art Institute of Chicago, the Field Museum, the Museum of Science and Industry, the Adler Planetarium, the Shedd Aquarium, and the Sears Tower Skydeck. You can buy the pass at any one of the participating attractions. The **Go Chicago Card** (🖷 617/742-5950 ⊕ gochicagocard.com) is good for 25 attractions and shopping, dining, and hotel discounts. The card can be purchased as a one- or a multiday pass with prices beginning at $49. Each card comes with a guidebook.

For savings on bus fare, **purchase a Visitor Pass** for $5 per day. It's good for unlimited rides. **Chicago Greeter** and **Insta-Greeter** (✉ Visitor Information Center at Chicago Cultural Center, 77 E. Randolph St. 🖷 312/744-8000 ⊕ www.chicagogreeter.com) are two free city services that match knowledgeable Chicagoans with visitors for tours of various sights and neighborhoods. Chicago Greeter is for small groups and requires advance registration. Insta-Greeter is available Friday and Saturday 10–4 and Sunday 11–4. Look for weekend package deals, itinerary ideas, and other special incentives at ⊕ www.877chicago.com or (877/244–2246).

DISCOUNT RESERVATIONS

To save money, look into discount reservations services with Web sites and toll-free numbers, which use their buying power to get a better price on hotels, airline tickets (⇨ Air Travel), even car rentals. When booking a room, always **call the hotel's local toll-free number** (if one is available) rather than the central reservations number—you'll often get a better price. Always ask about special packages or corporate rates.

⚡ Hotel Rooms 877Chicago 🖷 877/244-2246 ⊕ www.877chicago.com. **Accommodations Express** 🖷 800/444-7666 or 800/277-1064. **Central Reser-**

vation Service (CRS) ☏ 800/555-7555 or 800/548-3311 ⊕ www.crshotels.com. **Hotels.com** ☏ 800/246-8357 ⊕ www.hotels.com. **Quikbook** ☏ 800/789-9887 ⊕ www.quikbook.com. **Steigenberger Reservation Service** ☏ 800/223-5652 ⊕ www.srsworldhotels.com. **Turbotrip.com** ☏ 800/473-7829 ⊕ w3.turbotrip.com.

PACKAGE DEALS

Don't confuse packages and guided tours. When you buy a package, you travel on your own, just as though you had planned the trip yourself. Fly/drive packages, which combine airfare and car rental, are often a good deal. In cities, ask the local visitor's bureau about hotel and local transportation packages that include tickets to major museum exhibits or other special events.

GAY & LESBIAN TRAVEL

Gay and lesbian travelers will find Chicago a very welcoming, progressive city with a vibrant gay scene. Bars, coffeehouses, and publications serving the interests of gays and lesbians exist citywide, particularly in the adjoining neighborhoods of Lake View and New Town (aka "Boys Town"), bordered by Irving Park Road, Lincoln Avenue, Belmont Avenue, and Lake Shore Drive, and Andersonville, which is bordered by Devon Avenue, Ridge Avenue, Sheridan Road, and Lawrence Avenue.

Pick up *Gay Chicago Magazine* (☏ 773/327-7271 ⊕ www.gaychicagomag.com) to find out more information on the gay and lesbian scene in Chicago. The *Windy City Media Group* (☏ 773/871-7610 ⊕ www.wctimes.com) publishes gay and lesbian papers specifically on nightlife (*Nightspots*), the African-American community (*Blacklines*), and the Latin-American community (*En La Vida*).

For details about the gay and lesbian scene, consult *Fodor's Gay Guide to the USA* (available in bookstores everywhere). ▣ Gay- & Lesbian-Friendly Travel Agencies **Different Roads Travel** ✉ 1017 N. LaCienega Blvd., Suite 308, West Hollywood, CA 90069 ☏ 310/289-6000 or 800/429-8747 (Ext. 14 for both) ☏ 310/855-0323 ✉ lgernert@tzell.com. **Kennedy Travel** ✉ 130 W. 42nd St., Suite 401, New York, NY 10036 ☏ 800/237-7433 or 212/840-8659 ☏ 212/730-2269

⊕ www.kennedytravel.com. **Now, Voyager** ✉ 4406 18th St., San Francisco, CA 94114 ☏ 415/626-1169 or 800/255-6951 ☏ 415/626-8626 ⊕ www.nowvoyager.com. **Skylink Travel and Tour/Flying Dutchmen Travel** ✉ 1455 N. Dutton Ave., Suite A, Santa Rosa, CA 95401 ☏ 707/546-9888 or 800/225-5759 ☏ 707/636-0951, serving lesbian travelers.

HOLIDAYS

Major national holidays are New Year's Day (Jan. 1); Martin Luther King Jr. Day (3rd Mon. in Jan.); Presidents' Day (3rd Mon. in Feb.); Memorial Day (last Mon. in May); Independence Day (July 4); Labor Day (1st Mon. in Sept.); Columbus Day (2nd Mon. in Oct.); Thanksgiving Day (4th Thurs. in Nov.); Christmas Eve and Christmas Day (Dec. 24 and 25); and New Year's Eve (Dec. 31).

INSURANCE

The most useful travel-insurance plan is a comprehensive policy that includes coverage for trip cancellation and interruption, default, trip delay, and medical expenses (with a waiver for preexisting conditions).

Without insurance you'll lose all or most of your money if you cancel your trip, regardless of the reason. Default insurance covers you if your tour operator, airline, or cruise line goes out of business—the chances of which have been increasing. Trip-delay covers expenses that arise because of bad weather or mechanical delays. Study the fine print when comparing policies.

U.K. residents can buy a travel-insurance policy valid for most vacations taken during the year in which it's purchased (but check preexisting-condition coverage).

Always **buy travel policies directly from the insurance company**; if you buy them from a cruise line, airline, or tour operator that goes out of business you probably won't be covered for the agency or operator's default, a major risk. Before making any purchase, review your existing health and home-owner's policies to find what they cover away from home. ▣ Travel Insurers In the U.S.: **Access America** ✉ 2805 N. Parham Rd., Richmond, VA 23294 ☏ 800/284-8300 ☏ 804/673-1469 or 800/346-9265 ⊕ www.accessamerica.com. **Travel Guard International** ✉ 1145 Clark St., Stevens Point, WI

54481 ☎ 800/826-1300 or 715/345-1041 📠 800/
955-8785 or 715/345-1990 ⊕ www.travelguard.com.

FOR INTERNATIONAL TRAVELERS

For information on customs restrictions, *see* Customs & Duties.

CAR RENTAL

When picking up a rental car, non-U.S. residents need a reservation voucher for any prepaid reservations that were made in the traveler's home country, a passport, a driver's license, and a travel policy that covers each driver.

CAR TRAVEL

In Chicago, gas stations are plentiful. Most stay open late (24 hours along large highways and in big cities), except in rural areas, where Sunday hours are limited and where you may drive long stretches without a refueling opportunity. Highways are well paved. Interstate highways—limited-access, multilane highways whose numbers are prefixed by "I–"—are the fastest routes. Interstates with three-digit numbers encircle urban areas, which may have other limited-access expressways, freeways, and parkways as well. Tolls may be levied on limited-access highways, called tollways. These tollways snake around the outskirts of the city. I–294 runs north and south between Wisconsin and Indiana. I–90 runs northwest to western Wisconsin, including Madison and Wisconsin Dells. I–88 runs east–west and goes from Eisenhower to I–55. Traffic on all is sometimes just as congested as on the regular expressways. Most toll gates are unmanned, so bring lots of change if you don't have an I-Pass, which are sometimes included with rental cars. Even though tolls are double without the I-Pass, it's not cost-effective to purchase one for a couple of days. So-called U.S. highways and state highways are not necessarily limited-access but may have several lanes.

Along larger highways, roadside stops with restrooms, fast-food restaurants, and sundries stores are well spaced. State police and tow trucks patrol major highways and lend assistance. If your car breaks down on an interstate, pull onto the shoulder and wait for help, or have your passengers wait while you walk to an emergency phone (available in most states). If you carry a cell phone, dial 911, noting your location using the small green roadside mileage markers.

Driving in the United States is on the right. Do obey speed limits posted along roads and highways. Watch for lower limits in small towns and on back roads. Illinois law requires front-seat passengers to wear seat belts. On weekdays between 6 and 10 AM and again between 4 and 7 PM expect heavy traffic.

Bookstores, gas stations, convenience stores, and rest stops sell maps (about $3) and multiregion road atlases (about $10).

CONSULATES & EMBASSIES

🞄 Australia ✉ 123 N. Wacker St., Suite 1330, 60606 ☎ 312/419-1480 📠 312/419-1499 ⊕ www.dfat.gov.au.

🞄 Canada ✉ 2 Prudential Plaza, 180 N. Stetson, 60601 ☎ 312/616-1860 📠 312/616-1878 ⊕ www.chicago.gc.ca.

🞄 New Zealand ✉ 8600 Bryn Mawr Ave., Suite 500N, 60631 ☎ 773/714-8669 📠 773/714-9483 ⊕ www.mfat.govt.nz.

🞄 United Kingdom ✉ Wrigley Bldg., 400 N. Michigan Ave., 13th fl., 60611 ☎ 312/970-3800 📠 312/970-3852 ⊕ www.britainusa.com/chicago.

CURRENCY

The dollar is the basic unit of U.S. currency. It has 100 cents. Coins are the copper penny (1¢); the silvery nickel (5¢), dime (10¢), quarter (25¢), and half-dollar (50¢); and the golden $1 coin, replacing a now-rare silver dollar. Bills are denominated $1, $5, $10, $20, $50, and $100, all mostly green and identical in size; designs and background tints vary. In addition, you may come across a $2 bill, but the chances are slim. The exchange rate at this writing is US$1.81 per British pound, $1.20 per Euro, 81¢ per Canadian dollar, 77¢ per Australian dollar, and 71¢ per New Zealand dollar.

ELECTRICITY

The U.S. standard is AC, 110 volts/60 cycles. Plugs have two flat pins set parallel to each other.

EMERGENCIES

For police, fire, or ambulance, **dial 911** (0 in rural areas).

INSURANCE

Britons and Australians need extra medical coverage when traveling overseas.

🗊 Insurance Information In the U.K.: **Association of British Insurers** ✉ 51 Gresham St., London EC2V 7HQ ☎ 020/7600-3333 🖷 020/7696-8999 ⊕ www. abi.org.uk. In Australia: **Insurance Council of Australia** ✉ Level 3, 56 Pitt St. Sydney, NSW 2000 ☎ 02/9253-5100 🖷 02/9253-5111 ⊕ www.ica.com. au. In Canada: **RBC Insurance** ✉ 6880 Financial Dr., Mississauga, Ontario L5N 7Y5 ☎ 800/387-4357 or 905/816-2559 🖷 888/298-6458 ⊕ www. rbcinsurance.com. In New Zealand: **Insurance Council of New Zealand** ✉ Level 7, 111-115 Customhouse Quay, Box 474, Wellington ☎ 04/472-5230 🖷 04/473-3011 ⊕ www.icnz.org.nz.

MAIL & SHIPPING

You can buy stamps and aerograms and send letters and parcels in post offices. Stamp-dispensing machines can occasionally be found in airports, bus and train stations, office buildings, drugstores, and the like. You can also deposit mail in the stout, dark blue, steel bins at strategic locations everywhere and in the mail chutes of large buildings; pickup schedules are posted. You can deposit packages at public collection boxes as long as the parcels are affixed with proper postage and weigh less than one pound. Packages weighing one or more pounds must be taken to a post office or handed to a postal carrier.

For mail sent within the United States, you need a 39¢ stamp for first-class letters weighing up to 1 ounce (23¢ for each additional ounce) and 23¢ for postcards. You pay 80¢ for 1-ounce airmail letters and 70¢ for airmail postcards to most other countries; to Canada and Mexico, you need a 60¢ stamp for a 1-ounce letter and 50¢ for a postcard. An aerogram—a single sheet of lightweight blue paper that folds into its own envelope, stamped for overseas airmail—costs 70¢.

To receive mail on the road, have it sent c/o General Delivery at your destination's main post office (use the correct five-digit ZIP code). You must pick up mail in person within 30 days and show a driver's license or passport.

PASSPORTS & VISAS

When traveling internationally, carry your passport even if you don't need one (it's always the best form of ID) and **make two photocopies of the data page** (one for someone at home and another for you, carried separately from your passport). If you lose your passport, promptly call the nearest embassy or consulate and the local police.

Visitor visas aren't necessary for Canadian or European Union citizens, or for citizens of Australia who are staying fewer than 90 days.

🗊 Australian Citizens **Passports Australia** ☎ 131-232 ⊕ www.passports.gov.au. **United States Consulate General** ✉ MLC Centre, Level 59, 19-29 Martin Pl., Sydney, NSW 2000 ☎ 02/9373-9200, 1902/941-641 fee-based visa-inquiry line ⊕ usembassy-australia.state.gov/sydney. 🗊 Canadian Citizens **Passport Office** ✉ To mail in applications: 70 Cremazie St., Gatineau, Québec J8Y 3P2 ☎ 800/567-6868, 866/255-7655 TTY ⊕ www. ppt.gc.ca. 🗊 New Zealand Citizens **New Zealand Passports Office** ✉ For applications and information, Level 3, Boulcott House, 47 Boulcott St., Wellington ☎ 0800/22-5050 or 04/474-8100 ⊕ www. passports.govt.nz. **Embassy of the United States** ✉ 29 Fitzherbert Terr., Thorndon, Wellington ☎ 04/462-6000 ⊕ usembassy.org.nz. **U.S. Consulate General** ✉ Citibank Bldg., 3rd fl., 23 Customs St. E, Auckland ☎ 09/303-2724 ⊕ usembassy. org.nz. 🗊 U.K. Citizens **U.K. Passport Service** ☎ 0870/521-0410 ⊕ www.passport.gov.uk. **American Consulate General** ✉ Danesfort House, 223 Stranmillis Rd., Belfast, Northern Ireland BT9 5GR ☎ 028/9038-6100 🖷 028/9068-1301 ⊕ www.usembassy. org.uk. **American Embassy** ✉ For visa and immigration information or to submit a visa application via mail (enclose an SASE), Consular Information Unit, 24 Grosvenor Sq., London W1A 2LQ ☎ 090/5544-4546 or 090/6820-0290 for visa information (per-minute charges), 0207/499-9000 main switchboard ⊕ www.usembassy.org.uk.

TELEPHONES

All U.S. telephone numbers consist of a three-digit area code and a seven-digit local number. Within many local calling areas, you dial only the seven-digit number. Within some area codes, you must dial "1" first for calls outside the local area. To call between area-code regions, dial "1" then all 10 digits; the same goes for calls to numbers prefixed by "800," "888," "866," and "877"—all toll-free. For calls to numbers preceded by "900" you must pay—usually dearly.

For international calls, dial "011" followed by the country code and the local number. For help, dial "0" and ask for an overseas operator. The country code is 61 for Australia, 64 for New Zealand, 44 for the United Kingdom. Calling Canada is the same as calling within the United States, although you might not be able to get through on some toll-free numbers. Most local phone books list country codes and U.S. area codes. The country code for the United States is 1.

For operator assistance, dial "0." To obtain someone's phone number, call directory assistance at 555–1212 or occasionally 411 (free at many public phones). To have the person you're calling foot the bill, phone collect; dial "0" instead of "1" before the 10-digit number.

At pay phones, instructions often are posted. Usually you insert coins in a slot (usually 25¢–50¢ for local calls) and wait for a steady tone before dialing. When you call long-distance, the operator tells you how much to insert; prepaid phone cards, widely available in various denominations, are easier. Call the number on the back, punch in the card's personal identification number when prompted, then dial your number.

MAIL & SHIPPING
Chicago post offices are open 8–5 during the week and 8–1 on Saturday. Some downtown locations open as early as 7. Post offices are closed on Sunday. There are several locations, some called postal stores, in the downtown area.
🔏 **Post Offices Cardiss Collins Postal Store** ✉ 433 W. Harrison St., 60607 ☎ 800/725-8777. **Nancy B. Jefferson (Midwest Station)** ✉ 116 S. Western, 60612 ☎ 800/725-8777. **Wacker Drive Postal Store**

✉ 233 S. Wacker Dr., Suite L1a, 60606 ☎ 800/725-8777.
🔏 **Major Services FedEx** ☎ 800/463-3339. **UPS** ☎ 800/742-5877.

MEDIA
NEWSPAPERS & MAGAZINES
Chicago is served by two daily metro newspapers, the *Chicago Tribune* and the *Chicago Sun-Times*. Also be sure to check out the two alternative newsweeklies, *Chicago Reader,* which comes out on Thursday, and *New City,* which is available on Wednesday. Two features-oriented monthly periodicals, *Chicago Magazine* and *Chicago Social,* are sold at most newsstands.

RADIO & TELEVISION
Local radio stations include: **Q101 101.1 FM** and **WXRT 93.1 FM** for alternative rock; **WFMT 98.7 FM** and **WDRV 97.1 FM** for classic rock; **WFMT 98.7 FM** for classical music; **WUSN 99.5 FM** for country; **WCKG 105.9 FM** and **WLUP 97.9 FM** for rock; **WGCI 107.5 FM** for R&B; **B-96 96.3 FM** for Top-40 hits; and **WNUA 95.5 FM** for jazz. The National Public Radio affiliate is **WBEZ 91.5 FM. WBBM 780 AM** and **WMAQ 670 AM** are both news stations. For talk radio and local sports turn to **WGN 720 AM.**

Local television stations include **WBBM Channel 2** (CBS), **WMAQ Channel 5** (NBC), **WLS Channel 7** (ABC), **WGN Channel 9** (WB), and **WFLD Channel 32** (Fox). **WTTW Channel 11** and **WYCC Channel 20** are public television stations.

MONEY MATTERS
Costs in Chicago are quite reasonable compared to other large cities such as San Francisco and New York. Restaurants, events, and parking costs are markedly higher in the Loop than in any other area of the city.

Prices throughout this guide are given for adults. Substantially reduced fees are almost always available for children, students, and senior citizens. For information on taxes, *see* Taxes.

ATMS

ATMs are plentiful. You can find them in banks, grocery stores, and hotels, as well as at some drug stores, gas stations, and convenience stores.

CREDIT CARDS

Throughout this guide, the following abbreviations are used: **AE,** American Express; **D,** Discover; **DC,** Diners Club; **MC,** MasterCard; and **V,** Visa.

🔁 Reporting Lost Cards **American Express** ☎ 800/992-3404. **Diners Club** ☎ 800/234-6377. **Discover** ☎ 800/347-2683. **MasterCard** ☎ 800/ 622-7747. **Visa** ☎ 800/847-2911.

PACKING

In general, Chicago's out-and-about look is casual—jeans, a polished top, and comfortable shoes should be fine for touring around the city. The weather can change abruptly, so it's a good idea to dress in layers. Summers can be very hot and winters very cold and windy—hat, gloves, a scarf, and a warm coat are vital. Don't forget an umbrella.

For dining out, most elegant restaurants in the city require a shirt and tie for men and a dressy look for women. For mass, church, or synagogue services, people usually dress in nice slacks or skirts or dresses. Men do not always wear a suit or a sport jacket, but rarely wear jeans.

In your carry-on luggage, pack an extra pair of eyeglasses or contact lenses and enough of any medication you take to last a few days longer than the entire trip. You may also ask your doctor to write a spare prescription using the drug's generic name, as brand names may vary from country to country. In luggage to be checked, **never pack prescription drugs, valuables, or undeveloped film.** And don't forget to carry with you the addresses of offices that handle refunds of lost traveler's checks. Check *Fodor's How to Pack* (available at online retailers and bookstores everywhere) for more tips.

To avoid customs and security delays, carry medications in their original packaging. Don't pack any sharp objects in your carry-on luggage, including knives of any size or material, scissors, nail clippers, and corkscrews, or anything else that might arouse suspicion.

To avoid having your checked luggage chosen for hand inspection, don't cram bags full. The U.S. Transportation Security Administration suggests packing shoes on top and placing personal items you don't want touched in clear plastic bags.

CHECKING LUGGAGE

You're allowed to carry aboard one bag and one personal article, such as a purse or a laptop computer. Make sure what you carry on fits under your seat or in the overhead bin. Get to the gate early, so you can board as soon as possible, before the overhead bins fill up.

Baggage allowances vary by carrier, destination, and ticket class. On international flights, you're usually allowed to check two bags weighing up to 70 pounds (32 kilograms) each, although a few airlines allow checked bags of up to 88 pounds (40 kilograms) in first class. Some international carriers don't allow more than 66 pounds (30 kilograms) per bag in business class and 44 pounds (20 kilograms) in economy. If you're flying to or through the United Kingdom, your luggage cannot exceed 70 pounds (32 kilograms) per bag. On domestic flights, the limit is usually 50 to 70 pounds (23 to 32 kilograms) per bag. In general, carry-on bags shouldn't exceed 40 pounds (18 kilograms). Most airlines won't accept bags that weigh more than 100 pounds (45 kilograms) on domestic or international flights. Expect to pay a fee for baggage that exceeds weight limits. Check baggage restrictions with your carrier before you pack.

Airline liability for baggage is limited to $2,500 per person on flights within the United States. On international flights it amounts to $9.07 per pound or $20 per kilogram for checked baggage (roughly $640 per 70-pound bag), with a maximum of $634.90 per piece, and $400 per passenger for unchecked baggage. You can buy additional coverage at check-in for about $10 per $1,000 of coverage, but it often excludes a rather extensive list of items, shown on your airline ticket.

Before departure, itemize your bags' contents and their worth, and label the bags with your name, address, and phone number. (If you use your home address, cover it so potential thieves can't see it readily.) Include a label inside each bag and **pack a copy of your itinerary.** At check-in, make sure each bag is correctly tagged with the destination airport's three-letter code. Because some checked bags will be opened for hand inspection, the U.S. Transportation Security Administration recommends that you leave luggage unlocked or use the plastic locks offered at check-in. TSA screeners place an inspection notice inside searched bags, which are re-sealed with a special lock.

If your bag has been searched and contents are missing or damaged, file a claim with the TSA Consumer Response Center as soon as possible. If your bags arrive damaged or fail to arrive at all, file a written report with the airline before leaving the airport.

🔳 Complaints **U.S. Transportation Security Administration Contact Center** ☎ 866/289-9673 ⊕ www.tsa.gov.

PUBLIC TRANSPORTATION

Chicago's extensive public transportation network includes rapid transit trains, buses, and a commuter rail network. The Chicago Transit Authority, or CTA, operates the rapid transit trains (the El), city buses, and suburban buses (PACE). Metra runs the commuter rail.

The Regional Transportation Authority (RTA) for northeastern Illinois oversees and coordinates the activities of the CTA and Metra. The RTA's Web site can be a useful first stop if you are planning to combine suburban and city public transit while in Chicago.

🔳 **RTA Travel Information Center** ☎ 312/836-7000 ⊕ www.rtachicago.com.

CTA: THE EL & BUSES

The Chicago Transit Authority (CTA) operates rapid transit trains and buses.

Chicago's rapid transit train system is known as the El. Each of the seven lines has a color name as well as a route name:

Blue (O'Hare–Congress–Douglas), Brown (Ravenswood), Green (Lake–Englewood–Jackson Park), Orange (Midway), Purple (Evanston), Red (Howard–Dan Ryan), Yellow (Skokie–Swift). In general, the route names indicate the first and last stop on the train. Chicagoans refer to trains both by the color and the route name. Most, but not all, rapid transit lines operate 24 hours; some stations are closed at night. The El, though very crowded during rush hours, is the quickest way to get around (unless you're coming from the suburbs, in which case the Metra is quicker but doesn't run as often). Trains run every 15 minutes, though during rush hour they run about every 10 minutes and on weekends, every 30 minutes. Pick up the brochure "Downtown Transit Sightseeing Guide" for hours, fares, and other pertinent information. In general, late-night CTA travel is not recommended. Note that the Red and Blue lines are subways; the rest are elevated. This means if you're heading to O'Hare and looking for the Blue Line, look for a stairway down, not up.

Exact fares must be paid in cash (dollar bills or coins; no change given by turnstiles on train platforms or fare boxes on buses) or by transit card. Transit cards are flimsy plastic and credit-card size and can be purchased from machines at CTA train stations as well as at Jewel and Dominicks grocery stores and currency exchanges. These easy-to-use cards are inserted into the turnstiles at CTA train stations and into machines as you board CTA buses; directions are clearly posted. Use them to transfer between CTA vehicles. To transfer between the Loop's elevated lines and the subway or between rapid transit trains and buses, you must either use a transit card with at least 30¢ stored on it, or, if you're not using a transit card, **buy a transfer when you first board.** If two CTA train lines meet, you can **transfer for free.** You can also **obtain free train-to-train transfers** from specially marked turnstiles at the Washington/State subway station or the State/Lake El station, or ask for a transfer card, good on downtown trains, at the ticket booth.

Buses generally stop on every other corner northbound and southbound (on State Street they stop at every corner). Eastbound and westbound buses generally stop on every corner. Buses from the Loop generally run north–south. Principal transfer points are on Michigan Avenue at the north side of Randolph Street for northbound buses, Adams Street and Wabash Avenue for westbound buses and the El, and State and Lake streets for southbound buses.

Buses are crowded during rush hour. Schedules vary depending on the time of day and route, and run every eight to 15 minutes, though service is less frequent on weekends, very early in the morning, and late at night. Schedules are available online at www.transitchicago.com.

Pace runs suburban buses in a six-county region; these connect with the CTA and use CTA transit cards, transfers, and passes.

CTA Fares: The CTA fare structure is as follows: the basic fare for rapid transit trains and buses is $1.75, and transfers are 25¢. Transit cards can be purchased in preset denominations of $10 ($11 worth of rides) or $20 ($22 worth of rides) at many local grocery stores, currency exchanges, and stations. You can also purchase a transit card of any denomination over $1.50 at any CTA stop. If you pay cash and do not use a transit card, you must buy a transfer when you first board the bus or train. Transfers can be used twice within a two-hour time period. Transfers between CTA train lines are free—no transfer card is needed. Transit cards may be shared.

For $5, a one-day Visitor Pass offers 24 hours of unlimited CTA riding from the time you first use it. Visitor Passes are sold at hotels, museums, and other places tourists frequent, plus all transit card booths. A two-day pass is $9, a three-day pass is $12, and a five-day pass is $18.
🚉 **CTA** ✉ Merchandise Mart, 350 N. Wells St., 60654 ☎ 888/968-7282 advance sales of visitor passes, 312/836-7000 ⊕ www.transitchicago.com.

METRA: COMMUTER TRAINS
Metra commuter trains serve the city and surrounding suburbs. The Metra Electric railroad has a line close to Lake Michigan; its trains stop in Hyde Park. The Metra commuter rail system has 11 lines to suburbs and surrounding cities including Aurora, Elgin, Joliet, and Waukegan; one line serves the North Shore suburbs, and another has a stop at McCormick Place. Trains leave from a number of downtown terminals.

Metra trains use a fare structure based on the distance you ride. A Metra weekend pass costs $5 and is valid for rides on any of the eight operating lines all day on weekends, except for the South Shore line.
🚉 **Metra information line** ☎ 312/322-6777 ⊕ www.metrarail.com.

RESTROOMS
Facilities are readily available in tourist areas and throughout the downtown malls, Navy Pier, North Pier, and in many larger department stores. For the most part, restrooms are quite clean. Along the lakefront and in the park districts, public facilities close in wintertime. Most gas stations have restrooms, though sanitation standards vary.

SAFETY
The most common crimes in public places are pickpocketing, purse snatching, jewelry theft, and gambling scams. Men: keep your wallet in a front coat or pants pocket. Women: close your purse securely and keep it close to you. Also **beware of someone jostling you and of loud arguments**; these could be ploys to distract your attention while another person grabs your wallet. **Leave unnecessary credit cards at home and hide valuables and jewelry** from view.

Although crime on CTA buses and trains has declined, several precautions can reduce the chance of your becoming a victim: look alert and purposeful; **know your route** ahead of time; have your fare ready before boarding; and **keep an eye on your purse or packages** during the ride. Avoid taking public transit late at night.

SENIOR-CITIZEN TRAVEL

The Chicago Department on Aging provides information and referrals to senior citizens 60 years of age and older. The department's Renaissance Court offers free programs for senior citizens every weekday, including exercise classes, arts and crafts, and games. Trips and tours are available at additional cost.

To qualify for age-related discounts, mention your senior-citizen status up front when booking hotel reservations (not when checking out) and before you're seated in restaurants (not when paying the bill). Be sure to have identification on hand. When renting a car, ask about promotional car-rental discounts, which can be cheaper than senior-citizen rates.

🔢 Local Resources Chicago Department on Aging ✉ 121 N. LaSalle St. ☎ 312/744-4016. Renaissance Court ✉ 8 E. Washington St. ☎ 312/744-4550.
🔢 Educational Programs Elderhostel ✉ 11 Ave. de Lafayette, Boston, MA 02111 ☎ 877/426-8056, 978/323-4141 international callers, 877/426-2167 TTY 🖥 877/426-2166 ⊕ www.elderhostel.org.

SIGHTSEEING TOURS

BOAT TOURS

Get a fresh perspective on Chicago by taking a water tour or cruise. Boat tour schedules vary by season; be sure to **call for exact times and fares**. The season usually runs from May 1 through October 1. Two cruises stand out, though they're a bit more expensive than the rest: the Chicago Architecture Foundation river cruise and a trip on *Chicago's First Lady*. The CAF tour highlights more than 50 sights. The cost is $23 weekdays, $25 on weekends including Friday and holidays; reservations are recommended.

You can get a blast from the past on the *Windy*, a 148-foot ship modeled on old-time commercial vessels. Passengers may help the crew or take a turn at the wheel during sailing cruises of Lake Michigan. The cost is $27.

You can use the Shoreline Water Taxi to see some of Chicago's favorite destinations: Sears Tower, Navy Pier, and Shedd Aquarium. The fleet of taxis makes frequent departures from 10:30 until 6 daily

from Memorial Day to Labor Day. The fare is $6. To see the city aboard a WW II amphibious, take **MetroDucks** tour. It covers a lot of land sights then splashes into Lake Michigan for another view of the city.

🔢 Boat Tours Chicago Architecture Foundation river cruise ☎ 312/922-3432 information, 312/902-1500 tickets ⊕ www.architecture.org. **Mercury Chicago Skyline Cruiseline** ☎ 312/332-1353 recorded information ⊕ www. mercuryskylinecruiseline.com/. **MetroDucks** ☎ 800/298-1506 ⊕ www.metroducks.com. **Shoreline Marine** ☎ 312/222-9328 ⊕ www. shorelinesightseeing.com. **Wendella Sightseeing Boats** ✉ 400 N. Michigan Ave. ☎ 312/337-1446 ⊕ www.wendellaboats.com. **Windy of Chicago Ltd.** ☎ 312/595-5555 ⊕ www.tallshipwindy.com.

BUS & TROLLEY TOURS

A narrated bus or trolley tour can be a good way to orient yourself among Chicago's main sights. Tours cost roughly $20 and normally last two hours. American Sightseeing offers two routes; combined, they cover the city quite thoroughly. The double-decker buses of Chicago Motor Coach Company tour downtown Chicago and the lakefront.

Chicago Trolley Charters schedules stops at all the downtown attractions. You can get on and off the open-air trolleys as you like; these tours vary in price, so call for details. The Chicago Architecture Foundation's bus tours often go farther afield, exploring everything from cemeteries to movie palaces.

🔢 Bus & Trolley Tours American Sightseeing ☎ 312/251-3100 ⊕ www.grayline.com. **Chicago Architecture Foundation** Tour Centers ✉ Santa Fe Bldg., 224 S. Michigan Ave. ✉ John Hancock Center, 875 N. Michigan Ave. ☎ 312/922-3432 ⊕ www. architecture.org. **Chicago Trolley Charters** ☎ 773/648-5000 ⊕ www.chicagotrolley.com.

FOREIGN-LANGUAGE TOURS

🔢 Foreign-Language Tours Chicago Tour Guides Institutes, Inc. ☎ 773/276-6683 ⊕ www. chicagoguide.net.

SPECIAL-INTEREST TOURS

🔢 African-American Black Coutours ☎ 773/233-8907 ⊕ www.blackcoutours.com. **Tour Black**

Chicago ☎ 773/684-9034 ⊕ www.
tourblackchicago.com.
🎧 **Architecture** ⇨ Walking Tours.
🎧 **Gangsters Untouchable Tours** ☎ 773/881-1195
⊕ www.gangstertour.com.
🎧 **Ghosts Chicago Supernatural Ghost Tours**
☎ 708/499-0300 ⊕ www.ghosttours.com.
🎧 **Horse & Carriage Rides Antique Coach and
Carriage** ☎ 773/735-9400 ⊕ www.antiquecoach-
carriage.com. **Chicago Horse & Carriage Ltd.**
☎ 312/953-9530 ⊕ www.chicagocarriage.com.
Noble Horse ☎ 312/266-7878 ⊕ www.
noblehorsechicago.com.
🎧 **Historic Neighborhoods Black Metropolis Convention and Tourism Council** ☎ 773/548-2579
⊕ www.bronzevilleonline.com/bvic.htm. **Chicago
Neighborhood Tours** ☎ 312/742-1190 ⊕ www.
chicagoneighborhoodtours.com.

WALKING TOURS

The Chicago Architecture Foundation has
by far the largest selection of guided tours,
with more than 50 itineraries covering
everything from department stores to
Frank Lloyd Wright's Oak Park buildings.
Especially popular walking tours of the
Loop are given daily throughout the year.
Chicago Greeter and InstaGreeter are two
free city services that match knowledgeable Chicagoans with visitors for tours of
various sights and neighborhoods. Friends
of the Chicago River has Saturday-morning walking tours along the river. The organization also has maps of the walking
routes, available for a small donation.
🎧 **Chicago Architecture Foundation** Tour Centers
✉ Santa Fe Bldg., 224 S. Michigan Ave. ✉ John
Hancock Center, 875 N. Michigan Ave. ☎ 312/922-
3432 ⊕ www.architecture.org. **Chicago Greeter and
InstaGreeter** ✉ Visitor Information Center at
Chicago Cultural Center, 77 E. Randolph St. ☎ 312/
744-8000 ⊕ www.chicagogreeter.com. **Friends of
the Chicago River** ✉ 407 S. Dearborn St., Suite
1580 ☎ 312/939-0490 ⊕ www.chicagoriver.org.

STUDENTS IN CHICAGO

Most museums and attractions offer special rates to persons with valid student
IDs. Ask if the special rate is not posted.
🎧 **IDs & Services STA Travel** ✉ 10 Downing St.,
New York, NY 10014 ☎ 212/627-3111, 800/777-0112
24-hr service center 🖷 212/627-3387 ⊕ www.sta.
com. **Travel Cuts** ✉ 187 College St., Toronto, Ontario M5T 1P7, Canada ☎ 800/592-2887 in U.S.,
416/979-2406 or 866/246-9762 in Canada 🖷 416/
979-8167 ⊕ www.travelcuts.com.

TAXES

At restaurants, you'll pay approximately
10% meal tax (thanks to special taxing
initiatives, some parts of town are higher
than others).

The hotel tax in Chicago is 15.39%, and
slightly less in suburban hotels.

SALES TAX

In Chicago a 9% state and county sales
tax is added to all purchases except groceries, which have a 2% tax. Sales tax is
already added into the initial price of prescription drugs.

TAXIS

You can hail a cab on just about any busy
street in Chicago. Hotel doormen will hail
a cab for you as well. Available taxis are
sometimes indicated by an illuminated
rooftop light. Chicago taxis are metered,
with fares beginning at $2.25 upon enter-
ing the cab and $1.90 for each additional
mile. A charge of $1.00 for the first addi-
tional passenger and 50¢ is made for each
additional passenger between the ages of
12 and 65. There's no extra baggage
charge. Taxi drivers expect a 15% tip.
🎧 **Taxi Companies American United Cab Co.**
☎ 773/248-7600. **Checker Taxi** ☎ 312/243-2537.
Flash Cab ☎ 773/561-1444. **Yellow Cab Co.** ☎ 312/
829-4222.

TIME

Chicago is in the Central Standard Time
zone. It's 1 hour behind New York, 2
hours ahead of Los Angeles, 6 hours
behind London, and 16 hours behind
Sydney.

TIPPING

You should tip 15% for adequate service
in restaurants and up to 20% if you feel
you've been treated well. At higher-end
restaurants, where there are more service
personnel per table who must divide the
tip, up these measures by a few percentage
points. An especially helpful wine steward
should be acknowledged with $2 or $3.
It's not necessary to tip the maître d' unless you've been done a very special favor

and you intend to visit again. Tip $1 per checked coat.

Taxi drivers, bartenders, and hairdressers expect about 15%. Bellhops and porters should get about $1 per bag; valet-parking attendants $1 or $2 (but only after they bring your car to you, not when they park it), and hotel maids about $1 to $2 per room per day of your stay. On package tours, conductors and drivers usually get about $2–$3 per day from each group member. Concierges should get tips of $5–$10 for special service.

TOURS & PACKAGES

Because everything is prearranged on a prepackaged tour or independent vacation, you spend less time planning—and often get it all at a good price.

BOOKING WITH AN AGENT

Travel agents are excellent resources. But it's a good idea to collect brochures from several agencies, as some agents' suggestions may be influenced by relationships with tour and package firms that reward them for volume sales. If you have a special interest, find an agent with expertise in that area. The American Society of Travel Agents (ASTA) has a database of specialists worldwide; you can log on to the group's Web site to find one near you.

Make sure your travel agent knows the accommodations and other services of the place being recommended. Ask about the hotel's location, room size, beds, and whether it has a pool, room service, or programs for children, if you care about these. Has your agent been there in person or sent others whom you can contact?

Do some homework on your own, too: local tourism boards can provide information about lesser-known and small-niche operators, some of which may sell only direct.

BUYER BEWARE

Each year consumers are stranded or lose their money when tour operators—even large ones with excellent reputations—go out of business. So check out the operator. Ask several travel agents about its reputation, and try to **book with a company that**

has a consumer-protection program. (Look for information in the company's brochure.) In the United States, members of the United States Tour Operators Association are required to set aside funds (up to $1 million) to help eligible customers cover payments and travel arrangements in the event that the company defaults. It's also a good idea to choose a company that participates in the American Society of Travel Agents' Tour Operator Program; ASTA will act as mediator in any disputes between you and your tour operator.

Remember that the more your package or tour includes, the better you can predict the ultimate cost of your vacation. Make sure you know exactly what is covered, and beware of hidden costs. Are taxes, tips, and transfers included? Entertainment and excursions? These can add up.

⏎ Tour-Operator Recommendations **American Society of Travel Agents** (⇨ Travel Agencies). **CrossSphere–The Global Association for Packaged Travel** ⊠ 546 E. Main St., Lexington, KY 40508 ☎ 859/226-4444 or 800/682-8886 ⊟ 859/226-4414 ⊕ www.CrossSphere.com. **United States Tour Operators Association** (USTOA) ⊠ 275 Madison Ave., Suite 2014, New York, NY 10016 ☎ 212/599-6599 ⊟ 212/599-6744 ⊕ www.ustoa.com.

TRAIN TRAVEL

Amtrak offers nationwide service to Chicago's Union Station, located at 225 South Canal Street. Some trains travel overnight, and you can sleep in your seat or book a sleeper car at an additional cost. Train schedules and payment options are available by calling Amtrak directly or consulting its Web site. Amtrak trains tend to fill up, so if you don't purchase a ticket in advance at least **make a reservation.**

⏎ Train Information **Amtrak** ☎ 800/872-7245 ⊕ www.amtrak.com.

TRANSPORTATION AROUND CHICAGO

Considering the difficulties of driving in Chicago, try other means of exploring the city. Public transit is inexpensive and convenient; taxis are generally easy to come by. And many areas of the city are a pleasure to walk through, even in unpredictable weather conditions.

Convention goers can **take advantage of several alternatives to cabs or shuttle buses.** CTA trains do not serve Mc-Cormick Place, but CTA Bus 3 (King Drive), Bus 4 (Cottage Grove), and Bus 21 (Cermak) stop at 23rd Street and Martin Luther King Jr. Drive and travel north to downtown Chicago. Another option is the Metra commuter train, which has a 23rd Street stop, accessible from the North Building, on the Metra Electric and South Shore lines. Visitors going downtown can get off at one of two stations: Van Buren Street or the northernmost and final stop, Randolph Street. On weekdays Metra trains run fairly often, but weekend service is less frequent.

TRAVEL AGENCIES
A good travel agent puts your needs first. Look for an agency that has been in business at least five years, emphasizes customer service, and has someone on staff who specializes in your destination. In addition, **make sure the agency belongs to a professional trade organization.** The American Society of Travel Agents (ASTA) has more than 10,000 members in some 140 countries, enforces a strict code of ethics, and will step in to mediate agent-client disputes involving ASTA members. ASTA also maintains a directory of agents on its Web site; ASTA's TravelSense.org, a trip planning and travel advice site, can also help to locate a travel agent who caters to your needs. (If a travel agency is also acting as your tour operator, *see* Buyer Beware *in* Tours & Packages.)

🏲 Local Agent Referrals **American Society of Travel Agents (ASTA)** ✉ 1101 King St., Suite 200, Alexandria, VA 22314 ☎ 703/739–278, 800/965–2782 24-hr hotline 🖷 703/684–8319 ⊕ www. astanet.com and www.travelsense.org. **Association of British Travel Agents** ✉ 68–71 Newman St., London W1T 3AH ☎ 020/7637–2444 🖷 020/7637–0713 ⊕ www.abta.com. **Association of Canadian Travel Agencies** ✉ 130 Albert St., Suite 1705, Ottawa, Ontario K1P 5G4 ☎ 613/237–3657 🖷 613/237–7052 ⊕ www.acta.ca. **Australian Federation of Travel Agents** ✉ Level 3, 309 Pitt St., Sydney, NSW 2000 ☎ 02/9264–3299 or 1300/363–416 🖷 02/9264–1085 ⊕ www.afta.com.au. **Travel Agents' Association of New Zealand** ✉ Level 5, Tourism and Travel House, 79 Boulcott St., Box 1888, Wellington 6001 ☎ 04/499–0104 🖷 04/499–0786 ⊕ www.taanz.org.nz.

VISITOR INFORMATION
Learn more about foreign destinations by checking government-issued travel advisories and country information. For a broader picture, consider information from more than one country.
🏲 Tourist Information **Chicago Convention and Tourism Bureau** ✉ 2301 S. Lake Shore Dr., 60616 ☎ 312/567–8500 🖷 312/567–8533, 312/567–8528 automated Fax Back Information Service ⊕ www.choosechicago.com. **Chicago Cultural Center** ✉ 77 E. Randolph St., 60602. **Chicago Water Works** ✉ 163 E. Pearson, 60610 ☎ 877/244–2246, 866/710–0294 TTY ⊕ www.877chicago.com.

Illinois Bureau of Tourism ✉ 100 W. Randolph St., Suite 3-400, 60601 ☎ 800/226–6632 brochures ⊕ www.enjoyillinois.com. **Illinois Travel and Tourism Association** ✉ 27 E. Monroe St. ☎ 312/814–2732. **Mayor's Office of Special Events, General Information, and Activities** ✉ 121 N. LaSalle St., Room 703, 60602 ☎ 312/744–3315 🖷 312/744–8523 ⊕ www.cityofchicago.org. **Navy Pier Welcome Center** ✉ 700 E. Grand Ave. ☎ 800/595–7437 or 312/595–7437 ⊕ www.navypier.com.
🏲 Government Advisories **Consular Affairs Bureau of Canada** ☎ 800/267–6788 or 613/944–6788 ⊕ www.voyage.gc.ca. **U.K. Foreign and Commonwealth Office** ✉ Travel Advice Unit, Consular Directorate, Old Admiralty Bldg., London SW1A 2PA ☎ 0870/606–0290 or 020/7008–1500 ⊕ www.fco.gov.uk/travel. **Australian Department of Foreign Affairs and Trade** ☎ 300/139–281 travel advisories, 02/6261–1299 Consular Travel Advice ⊕ www.smartraveller.gov.au or www.dfat.gov.au. **New Zealand Ministry of Foreign Affairs and Trade** ☎ 04/439–8000 ⊕ www.mft.govt.nz.

WEB SITES
Do check out the World Wide Web when planning your trip. You'll find everything from weather forecasts to virtual tours of famous cities. Be sure to visit Fodors.com (⊕ www.fodors.com), a complete travel-planning site. You can research prices and book plane tickets, hotel rooms, rental cars, vacation packages, and more. In addition, you can post your pressing questions in the Travel Talk section. Other planning tools include a currency con-

verter and weather reports, and there are loads of links to travel resources.

To find out more about cultural and sightseeing offerings, go to ⊕ www.877chicago.com. The Chicago Convention and Tourism Bureau's site, ⊕ www.choosechicago.com, has plenty of general tips on the city and local events, plus helpful information on convention facilities. To sort out the public-transit system, log on to the CTA's site at ⊕ www.transitchicago.com. The Web sites of the city's daily newspapers, the *Tribune* (⊕ www.chicagotribune.com) and the *Sun-Times* (⊕ www.suntimes.com/index) are great sources for reviews and events listings. The *Chicago Reader*'s site ⊕ www.chireader.com is rich in arts, entertainment, and dining reviews. *Chicago* magazine's site ⊕ www.chicagomag.com carries a few Web-exclusive features along with articles from the monthly. Metromix's site ⊕ www.metromix.com thoroughly covers Chicago's entertainment scene, from arts festivals to TV. Another good online entertainment reference is ⊕ chicago.citysearch.com.

INDEX

PHOTO CREDITS

Cover Photo (Millenium Park): *Kim Karpeles*. **Chapter 1: Experience Chicago:** 1, *Andre Jenny/Alamy*. 2, *Corbis*. 3, *Kim Karpeles/Alamy*. 4 (left), *Ken Ross/viestiphoto.com*. 4 (top center), *Richard Cummins/viestiphoto.com*. 4 (bottom center), *Edward Hatters-ley/Alamy*. 4 (right), *Chicago Convention & Tourism Bureau*. 5 (top left), *Jon Arnold/ Agency Jon Arnold Images/age fotostock*. 5 (bottom left), *Kim Karpeles/Alamy*. 5 (right), *Adler Planetarium & Astronomy Museum*. 6 (top left), *Scott Brownell/Museum of Science and Industry*. 6 (bottom left), *Ed Lines Jr. and Patrice Ceisel/Shedd Aquarium*. 6 (right), *Richard Cummins/viestiphoto.com*. 8, *José Fuste Raga/age fotostock*. 9-12, *Richard Cummins/viestiphoto.com*. 13, *José Fuste Raga/age fotostock*. 15, *Richard Cummins/viestiphoto.com*. 16, *Todd Bannor/age fotostock*. 17-18, *Richard Cummins/viestiphoto.com*. 19, *San Rostro/age fotostock*. 20 (all), *National Baseball Hall of Fame Library, Cooperstown, NY*. 21 (top left), *National Baseball Hall of Fame Library, Cooperstown, NY*. 21 (center), *Library of Congress Prints and Photographs Division*. 21 (top right), *Bettmann/Corbis*. 21 (bottom), *Ken Ross/viestiphoto.com*. 22, *Joe Viesti/viestiphoto.com*. 24, *Richard Cummins/viestiphoto.com*. 25 (left), *Graphics and Reproduction/City of Chicago*. 25 (right), *Cathy Bazzoni/City of Chicago*. 26, *Corbis*. 27 (left and right), *Richard Cummins/viestiphoto.com*. 28 (top), *Hisham F. Ibrahim/Photodisc*. 28 (bottom), *Library of Congress Prints and Photographs Division*. 29 (top left), *Bill Brooks/Alamy*. 29 (top right), *Richard Cummins/viestiphoto. com*. 29 (bottom), *Library of Congress Prints and Photographs Division*. **Chapter 2: Neighborhoods:** 31, *Linda Matlow/Pix Int'l./Alamy*. 33, *Ken Ross/viestiphoto.com*. 35, *Graphiics and Reproduction/City of Chicago*. 38, *Kim Karpeles/Alamy*. 41, *Andre Jenny/Alamy*. 43, *Chicago Antique Market*. 45, *Richard Cummins/viestiphoto.com*. 48, *Linda Matlow/Pix Int'l./Alamy*. 51, *Andrew Woodley/Alamy*. 53, *Peter J. Schulz/City of Chicago*. 55, *Kim Karpeles/age fotostock*. 58, *Richard Cummins/viestiphoto.com*. 61, *Richard Cummins/viestiphoto.com*. 63, *Igor Litvak/Wicker Park & Bucktown Chamber of Commerce*. 65, *Subterranean*. 68, *Visions of America, LLC/Alamy*. 71, *Sarah Hadley/Alamy*. 73, *Kim Karpeles/Alamy*. 75, *chicagoview/Alamy*. 78, *Cheryl Tadin/City of Chicago*. 81, *Steve Skjold/Alamy*. 83, *Cathy Bazzoni/City of Chicago*. 85, *Danita Delimont/Alamy*. 88, *Scott Brownell/Museum of Science and Industry*. 91, *Chicago Neighborhood Tours*. **Chapter 3: Museums:** 93, *Chicago Convention and Tourism Bureau*. 96, *The Art Institute of Chicago: Friends of American Art Collection, 1930.934. All rights reserved by The Art Institute of Chicago and VAGA, New York, NY*. 98, *Ken Ross/viestiphoto.com*. 99 (top), *Bruno Perousse/age fotostock*. 99 (bottom), *Chicago Convention and Tourism Bureau*. 100 (top), *The Art Institute of Chicago: Friends of American Art Collection, 1930.934. All rights reserved by The Art Institute of Chicago and VAGA, New York, NY*. 100 (top center), *The Art Institute of Chicago, Friends of the American Art Collection, 1942.51*. 100 (bottom center), *The Art Institute of Chicago, Robert A. Waller Fund, 1910.2*. 100 (bottom), *The Art Institute, Gift of Arthur M. Wood in memory of Pauline Palmer Wood 1985.1103*. 101 (top), *The Art Institute of Chicago: Helen Birch Bartlett Memorial Collection, 1926.224*. 101 (top center), *Ken Ross/viestiphoto.com*. 101 (bottom center and bottom), *The Art Institute of*

NOTES

NOTES

NOTES

NOTES

NOTES

NOTES

ABOUT OUR WRITERS

Kelly Aiglon is a Chicago-based freelance writer who loves to write about hotels—including those within blocks of her home! She is a freelance writer whose work appears in *Chicago Tribune, Midwest Living,* and *Chicago Magazine.*

Thomas Connors writes regularly on architecture and design. His work has appeared in a number of publications, including *Architectural Record, House Beautiful, Interior Design, Chicago Magazine, Chicago Tribune,* and *Time Out Chicago.*

Elaine Glusac writes about food and travel for the *International Herald Tribune, Travel & Leisure, American Way, Southwest Spirit, National Geographic Traveler,* and *Cooking Light.* Her Chicago dining reviews appear in the *Chicago Tribune.*

Roberta Sotonoff, a confessed travel junkie, writes to support her habit. Over 30 domestic and international newspapers, magazines, online sites, and guidebooks have published her work. One of her favorite destinations is her hometown, Chicago.

Perpetually in search of the newest, most exciting things Chicago has to offer, freelance writer **Judy Sutton Taylor** has spent the last 14 years scouring the shops and neighborhoods of her adopted hometown. A mother of twin toddlers, Judy is also the kids editor for *Time Out Chicago.*

Jennifer Vanasco has lived by the lake for 10 years. She writes about theater and culture for the *Chicago Reader, Chicago Free Press,* and *Chicago Tribune.* Her syndicated column on gay and lesbian issues is a three-time award winner with the Society of Professional Journalists.

Jessica Volpe is a Chicago-based freelance writer whose writing credits include *Chicago Tribune* publications RedEye and Metromix.com.